Additional Advance Praise for *Meeting China Halfway*

"Lyle Goldstein's book on China delivers a bracing synthesis on the dangers the United States faces and the options it has in the face of China's military rise. It will be required reading for Asia specialists."
  —**Robert Kaplan**, author of *Asia's Cauldron: The South China Sea and the End of a Stable Pacific* and chief geopolitical analyst for Stratfor

"Goldstein proposes a bold call for the US—accommodate China's interests in Asia instead of clinging to the status quo. Based on his thorough research in Chinese writings, Goldstein proposes mutual compromises to set in motion a spiral of cooperation. This valuable book will frame the China policy debate for years to come."
  —**Susan Shirk**, Chair, 21st Century China Program, UC-San Diego

"The most consequential dyad in an increasingly polycentric world is the Sino-American relationship. But this relationship is strategically and intellectually in irons and drifting toward possible shipwreck. Goldstein offers a gale of fresh thinking to redirect it toward mutually advantageous problem solving. He addresses apparently intractable problems with meticulous research and uncommon ingenuity, drawing on Chinese as well as American sources. His recommendations balance suggested actions by both countries. *Meeting China Halfway* is thus a very thought-provoking manual for the re-imagination of engagement between America and China. Its proposals are clear and specific and invite those inclined to inaction to come up with better alternatives."
  —**Amb. Chas W. Freeman, Jr. (USFS, Ret.)**, former assistant secretary of defense for international security affairs

"If one foresees the future of this key bilateral relationship to be a protracted negotiation, Goldstein's proposal of spirals of cooperation lays out a plausible way to take constructive steps. His ideas merit serious thought and discussion."
  —**Adm. Joseph Prueher (USN, Ret.)**, former commander of US Pacific Command and former ambassador to China

"Creative thinking, innovative ideas… While one may not agree to everything Lyle Goldstein wrote in this imaginative book, he did a great job in broadening our scope in thinking about how to build toward a new type of major power relationship between China and the United States. Mutual compromise, mutual adaptation, mutual accommodation, those steps he recommended are not easy for both sides, but if taken, the end result would be win-win."

—**Wu Xinbo**, professor and director, Center for American Studies, Fudan University

"The downward spiral in US-China relations is the most dangerous trend in international politics. Preventing it from ending in crisis, miscalculation, and war should be the highest priority. Lyle Goldstein brings not just punditry but genuine expertise on China to the problem, and applies impressive energy to finding a way out. His ambitious exploration of 'cooperation spirals' will be controversial, should provoke sharp debate about options for conflict avoidance, and deserves attention because it is among the few optimistic approaches that engage the obstacles to peace rather than dismissing them."

—**Richard Betts**, director, Saltzman Institute of War and Peace Studies, Columbia University

"Lyle Goldstein is in a unique positon to witness firsthand in both Washington and Beijing the rising distrust. He produced this unique book to explore the new paths of US-China relations leading toward cooperation spirals and avoiding escalation spirals. A timely and compelling work, it's a must read for anyone interested in the most important bilateral relations and great power politics in the 21st century."

—**Suisheng Zhao**, director, Center for China-US Cooperation, editor of the *Journal of Contemporary China*, University of Denver

"*Meeting China Halfway* is a serious and thoughtful attempt to guide the US-China rivalry away from militarized and zero-sum confrontation and toward policies that would be helpful not only bilaterally but more generally to East Asia and the world. Goldstein is a senior analyst of Chinese maritime policy who is well known for his familiarity with Chinese writing on security and environmental issues. He brings both a wealth of Chinese sourcing to the project and, more importantly, a respect for China as an intelligent counterpart with distinctive perspectives."

—**Brantly Womack**, professor of foreign affairs and C. K. Yen Chair, the Miller Center at the University of Virginia, author of *China among Unequals: Asymmetric Foreign Relations in Asia*

"This book is admirable for both breadth and depth, examining an exhaustive spectrum of the issue areas that both drive and condition rivalry between the United States and China. The author does a remarkable job at driving home his urging for a 'cooperation spiral.' A sensible and practicable guide away from making conflict a viable choice."

—**Zha Daojiong**, professor, School of International Studies, Peking University

"Goldstein takes the debate about US-China relations in a quite new and vitally important direction. Combining deep scholarship with a keen sense of practical policy, he offers a detailed plan for the two powers to step back from escalating rivalry through mutual accommodation. Sooner or later, if America and China are to stay at peace, they will have to take steps very much like those Goldstein proposes. And the sooner the better."

—**Hugh White**, professor of strategic studies, Australian National University

"In this painstakingly researched book, Dr. Goldstein provides valuable insight into the often overlooked Chinese point of view on a range of important issues facing the bilateral relationship today. Wherever one falls on the debate over how to shape US-China relations, this book is an important and unique addition to the China field, and it should be considered by policymakers in both Washington and Beijing."

—**Kristen Gunness**, senior China policy analyst

"This important new book pulls it all together: the forces that drive the United States and China toward a war; the facts that reveal that these two nations have many shared interests and few valid reasons to confront each other; and specific and valuable suggestions about moves both sides can make to pull away from a major catastrophic confrontation. Well written and thoroughly documented. A book for academics, policy makers, and concerned citizens alike."

—**Amitai Etzioni**, University Professor, George Washington University, and author of *Security First: For a Muscular, Moral Foreign Policy*

MEETING CHINA HALFWAY

MEETING CHINA HALFWAY

How to Defuse the Emerging US-China Rivalry

Lyle J. Goldstein

Georgetown University Press
Washington, D.C.

Library of Congress Cataloging-in-Publication Data

Goldstein, Lyle, author.
  Meeting China halfway : how to defuse the emerging US-China rivalry / Lyle J. Goldstein.
    pages cm
  Includes bibliographical references and index.
  ISBN 978-1-62616-160-3 (alk. paper) — ISBN 978-1-62616-162-7
  1. United States—Foreign relations—China. 2. China—Foreign relations—United States. 3. United States—Military relations—China. 4. China—Military relations—United States. 5. United States—Foreign economic relations—China. 6. China—Foreign economic relations—United States. I. Title.
  E183.8.C5G635 2015
  327.7305—dc23
                        2014029714

♾ This book is printed on acid-free paper meeting the requirements of the American National Standard for Permanence in Paper for Printed Library Materials.

16 15   9 8 7 6 5 4 3 2
First printing

Printed in the United States of America

Jacket design by Faceout Studio.
Image source / akg-images: Chinese soldier in Beijing
Image source / Alamy: Serviceman in dress blues by US flag

CONTENTS

1 Introduction
  Reversing the Escalation Spiral   1

2 Bad Blood
  The Legacy of History for US-China Relations   26

3 Imagine
  The Taiwan Question and US-China Relations   46

4 Mutually Assured Dependence
  Economic Aspects of US-China Relations   79

5 Toxic Embrace
  The Environment and US-China Relations   109

6 "South–South" Pivot
  The Developing World and US-China Relations   137

7 Persian Spring
  The Middle East and US-China Relations   163

8 Bipolarity Reconsidered
  The Korean Peninsula and US-China Relations   191

9 Keystone
  Japan and US-China Relations   225

10 The New "Fulda Gap"
   Southeast Asia and US-China Relations   263

11 Alter Ego
    India and US-China Relations   305

12 Conclusion: Rebalancing the Rebalance
    Mitigating Strategic Rivalry in US-China Relations   330

Index   371

About the Author   389

1

INTRODUCTION
Reversing the Escalation Spiral

More than six decades have now passed since young Lieutenant John Yancey of the Seventh Marine Infantry Regiment watched half his platoon mowed down by Chinese bullets on an obscure ridge in Northeast Asia. He turned to his surviving men and said: "Stand fast and die like Marines." More than one thousand fellow Americans would perish in the frozen onslaught of the Chosin Reservoir campaign in late 1950. That battle was not supposed to happen. Two weeks earlier, Far East commander General Douglas MacArthur had assured President Harry Truman in a face-to-face meeting on Wake Island that the chance of Chinese military intervention in the Korean War was "very small," despite high-level warnings from Beijing that US forces crossing the 38th Parallel represented a "menace to the security of China."[1]

As US-China rivalry continues to build a dangerous momentum in our own time, it will be important for those interested in the future of this crucial relationship to somberly reflect on the roughly 35,000 Americans killed in the Korean War—the first and only major US-China conflagration.[2] They may also consider that in the fall of 1950, "no one in the Pentagon, the State Department, or the White House took [Chinese warnings] any more seriously than MacArthur did."[3] Today, similar warnings are worryingly common in Chinese discourse on strategic affairs.[4] The Cold War and related ideological struggles are now long past, of course, but the potential for a US-China military conflict has increased markedly in the past ten years and now encompasses scenarios ranging from the South China Sea, to the East China Sea, back to the

Korean Peninsula, and even into the Indian Ocean and much further afield. In comparing the present era of geopolitical rivalry with the early Cold War, however, one difference is most prominent. In 1950 the United States was at the apex of its strength, and China had been gravely weakened by decades of war and internal turmoil. Today the United States confronts a China that is vastly strengthened. The concomitant risks, therefore, are that much greater. Indeed, given the strength of both powers, a military conflict today between China and the United States could resemble not so much the "limited" Korean War but the even graver tragedy of World War I, which has been the subject of so much discussion during its recent centenary.

Scholars who research US-China relations on both sides of the Pacific are nearly universal in concluding that such a catastrophic conflict today is far from inevitable. But what they have not done thus far is to provide concrete intellectual paradigms and accompanying policy proposals to lead this troubled relationship away from the brink of disaster. Therefore, this book seeks to be dramatically different from any other in the field in its treatment of US-China relations, by explicitly focusing on how to realize new paths to bilateral cooperation via "cooperation spirals"—the opposite of an escalation spiral. One hundred policy proposals are made throughout the chapters of this book, not because these are the only solutions to arresting the alarming course toward conflict, but rather to inaugurate a genuine debate regarding policy solutions to the most vexing problems in bilateral relations.

At present, unfortunately, the two nations' rivalry continues to unfold across geopolitical, economic, and even cultural realms and is now extant in all corners of the globe. As China seeks to pursue its "New Silk Road Strategy" with a raft of new projects and initiatives, American strategists might do well to reflect on the obvious fact that China's new "lean to the west," in part at least, seems to reflect a disposition not to "lean to the east," an alternative that would have meant seeking to meet the American rebalance directly in East Asia but was ultimately rejected. Beijing thus appears to be intentionally avoiding a kind of "head-on" collision by focusing China's energies in a different direction. However, strategists with a zero-sum disposition are all but certain to try to conjure up a clever series of strategic countermoves to prevent the growth of Chinese influence in Central Asia, South Asia, the Middle East, and beyond. The author has had the unique opportunity to witness firsthand, in both Washington and Beijing, the intense fear and loathing that drive zero-sum mentalities in both countries and the competitive and increasingly dangerous policies that have resulted. Of course, the combination of the "balance of financial terror" with the "balance of nuclear terror" thankfully lends considerable ballast to the relationship. But it would be foolhardy in the extreme to rely on these largely hypothetical shock absorbers to prevent a catastrophe. Moreover, the rivalry between the United States and China not only carries the risks of conventional or even nuclear warfare but, apart from these most obvious risks, also bears the immensely costly burdens of an arms race and proxy conflicts below the threshold of direct hostilities. And then there are the opportunity costs of this rivalry—in crucial areas, such as responses to nuclear proliferation or pandemic outbreaks—where cooperative opportunities have, far too often, been crowded out by the tendency toward rivalry. Of late, the US-China rivalry has been eclipsed, at least in the headlines, by tensions in US-Russian relations resulting from the 2014 crisis in Ukraine. But this trend is not likely to be durable since Russia is hardly strong enough to compete against the West on its own. The same cannot be said of China.

Within five years, if it has not already occurred, China's economy will surpass that of the United States in size. And China has steadily improved its military prowess and weapons technology, such that it has even moved ahead of the US military in certain domains, for example, the not insignificant area of antiship cruise missiles.[5] The ideological factor in the bilateral relationship, moreover, which pits democratic and market principles against authoritarian state capitalism, has the frequent effect of spraying gasoline over already-red-hot coals. A rather typical, ideologically tinged American analysis of the strategic dilemma posed by China's rise ends as follows: "Only a fully democratic China would undoubtedly seek to . . . maximize the happiness of the population rather than [its] . . . own power."[6] In other words, the dilemma, as understood by many if not most Americans, can be resolved only if China embraces American values and institutions. But might there be other ways to mitigate the two countries' "natural" tendency toward rivalry, with its myriad costs and dangers?

A spring 2011 Brookings Institution report by Kenneth Lieberthal and Wang Jisi marked an important reality check for observers of US-China relations. Their dismaying conclusion revealed that relations were plagued with "strategic distrust," despite more than sixty bilateral dialogues intended to foster greater trust. In explaining the Chinese perspective on strategic distrust, Wang reports candidly that "some high-ranking officials have openly stated that the United States is China's greatest national security threat. This perception is widely shared in China's defense and security establishments and in the Communist Party's ideological organizations." Lieberthal likewise offers a similarly suspicious American perspective: "Americans . . . worry . . . that China seeks to displace the United States as Number 1, and [Beijing] views

US-China relations in fundamentally zero-sum terms." This book adopts and seeks to carry forward several recommendations made in Lieberthal and Wang's path-breaking report, but it also draws inspiration from their attempt "to spark creative thinking."[7]

The June 2013 meeting of presidents Barack Obama and Xi Jinping at Sunnylands in Rancho Mirage, California illustrated the top-level recognition on both sides that the bilateral relationship is evolving in troubling directions. The concept of the meeting—that the two leaders would spend extended "free time," without a formal agenda or large groups of advisers—was undoubtedly positive. As one wise commentary on the Sunnylands summit observed: "It is extraordinary that the leaders of the world's two great powers meet so rarely in this way," and further noted that "it is easy to mock the idea of meetings for the sake of meetings," but quite correctly concluded that personal trust between the leaders could amply facilitate much-needed diplomatic breakthroughs and also help mitigate the most severe crises.[8] A breakthrough of sorts could even be seen in President Xi's proposed "新型大国关系" (new-type major power relations). Although many will undoubtedly criticize the term as frustratingly lacking in specific frameworks regarding how to proceed, what the term does usefully provide is a strong recognition that, on one hand, the relationship is of supreme importance to both powers and indeed to the world. On the other hand, and perhaps even more important, the term illustrates the clear understanding by Beijing of the inherent dangers of unbridled great power competition and the imperative, therefore, to break with patterns of past great power rivalries.[9] Since the Sunnylands summit, a string of positive, albeit small-scale joint activities has been undertaken by the US and Chinese armed forces. And yet troubling military confrontations have also continued—for example, in December 2013, involving warships from the two countries in the South China Sea; and in August 2014, involving US and Chinese military aircraft over the East China Sea. Regrettably, US-China relations are still lacking fundamental stability. A second major Obama-Xi summit occurred in November 2014 in Beijing. Encouragingly, this meeting seemed to yield some tangible results in key areas, such as carbon emissions, trade, easing visa requirements, and military confidence-building. President Xi said that "a pool begins with many drops of water," while President Obama remarked that "when the U.S. and China are able to work together effectively, the whole world benefits."

Yet the Washington foreign policy establishment greeted the late 2014 summit with ample skepticism. As one representative commentary published a couple of weeks after the summit reflected, "The atmospherics were cordial,

[but] there were no substantive changes . . . [regarding] any of the most neuralgic security issues driving strategic competition in the Asia-Pacific. China committed itself to nothing specific or binding. It is difficult not to think that China wants the appearance of peaceful rise, not the reality." In this same piece from a commentator at a think tank closely aligned with the current administration, the author states, "We need to think through China's strengths and vulnerabilities [and] determine our best points of leverage." In the end, the author calls upon the "United States and its allies and partners . . . to think through the full panoply of countermeasures available to help fashion a concerted strategy for countering coercion."[10]

A similar skepticism seemed to pervade Obama administration thinking in the lead-up to the November 2014 summit as it was publicly revealed that "Mr. Xi's push for a 'new type of great power relations' . . . has clearly fallen out of favor with Mr. Obama and his aides."[11] Dismissing this phrasing altogether could have major negative consequences for this all-important relationship over the long term. In short, rejection of this concept may well imply to Chinese strategists that only Washington can develop overall concepts to govern the relationship, or worse: that Washington is quite comfortable with "new type" great power relations, even if that means rivalry and military conflict. These are the wrong messages to convey to Beijing and suggest that the relationship today is very far from set on a firm foundation, unfortunately. This book takes a different approach with the clear realization that one of the most basic principles of cooperation is the ability to listen and try to comprehend the other side's ideas. Where the vision of "new-type major power relations" is presently lacking in specifics, this book has the considerable ambition to provide them in a forthright and succinct manner.

Relying on the evidence and ideas from a broad array of Chinese and American thinkers, this book seeks to provide the intellectual framework, in the form of concrete proposals, that is necessary to put this most vital of relationships on a solid footing for the twenty-first century and beyond. As such, the book, which surveys all major points of tension in the relationship—from currency practices to green technology development to the South China Sea issue—aspires to serve as a practitioner's guide for a step-by-step strengthening of US-China relations.

Scholars are frequently reticent about making clear and specific prescriptions, preferring to emphasize positive description and value-neutral theorizing in order to answer puzzles in the study of international relations. This is often vital work, but the author's experience in government and around decision makers reinforces the perception that what is required more urgently is the development of specific, actionable policy recommendations that are informed by rigorous political science analysis. In short, there is ample room for a normative treatment of US-China relations—that most critical of bilateral relationships to world order for the current century, and likely the ones that follow as well.

How to Respond to China's Rise? The Debate

A major debate has been ongoing in Washington regarding how to respond to China's rapid rise. Regrettably, US policy in Asia in recent years had seemed troublingly ad hoc and lacking a set of clear objectives, with accompanying resources and explicit bottom lines. Indeed, as one insider account of the ever-more-frequent crises in East Asia relates, "In reality, there's no such thing as strategy. There are just a series of tactical decisions."[12]

The wide acceptance of the "rebalance to the Asia-Pacific" during the years 2011–12 seems to indicate the ascendance of those in the debate arguing that China's influence needed to be balanced by that of the United States, not least in the military realm. Perhaps the most eloquent and logically argued of the exponents for a more forceful US approach in countering China is Aaron Friedberg and his book *Contest for Supremacy* (2012). This book has gained a major following in Washington because of the clarity of his argument and the specificity of his recommendations. Friedberg states emphatically that "China is too important to be left to the China hands," suggesting that a "Shanghai coalition" made up of scholars and interests that receive material benefits or other "psychic rewards" from favoring engagement is "speeding the day when China will emerge as Asia's preponderant power."[13] He concludes: "The 'natural antagonism' between a rising power and an established hegemonist has not been, and cannot easily be, extinguished. Nor can the 'massive' ideological differences between America and China be put aside."[14] Contemptuous of most attempts at cooperation with China, Friedberg warns, "Beijing wants to ease Washington's anxieties and to dull its competitive reflexes, preventing or at least slowing a vigorous response to China's growing power."[15] There are strengths and weaknesses to Friedberg's important book. In the latter category, he seems to actually understate China's growth in power. For example, he does not expect China's economy to surpass that of the United States until midcentury, but most economists expect that event by 2020, if not before.[16] As for strengths, his use of Chinese sources is impressive, especially because he is not a China expert.

A second virtue of Friedberg's work, as suggested above, is that it proposes an actionable set of policy recommendations. With regard to economic policy, he makes the relatively uncontroversial suggestion that the United States must increase its savings rate, but he goes much further to also suggest that Washington should tighten its technology export controls as well as limit China's role in the sensitive communications sector. Most of his policy recommendations relate to defense and deterrence, and the following list is not complete: disperse US forces and harden US bases; reinforce Chinese doubts about their own weapons and war plans; and develop and deploy long-endurance unmanned aerial vehicles, arsenal ships, stealthy intercontinental bombers, and long-range conventional missiles, because "modern wars are not won on the defensive." Friedberg advocates that the United States prepare in earnest to undertake a blockade of China if necessary. On the diplomatic side, he says that, though "an Asian equivalent of NATO" is not feasible at present, a "community of Asian democracies" could effectively balance Chinese power.[17]

A comprehensive critique of Friedberg's book is offered in chapter 12, but for now, we may simply observe that many of his policy recommendations are being realized in the form of the present "rebalancing to Asia," as well as the related "Air–Sea Battle" strategy developed by the Pentagon. A window into the Obama administration's China policy is provided by Jeffrey Bader's account *Obama and China's Rise* (2012). Interestingly, that book makes no mention of "rebalancing," or of the so-called pivot to the Asia-Pacific region, or of the Air–Sea Battle strategy. Bader seems to call, above all, for "balance" in Washington's China policy, and he warns against falling "into the classic security dilemma" with Beijing. However, he suggests that the Obama administration was perfectly prepared to "push back . . . [by] . . . throwing around a few elbows ourselves."[18] Overall, the account gives a somewhat disturbing impression of an administration seemingly more concerned with its image and avoiding criticism. Bader is proud to have stamped out any possibility of "excessive accommodation," and he even crows about reining in the president's campaign-trail penchant for intensifying engagement with former US adversaries in East Asia.[19] Indeed, with the full flowering of the rebalancing and of the Air–Sea Battle strategy since Bader's departure, it is quite clear that a major reason why the political right has apparently not jumped on the administration's Asia-Pacific policy is that the Obama administration has in fact largely endorsed the program advocated by those seeking to balance against China's rise.[20]

By contrast, the challenge of avoiding an escalation spiral toward the abyss of conflict in US-China relations will require a concerted and purposeful endeavor. The effort to propose a genuinely progressive alternative to current policies is, in large part, the purpose of the present book. Henry Kissinger's *On China* offers a compelling vision of a cooperative future built on his deep understanding of Chinese strategic culture, which he developed over the course of decades as he interacted directly with Chinese leaders. His invocation of the 1907 Crowe Memorandum (an influential assessment of German aims and possible British responses that was written by a senior official in the British Foreign Office) is haunting:

> The reader of the Crowe Memorandum cannot fail to notice that the specific examples of mutual hostility being cited were relatively trivial compared to the conclusions drawn from them. It was not what either side had already done that drove the rivalry. It was what they might do. . . . [Washington and Beijing] . . . need to ask themselves the question apparently never formally posed at the time of the Crowe Memorandum: Where will a conflict take us? Was there a lack of vision on all sides, which turned the operation of the equilibrium into a mechanical process, without assessing where the world would be if the maneuvering colossi missed a maneuver and collided?[21]

However, Kissinger's fine book does not offer up specific policy proposals, recommending only that US and Chinese leaders must develop a "tradition of consultation and mutual respect."[22]

Michael Swaine's book, *America's Challenge: Engaging a Rising China in the 21st Century* (2011), represents a crucial step in analysis of US-China relations, in that it raises the important possibility that "to maintain an effective strategy overall, US interests . . . might also need to change as China's capabilities increase." Examining a range of possible strategies that Washington could pursue in cooperation with China, Swaine concludes that a broad consensus supports a balance between hedging and engagement. However, he seems to break rather decisively with the current policy paradigm, calling for "alternatives to the current emphasis on predominance in the Western Pacific." Indeed, he argues that asserting "US maritime predominance in the Western Pacific is probably unsustainable over the long term, . . . [and] attempts to sustain this predominance . . . are likely to prove . . . destabilizing."[23]

Another new and extremely useful book is *Strategic Reassurance and Resolve: US-China Relations in the 21st Century* (2014), by James Steinberg and Michael O'Hanlon. The book shares many assumptions and recommendations with the present endeavor. The authors note that in various obvious scenarios, "the risks of serious US-China war could be far greater than many now appreciate." In common with the present volume, Steinberg and O'Hanlon offer a large number of concrete proposals to mitigate US-China tensions. In using a methodology quite similar to the one employed here, they express the hope that "Washington can craft its own policies in ways that will call forth reciprocal, positive Chinese actions," and they also advocate a "virtuous cycle of cooperative restraint."[24] Significantly, they emphasize that advocating cooperative approaches is frequently not popular, and, moreover, they assert that "there are powerful forces in the United States . . . that will tend to favor US policies that could accentuate . . . [the] rivalry between the United States and China. The same is true in key allied capitals, perhaps most notably in Tokyo."[25]

However, there are also major differences between the present volume and the one by Steinberg and O'Hanlon. They put a high premium on maintaining America's system of overseas bases in the Western Pacific, though it is argued here that this system should be reformed. And they may understate the vulnerability of that basing structure, underrate the pace of progress in Chinese military modernization, and overrate the pertinence of the United States' experience with recent counterinsurgency wars for any major power war.[26] Another significant difference is that Steinberg and O'Hanlon put the major onus on Beijing for improving the troubled bilateral relationship, whereas this book seeks a more equal, bilateral modus vivendi and even calls upon Washington, with its strength and maturity, to make the difficult first moves toward reconciliation in crucial areas of contention.[27] Nevertheless, Steinberg and O'Hanlon have made a superb contribution to the debate, and their call for "nonmilitary responses" to counter Chinese actions in the East China Sea and South China Sea areas is particularly brave, sober, and significant.[28]

The recent book on US-China relations that comes closest to the present effort is Hugh White's *The China Choice: Why America Should Share Power* (2012). White presents a disquieting picture of current US-China relations: "Active rivalry between America and China over their future roles in Asia is no longer a future risk, but a present reality." He sees a collision as ever more likely, because both states appear to be seeking unachievable and conflicting goals: "The hope that America can maintain uncontested leadership in Asia is . . . as illusory as the fear that China will be able to dominate Asia in its place." He might be quite correct in observing, moreover, that "the Chinese military has been preparing for war with the United States. Now the principal task of the US military is preparing for war with China." In this most sober volume, he warns that "those who cannot imagine a catastrophe have no capacity to prevent it."[29] Where the present volume seeks to improve upon White's incisive analysis, along with the analyses of the other books discussed above that have sought to elaborate a viable cooperative approach vis-à-vis China, is in both providing a much wider discussion of Chinese sources—and thus a firmer basis for cooperation—and also, more particularly, offering a series of specific, balanced, and sequential policy recommendations.

As suggested above, a major ambition of the present book is to take Chinese voices seriously—a shortcoming of all too much scholarship on China and US-China relations. Chinese foreign policy experts have reacted with alarm and dismay regarding the developments in bilateral relations during the last several years. Chen Jian, of People's University in Beijing, wrote in mid-2012 that the "US seems to have undertaken hostile measures. . . . From 2012 to 2024 will be the most dangerous period for US-China relations. . . . The actions of small states could drag the United States and China into an armed conflict."[30] Another scholar, Pang Zhongying, also at People's University, observed that "under the circumstances of the US strategic pivot, . . . 'East Asian cooperation' confronts its greatest external attack."[31] Wu Xinbo of Fudan University concluded that "the Obama administration's balancing strategy has already had an obviously negative impact on China's security interests."[32] Although counseling patience, Shen Dingli, also of Fudan, wrote in late 2012 that no matter how hard the United States tries to "create trouble for China, . . . [and] maneuvers by various means to surround China, . . . this will not change the fact that the sun is setting on American superiority."[33]

Less moderate voices are also evident in Chinese discourse, for example, Chinese Air Force general Chao Liang. He stated explicitly in a mid-2013 interview that China must "rebalance" against the US "rebalancing policy," calling, among other steps, for China to greatly enhance its "strategic power projection," including both nuclear and long-range conventional strike capabilities.[34] Likewise, Chinese admirals call openly for measures "with respect to near sea areas to control firmly, control well, control strictly, and to eliminate near seas threats, confirming [China's] sovereignty, . . . and that it will not accept invasion and encroachment."[35] Another important Chinese admiral called in mid-2014 for enhanced 积极长远的力量运用规划 (plans for the active wielding of long-range power) or what might be termed simply "power projection" as a means to cope with perceived threats to China's maritime security.[36] There is also open discussion in 2014 within Chinese foreign policy journals about a perceived imperative to "undermine, weaken, or destroy" alliances that are viewed as hostile to China.[37] A question often asked in the course of 2014 has been whether Beijing might be studying the lessons of the volatile Ukraine Crisis that has dominated headlines in that year. Indeed, preliminary evidence is that, not only is President Vladimir Putin much admired in China, but also that Chinese strategists have observed that "Russia does not fear." As one Chinese senior colonel explains in an interview: "[A US] aircraft carrier group daring to enter the Black Sea . . . would be akin to a person locked inside a house."[38] For the moment at least, the study of key Mandarin-language sources seems to reveal that cooler heads still prevail, and that China is not seeking to follow the belligerent and risky Russian model. The overall guidance in Beijing with respect to US-China relations still seems to be 斗而不破 (struggle, but do not break).[39] Nevertheless, it is quite evident that Chinese discourse regarding the United States has become more bellicose, even as a similar trend has developed in the United States, reflecting a clear and dangerous evolution toward intensified rivalry. Chinese voices are not unknown in the West. However, much more can and must be done to understand Chinese perspectives on US-China relations and the new global order—in part, through a close analysis of Mandarin-language texts.

Therefore, embedded within each chapter that follows is a lengthy analysis of a variety of writings on the key issues by leading Chinese scholars. To the maximum extent, this book draws upon direct translations of the key passages from these writings. The concept is to allow Western readers direct access to these Chinese assessments—which heretofore were almost completely inaccessible to Western analysts. It is crucial to state that by quoting from this expansive variety of Chinese thinkers on key subjects, the author emphatically is *not* implying endorsement of these assessments. On the contrary, some of these Chinese assessments are highly subjective and even spurious. Yet it would be a mistake to ignore these viewpoints or dismiss them altogether. The tendency to scorn one's adversary's ideas as "propaganda" is all too common in the practice of international diplomacy. Such an approach not only smacks of xenophobia but is also likely to feed the tendency toward "misperception" and enhanced subjectivity in policy judgment. Recently, in fact, a mark of the quality and openness of Chinese writings on foreign affairs and defense matters has been a new tendency toward self-criticism and demand for accountability, as in a 2014 Chinese article that criticized Chinese assessments of the Iraq and Afghanistan wars, suggesting that these appraisals were critically weakened by group-think and a lack of diverse perspectives.[40] The failure to adequately consult a wide variety of Chinese-language materials can create cultural blindness to actual opportunities for cooperation and the peaceful resolution of difficult issues. In sum, this book seeks to improve on its predecessors by analyzing hundreds of important Chinese writings that have not been evaluated by Western scholars. It is hoped that a better understanding of Chinese viewpoints may facilitate enhanced US-China cooperation on critical issues of mutual concern.

Cooperation Spirals

In addition to the commonsense methodological approach of surveying a wide body of Chinese-language writings, this book also presents the conceptual innovation of "cooperation spirals," in order to provide bilateral policy "moves" for achieving substantive progress in US-China relations across a range of difficult issues. A cooperation spiral may be considered the precise opposite of an escalation spiral—which is frequently interpreted as the result of fear and misperception when leaders confront security dilemmas.[41] In a cooperation spiral, trust and confidence are built over time through incremental and reciprocal steps that gradually lead to larger and more significant compromises. To be sure, these proposed steps will be difficult—and thus their related challenges are fully analyzed in the chapters that follow—but their gradual, evolutionary, and reciprocal nature make them a feasible guide for practitioners.

Unfortunately, the leading journals in East Asian international relations, such as *Asian Survey* and *International Security*, appear to neglect the issue of how to foster US-China cooperation.[42] Alternatively, academic journals that do take international cooperation as their focus, such as *Conflict Management and Peace Science*, have tended to disregard the issue of China, and US-China relations in particular. A veritable intellectual chasm has therefore seemed to open up with respect to fresh scholarship on how Beijing and Washington might cooperate in the twenty-first century.

Nevertheless, a number of relevant insights from the quite extensive theoretical debate—which generally pits "neoliberals" against "neorealists"— regarding the nature of cooperation in world politics are summarized here. Two pioneers in the study of international cooperation, Robert Axelrod and Robert Keohane, warn at the outset that "achieving cooperation is difficult in world politics, . . . [where] cheating and deception are endemic." They highlight the importance of the "mutuality of interests," as expressed in "payoff structures," the "shadow of the future," and the number of actors involved.

Each of these issues is pertinent to the prospects for US-China cooperation, given that one may evaluate whether Beijing and Washington indeed prefer "mutual cooperation" to "mutual defection," because that cannot be assumed. They emphasize, moreover, that the "mutuality of interests is not based simply on objective factors, but is grounded upon the actors' perception of their own interests. Perceptions define interests." These scholars evaluate both the possibilities and risks of "issue linkage" in facilitating cooperation, and also the likely constraints posed by domestic politics. They appear to offer strong support for the proposed cooperation spiral model, when they assert that "a strategy based on reciprocity—such as tit for tat—can be remarkably effective in promoting cooperation, . . . even among pure egoists." Still, even these foremost advocates of cooperation are quite cognizant that attempts at reciprocity can devolve into "acrimonious and frustrating patterns of bargaining," but also that the most effective motive for cooperation between rivals in world politics has generally been the "activities of a third power."[43] Cheating and the problem of relative gains also pose significant challenges for policymakers that seek mutual accommodation by employing cooperation spirals. Nevertheless, Asia specialists are still very much intrigued by the possibilities for reinvigorated engagement, as one scholar explained in the summer of 2013 in the leader article of *Global Asia*: "Engagement invites reciprocity, thus setting in motion a succession of positive changes in policy and outlook quite opposite from the ladder of escalation that characterizes all too many international conflicts."[44]

Skeptics are likely to counter that the "cooperation spirals" confer a distasteful moral equivalence to the developing rivalry between the United States and China. From that perspective, the nature of the conflict between these two powers over the Asia-Pacific region is not so much the inevitable structural result of an increasingly bipolar system, but rather is determined by the alleged nationalism and "inherent aggressiveness" of the contemporary Chinese regime. Many in the West, as Friedberg contends, consider the Chinese regime to be "evil," and thus inherently untrustworthy. Numerous Western analysts have pointed to "Chinese nationalism" as a major driver of future conflict, whether in the South China Sea or elsewhere.[45] Undoubtedly, the contemporary Chinese regime leans on Chinese nationalism to retain its governing legitimacy. Likewise, the state-controlled media is able to stifle dissenting opinions, including voices promoting compromises.[46] Nevertheless, this book does not take up this major theme of the connection between China's form of polity and its predisposition (or not) toward armed conflict, chiefly for two reasons. First, books that closely examine the internal workings of the

Chinese government and the Chinese Communist Party are quite common in the West.[47] Second, my view is that this book can have more of an impact on the "rivalry dynamics" aspect of US-China relations, rather than seeking more ambitiously to bring about fundamental change in Beijing. In my estimate, the reform of China's governing apparatus is a job best left to the Chinese people.

The cooperation spiral model, as applied in this book across a wide variety of difficult policy dilemmas in US-China relations, draws on all major traditions in international relations theory. From the constructivist tradition, the model relies on the conception that ideas and norms have force unto themselves, and therefore creative diplomacy and focused leadership can potentially break divisive deadlocks and prevent the tragedy of great power conflict. From the liberal tradition, the model adopts certain precepts related to processes, and specifically to those institutions that can guide expectations and behavior—thus building trust and enabling further cooperation. Finally, though in somewhat obvious contradiction to realist predictions of rivalry, the cooperation spiral also takes certain realist principles as essential, including the principles that cooperative measures must be consistent with state interests, must accord with tendencies in the balance of power, and must also be reciprocal in nature to the extent possible. Therefore, the proposed model also represents a realist form of cooperation. Stimulating a wider discussion of alternative steps within the proposed cooperation spirals would constitute, in itself, a major contribution to this field. After all, this author hardly purports to be Moses with a Hundred Commandments. The twin key points of this approach are that reciprocity is necessary and that practical first steps must be found. The endpoints only seem utopian in the absence of the accomplishments that result from climbing the earlier steps, and even if the endpoints remain out of reach, each step represents a significant advance. For instance, the European Union could not have emerged except at the end of a path of cooperation that began with small and tentative cooperative efforts that proved themselves intrinsically useful.[48]

Turning from the proposed model of the cooperation spiral to the logic of this book's argument and the progression of its chapters, it is suggested at the outset that this book is built on the premise that history cannot be overlooked or papered over. Therefore, chapter 2 draws upon the findings of a number of cutting-edge historical treatments of East Asia—both Western and Chinese. The central issues of Taiwan and of economic relations are, respectively, the subjects of chapters 3 and 4. These chapters introduce the concept of the cooperation spiral—a pattern that continues throughout the rest of the book. Chapter 5 highlights the rather significant progress that has been achieved in the environmental domain, but it also puts a purposeful focus on the all-important issue of climate change. Chapter 6, on US-China interactions in the developing world, naturally follows the prior discussions regarding economic and environmental relationships. A turn toward geopolitics on the world stage is made in chapter 7, where the Middle East is discussed as a region beset by instability for which US-China strategic cooperation offers significant promise. From a wider discussion of the global possibilities for US-China cooperation, the book then turns to the key issues that have roiled the politics of East Asia in the last decade—threatening the region's new prosperity, which has so dazzled and impressed the rest of the world in the current era. Thus, collaborative US-China cooperation cycles are promoted to cope with the ongoing crisis on the Korean Peninsula (chapter 8), the dangers of China/Japan enmity (chapter 9), and new tensions that have recently escalated in Southeast Asia (chapter 10). With a nod toward a future world where India's role may come to approximate that of contemporary China, chapter 11 develops possibilities for an India-US-China triangular relationship that might promote stability and peace instead of the current course toward escalating great power rivalry.

Chapter 12, the conclusion, develops a number of key linkages among issue areas (e.g., Taiwan and the Korean Peninsula) and also presents the final cooperation spiral, which focuses on the key security dimension of the overall US-Chinese relationship. Crucially, the conclusion also discusses in some detail three major critiques that may undermine the promise of cooperation spirals for US-China cooperation. The first critique concerns China's record on human rights. Should the United States seek active cooperation with a rising power that does not share its most cherished values? The second critique holds that a Group of Two (commonly referred to as the "G-2") condominium in world decision making is inherently unfair and also likely premature in many respects. What will be the reaction of other major powers (e.g., Japan), not to mention those small states seemingly squeezed between the two whales? And finally, the third critique is the most iconic of all arguments made against enhanced US-China engagement: the charge of "appeasement." If China's security concerns are to be accommodated to a significant extent, as recommended in this book, will Beijing not 得寸进尺 (given an inch, take a yard) and demand ever more concessions? Full answers to these wholly reasonable critiques are given in the book's conclusion, but here it is enough to assert that China's human rights situation and the vital question of relations with "third parties" would both benefit substantially from the stabilizing impact of the development of a genuinely cooperative bilateral relationship between the two emergent superpowers. As for the charge of appeasement, this book is likely to incense nationalists in Beijing as much as or perhaps more than it will infuriate hawks in Washington, because it calls for mutual accommodation or concessions in *equal* measure from both sides—the only realistic way forward, because neither side can now hope to impose its will on the other.

A few additional caveats must be stated at the outset. Regarding the rather extensive employment of Chinese sources throughout the chapters that follow, a couple of methodological issues may be considered. First, which Chinese sources are examined, and how is their credibility evaluated? A weakness of some other studies in this field is a tendency to rely exclusively upon a single set of sources. As much as possible, therefore, this book relies on the widest possible array of sources, prioritizing academic writings above magazine-type articles, but hardly dismissing the import of the latter. Second, why does the book focus almost exclusively on Chinese and US sources? For example, Taiwanese sources are not generally examined for the chapter on Taiwan, Korean sources are not considered for the chapter on Korea, and so on. On one hand, this reflects a simple limit on the scope of the project and the difficult requirements of restricted space in a book covering such a broad range of topics. On the other hand, the reader will also quite correctly discern a certain "G2" (Group of Two) aspect to the prioritization of American and Chinese sources, vice those of "third parties." In defense of this approach, one may say first that the views of Seoul, Tokyo, Manila, Taipei, Canberra, Jakarta, New Delhi, and so on are quite well represented among the Washington foreign policy elite. To take but one obvious example, in the last decade the Tokyo-based English-language magazine *The Diplomat* has become a leading forum for American strategic thinking about the Asia-Pacific region's security. True enough, it is not quite fair to prioritize Chinese and American perspectives over those from other nations, but then international affairs is also not quite fair either. It is, moreover, suggested in this book that a substantial amount of the tension in the Asia-Pacific region today results from a failure to create decision frameworks that are in accord with the genuine balance of power, and its obvious tendencies. This book reflects the fact that ultimately peace and stability will flow, first and foremost, from a carefully negotiated consensus among the two leading superpowers that is then shaped and further modified by the other powers and lesser states. The new balance of power in the world dictates such a structure and process for the emerging world order. This book conforms to this new reality of world politics.

Two additional assumptions that need to be addressed at this point include the key foreign policy concepts of "linkage," on one hand, and that of "spheres of influence," on the other hand. Each of these concepts is critical to the book's argument. At the most basic level, the term "linkage" in a foreign policy context simply implies that issues are related in various ways. Most fundamentally, for example, a whole variety of issue areas can benefit from the general strengthening of a given relationship. Intuitively, it seems quite plain that a leadership summit between two rivals can serve to break through a series of policy logjams because the leaders are seen to value the overall relationship above the minor costs of mutual accommodation on any given issue. During the Cold War the term "linkage" first came into vogue during the 1970s, as the Nixon administration attempted to link progress in arms control and economic issues with Soviet behavior in the developing world. Paradoxically, the opposite policy currently seems to be fashionable in US-China relations— "delinkage," perhaps dating from the 1990s, when the Clinton administration prudently chose to delink economic cooperation from the sensitive human rights issue. Within the conceptual framework of "delinkage," there are certain issues on which the United States and China remain deadlocked or engage in strategic competition, while simultaneously pursuing robust cooperation in other areas where US and Chinese interests closely align. I do not dismiss the value of isolating certain issues in order to make progress where possible. Indeed, the discussion of environmental cooperation in chapter 5 showcases the considerable success of that tactic. However, the general approach adopted here is that there are real limits to delinkage, and, moreover, that progress on the most substantive and difficult questions presently dividing Beijing and Washington would benefit not only from a general improvement in the relationship but also, in particular, from the linking of certain critical issues. For example, there could be a mutually advantageous linking of the Taiwan and Korean Peninsula issues, as discussed in the book's concluding chapter.

A second key theme that emerges in the chapters that follow is that of "spheres of influence." Going against the grain of much contemporary commentary regarding international relations in the twenty-first century, my analysis accepts spheres of influence as an integral and natural organizing principle of world politics that follows from the continued deep relevance of geography to almost all interactions in international affairs—not least those of a strategic nature. The Ukraine crisis that developed in the spring of 2014 seems to have shown that spheres-of-influence principles may substantially trump those of universalist principles, even within the comparatively stable and prosperous European context. The larger point is that the general phenomenon of states, and often great powers, seeking a larger voice on issues that are immediately proximate to them cannot be ignored or wished away. Alternatively, it is also conceivable that spheres of influence can play a stabilizing, and indeed positive, role in global politics. As conceptualized in this book, the immutable process of the diffusion of global power, or "multipolarization," will of necessity involve a greater salience for spheres-of-influence-type diplomacy. Although Americans, imbued with a liberal internationalist ideology, are prone to deep suspicion regarding spheres of influence, Christopher Layne recently reminded us that this concept was a key part of George Kennan's crucial theorizing during the early Cold War, and that a closer adherence to this conception during that long struggle might well have saved the United States considerable blood and treasure.[49] Similarly, Steinberg and O'Hanlon observe that American strategists during the Cold War "recognized the need to develop a modus vivendi with the Soviet Union to limit the dangers of inadvertent conflict or the escalation of peripheral conflicts to a direct confrontation between the two nuclear powers themselves, . . . [and they were] . . . willing to tolerate . . . Soviet spheres of influence."[50]

Thus, readers should not be surprised in the chapters that follow to see a considerable willingness to accord Beijing a sphere of influence in the Asia-Pacific region. As is discussed in much greater detail throughout the book, this judgment is premised not only on the realities of the evolving global and regional balances of power but also on a reasonably positive outlook with respect to Chinese intentions. It is important to recall that China has no military bases abroad; nor has it resorted to a large-scale use of force for more than three decades. Whether this quite remarkable restraint continues without exception is less important than the overall trend, which is clearly favorable. Connecting the themes of linkage and spheres of influence, one might crudely summarize the book's general thesis to suggest that bestowing or even deputizing Beijing with a larger role in the Asia-Pacific region, and especially in its backyard, will yield a higher degree of successful bilateral cooperation across a whole gamut of global issues, from nuclear proliferation to climate change. Is this not how London courted Washington so that the two could put their long history of militarized rivalry and contentious squabbling behind them to become effective partners on the world stage?[51] In effect, making room for China on the global stage, but especially within the Asia-Pacific region, will actually benefit both US prosperity and US national security.

A somewhat perverse impression, however, can result, and this is the notion that the United States is giving up distinctly more within each cooperation spiral than is Beijing. Although none of the related spirals call upon the United States to reduce its military outlays more than China does, many American readers are sure to be uncomfortable with the fact that the various spirals proposed in this book call for drawing down certain of the the US forces deployed to the Western Pacific. Elsewhere, the spirals call for reduced US military surveillance in areas close to China (chapter 10) and also for halting US drone attacks in Pakistan (chapter 11). It is quite true that Beijing is not asked in this book to decrease its presence at various far-flung bases, nor to halt drone attacks. However, China's national defense posture is quite different than that of the United States: There are no far-flung bases (or any overseas actually); nor are there any drone strikes (at least not yet). Given these asymmetrical postures, it is only natural that the scope and scale of measures to reach accommodation in each would be quite different. Put another way, if China maintained bases in Cuba, Mexico, and other areas proximate to the United States, then such deployments would quite obviously also be part of a package negotiation, but China's posture is already quite defensive. As Ambassador Chas Freeman explains, "We seem to think that if we Americans don't provide it, there can be no balance or peace in Asia. . . . [However, the] . . . bottom line is that the return of Japan, South Korea, and China to wealth and power and the impressive development of other countries in the region should challenge us to rethink the entire structure of our defense posture in Asia."[52] American readers should also keep in mind that the cooperation spirals described herein are, in fact, also quite exceptionally demanding from a Chinese perspective. In each of the extremely sensitive territorial disputes on China's maritime flank, Beijing is asked to significantly adjust its current and long-held positions: reforming the so-called nine-dash line in the South China Sea, adopting the median line in the East China Sea, and renouncing the use of force on Taiwan. Indeed, the book has been designed such that the author expects to be equally unpopular in both Beijing and Washington. But that is the nature of asking statesmen to "meet halfway"—to take the long view for the sake of future generations and thus make brave and hard choices for peace.

Thucydides' Trap

More than two thousand years ago, Thucydides explained how the Peloponnesian Wars resulted from the rapid growth of Sparta and the fear that this growth precipitated in Athens.[53] Quite remarkably, this important historical analogy is now apparently being considered by the most senior Chinese foreign policy decision makers.[54] From the experience of Athens and Sparta, as well as a plethora of other rivalries in history, the dominant realist paradigm has been developed to explain why major wars have accompanied the rise of new great powers. This theory has been justly criticized from a variety of perspectives, perhaps most effectively by David Kang, who characterizes realist theorizing as ethnocentric—that is, as overly based on the European experience and thus quite inapplicable to contemporary East Asia.[55] Other intellectual traditions, including obviously various strands of liberal theorizing, call into question the dire realist prediction regarding China and the inevitable rivalry that it predicts. Even realist theorizing itself, on the margins at least, may provide some possibilities for mitigated power competition through enhanced security and deterrence. And yet the undercurrents of rivalry in US-China relations are deep and actually intensifying.

Confronted with intensifying rivalry, the United States faces certain stark choices. It can either seek to preserve the status quo of American global hegemony—necessitating a massive arms buildup and requiring more active and risky "brinkmanship" to hold rising powers firmly in check. Or it can assume the much more rational and practical vision of its original founders: preserving first and foremost its own security and the liberties of its citizens, adopting a demeanor that is slow to anger, and steadfastly refusing to go "abroad in search of monsters to destroy."[56] Indeed, such monsters or dragons as lurk among the reefs and shoals of China's proximate waters are actually no more worthy than those that haunt the footpaths of obscure valleys in Afghanistan. Those calling for the United States to maintain the utmost vigilance against challengers and to take up arms at the slightest affront must understand that the United States today is in a manifestly different position than was Britain when it was confronted with the aggressive Nazi regime in the late 1930s. In fact, the United States is immensely strong and has an almost unassailable strategic position. From this position of strength, Washington can afford to take the lead, demonstrating its maturity and taking brave risks for the sake of peace. As theorists who have considered the problem of "power transition" in world politics have concluded, "The goal is to embark on a long-term process of rapprochement that will eventually succeed in fostering the mutual attribution of benign character."[57] Such a process will benefit American security and prosperity most directly. The November 2014 Obama-Xi Summit in Beijing may hint at a positive turn in the relationship. The numerous agreements that emerged from that meeting suggest that both sides emphatically decided to prioritize pressing global problems such as climate change above petty and ultimately nonsensical disputes over reefs and shoals. Such farsighted states-manship should be applauded and will hopefully initiate a much-needed trend in managing US-China relations.

In order to shift the daunting intellectual tide against rivalry and toward cooperation in pursuit of "peaceful systemic change," scholars must climb down from the ivory tower and enter the realm of subjective argumentation and normative judgment. And they cannot do this armed only with elegant models and esoteric analyses. Rather, it is imperative for them to develop an academically defensible set of proposals—here presented in the form of "cooperation spirals." In the pages that follow, ten separate cooperation spirals are elaborated, each with a graphic figure and text explaining the recommendations. The author readily admits that certain proposals require greater specificity, although this has been provided to the extent possible here, given space limitations. Also, the author in no way believes that just one set of steps should constitute these cooperation spirals, or that they should be limited to just a hundred steps in ten issue areas. Issue area experts are certainly welcome to propose superior cooperation spirals, with greater specificity, realism, and thus promise to improve the relationship. The book is thus intended to spark a debate and perhaps further research about how such spirals should be correctly structured—above all, to incorporate the principles of gradualism, reciprocity, fairness, and enforceability. The aim is to move bilateral diplomacy in this most crucial relationship beyond the red-faced wagging of fingers and the bland and seemingly useless recitation of well-worn talking points. A creative dialogue among scholars and strategists on both sides of the Pacific may seek to perfect these cooperation spirals with the ambitious goal of moving the relationship to a better place—enabling a modus vivendi built on the principles of negotiation and compromise that will undergird global peace and development in the decades and centuries to come.

Notes

1. This paragraph is drawn from Martin Russ, *Breakout: The Chosin Reservoir Campaign, Korea 1950* (New York: Penguin, 1999), 1–2, 31.
2. US Department of Veterans Affairs, "America's Wars," www.va.gov/opa/publications/factsheets/fs_americas_wars.pdf.
3. Russ, *Breakout*, 2–3.
4. See, e.g., 郑明 [Zheng Ming, PLA Navy Admiral (ret.)], "钓鱼岛, 黄岩岛事件: 或可成为我国制定和实施海洋发展战略的一个切入点" [The Events

Related to the Diaoyu and Huangyan Islands: How They Might Become Defining Points for Laying Out and Realizing Our Country's Maritime Development Strategy], 现代舰船 [Modern Ships], September 2012, 12–17: or more recently 何雷 [He Lei, PLA general] "反思甲午战争历史教训凝聚强军胜战智慧力量" [Reflections on Historical Lessons of the Sino-Japanese War of 1894–95 and on Concentrating Wisdom Concerning Strengthening the Military for Gaining Victory] 中国军事科学 [China Military Science] (March 2014), 53.

5. See, e.g., John Patch, "Regain ASCM Standoff: Improve the Harpoon," *United States Naval Institute Proceedings*, June 2010, 78–80.

6. Edward N. Luttwak, *The Rise of China vs. the Logic of Strategy* (Cambridge, MA: Harvard University Press, 2012), 270.

7. Kenneth Lieberthal and Wang Jisi, *Addressing US-China Strategic Distrust* (Washington, DC: Brookings Institution Press, 2012), xi, 13, 22.

8. "The Summit: Barack Obama and Xi Jinping Have a Chance to Recast This Century's Most Important Bilateral Relationship," *The Economist*, June 8, 2013, 11.

9. On Chinese studies of great power rivalries, see, e.g., Andrew S. Erickson and Lyle Goldstein, "China Studies the Rise of Great Powers," in *China Goes to Sea: Maritime Transformation in Comparative Historical Perspective*, ed. Andrew S. Erickson, Lyle Goldstein, and Carnes Lord (Annapolis: Naval Institute Press, 2009), 401–25.

10. Patrick M. Cronin, "How to Deal with Chinese Assertiveness: It's Time to Impose Costs," *National Interest*, December 4, 2014, http://nationalinterest .org/feature/how-deal-chinese-assertiveness-its-time-impose-costs-11785.

11. Jane Perlez, "China's 'New Type' of Ties Fails to Sway Obama," *New York Times*, November 9, 2014, http://www.nytimes.com/2014/11/10/world/asia /chinas-new-type-of-ties-fails-to-sway-obama.html.

12. Jeffrey A. Bader, *Obama and China's Rise: An Inside Account of America's Asia Strategy* (Washington, DC: Brookings Institution Press, 2012), 141.

13. Aaron L. Friedberg, A *Contest for Supremacy: China, America, and the Struggle for Mastery in Asia* (New York: W. W. Norton, 2012), 197–99, 269.

14. Ibid., 141.

15. Ibid., 183; see also 167.

16. Ibid., 35. See, e.g., Malik Singleton, "OECD Report Says China's Economy Will Overtake the US by 2016," *International Business Times*, March 13, 2013, available at www.ibtimes.com; and "Rancho Eclipse: We Invite You to Predict When China's Economy Will Overtake America's," *The Economist*, June 6, 2013, www.economist.com/blogs/graphicdetail/2013/06/daily-chart-0.

17. Friedberg, *Contest*, 271–82.

18. Bader, *Obama*, 113, 116, 149–50.

19. Ibid., 29, 79.

20. Bader states that criticism of the Obama administration by Republicans was muted and attributes that to his "thorough grounding in US national interests"; Bader, *Obama*, 141. Further evidence of the right-wing turn in administration policy toward China is, e.g., a Heritage Foundation analyst heaping praise on Secretary of State Hillary Clinton's approach to the South China Sea. See Walter Lohman, "Secretary Clinton's Asia Trip: Keep the Pressure on South China Sea," September 4, 2012, http://blog.heritage.org/2012/09/04/secretary-clintons-asia-tour-keep-the-pressure-on-south-china-sea/.

21. Henry Kissinger, *On China* (New York: Penguin Press, 2011), 522–27.

22. Ibid., 529.

23. Michael D. Swaine, *America's Challenge: Engaging a Rising China in the Twenty-First Century* (Washington, DC: Carnegie Endowment for International Peace, 2011), 8, 15, 352.

24. James Steinberg and Michael O'Hanlon, *Strategic Reassurance and Resolve: US-China Relations in the 21st Century* (Princeton, NJ: Princeton University Press, 2014), 47, 148, 157.

25. Ibid., 71–73.

26. Ibid., 88, 93, 99, 183, 188.

27. Ibid., 203.

28. Ibid., 142–49.

29. Hugh White, *The China Choice: Why We Should Share Power* (New York: Oxford University Press, 2013), 6, 55, 116–18, 127.

30. 陈建 [Chen Jian], "讨论新型大国关系" [A Discussion of New-Type Great Power Relations], 国际问题研究 [International Studies], November–December 2012, 11, 13.

31. 庞中英 [Pang Zhongying], "'东亚合作'向何处去? 论东亚地区秩序的困境与中国的战略选择" [Where Is "East Asian Cooperation" Heading? On the Challenges Facing the East Asian Order and China's Strategic Choice], 中国外交 [Chinese Foreign Policy], November 2012, 43.

32. . 吴心伯 [Wu Xinbo], "论奥巴马政府的亚太战略" [On the Obama Administration's Asia-Pacific Strategy], 国际政治 [International Politics], September 2012, 90.

33. 沈丁立 [Shen Dingli], "中国无需担忧'再平衡'" [China Need Not Be Anxious regarding "Rebalancing"], 东方早报 [Oriental Morning Post], November 22, 2012.

34. 乔良 [Gen. Qiao Liang, PLA Air Force], "洞察美国'2013年中国军力报告" [A Clear View regarding the US "2013 Report on Chinese Military Power"], 航空知识 [Aerospace Knowledge], August 2013, 26.

35. See, e.g., 段昭显 [Duan Zhaoxian, PLA Navy Admiral], "论建设海洋强国的战略目标" [On the Strategic Objective of Building China into a Maritime Power], 中国军事科学 [China Military Science], March 2013, 14.

36. 蒋伟烈 [Jiang Weilie, PLA Navy Vice Admiral], 甲午海战的历史启示 [Historical Implications of Naval Battles During the Sino-Japanese War of 1894–95], 中国军事科学 [China Military Science] (March 2014), 60.

37. See, e.g., 刘丰 [Liu Feng], "分化对手联盟: 战略, 机制与案例" [Splitting Up Alliances: Strategy, Mechanism, and Cases], 国际政治 [International Politics], March 2014, 37–48.

38. 房兵 [Fang Bing, PLA Senior Colonel], "战还是和? 俄乌克里米亚地区军事局势分析" [War or Peace? An Analysis of the Military Situation in the Russia-Ukraine Crimea Area], 兵工科技 [Ordnance Science and Technology], no. 7 (2014): 10; and also on Putin, see 马国川 [Ma Guochuan], "王缉思: 中美应 '共同进化'" [Wang Jisi: The US and China Should 'Evolve Together'], 财经 [*Finance and Economics*] (June 2014), 37.

39. 张任荣 [Zhang Renrong], "美国的世界领导地位与中国的战略定力" [America's Position of World Leadership and China's Strategic Self-Control], 学习时报 [Study Times], June 9, 2014.

40. 牛新春 [Niu Xinchun], "集体性失明: 反思中国学者对伊战, 阿战的预测" [Collective Blindness: Recollecting the Predictions of Chinese Scholars with Respect to the Iraq and Afghan Wars], 现代国际关系 [Contemporary International Relations], April 2014, 1–9.

41. Regarding inadvertent escalation and security dilemmas, the most classic work is by Robert Jervis, *Perception and Misperception in International Politics* (Princeton, NJ: Princeton University Press, 1976).

42. The author's survey of articles published in the prestigious journal *International Security* in the years 2006–11 yielded not a single China-related article with "cooperation" in the title.

43. Robert Axelrod and Robert Keohane, "Achieving Cooperation under Anarchy: Strategies and Institutions," in *Neorealism and Neoliberalism: The Contemporary Debate*, ed. David A. Baldwin (New York: Columbia University Press, 1993), 85–89, 101, 103.

44. Mel Gurtov, "Engaging Enemies: Fraught with Risk, Necessary for Peace," *Global Asia*, Summer 2013, 8–9.

45. See, e.g., Michael Yahuda, "China's New Assertiveness in the South China Sea," *Journal of Contemporary China* 22, no. 81 (2013): 454–55.

46. However, it should be stated clearly that in every chapter of this book, one can readily find Chinese voices supporting compromise. Therefore, it seems unlikely that such voices are being censored generally.

47. See, e.g., Andrew Nathan and Bruce Gilley, *China's New Rulers: The Secret Files* (New York: New York Review of Books, 2003); and Richard McGregor, *The Party: The Secret World of China's Communist Rulers* (New York: Harper-Collins, 2010).

48. The author thanks an anonymous reviewer for these insights and reflections on the proposed model.

49. Christopher Layne, "The Global Power Shift from West to East," *The National Interest*, May–June 2012, http://nationalinterest.org/article/the-global-power-shift-west-east-6796?page=show. Another scholar, reflecting on the differences between the "Long Peace" between the USSR and the US during the Cold War, observes that "whatever the reason, it is the case that the US and the USSR managed their relationship in such a way as to respect the lines drawn around their spheres of influence." Peter Shearman, "The Rise of China, Power Transition, and International Order in Asia," in *Power Transition and International Order in Asia*, ed. Peter Shearman (New York: Routledge, 2014), 15.

50. Steinberg and O'Hanlon, *Strategic Reassurance*, 52.

51. See, e.g., Lionel Gelber, *The Rise of Anglo-American Friendship: A Study in World Politics, 1898–1906* (Hamden, CT: Archon Books, 1966), 136–40.

52. Chas Freeman, *Interesting Times: China, America, and the Shifting Balance of Prestige* (Charlottesville, VA: Just World Books, 2012), 24.

53. On the applicability of Thucydides' writings to US-China relations, see Graham Allison, "Thucydides Trap Has Been Sprung in the Pacific," *Financial Times*, August 21, 2012.

54. See, e.g., 王毅 [Wang Yi], "坚定不移走和平发展道路，为实现民族复兴中国梦营造良好国际环境" [Adhere to the Path of Peaceful Development and Foster a Favorable International Environment for the Rejuvenation of the Chinese Nation], *中国外交* [Chinese Foreign Policy], March 2014, 4. Wang is currently foreign minister of the People's Republic of China.

55. David Kang, *China Rising: Peace, Power, and Order in East Asia* (New York: Columbia University Press, 2007), 37.

56. President John Quincy Adams, July 4, 1821.

57. Charles A. Kupchan, "Conclusion: The Shifting Nature of Power and Peaceful Systemic Change," in *Power in Transition*, ed. Charles A. Kupchan, Emanuel Adler, Jean-Marc Coicaud, and Yuen Foong Khong (Tokyo: United Nations University Press, 2001), 171.

2

BAD BLOOD
The Legacy of History for US-China Relations

To most visitors to China, the history of the civilization is presented as a series of proud symbols from the majestic Great Wall to the extraordinary Terracotta Warriors. Modern history generally does not rate a mention, except for the occasional allusion to China's space program or some such recent achievement, which may demonstrate the teleological conclusion of China's "long march" back. Indeed, the preceding two hundred years of China's history are, at best, the topic for an awkward discussion or, at worst, a humiliating and indignant theme to broach with the Chinese today. In a startling contrast, Americans revel in the details of the two hundred years that helped to build the "Arsenal of Democracy" and resulted in the unmatched superpower of the post–Cold War period, but they tend to be much less interested in the cultures, and indeed the often inglorious struggles, that preceded 1776.

If modern history quite rarely presents itself directly in contemporary China, it may still come into view at bizarre moments. Strolling in the small, albeit charming, seaside city of Yantai in Northern Shandong, for example, one may come upon a building labeled the "Former Residence of the American Consulate General in Yantai." As in most Chinese cities, such foreign settlements were generally located on a hill or near a body of water so as to be maximally defensible, lest the "natives become restless." Today, the US government maintains five consulates in China's largest cities; but how could it be that more than a hundred years ago, a consulate was maintained in this rather obscure corner of China? A somewhat similar vignette is suggested by any traveler to the megalopolis of Wuhan, along the Yangtze River in the very center of China. Here, the visitor to this industrial hub will find a "bund," a row of grand and imposing Western-style buildings, which is only slightly less impressive than its famous cousin in Shanghai—the most obvious symbol of the extraordinary role of foreign powers in Chinese modern history. How is it possible that this city in the middle of China more than a century ago also had such a major foreign settlement, not coincidentally located along the river, for protection if necessary by the gunboats? The answer to these curiosities is that foreign penetration of China at that time was deeper than is commonly appreciated and, moreover, that the American role, by turns onlooker and occasionally even "defender" of China's sovereignty, merits closer scrutiny.

In a corner of the newly refurbished National Museum in Beijing is an exhibit portraying the much less subtle viewpoint of the Chinese regime; one of the first images in this large exhibit detailing the so-called Century of Humiliation is of a US Marine sitting on the throne chair of the Chinese emperor in the Forbidden City after the suppression of the Boxer "Rebellion" in 1900. The complex story of just how a young Marine came to strike such a pose is discussed below. But here we may surmise that this picture and its prominent placement in China's new display in the National Museum may pose significant challenges for US-China relations.

The journalist Rob Gifford writes: "History hangs over China. Like a vapor that used to be sweet but has somehow imperceptibly turned bad, it seeps into every corner and silently makes its way into the mind of every Chinese person. . . . In 1793, China was the export superpower; its silk, tea, and porcelain were in demand around the world. . . . [But] . . . along came the hairy barbarians from the ocean, and everything that Chinese people previously thought was magnificent and a sign of their superior culture suddenly became a symbol of backwardness, . . . as the ocean people semicolonized China."[1]

Practical people are often not especially concerned with history, and it is natural to ask at this point why a pragmatic guide to substantive progress in US-China relations would take up the nagging questions of history at all when these pages could reasonably be devoted to the dissection of competing policy proposals and various contending interests. The reason, simply stated, is that the relationship is afflicted by history and that this historical baggage, underlying as it does two very distinct visions of the present and future, now forms a major barrier to genuine reconciliation and thus also practical progress. The Chinese are continually confronted with the difficulties and ironies of Beijing's conventional historical narrative—one need only consider the respective economic successes of entities such as Taiwan and Hong Kong to recognize flaws in the logic of the Chinese Communist Party's teleological narrative. But Americans rarely reflect on the roots of US diplomacy in the Asia-Pacific region, particularly those roots preceding the brilliant victories of World War II. As in the other chapters of this book, the text here endeavors to present certain new points of view—where possible, from Chinese authors. After all, the practice of history in contemporary China has come a long way from the era of tedious and exasperating discourses on Marx and class warfare. Recall that the discussion of Chinese sources here does not imply an endorsement of these assessments, but they are discussed in order to fully explain Chinese perspectives, which may be safely assumed to be often quite different from Western perspectives. This chapter is generally aimed at stirring such a reflection, coming to terms with the very significant bad blood in US-China relations. As the eminent historian of China John Fairbank has written, "A new perspective requires . . . that we recognize certain basic features of our past relations with East Asia."[2]

Origins

Although the diplomatic record suggests that official US-China interaction began in 1844 with the Treaty of Wangxia, it is quite clear that intense commercial interaction between the United States and China predated that treaty by almost a half century. American ships in Canton's harbor apparently vastly outnumbered British ones during the period 1805–14, obviously taking advantage of London's preoccupation with Napoleon in that turbulent period of European history.[3] A Peking University Press 2011 textbook on US-East Asian relations notes that US interactions with China were led by private interests and were somewhat different in character than those of the European imperialist powers, partly because the United States lacked " at that time . . . sufficient force."[4] The same source notes that by the 1820s, American traders were annually bringing into China two thousand boxes of opium.[5] A recent historical appraisal of this period by an American scholar confirms the major role of American merchants in this nefarious trade. John Haddad concludes that "British and American traders, by flooding China with opium, taught the Chinese to distrust all things Western."[6]

The Opium War remains the preeminent symbolic turning point in modern Chinese history and continues to be actively discussed by Chinese historians.[7] For example, one 2012 Chinese scholarly study raises the delicate issue of how China was defeated when it wielded roughly 887 warships, compared with just 50 warships deployed by the British.[8] Another similar analysis blames poor integration among the relevant forces, backward armaments, and a general paucity of resources as some of the factors determining that China could not "withstand the Western assault."[9]

It is certainly not a coincidence that Washington's first treaty with China, in 1844, came just two years after the Treaty of Nanjing that ended the Opium War in 1842. Fairbank cogently explains that a wide gulf separated American rhetoric, which often condemned European and especially British imperialism, from practice, whereby US citizens enjoyed the many fruits of semicolonial status. He writes:

> The British sponsored unequal treaty system in East Asia made foreigners a privileged class on a par with the local ruling class, and certainly had some attributes of empire. The system was maintained by the presence of foreign naval firepower and gunboat diplomacy. . . . Americans got the fruits of informal empire without the hard work. . . . Even the most undistinguished American citizens—deadbeats, . . . stowaways, and adventurers—once they disembarked at Shanghai, had upper-class status thrust upon them. Like the Chinese gentry, they were set above the masses, not subject to local police coercion. Embarrassed at first to be pulled by a human horse in a rickshaw, the average American soon accepted his superiority and found Oriental life and its inexpensive personal services enjoyable. Even the most egalitarian missionary had to compromise.[10]

Current scholarship has reexamined some aspects of Fairbank's assessment, suggesting that it minimizes Anglo-American rivalry, especially with respect to access to East Asian markets, as the chief motivating impulse for American diplomacy toward China. True, America's first envoy, Caleb Cushing, described the Opium War as an incident of "base cupidity and violence, and [a] high-handed infraction of all law, human and divine, which have characterized the British . . . in the seas of China."[11] But the fact of Anglo-American rivalry does not so much undermine as qualify and modify Fairbank's thesis that US interests benefited from and acquiesced to British actions in China.

According to an authoritative account of US Navy operations in Chinese waters by retired US Navy admiral Kemp Tolley, by the 1850s "American warships in numbers greater than ever before visited [Canton], the jumping off place for Perry's operations directed toward opening first the Ryukyus and then Japan." Tolley describes numerous incidents of high-handed action by US forces in China, for example, the actions of the crew of the USS *Plymouth*, working with British Royal Navy Marines in March 1853 to confer "joint educational measures . . . [upon a group of] Chinese soldiery [who had] moved in on the Shanghai race course, having first inflicted indignities on several foreign ladies and gentlemen." In the Battle of Muddy Flats, the Chinese soldiers, after being shelled and flanked, "fled in great disorder, leaving behind them a number of wounded and dead."[12]

Autumn in the Heavenly Kingdom, a new book on the Taiping Rebellion by Stephen Platt, sheds considerable new light on chaotic and confusing mid-nineteenth-century China and the not insignificant role that foreigners, including Americans, had in it. One puzzle described in the book is that the British government was almost simultaneously attacking the Chinese government in the so-called Arrow War (or Second Opium War), while shortly thereafter coming to the aid of the beleaguered Qing Dynasty in suppressing the Taiping rebels. Platt describes the British actions in the Arrow War as launched on the "slimmest of pretexts" and led by Lord Elgin, who himself "found the conduct of his countrymen in Asia morally repulsive."[13]

An extraordinary episode symbolic of the evolving US role in China is related in the course of the Battle of the Taku Forts (near present-day Tianjin), on June 25, 1859, during the Arrow War. The British commanders, who were battle-hardened veterans of the Crimean War, did not expect a serious contest, but they were surprised by stiff and determined Chinese resistance, which resulted in the "disaster of the Peiho," where 400 British were killed or wounded, of whom 29 were officers. Observing this ignominious defeat was the USS *Powhatan*, whose commander, Josiah Tattnall, decided at that moment to cast neutrality aside with the famous statement that "blood is thicker than water!" Moreover, he was quoted by a reporter at the scene to have said that "he'd be damned if he'd stand by and see white men butchered before his eyes." However, Platt concludes that Tattnall's intervention only succeeded in towing "more British Marine reserves forward to their deaths in the disastrous landing; . . . [but] it gave Americans a taste of blood in China and set a new tone for British–American friendship."[14]

Much more important to the course of the Taiping Rebellion, however, was the role of another American, Frederick Ward, a mercenary who arrived in China only after departing Nicaragua, where he and his colleagues had worked to foment a civil war and create a "Yankee state." According to Platt, Ward's army was recruited among "a mélange of Europeans, Americans, and Filipinos to fight in the region just outside Shanghai. . . . His army was strictly illegal, a bald violation of the neutrality ordinance."[15] After a mixed military record—but one that had a definite impact on the course of this Chinese civil war, which happened to coincide temporally with the American Civil War—Ward was killed near Ningbo in September 1862. Platt writes that "Ward's dying words, fittingly enough, were a demand for money."[16] In the larger scheme of modern Chinese history, this new research reveals conclusively that the Qing Dynasty might well have collapsed in the mid–nineteenth century without foreign support, which raises a further compelling question of whether so much bloodshed in twentieth-century century China could have been avoided if the Taiping Rebellion had actually succeeded. One can only speculate on this intriguing historical counterfactual, but there seems little question that foreign intervention did play a significant role in determining the final outcome and that the American role in this story was of some importance.

American Exceptionalism in Practice

To be sure, profits and geopolitical rivalry formed major motives for the Western onslaught against China during the nineteenth century, but the missionary impulse played a definite role as well. Indeed, in *Autumn in the Heavenly Kingdom* Platt recounts that Chinese converts to Christianity were included in the leadership of the Taiping movement and, as is well known, the rebellion was led by Hong Xiuquan, who claimed to be the younger brother of Jesus Christ.

As the Peking University textbook on US history in Asia indicates, China became the preeminent "target for conquest" among American missionaries in the nineteenth century.[17] The same history relates: "The schools founded by American missionaries in East Asia spread the concepts of modern, Western civilization, thus forming an important and special, independent progressive role. . . . The US missionaries and the process of societal transformation and modernization in East Asia can hardly be separated."[18] Specifically, the history points out that many modern Chinese hospitals were actually founded by American missionaries.[19] At the same time, it is not clear that this rather enlightened conclusion is widely held. Contemporary Chinese military elites may have a very different perspective, as suggested by a 2009 scholarly paper published in the journal 军事历史研究 (*Military Historical Research*), where the foreign churches established in China during the nineteenth century are described as "strong points for the Western invasion." The missionaries are accused of "going out in every direction, secretly gathering [military] intelligence, bullying and humiliating virtuous people, quibbling over trivia, threatening blackmail, seizing means of production, lending at high rates of interest, exploiting peasants, and . . . generally causing significant harm."[20]

Although many Americans were no doubt engaged in good works in China, a recent history of the US role in the Asia-Pacific region appropriately recognizes that Chinese immigrants simultaneously confronted major racist barriers and also significant violence in their quest to make a new life in America. James Bradley quotes a Wyoming state official who arrived first on the scene of the Rock Springs Massacre in September 1885: "Not a living Chinaman—man, woman, or child—was left in the town. . . . The smell of burning human flesh was sickening . . . and plainly discernible for more than a mile along the railroad." Bradley adds that during the court trials that followed, there were no convictions.[21] Indeed, the Peking University history textbook on the US role in East Asia notes that the number of Chinese killed in outbreaks of anti-Chinese violence in the United States during this period "was not small."[22]

On the cusp of a new century, the United States began to exert newfound muscle in the region in earnest, beginning with the conquest of the Philippines in 1898. It is widely recognized that this less-than-glorious episode of imperialism, which featured not only massacres of Philippine civilians on a large scale but also saw the invention of "waterboarding" by US soldiers, was tied to US ambitions for increasing access to markets in China. Thus it is perhaps not surprising that the US naval squadron that defeated the Spanish fleet at Manila had come directly and expeditiously from Hong Kong rather than from US home waters. Shortly thereafter, Washington dispatched a substantial force of Marines to join the eight-nation expeditionary force sent to Beijing to repress the xenophobic uprising of the Boxer Rebellion in 1900. Although the Boxers were clearly guilty of grave atrocities against both Westerners and Chinese Christians, in contemporary China the Boxers tend to be viewed as patriotic fighters struggling against imperialism. For example, in the art on display at the Tianjin City Museum, near where the largest battles of the Boxer Rebellion were fought, an enormous canvas portrays the Boxers as heroic warriors rising up to defend China against the Western invaders.[23] Also, that picture of the US Marine sitting atop the Chinese Emperor's throne in the Forbidden City, described at the beginning of this chapter and now prominently on display in the Chinese National Museum in Beijing, dates from this period.

Bradley's account of pre–World War I American diplomacy in East Asia also reveals a darker side of the Open Door policy that characterized US policy at the time. A US diplomatic mission including both Secretary of State William Taft and President Theodore Roosevelt's daughter, Alice Roosevelt, was greeted in a Canton [Guangzhou] that "was plastered with anti-American posters. . . . Taft ordered Alice to remain in the fortress safety of America's island consulate."[24] This immediate outbreak of anti-American feeling was prompted by perceived unfair trade and immigration laws. A boycott of American exports undertaken by the Chinese that year may have cut those exports by as much as half. According to Bradley, "Unable to imagine that the Chinese would behave as patriots and assuming that they'd always react as merchants, Roosevelt had fundamentally underestimated the Chinese character and had lit another long fuse."[25]

Admiral Tolley explains the deep antiforeign and indeed anti-American sentiments pervasive in China at the beginning of the twentieth century: "Most newcomers to China . . . found it difficult to believe that fundamentally, the Chinese did not like Americans. But why should they? . . . [It] is possible to outrage the spirit and antagonize the nature of a people. . . . That, the Americans had managed to accomplish with signal success. . . . Businessmen pressed trade at the point of a gun. . . . Missionaries in their thousands, zealous and well-intentioned, nonetheless manifestly felt and acted superior to the 'heathen Chinee,' who felt that what they considered culturally inferior people were attempting to foist on them inappropriate morals and dogma."[26]

A certain bright farmer's son studying at a middle school in the Hunan provincial capital, Changsha, felt the influence of these tensions. As Jonathan Spence relates, Mao Zedong, at the age of eighteen years in 1912, just one year after the collapse of the Qing Dynasty, wrote an essay discussing leadership in the ancient Qin Dynasty. His conclusion was that the story illustrated "the stupidity of the people in our country [of China]," which had delivered China "to the brink of destruction." Mao wrote that "if those in the Western nations . . . heard of [this story], they would laugh uncontrollably . . . and make derisive noise with their tongues." Spence observes: "That the derision of foreigners should be seen as a potent factor to Mao is interesting; . . . by the first decade of the twentieth century the Chinese were circulating translations of various sharp critiques of their own country made by foreign missionary observers, as if to rub salt into their wounds, and Mao had probably seen these in the newspapers he read so avidly."[27]

Another new history of pre–World War II US policy in China by William Braisted is also revealing and explains how "the operations of US naval forces in China, though motivated by the best intentions toward China, were viewed by the people of China in the same way they viewed the actions of other foreign nations, that is, as violations of Chinese sovereignty. . . . Those actions contributed to Chinese resentment, . . . which continues to the present."[28] Braisted shows that the US Navy in the interwar period frequently cooperated closely with both the British and also the Japanese—rather an embarrassment, considering the tendency of both London and Tokyo, but increasingly the latter, toward rapacious and destructive behavior in China. Of the former, Braisted says that "the American and British navies [in China sometimes] responded as if they were one service."[29] Reflecting on this close naval cooperation in China during the 1920s, US Navy admiral William Phelps is said to have quoted a Chinese general complaining to a British official as follows: "You have seen barges on the Thames deeply laden. But you do not see any Chinese steamers madly rushing up and down the Thames sinking British barges and drowning their crews. Well, we're going to stop foreign ships rushing heedlessly up our river sinking our junks and drowning their crews." Braisted then comments: "Admiral Phelps might have reflected that there were no Chinese ships or protecting gunboats on American rivers and coastal waters."[30] In the afterglow of the World War II victory, it is easy to forget that the chief of the US Navy Asiatic Fleet, Admiral Montgomery Taylor, in the early 1930s "was regarded at least in the Japanese navy as a friend who deserved appreciation," in part because of his inclination to cooperate closely with Japan in Chinese waters.[31]

World War II, for all its catastrophic bloodletting, was a kind of silver lining for US-China relations. There is little doubt that the American heroes of Midway, Guadalcanal, and thousands of other battles scattered across the Asia-Pacific region were significantly responsible for China's liberation following the defeat of the Japanese Empire. The history of the American Volunteer Group, or the Flying Tigers, is a particularly compelling story for US-China relations because it involved not only intense cooperation but also, through major sacrifices, achieved tremendous combat results during a time when the specter of a Japanese victory was extremely vivid in the immediate aftermath of Pearl Harbor. Today, China holds the Flying Tigers in high regard.[32] A contemporary Chinese scholarly analysis of the origins of the Chinese Air

Forces notes the significant role of the Flying Tigers and the US Fourteenth Air Force that followed, though the author also observes that the numbers of planes sent to China were insufficient and did not fulfill the many promises of the US government.[33] A recent Chinese scholarly paper published in another military journal relates in admirable detail how Chinese Communist soldiers rescued an American P-51 pilot, who was shot down in the vicinity of Shanghai in January 1945.[34] General Joseph Stillwell is similarly revered and is also the topic of current Chinese scholarship.[35] Given Stillwell's deep and quite unparalleled knowledge of and experience in China, another fascinating counterfactual for scholars of US-China relations is to reflect on how and whether this extraordinary persona might have made further contributions to that relationship if he had lived beyond 1946.

From Brief Collaboration to Intense Conflagration

A debate among US scholars has concerned whether the Cold War break between the United States and China was inevitable or was instead caused by poor policy choices. Chen Jian argues quite convincingly that the "lost chance" for a working diplomatic relationship between the new Communist regime in Beijing and Washington is "a myth." He writes: "The CCP's [Chinese Communist Party's] adoption of an anti-American policy in 1949–50 had deep roots in both China's history and its modern experiences. Sharp divergences in political ideology . . . and perceived national interests contributed to the shaping of the Sino-American confrontation."[36] Indeed, such a result is hardly surprising, given the vast material support that the United States had given to Chiang Kai-shek's forces—including, for example, a major airlift and sealift of half a million Nationalist troops into areas previously occupied by the Japanese to forestall their likely domination by Communist forces.[37] America's propensity to "lean to one side" is also strongly suggested by a recent account published by an American eyewitness to one set of the truce negotiations that Washington attempted to facilitate with the famous, but failed, mediation mission of General George Marshall during the years 1946–47.[38] At least some contemporary Chinese scholarship, however, suggests that the CCP went to great lengths in 1949 to engage with the United States, including making strenuous efforts to ensure that no Americans were killed and no damage was done to US property in the final phases of China's civil war.[39]

The Korean War is exceptionally important to modern Chinese history because it followed the founding of the People's Republic of China by less than a year and thus shaped many of its key institutions, not least the Chinese military. However, the salience of that conflict is also clear, given that the three-year war claimed the lives of 37,000 Americans and perhaps 250,000 or more Chinese, not to mention hundreds of thousands wounded and many more than 1 million Korean casualties on both sides. The Korean War assumes special importance for the purposes of this book, given that it was the last time Washington and Beijing came to heavy military blows and, perhaps more particularly, because this war represented a conflict that neither side sought directly but that occurred anyhow.

A more complete review of recent revelations and conclusions regarding the war from both Chinese and US sources is made in chapter 8, but a few general issues can be raised at this point. First, it is widely known that a consensus among the Chinese Communist leadership held that China should not intervene in the Korean War. Marshal Lin Biao, for example, "argued that the firepower of an American division was perhaps ten to twenty times more powerful than its Chinese equivalent."[40] Mao overruled his colleagues in a risky gambit based on "geopolitical and historical considerations."[41] Mao certainly bears some culpability for the war, together with Joseph Stalin, but the real impetus clearly came from Kim Il-sung himself. Chen claims that Mao had told Stalin during his visit to Moscow in 1949–50 that he did not expect the United States to become involved "in a revolutionary war in East Asia," but he also apparently sent 50,000 to 70,000 ethnic Korean soldiers from the ranks of the People's Liberation Army to assist Kim in his war preparations. Thus, Chen concludes that "Mao virtually gave Kim's plan a green light."[42] Mao suffered the personal tragedy of having his son killed in combat, but China also lost what in retrospect was a golden opportunity to achieve unification with Taiwan. As Thomas Christensen's account of US decision making in the early 1950s suggests, before the outbreak of the Korean War, President Harry Truman had endorsed the recommendations of his State Department that Taiwan should not be defended by American forces because that would "deflect upon ourselves the righteous wrath of the Chinese people."[43] However, that policy direction was quickly reversed, as the advocates of Taiwan as an "unsinkable aircraft carrier" gained new salience upon the outbreak of hostilities in Korea because Washington viewed this as a prelude to a global war with a united Communist Bloc. Those historical deliberations regarding Taiwan are reviewed in greater detail in chapter 3.

The most important point to make regarding the Korean War concerns its historiography, particularly that of Chinese scholars. Although in the United

States, it is commonly referred to as the "forgotten war," this is not the case in China, where discussions of what is there called the War to Resist America are quite ubiquitous. Many Americans will be taken aback to learn that the Chinese consider the Korean War to have been a great victory. As Peter Gries explains, the Korean War narrative plays an important role in contemporary Chinese self-identity and nationalism: "Recent Chinese accounts of the Korean War construct America as the best, and China as a victor over America, thus making China 'better than the best.'"[44] Nonetheless, one can find some introspection among Chinese depictions of this bloody conflict. For example, an interview appearing in the progressive 财经 (*Finance and Economics*) magazine with a former high-level diplomat makes the radical suggestion (for the Chinese context) that the Sino-Soviet alliance was a mistake that precipitated the Korean War.[45]

China's economic failures during the period of Maoism, and especially resulting from the great excesses of both the Great Leap Forward and the Cultural Revolution, are well documented, at least in the West. The human tragedy resulting from these failed policies has been better recorded in the case of the Cultural Revolution, in part because those it most severely affected were intellectuals, who are naturally positioned to share and reflect on their experiences. And it is particularly important to consider that many of those intellectuals who suffered grave harm were various leadership cadres—including, for example, the father of Xi Jinping. In recent years, several treatments of the Great Leap Forward have brought the full dimensions of the human-made tragedy into clearer relief based on new data and interview evidence. Jasper Becker, for example, demonstrates the enormous reach of the famine caused by Mao's ideological zealotry. He describes how millions died, even in Sichuan, which possesses some of the richest arable land in the world. In but one small example from his epic study of the 1959–60 famine, Becker writes of the situation in Henan: "Traveling around the region over thirty years later, every peasant that I met aged over fifty years said he personally knew of a case of cannibalism in his production team."[46] Chinese scholarship is far from open in discussing this period. However, one noteworthy and somewhat remarkable exception is a 2010 article published in 中共党史研究 (*Chinese Communist Party History Studies*), which examined declassified American intelligence estimates for China during this period. Rather surprisingly, the author praises the estimates by the US Central Intelligence Agency (CIA) during this period for certain "profound and incisive insights . . . that were not actually much different from internal Chinese estimates." The author only criticizes the CIA's analyses for underestimating the "irrational aspects of the Great Leap," and he is not coy with respect to its dramatic economic failure, though he does not mention the catastrophic famine.[47]

If the quality of the CIA's estimates comes in for praise from certain CCP scholars, other American intelligence operations from the early Cold War period have also come under new scrutiny, both in the United States and in China. Many Americans may be surprised to realize the important role played by the CIA in developing the international following for the current Dalai Lama. According to a 2002 book by two former CIA agents that details the history of the CIA's operations into Tibet, the CIA not only played a key role in getting the Dalai Lama out of Tibet in 1959 but also provided him and his associates with funds for "rice and robes" for an indefinite period afterward.[48] The repeated failures and high costs of the CIA's efforts in Tibet apparently caused President Dwight Eisenhower to wonder in early 1960 if "stoking resistance . . . only invite[ed] greater Chinese repression?"[49] A story detailing these revelations about the CIA's activities in Tibet were described in a 2011 Chinese article, which featured, among several stories connecting historical events to current US surveillance practices, the cover story from a popular magazine with the title "The Intelligence War of the US against China through History."[50]

Throughout the 1950s and 1960s, US-China relations continued to boil on rancorously, always on the verge of new hostilities. Although Chinese behavior in the two Taiwan Strait disputes during the 1950s evinced certain cautious tendencies, aiming not to prompt direct conflict with the United States, actions such as the firing of 7,000 artillery rounds onto the tiny island of Jinmen on one day in September 1954 could not quite be called risk-averse.[51] Similarly, it is not widely known that Beijing intervened quite actively to assist North Vietnam against the United States. According to Qiang Zhai, "Beginning in 1965, China sent ground-to-air missiles, anti-aircraft artillery, railroad, engineering, minesweeping, and logistics units . . . to help Hanoi. The total number of Chinese troops in North Vietnam . . . amounted to over 320,000 [over a three year span]," of which 1,000 were killed.[52] The significance of this history is not at all obscure in Chinese military circles—as revealed, for example, in the mid-2014 cover story for a prominent quasi-military Chinese journal. That story featured a number of detailed interviews with Chinese soldiers who had participated in the air defense of Vietnam, and it included the claim that Chinese units brought down a sum total of 597 US aircraft during the Vietnam War.[53] US-China crisis interaction during this period witnessed several instances when American leaders contemplated the possibility of employing nuclear weapons against China and actively considered preventive strikes against Chinese nuclear facilities in the early 1960s. Indeed, the frequency of such deliberations may have contributed to the process whereby China's approach to nuclear weapons and to national security generally resembles an adolescent who was abused in his youth.

A Bewildering and Fortunate Turn of Events

In the dark days at the height of the Vietnam War, the Nixon–Kissinger opening to China represented a creative strategic gambit with extraordinary consequences. The consequences for US-China relations have been quite well appreciated, but the larger impact on the course of the Cold War may be understated, given the immense resources Moscow henceforth had to devote to its underdeveloped Far Eastern flank. Among several interesting revelations to emerge in recent times is Kissinger's brave admission that the conclusion by the American leadership at the time that "the Soviet Union was the probable aggressor, . . . [which] hid a larger design, . . . was mistaken. . . . Recent historical studies have revealed that the Zhenbao Incident . . . [was] initiated by the Chinese; . . . they had laid a trap."[54] Despite this apparent analytical error, he relates, "It was a case of mistaken analysis leading to a correct judgment." Indeed, both Washington and Beijing have benefited enormously from the four decades of peace and dynamic development that flowed from these initial steps to break down the Cold War stalemate.

Much greater insight is now available concerning Chinese internal politics and the key roles of various Chinese leaders in developing this completely novel policy direction. Li Jie, a research professor for the CCP Central Committee, explains: "During this period, the domestic situation in China interacted with the Sino-US relationship, both as cause and as effect. National security was the main consideration behind China's decision to improve relations with the United States, but changes in China's diplomacy, away from the leftist emotionalism and toward pragmatism, also had an important impact."[55] Rosemary Foot's assessment of US diplomacy in this period also stresses the impact of domestic politics and its close interrelationship with the very sensitive Taiwan issue. She is critical of the "US tendency to engage in verbal acrobatics that succeeded only in dizzying the spectators rather than clarifying US objectives."[56] But she also suggests that "pursuit of . . . larger global aims prompted US officials to give too much away."[57] The primary issue to which she is referring—Taiwan, of course—is taken up in much more detail in chapter 3. Nevertheless, Kissinger's recent account is certainly worth considering as one ponders the kind of leadership and bureaucratic skill that might be required to broker a more effective modus vivendi between Washington and Beijing for the twenty-first century. Recalling the delicate steps that enabled the opening, he writes, "Each side leaned over backward to avoid being perceived as having made the first public move. . . . The result was a minuet so intricate . . . that neither country needed to bear the onus of an initiative that might be rejected."[58] It is worth emphasizing that during this period of intense Chinese vulnerability vis-à-vis the Soviet threat, Beijing began to find shelter—albeit with considerable uncertainty—under the conflict deterrence system offered by US global strength and leadership, as so many other countries had done during the Cold War.

Today, it is perhaps a sad commentary on US-China relations that scholars on both sides of the Pacific are looking to apply lessons from that intense rivalry in order to moderate tendencies toward rivalry in the contemporary US-China relationship. In early May 2012 the *New York Times* sponsored a forum to debate the question "Are we headed for a Cold War with China?"[59] One Chinese scholar recently probed the significance of the so-called long peace (特久和平), observing that this long peace existed under "the threat of terror." This Chinese analysis highlights the deleterious role of ideology in intensifying the Cold War and prompting major policy errors, along with the enormous waste of resources that resulted from the arms race. It concludes, moreover, that Soviet attempts to build security belts (e.g., in Eastern Europe) and American attempts to employ proxies in the developing world both backfired strategically.[60] This understanding of the Cold War and all its related costs may yet help China and the United States avoid such a similar outcome of intense rivalry.

President Xi Jinping is said to have a major interest in modern history.[61] A speech he gave on September 1, 2011, titled "Leadership Cadres Should Read Up on History," may be somewhat revealing regarding how modern Chinese history has affected his worldview. Although he states emphatically that one of China's mistakes has been its failure to embrace foreign ideas, he dwells on the impact of imperialism on China. He explains, "After the Opium War, . . . the imperialist countries . . . relied on gunboats to conduct a military invasion, causing innumerable massacres and butchering Chinese people. They forced China to sign unequal treaties, ravaged Chinese territory, and destroyed its judiciary, its customs, its trade, and its sovereignty over its own transportation system. They set up concessions, established military garrisons, propped up and bribed proxies to support imperialism, and thus controlled the Chinese government."[62]

The speech goes on at length in this fashion and embraces both the Taiping movement and the Boxer movement discussed earlier in this chapter. Historians will debate the details of this interpretation—and so they should—but for the purposes of this book, the central point is that the current Chinese leadership holds this perspective on history, and this perspective is mainstream "conventional wisdom" in contemporary China.

The United States did not play a leading role in most of these events, but it did play a large role—for example, in the suppression of the Boxer Rebellion. Even after the World War II victory that finally liberated China from foreign oppression, the United States, under the guise of the struggle against global communism, intervened frequently and on a large scale around China's periphery, eliciting strong hostility from Chinese nationalists that lingers to this day. A Chinese worldview conditioned by the "century of humiliation" strongly influences Chinese perspectives on the feasibility of building a stable and constructive partnership with the United States.

Americans do not like apologies, and that path is not advocated here. As a nation, the United States has done little to reflect on, and much less to seek amends for, the glaringly obvious past wrongs of slavery and the subjugation of native peoples.[63] The Chinese leadership also has much to answer for in its modern history. These issues are not immediately germane to the question of how to create the conditions for substantive progress in US-China relations. What is necessary to enable understanding and consideration of the solutions advocated in this book is to simply realize that there is significant bad blood in US-China relations. Because the United States, for better or worse, bears the standard of the West in its role as a global leader generally and in East Asia in particular, it must also accept that, as Fairbank put it, "The West expanded into China, not China into the West."[64] Keeping this historical fact closely in mind, and adding that the United States is still the much more powerful party, I suggest that Washington both create the appropriate conditions for cooperation spirals and also, crucially, make the first moves.

Notes

1. Rob Gifford, *China Road: A Journey into the Future of a Rising Power* (New York: Random House, 2007), 41–42.

2. John King Fairbank, *The United States and China, Fourth Edition* (Cambridge, MA: Harvard University Press, 2009), 308.

3. Macabe Keliher, "Anglo-American Rivalry and the Origins of US/China Rivalry," *Diplomatic History* 31 (April 2007): 237.

4. 张小明 [Zhang Xiaoming], 美国与东亚关系导论 [An Introduction to the History of US-East Asian Relations] (Beijing: Peking University Press, 2010), 19.

5. Ibid., 22.

6. John R. Haddad, *America's First Adventure in China: Trade, Treaties, Opium, and Salvation* (Philadelphia: Temple University Press, 2012), 135.

7. Conversely, a legitimate school of thought maintains that China's relative decline versus Europe antedates this conflict. According to this logic, the Opium War was a symptom rather than a cause of China's precipitous decline.

8. 胡斌 [Hu Bin], "鸦片战争时期梁章钜海防思想浅论" [A Brief Discussion of Liang Zhangju's Coastal Defense Thinking at the Time of the Opium War], 军事历史研究 [Military Historical Research], March 2012, 69.

9. 曲庆玲 [Qu Qingling], "试论第一次鸦片战争时期的虎门海防要塞建设" [A Preliminary Discussion Regarding the Coastal Fortifications Built at Humen during the First Opium War], 军事历史研究 [Military Historical Research], March 2012, x. A broader conception of modern Chinese history, however, might also note that the Han Chinese have themselves resorted to occasional aggression; e.g., "the Jungars, . . . a Mongol people, . . . were virtually exterminated by Manchu troops in 1758–59." Svat Soucek, *A History of Inner Asia* (New York: Cambridge University Press, 2000), 18.

10. Fairbank, *United States and China*, 312–15.

11. Keliher, "Anglo-American Rivalry," 245–46.

12. Kemp Tolley, *Yangtze Patrol: The US Navy in China* (Annapolis: Naval Institute Press, 1971), 12–13.

13. Stephen R. Platt, *Autumn in the Heavenly Kingdom: China, the West, and Epic Story of the Taiping Civil War* (New York: Random House, 2012), 28.

14. Ibid., 47.

15. Ibid., 75–76.

16. Ibid., 314.

17. 张小明 [Zhang Xiaoming], 美国与东亚关系导论 [An Introduction to the History of US-East Asian Relations], 24.

18. Ibid., 33.

19. Ibid., 29. The extraordinary medical feats of Dr. Peter Parker, an American missionary, in Canton before the Opium War are detailed by Haddad, *America's First Adventure*, 99–109.

20. 魏延秋 [Wei Yanqiu], "近代外国势力对我国边疆之文化侵略浅析" [A Cursory Analysis of the Cultural Invasion of Our Country's Borders by Foreign Forces], 军事历史研究 [Military Historical Research], no. 2 (2009): 95.

21. James Bradley, *The Imperial Cruise: A Secret History of Empire and War* (Boston: Little, Brown, 2009), 284–85.

22. 张小明 [Zhang Xiaoming], 美国与东亚关系导论 [An Introduction to the History of US-East Asian Relations], 45.

23. This is from the author's visit to the Tianjin City Museum in March 2010.

24. Bradley, *Imperial Cruise*, 292–93.

25. Ibid., 297.

26. Tolley, *Yangtze Patrol*, 169.

27. Jonathan Spence, *Mao Zedong* (New York: Penguin 1999), 18–19.

28. James C. Bradford, "Epilogue," in *Diplomats in Blue: US Naval Officers in China, 1922–1933*, by William Braisted (Gainesville: University Press of Florida, 2009), 350.

29. Ibid., 139.

30. Ibid., 67.

31. Ibid., 341.

32. See, e.g., "The Flying Tigers Hold High Honor in China," China Net, www.china.org.cn/english/NM-e/142991.htm.

33. 古琳晖 [Gu Linhui], "全面抗战时期中国空军建设述评" [Commentary on the Many Aspects of Air Force Building during the War of Resistance], 军事历史研究 [Military Historical Research], no. 2 (2009): 73, 77.

34. 高志林, 张德义 [Gao Zhilin and Zhang Deyi], "新四军浙东游击纵队救护美国飞行员始末" [The Course of the Rescuing of an American Pilot by the Guerrilla Column of the New Fourth Army in Eastern Zhejiang], 军事历史 [Military History], no. 5 (2007): 72–74. In Mainland China, historians are also reappraising the delicate issue of the contribution of the Kuomintang to Japan's defeat. On that issue, see Qiang Zhang and Robert Weatherley, "Owning Up to the Past: The KMT's role in the War against Japan and the Impact on CCP Legitimacy," *Pacific Review* 26 (2013): 221–42.

35. 范德伟 [Fan Dewei], "将介石和史迪威的分歧与中国远征军入缅作战失败" [The Divergent Opinions of Jiang Jieshi and Stillwell and the Battle Lost by the Chinese Expeditionary Force in Burma], 军事历史 [Military History], May 2010, 38–45.

36. Chen Jian, *Mao's China and the Cold War* (Chapel Hill: University of North Carolina Press, 2001), 48.

37. Fairbank, *United States and China*, 342.

38. Sidney Rittenberg and Amanda Bennett, *The Man Who Stayed Behind* (Durham, NC: Duke University Press, 2001), 62.

39. 杨斐, 李莹 [Yang Fei and Li Ying], "试论渡江役与中美关系" [Regarding the Campaign to Cross the Yangtze River and US-China Relations], 军事历史 [Military History], no. 2 (2010): 41.

40. Yu Bin, "What China Learned from Its 'Forgotten War,'" in *PLA Warfighting: The PLA Experience since 1949*, eds. Mark Ryan, David Finkelstein, and Michael McDevitt (London: M. E. Sharpe, 2003), 124.

41. Ibid., 124.

42. Chen Jian, *Mao's China*, 54–55.

43. Thomas Christensen, *Useful Adversaries: Grand Strategy, Domestic Mobilization, and Sino-American Conflict, 1947–58* (Princeton, NJ: Princeton University Press, 1996), 120.

44. Peter Hays Gries, *China's New Nationalism: Pride, Politics, and Nationalism* (Berkeley: University of California Press, 2004), 57.

45. 马国川 [Ma Guochuan], "何方: 中苏同盟的历史启示" [He Fang: Revelations concerning the History of the Sino-Soviet Alliance], 财经 [Finance and Economics], April 1, 2013, 97–98.

46. Jasper Becker, *Hungry Ghosts: Mao's Secret Famine* (New York: Holt, 1996), 118, 150.

47. 姚昱 [Yao Yu], "二十世纪五六十年代美国中央情报局对中国经济状况情报评估" [Intelligence Estimates of the American Central Intelligence Agency regarding the Chinese Economy in the 1950s and 1960s], 中共党史研究 [Chinese Communist Party History Studies], no. 1 (2010): 38, 42–43.

48. Kenneth Conboy and James Morrison, *The CIA's Secret War in Tibet* (Lawrence: University of Kansas Press, 2002), 157.

49. Ibid., 134.

50. 益多 [Yi Duo], "中情局与'藏独'秘密战" [The CIA and the Secret War for Tibetan Independence], 军事世界 [Military World], July 2011, 31.

51. Regarding the Taiwan Strait crises, see Xiaobing Li, "PLA Attacks and Amphibious Operations during the Taiwan Strait Crises of 1954–55 and 1958," in *Chinese Warfighting*, 150; and Niu Jun, "Chinese Decision Making in the Three Military Actions across the Taiwan Strait," in *Managing Sino-American Crises: Case Studies and Analysis*, ed. Michael Swaine and Zhang Tuosheng (Washington, DC: Carnegie Endowment for International Peace, 2006), 293–326.

52. Qiang Zhai, *China and the Vietnam Wars, 1950–1975* (Chapel Hill: University of North Carolina Press, 2000), 137.

53. 吴佩新 [Wu Peixin], "中国人的越战" [A Chinese Man's Vietnam War], 航空知识 [Aerospace Knowledge], May 2014, 44–49.

54. Henry Kissinger, *On China* (New York: Penguin Press, 2011), 217. See also Lyle Goldstein, "Return to Zhenbao Island: Who Started Shooting and Why It Matters," *China Quarterly* 168 (December 2001): 985–97.

55. Li Jie, "China's Domestic Politics and Sino-US Normalization," in *Normalization of US-China Relations*, ed. William R. Kirby, Robert S. Ross, and Gong Li (Cambridge, MA: Harvard University Press, 2005), 63.

56. Rosemary Foot, "Prizes Won, Opportunities Lost: The US Normalization of Relations with China, 1972–79" in *Normalization of US-China Relations*, ed. Kirby, Ross, and Gong Li, 99.

57. Ibid., 114.

58. Kissinger, *On China*, 220.

59. "Are We Headed for a Cold War with China?" *New York Times*, May 2, 2012, www.nytimes.com/roomfordebate/2012/05/02/are-we-headed-for-a-cold-war-with-china/.

60. 吕雪 [Lu Xue], "对冷战时期美苏两国国家战略选择经验和教训的思考" [Experience and Lessons of American and Soviet National Strategic Choices during the Cold War], 军事历史 [Military History], no. 2 (2008): 50–51.

61. From the relevant US diplomatic notes, it is said that Xi "particularly likes Hollywood movies about World War II and hopes Hollywood will continue to make them. Hollywood makes those movies well, and such Hollywood movies are grand and truthful." See "US Embassy Cables," *The Guardian*, December 4, 2010, www.guardian.co.uk/world/us-embassy-cables-documents/100934.

62. 习近平 [Xi Jinping], "领导干部要读点历史" [Leadership Cadres Should Read a Little History], 中共党史研究 [Historical Research on the Chinese Communist Party], October 2011, 8.

63. See, e.g., Ta-Nehisi Coates, "The Case for Reparations," *The Atlantic*, May 21, 2014, www.theatlantic.com/features/archive/2014/05/the-case-for-reparations/361631/.

64. Fairbank, *United States and China*, 170.

3

IMAGINE

The Taiwan Question and US-China Relations

This book is partially premised on the perplexing development that, even as relations across the Taiwan Strait have improved significantly since 2008, US-China relations have not seen parallel gains, but rather have tended toward even more intense geopolitical rivalry. This strange disjunction suggests that an enormous opportunity has been missed by decision makers in both Washington and Beijing. Indeed, the dramatic warming of cross-Strait ties should form a strong foundation for deepening and broadening strategic US-China cooperation. As Chas Freeman writes: "Successful management of the Taiwan problem is the key to a sound US-China relationship. And the door that key can open is one that leads to a better century than the last one for all concerned."[1] From the perspective advocated in this book—that US-China relations could be enhanced by gradual, sequential, and reciprocal steps toward accommodation—the case of Taiwan represents both low-hanging fruit and also the prospect for building a model that demonstrates how the most vexing problems in the bilateral relationship can be alleviated through the process of realizing a cooperation spiral.

Not long ago, China and the United States stood on an exceedingly dangerous precipice concerning the fate of Taiwan. In 2007 two respected defense analysts at the Brookings Institution published a book with the provocative and sobering title *A War Like No Other: The Truth about China's Challenge to America*, which spelled out in graphic terms how a conflict over Taiwan could easily spin out of control, with catastrophic consequences for both great powers.[2] That same year, the scholar Alan Wachman described the "tragic dimension of the security dilemma," with respect to Taiwan. He observed that "every act by the United States . . . that Beijing interprets as encouraging or exploiting the autonomy of Taiwan is a strike at the heart of the PRC's [People's Republic of China's] sense of security." Conversely, he notes that "in a zero sum framework, . . . strategists and statesmen in . . . Washington . . . decry the PRC's militarization of the controversy with Taiwan . . . as provocative and destabilizing."[3]

Although tensions certainly remain with respect to Taiwan's future status, not least as illustrated by the instability in Taipei in the spring of 2014 and also electoral setbacks for the ruling party later that year in that city's important bellwether mayoral contest, there has generally been a remarkable calming of tensions across the Strait; and the explanation for this trend is rather straightforward, at least on a superficial level. The election in 2008 of the candidate of the Nationalist Party (Kuomintang, KMT), Ma Ying-jeou, after eight years of major cross-Strait tensions, ushered in a new era of cross-Strait cooperation. Thus, after a brief discussion of Taiwan's history and the key role that the island has played in US-China relations, the bulk of this chapter elaborates on the views of various scholars, especially contemporary Chinese thinkers but also American researchers, about this new situation, addressing both the strategic opportunities and related risks. Then, as in all the chapters to follow, before offering its conclusion, the chapter describes a detailed proposed cooperation spiral—in this case, with the ambitious aim to convert Taiwan from the painful thorn in the side of US-China relations into an elixir that will enable policymakers and practitioners to both see the way and simultaneously open the door to a more substantively cooperative US-China relationship.

Background

Taiwan has been at the center of US-China relations for many decades, as the preceding historical chapter made clear, and the most recent receding of its central position in the bilateral relationship raises a fascinating and difficult question: Is the former or the present situation more normal? This will be a question for future analysts, but here the central concern is how and why Taiwan came to play such a pivotal role in the relationship.

A new account of the history of Taiwan during the seventeenth century by Tonio Andrade that draws heavily on original Chinese and Dutch source material sheds significant light on the sensitive issue of the island's premodern history. Andrade writes that at that time, China's perspective on Taiwan was that "China traditionally ended at the ocean. . . . Most Chinese who bothered to think about Taiwan at all thought with some justification that it was filled with violent headhunters and miasmal swamps."[4] And yet he also acknowledges that by the 1650s, "there was a large and growing Chinese population," such that in 1652 there apparently was a Chinese peasant rebellion by five to six thousand, which was, however, suppressed efficiently by Dutch musketmen.[5] The Dutch had arrived as early as 1607 on "Formosa," and had set up various settlements and fortifications. But when the Ming loyalist Zheng Chenggong (Coxinga) attacked the Dutch on Taiwan in 1661, he is said to have demanded of the Dutch governor: "I have come to reclaim my land, which my father loaned to the [Dutch East India] Company. . . . You know that it is not proper to insist on occupying someone else's land."[6]

Andrade shows quite persuasively that the island might well have persisted as a Dutch colony or even become the "eastern capital" of a reinvigorated Ming Dynasty (as Zheng Chenggong hoped), but both these possibilities gave way before the expanding power of the Qing Dynasty. Taiwan was declared to be the ninth prefecture of Fujian Province in 1684, and thus it was officially incorporated into China based on what Wachman describes as the Shi Lang Doctrine (after the Qing admiral who led the invasion to rid the island of the "pirate" Zheng clan). According to Wachman, this doctrine, which eventually swayed apparently skeptical opinion in the Beijing court, held that "Taiwan was too close to China's coast to be allowed to remain autonomous when the waters were teeming with naval and commercial rivals. The strategy of maritime defense demanded that China secure the island for itself."[7] What is essential to take from this history, with the understanding that all borders and identities are everywhere rather fluid, is that China's claim to Taiwan dates back to almost a century before the American Revolution. Quite obviously, it is a strong claim.

Beijing's less-than-energetic rule over Taiwan drove the island once more into the international spotlight nearly two centuries later after a shipwrecked crew from one of the Ryukyu Islands was brutally massacred by Taiwan's aboriginal population. Concerned that Tokyo might covet that island, Beijing opted to finally restructure the governance of Taiwan to make it an independent province rather than a prefecture of Fujian Province. Before the Sino-Japanese War of 1894–95, the fate of the Ryukyu Islands themselves was not entirely clear, given that they simultaneously paid tribute to both Beijing and Tokyo. It is fascinating to note that China's leading diplomat and statesman of the time, Li Hongzhang, appealed to visiting former US president Ulysses

Grant in 1879 that "the Ryukyu chain has great strategic importance to China as a screen off the coast of China and predicted that Japanese absorption of the Liuchius [Ryukyus] would mean eventual loss of Formosa."[8] Taiwan "patriotic resistance" against foreign encroachments during the Sino-French War of 1884–85 is related in detail in contemporary Chinese history museums covering the "Century of Humiliation."[9] The Treaty of Shimonoseki, signed in April 1895, which ended the brief but decisive war between China and Japan, ceded Taiwan to Tokyo. If it had not been for the Triple Intervention, Shandong also would have been given to Japan, but the Western imperial powers showed their true colors when, for example, Germany took full possession of the port of Qingdao. In other words, the West did not object to Japanese aggression against China per se, but was only concerned that Japan should not get more than its "fair share" of the spoils. Of course, this was just the beginning of Japan's assertiveness in East Asia, but what is essential to realize here is that in the Chinese mind, there is a straight, direct, intersecting line connecting the cession of Taiwan in April 1895, the May 1919 endorsement of Japan's claim to Shandong in the Versailles Treaty, and of course the Nanjing Massacre in December 1937. In other words, the connection of Taiwan to modern Chinese nationalism is hardly obscure; rather it has become a potent—perhaps the most potent—symbol of modern Chinese nationalism.

Fifty years of Japanese rule on Taiwan had a powerful impact on the island's development, and indeed on its self-identity. Undoubtedly, some of Japan's legacy to the island is positive, whether in the domain of education or the engineering accomplishments of developing a durable and efficient road network—no small achievement, considering Taiwan's relatively backward status in the late nineteenth century. However, there were also obviously darker aspects of Japan's colonization. A recent academic study in a Mainland Chinese journal examines the role of Taiwan-born persons in supporting Japan's military effort during the Second World War. According to this study, 207,183 Taiwan-born persons served in various capacities—mostly in logistics support—for the Japanese war effort and 30,304 died in the Pacific War. The article also notes that Japan took "comfort women" from Taiwan, that Taiwan personnel were always considered as an inferior class in the Japanese military and "on Chinese battlefields, the Japanese government doubted the loyalty [of Taiwan-born soldiers] to Japan."[10] In today's cross-Strait warming, older Chinese soldiers who battled the Japanese in Chiang Kai-shek's Nationalist Army are returning to the Mainland to commemorate their efforts—a theme applauded in the Mainland Chinese press.[11]

Two fundamentally formative moments occurred not long after the Japanese surrender in May 1945. First, there was that moment when KMT soldiers first arrived on the island to accept the surrender of Japanese occupying forces and to enforce Chinese sovereignty over the island as specified by the Allied Conference at Cairo. According to Wachman, the spectacle of the bedraggled and undisciplined KMT soldiers was a rude awakening after decades living under the rule of the highly disciplined Imperial Japanese Army.[12] An even more important moment, however, in defining Taiwan's current identity politics was the so-called 228 incident that witnessed a brutal, all-out assault on February 28, 1947, by KMT security personnel against Taiwan intellectuals to prevent a fifth column on the island from subverting its rule during the Chinese civil war. With many thousands killed and many others imprisoned, this "white terror" left an indelible mark on Taiwan politics that remains to this day.

In considering Taiwan's relationship to the Mainland, it is essential to briefly consider a crucial debate related to US policy toward China and Taiwan during the important period of 1949–50. At that time two factions were contending to decide Taiwan's fate. The US secretary of defense, Louis Johnson, with strong support from the "MacArthur faction," argued that Taiwan represented an unsinkable aircraft carrier that could not be surrendered, no matter the outcome of the Chinese civil war. But the secretary of state, Dean Acheson, alternatively advocated a hands-off approach to Taiwan: "US military assistance enabling the [KMT] to continue the fight from Formosa would turn Chinese anti-foreign feeling against us. . . . We had extricated ourselves from the Chinese Civil War, and it was important that we not be drawn into it again."[13] Although President Harry Truman sided with Acheson in this debate, that decision was overturned after Kim Il-sung's forces crossed the 38th Parallel in June 1950, as discussed in chapters 2 and 8. A standard Chinese account of the Korean War generally suggests that Chinese intervention in Korea was inevitable after Truman's decision to place the US Seventh Fleet in the Taiwan Strait.[14] Documents from this period of deliberations remain a major point of interest for Mainland Chinese researchers.[15] The scholar He Di has shown that the People's Liberation Army (PLA) was poised to invade Taiwan in mid-1951, but the requisite force and resources were instead siphoned off to the war in Korea.[16]

Tensions across the Taiwan Strait hardly abated in the 1950s, as the Cold War reached peak intensity. It is widely known that Washington considered the use of nuclear weapons during the two cross-Strait crises, in 1954–55 and in 1958. Undoubtedly, this nuclear diplomacy played some role in prompting Beijing to commit major resources to acquiring its own nuclear arsenal. Nevertheless, recent reviews of these crises by historians on both sides of the Pacific illustrate cautious policies on both sides. The Chinese historian Niu Jun, for instance, writes that in the specific context of these two crises, "Mao Zedong stressed time and again that the PLA should avoid military conflicts with US troops."[17] Appraising American crisis behavior in the same circumstances, Robert Suettinger concludes that "in the face of often surprisingly confrontational policy recommendations from the Joint Chiefs of Staff, Eisenhower maintained a measured approach, recognizing the damage to other national values that war would cause."[18] Mainland Chinese scholars continue to study this period; for example, a 2010 article by a scholar at Peking University reveals the origins of both "strategic ambiguity" and "dual deterrence" in the US policy vis-à-vis Taiwan in the lesser-known Taiwan Strait Crisis of 1962, when the Mainland believed that an invasion by Chiang Kai-shek's forces was imminent and mobilized accordingly.[19]

The role of Taiwan in the US-China rapprochement of the 1970s has been well documented. If Beijing was looking for indirect security assurances after the Sino-Soviet border clash in 1969 and Washington was looking for Beijing's help in finding a way out of the Vietnam quagmire, it is somewhat remarkable how Taiwan remained a focal point of the initial talks, and also of the negotiations that eventually resulted in the final establishment of diplomatic relations by the end of the decade. Though neither side accomplished its primary objective, the necessary breakthrough in the relationship was achieved, and thus Washington agreed to remove its bases and troops from Taiwan and also to seat Beijing at the United Nations. According to a 2012 retrospective by the Chinese Academy of Social Sciences scholar Tao Wenzhao, the United States made these concessions because of perceived weakness in the wake of its difficulties in Vietnam, as well as an internal crisis of confidence.[20] In chapter 2 it was noted that the argument is made that Washington gave up too much at that time. Certainly, there was a pervasive perception in Taipei that Washington had stabbed its old friend in the back. But in retrospect, such steps seem eminently wise, and they have provided Washington with substantial strategic benefits, including the development of a formidable counterweight to Soviet power in the later part of the Cold War and also enabling more than three decades of peace in East Asia.[21]

And yet the situation has continued to evolve, perhaps in ways that could not have been predicted during the negotiations between Zhou Enlai and

Henry Kissinger in the early 1970s. Taiwan's spectacular economic growth in the 1960s and 1970s gave way to its evolution into a full-fledged democracy during the late 1980s—a development trajectory that contrasted starkly with the events on the Mainland culminating with the 1989 Tiananmen Square Massacre in Beijing. Despite some preliminary talks across the Strait that resulted in what some refer to as the "1992 Consensus" built on a "one-China principle," the 1995–96 crisis heralded a new era of tension across the Strait and in US-China relations more generally. This crisis, which was triggered by Taiwan president Lee Denghui's trip to his US alma mater, Cornell University, featured bellicose rhetoric on both sides, the provocative test-launching of Chinese missiles into areas of the ocean that are dangerously close to Taiwan's major ports, and the US deployment of the "largest armada [to the Western Pacific] since the end of the Vietnam War."[22] One detailed scholarly analysis of this crisis squarely blames the US Congress, and especially "Taiwan lobbying on behalf of independence diplomacy," noting that this "US/China confrontation, including the US show of force, was unnecessary and avoidable."[23]

For most of the first decade of the new century, relations across the Taiwan Strait continued to worsen, with predictable consequences for US-China relations. Chen Shuibian's election in 2000 brought the already-fraught relationship to a new boil because of the pro-independence platform of his Democratic Progressive Party. Chen provoked the bitter ire of Beijing with his initiatives to alter Taiwan's official name and its Constitution; to redirect its investments away from the Mainland; and to promote its membership, as Taiwan, in the United Nations. Although Washington clearly wanted to preserve a working relationship with Beijing in the years after the September 11, 2001, terrorist attacks, during this period it was not a stretch to suggest that China now sought to "challenge Pax Americana, . . . [in no small part because of its] narrow preoccupation with the question of national reunification [with Taiwan]."[24]

New Dawn for East Asian Security

Between 1995 and 2007 Taiwan was the preeminent East Asian security issue. Significant crises in 1996, 1999, and 2005 caused many analysts to conclude that the Taiwan Strait was the most dangerous flashpoint in the world. Moreover, a consensus among specialists held that this situation was the only possible scenario that could plausibly result in a war between the United States and China. Today, the situation looks very different. Few analysts, on either side of the Pacific, think that a Taiwan crisis will erupt into war. What explains this significant change in the regional security environment?

The simple explanation is that a new leader on Taiwan, Ma Ying-jeou, who was elected in 2008, adopted a policy seeking closer relations with the Mainland—a radical reversal of the confrontational, nationalist policies of his predecessor. Upon taking office, Ma immediately followed through on a promise to initiate the so-called three links, thus establishing direct air, cargo, and mail links between Taiwan and the Mainland for the first time. These steps alone had huge consequences, bringing a first-ever flood of Mainland tourists to Taiwan. For 2012 the number of Mainland tourists visiting Taiwan was projected to reach 2.3 million, up from 300,000 in 2008, and these tourists have served as a major engine of job creation on the island.[25]

Still more consequential has been Ma's effort to pass a free trade agreement with Beijing called the Economic Cooperation Framework Agreement (ECFA). In passing this controversial measure and opening the three links, Ma has further increased the already-very-high levels of interdependence between Taiwan and the Mainland. A study by the Peterson Institute for International Economics concluded that the ECFA would raise Taiwan's gross domestic product by 5.3 percent above the previous trend line.[26]

Taiwan's statistics demonstrate a clear "bounce" from the ECFA for its economy—for example, citing a 33 percent increase in agricultural exports to the Mainland during the first half of 2011, as well an increasing tendency among multinationals to view Taiwan as a "gateway" to the Chinese market that resulted in $3.7 billion of new investment on Taiwan during 2010.[27] Mainland appraisals are similarly bullish on the results of the ECFA, although it is noted that the Mainland's markets are now substantially more open to Taiwanese products than are Taiwan markets to the Mainland's products. More positively, it has also been observed that there has been a fresh wave of Taiwan investment in the Mainland since the ECFA was reached, including in areas previously starved of investment, such as central and western China. Thus, Taiwan investment is cited as a key factor in raising the profile of Sichuan Province in the information technology sector. Suggesting a "win–win" result, the same report cites the growth of Taiwan's agricultural exports to the Mainland as experiencing a fivefold increase during the first half of 2012. However, this economic analysis is not altogether optimistic, given that many obstacles to peaceful cross-Strait development still remain, including major "ideological contradictions." A sign of frustration and unfulfilled expectation is evident in the observation of a tendency toward "去统趋独" (steps toward unification create a tendency toward independence).[28]

While there are lingering concerns on both sides of the Taiwan Strait and an election of considerable import upcoming in 2016, it is essential to keep in mind that Ma's policies received a crucial validation by the people of Taiwan when he won a second term in January 2012. Despite major setbacks, including the catastrophic Typhoon Marakot and the very difficult 2008–9 economic downturn, Ma has succeeded in building a new consensus for his policies of accommodation with the Mainland, for four reasons: (1) Taiwan's citizens do not want to live under the constant shadow of war, and of the defense outlays that this situation would entail; (2) Washington has seemed to support Ma's policies; (3) Ma's position of "no independence, no unification" has convinced the Taiwanese that his accommodation with the Mainland will be very gradual; and (4), most important perhaps, Taiwan's economy has seen a significant boost with the inception of the ECFA, enjoying a handsome trade surplus with the Mainland and the new flood of Mainland tourists, as outlined above. What is essential to note, moreover, is that even the opposition Democratic Progressive Party (DPP), which had formerly favored independence, is now also creating links to Beijing.[29] All this suggests that Ma's policy transformation is not an aberration but rather a trend that is likely to endure, albeit with countercurrents that were newly visible in 2014 as part of the so-called Sunflower Movement, which has arisen in opposition to further steps toward Mainland–Taiwan integration. Undoubtedly, Taiwan politics have also been influenced to some degree by sympathy for the Hong Kong democracy protesters during 2014. This tendency and other factors may lead the Kuomintang to electoral defeat in 2016, but the new alignment of Taiwan-Mainland relations is, however, likely to be reasonably durable for the reasons outlined above.

Before offering policy prescriptions regarding opportunities for US-China relations accruing from the warming trend in cross-Strait relations since 2008, this chapter surveys additional Chinese and American perspectives on the dramatic developments outlined above. Recall that the discussion of Chinese sources here does *not* imply an endorsement of these assessments, but they are discussed in order to fully explain Chinese perspectives. Thus, with respect to the major 2012 election on Taiwan, a paper published in one of the major PRC journals dedicated to "Taiwan studies" just before the election betrays major anxieties with regard to the outcome. The analysis notes that the DPP's campaign was focused on bread-and-butter socioeconomic issues rather than cross-Strait relations, and it concludes that the "current atmosphere of cross-Strait peace and development has generally helped the KMT." This analysis also notes that Ma has had to deflect criticism that he is "倾中" (leaning toward the Mainland) by concentrating on US-Taiwan ties. Interestingly, the fact that youth unemployment on Taiwan is approaching 10 percent is highlighted as a wild card that could help the DPP. The analysis contends that the DPP will suffer from the perception that its return to power in Taipei might damage cross-Strait trade relations and thus the island's economic health overall.[30] In the afterglow of the KMT's victory in the 2012 elections, there was no mistaking Beijing's relief and pleasure. One Mainland report on the victory exulted: "Taiwan countrymen . . . chose peace and rejected upheaval, chose cooperation and rejected resistance. . . . [The result] will benefit peace and stability in the Taiwan Strait area. For realizing the near-term rejuvenation of the Chinese nation, this is an important moment."[31]

Despite warming trends across the Taiwan Strait, Chinese scholars continue to chip away at any intellectual underpinnings for Taiwan's independence. One academic study, for example, examines in considerable depth the writings of various Taiwanese authors who have advocated a distinct Taiwan identity based on either primordial ethnic ties or cultural development. Regarding the former argument that Taiwanese "blood" represents a mixing of Polynesian, Spanish, Dutch, Japanese, and Chinese ethnicities, the author concludes that Taiwanese nationalists themselves have rejected this argument, fearing it would be turned against their cause. The argument that Taiwan developed its own distinct culture, especially through the gradual accretion of Japanese culture, is similarly undermined, so it is argued, as "cultural imperialism." However dismissive, the analysis concludes that the influence of such ideas on Taiwan's society should not be underestimated.[32] Another recent academic treatment of the Taiwan issue, by a scholar at the Central Party School, warns of the threat of separatist movements operating "under the pretenses of self-determination." Russia's violent struggle against Chechen separatists and Canada's deliberations regarding Quebec's independence are investigated for lessons. According to this analysis, the US experience in the Civil War has a particular significance for contemporary China. Not only did the United States pay an "enormous cost" for unification, but it is asserted that Washington also historically implemented legal means quite similar to Beijing's 2005 Anti-Secession Law. Moreover, it is claimed, "for the United States' long-term development, unification provided beneficial strategic space, . . . created a vast market with vast resources, . . . enabled unprecedented capitalist production,

. . . and was primarily responsible . . . for its emergence in World War II as the world's strongest military power." Viewing the "low-cost military intervention" of the Western powers in Libya, the author advocates continuing Chinese military development to forestall foreign interference in China's antisecession strategy.[33]

There is unquestionably ample suspicion in China regarding the United States' motives with respect to its actions vis-à-vis Taiwan, many of which continue to focus on the issue of arms sales. One late 2011 Mainland analysis, for example, observes that US arms sales to Taiwan are ever more high-technology oriented, but also have a tendency to make Taiwan ever more dependent on the United States for defense. For example, AIM-120 air-to-air missiles were apparently purchased by Taipei but are maintained and stored on Guam. Another example concerns Patriot missile interceptor batteries, which are completely reliant on US satellite tracking for targeting information. Moreover, the author complains that the US Department of Defense will not verify how many American defense specialists are sent to the island on a regular basis, arguing that these defense linkages are now more important than the actual weapons purchased, which now amount to "just a pile of decorations."[34] An editorial in the official Chinese Navy newspaper 当代海军 (*Modern Navy*) takes note of the 2011 US decision to defer the sale of upgraded F-16 fighter planes, but it takes a decidedly dim view of US motives. It is suggested that the warming trend across the Strait has taken away Washington's "trump card" in the Taiwan situation, but that the United States is actively seeking to find new cards in the East China Sea and South China Sea. Moreover, it is asserted that Taiwan arms sales will continue to be popular in Washington because Taiwan is a major customer of the US armaments industry.[35] Finally, Mainland analysts who follow the Taiwan issue are quite concerned regarding the US "return to Asia" and what they invariably see as negative connotations for the cross-Strait relationship. One such analysis, in the journal 现代台湾研究 (*Modern Taiwan Studies*), foresees that the inevitable results of Washington's more active strategy "of fostering division" will be accelerating arms races and an increased chance of war. The author sees a subtle shift in the Obama administration's policy regarding Taiwan, from one that welcomed "negotiations, exchanges, and overall warming" to one that "is not willing to see cross-Strait relations move too quickly or get too close." In other words, the policy is viewed in Beijing as changing from "countering independence" to "countering unification."[36]

Other Mainland analyses of the Taiwan issue are examining possible trajectories for Mainland–Taiwan cooperation, especially in the security sphere. In mid-2012 a second maritime security exercise took place, joining the coast guard entities of Taiwan and the Mainland to practice search-and-rescue operations—a topic of considerable importance for peoples on both sides of the Taiwan Strait. This exercise apparently involved twenty-seven vessels, suggesting its scale and importance. Taipei and Beijing have agreed, moreover, to continue such confidence-building maritime security exercises on an annual basis.[37] The author has observed a new ease between the Mainland and Taiwanese security establishments, for example, encountering a whole clutch of experts from the Taiwan Coast Guard at a maritime technology and policy conference in Dalian in November 2010, and similarly at a sensitive South China Sea conference in Beijing mid-2013. However, these ever-more-routine interactions among internal security personnel are still different from direct security ties between the two military establishments. Demonstrating the salience of that issue, the lead academic article in a 2012 issue of 台湾 研究 (*Taiwan Studies*) by Shi Xiaodong sought to draw comparisons from the Middle East, especially the Egypt–Israel dyad, in order to investigate the possibilities for creating a "Cross-Strait Military Security Trust Mechanism." The author explains that today the major divergence of views exists because the Taiwan side has adopted a "European-style" perspective on military confidence building that focuses purely on military measures without political preconditions, though the Mainland's perspective holds that the precondition of endorsing the one-China principle is fundamental for building trust across the Strait. The article appears to argue that Beijing should be more flexible, and thus should consider security ties and even a "peace treaty" without preconditions—arguing that based on the Middle Eastern case, it is often easier to make concrete progress on narrow, technical military questions, and that though such steps would not constitute a "final agreement" on Taiwan's status, they would represent the initial steps in a long process.[38]

A 2014 Mainland analysis by the respected US-China relations expert Yuan Peng is cautiously optimistic. He notes, for example, that although the US "rebalance" has had a major impact on situations in the South China Sea and with respect to Japan in the East China Sea, "regarding the Taiwan area, the United States has up until the present generally exercised restraint." Interestingly, he notes that Taiwan's reunification is not China's main thrust among its "centenary strategic goals" (百年战略目标), and that "that may be a good thing." But he also suggests that the power disparity across the Taiwan Strait will continue to widen, fueling greater anxieties on Taiwan. Moreover, he fully expects the "current positive situation that was not easy to achieve" to come under major "assault" during the 2016 elections on Taiwan.[39]

A brief look at US perspectives regarding the Taiwan issue is also warranted, of course, though it is assumed here that Western readers are naturally more familiar with this literature, so this discussion does not constitute a complete literature survey. Interestingly, a major Mainland journal, 国际问题研究 (*International Issues Research*), undertook a similar survey in late 2012, evaluating the positions of various US analysts with respect to (1) the continuation of arms sales, (2) whether the Taiwan conflict could lead to war between the United States and China, (3) whether unification would amount to Chinese "expansionism," (4) whether abandoning Taiwan would have an impact on the US alliance's credibility, (5) what future Taiwan–Mainland relations might look like, and (6) whether abandonment of Taiwan would compromise core US values. In the end this study forecasts no major change in US policy likely in the short term, but medium- and long-term trends suggest the possibility of fundamental change.[40]

In the last few years a number of American scholars and even senior decision makers have indeed openly questioned Washington's commitment to Taiwan. For instance, the former vice chairman of the Joint Chiefs of Staff Admiral (retired) Bill Owens, wrote an op-ed article in November 2009 that proposed reexamining the Taiwan Relations Act: "Thoughtful review of this outdated legislation is warranted, and would be viewed by China as a genuine attempt to set a new course for [the] relationship."[41] Two major papers in the journal *Foreign Affairs*, in 2010 by Bruce Gilley and in 2011 by Charles Glaser, pointed to possible new directions for US policy regarding Taiwan. Gilley's innovative paper draws a comparison between Taiwan's position and that of Finland during the Cold War. Suggesting that "Finlandization" is in the interests of Taipei and Beijing, and also of Washington, he observes that Finland made "voluntary choices . . . by making strategic concessions to a superpower next door [because of] . . . geographic proximity, psychological threats . . . and cultural affinities." He explains that this was not the "cowering acquiescence" of a puppet state, but rather constituted "principled neutrality" that "posed a direct challenge to the dominant realist logic of the Cold War, which held that concessions to Soviet power were likely to feed Moscow's appetite for expansion."[42] Glaser is also focused on how resolution of the Taiwan issue could "[moderate] the security dilemma that haunts the Washington-Beijing relationship." Concerned about China's increased military capabilities, which "may make Beijing more willing to escalate," and also noting the "general poisoning of US-China relations" that has resulted from the Taiwan issue, Glaser argues that "not all adversaries are Hitler, and when they are not, accommodation can be an effective policy tool."[43] Because these arguments were published in what is perhaps America's most prestigious foreign policy journal, they cannot be dismissed as fringe or radical. Moreover, a rather wide spectrum of Washington policy analysts have recommended reform of US policy toward Taiwan.[44]

Against these arguments, numerous Washington analysts have suggested that altering current US policy and "abandoning Taiwan" would be counter to US strategic interests. For instance, Nancy Tucker and Bonnie Glaser argued in the fall of 2011 that such policies would go against traditional US support for democracies and "would not necessarily cause Beijing to be more pliable on other matters of importance to the United States, . . . [such as North] Korea and Iran."[45] Their suggestion that arms sales must continue in order to preserve American jobs, along with their decrying Taipei's loss of its "legendary clout" in Washington, are hardly persuasive.[46] But the concern that any change in US policy regarding Taiwan would cause China to view the United States as "weak, vacillating, and unreliable" is widely shared. Daniel Blumenthal also wrote a detailed critique of Charles Glaser's argument, suggesting that the Obama administration had tried a much softer approach toward China, including with respect to Taiwan, but had found that Beijing responded by becoming more assertive.[47] Other defense analysts have argued that the military balance across the Taiwan Strait is not hopeless and that Taipei can realize strategic benefits by pursuing "sea denial" versus the Chinese Navy.[48] Mark Stokes and Russel Hsiao go a step further, even advocating that Taiwan's defense should form a critical element of the Pentagon's evolving Air–Sea Battle doctrine. They turn Taiwan's difficult military situation into a virtue, arguing that "Taiwan faces the most stressing military challenge in the world—if selected operational problems could be solved for Taiwan, . . . they could be resolved everywhere."[49] Although such proposals have not been adopted, there is little doubt that some currents in Washington favor a more uncompromising approach vis-à-vis Beijing to the difficult Taiwan issue.

A final piece of recent US scholarship merits brief discussion. An article by Philip Saunders and Scott Kastner in the prestigious academic journal *International Security* is unusual in that it closely examines the outlines of a possible peace agreement between the Mainland and Taiwan. These authors see a variety of benefits stemming from such an agreement, including (1) the fact that audience costs would increase the penalty for belligerent behavior, (2) the reality of domestic institutional constraints, (3) the process of creating benchmarks for acceptable behavior, and (4) the resultant fostering of a "new dynamic" in cross-Strait relations.[50] Moreover, they conclude that the likelihood of a more powerful Mainland, coupled with the possible return of nationalists in Taipei, would create powerful incentives in the near and medium terms for compromise. According to Saunders and Kastner, "[A cross-Strait peace agreement] . . . would reduce the salience of the most contentious issue in Sino-US relations, potentially allowing for increased cooperation between the United States and China."[51] The next section of this chapter elaborates a set of proposals with respect to Taiwan to enable the involved parties to realize such possibilities of enhanced US-China relations while taking account of certain ideas and concerns identified above in discussions of the perceptions of both Chinese and American strategists.

A US-China Cooperation Spiral for the Taiwan Issue

Washington's move 1 on Taiwan: The United States should significantly reduce the planned redeployment of 8,000 Marines from Okinawa to Guam (figure 3.1). Since the 1990s the United States has been steadily building up forces on Guam, some 3,000 miles west of Hawaii. To date, this buildup has included significant forward basing of naval forces, including three nuclear attack submarines. Although the US Navy decided against basing an aircraft carrier group on the island, the June 2012 convergence of six nuclear submarines on the island's naval base at Apra Harbor illustrated Washington's intention to place significant combat capabilities forward on Guam. The US Air Force has also upgraded its facilities on Guam and has begun to rotate its premier units, including F-22 fighters and B-2 bombers, through Andersen Air Force Base on the island. No wonder Secretary of Defense Robert Gates said in 2008 that previous and planned deployments amount to "one of the largest movements of military assets in decades."[52] There are very significant problems with turning Guam into a giant armed fortress, however, not least the related environmental issues, morale questions, and infrastructure costs. Then there is also the dubious military strategy question of concentrating high-value assets in an era of precision strike. The buildup on Guam has been watched especially closely in Beijing and has attained a symbolic value as a gauge of Washington's preparations for military conflict with China.[53] Although air and naval assets

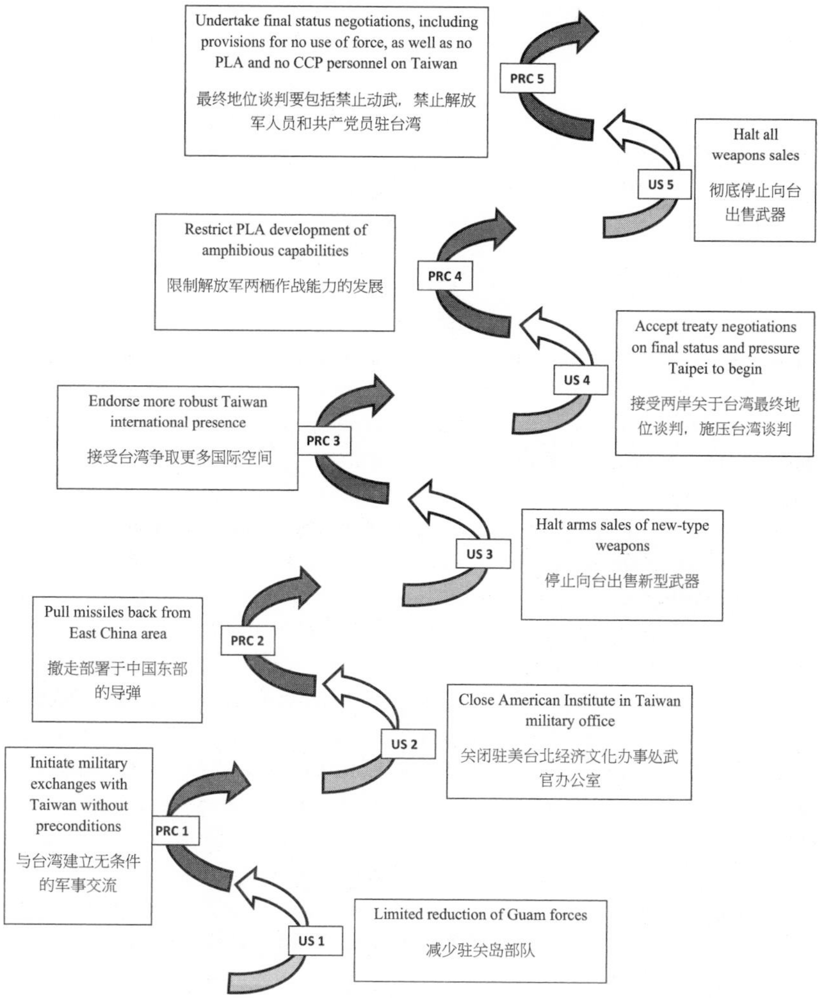

Figure 3.1 Cooperation Spiral: Taiwan 合作螺旋：台湾

Undertake final status negotiations, including provisions for no use of force, as well as no PLA and no CCP personnel on Taiwan

最终地位谈判要包括禁止动武，禁止解放军人员和共产党员驻台湾

PRC 5

Halt all weapons sales

彻底停止向台出售武器

US 5

Restrict PLA development of amphibious capabilities

限制解放军两栖作战能力的发展

PRC 4

Accept treaty negotiations on final status and pressure Taipei to begin

接受两岸关于台湾最终地位谈判，施压台湾谈判

US 4

Endorse more robust Taiwan international presence

接受台湾争取更多国际空间

PRC 3

Halt arms sales of new-type weapons

停止向台出售新型武器

US 3

Pull missiles back from East China area

撤走部署于中国东部的导弹

PRC 2

Close American Institute in Taiwan military office

关闭驻美台北经济文化办事处武官办公室

US 2

Initiate military exchanges with Taiwan without preconditions

与台湾建立无条件的军事交流

PRC 1

Limited reduction of Guam forces

减少驻关岛部队

US 1

should remain, the Marines on Guam no longer have a valuable role to play in the most relevant contingencies, especially in a Taiwan scenario. In the face of China's buildup, any attempted deployment to Taiwan in the thick of a fight would be a recipe for a military disaster. As a recognition of the strategic importance and value of better cross-Strait relations since 2008, an opening move by Washington to limit the buildup on Guam would not only represent relief for Guam residents, Marine families, and US taxpayers but would also have major positive results for US-China relations, especially if directly and publicly linked to clearly evident progress on cross-Strait relations, thus initiating this key cooperation spiral.

Beijing's move 1 on Taiwan: China should agree to initiate military confidence-building measures without political preconditions. In general, first steps within the proposed cooperation spirals are not so difficult, but agreeing to such a relationship would not be easy for Beijing, especially because a relatively clear policy line has been drawn that makes explicit acceptance of the one-China principle a part of any military security agreement between the Mainland and Taiwan. Thus, a change to "no preconditions" would represent a definite concession by Beijing. However, given some momentum from Washington's initial move to limit its buildup on Guam, such a concession would likely be feasible, for several reasons. First of all, there have already been four rounds of coast guard joint exercises. Coast guards are quite similar in nature to military organizations, especially in their culture. The fact that Taipei and Beijing agreed in mid-2012 to continue such paramilitary exercises on a regular basis certainly provides grounds for optimism regarding a military-to-military breakthrough in the near or medium term. Second, there appears to be a "natural affinity" between the two defense establishments, as demonstrated by very frequent visits by retired Taiwan military officers to the Mainland, as well as the not-infrequent efforts to coordinate policies with respect to South China Sea claims.[54] Finally, the 2012 publication of the article by Shi Xiaodong on developing cross-Strait military relations (discussed extensively above) argued quite openly for initiation of these relations without preconditions. Given that it was the lead article in an important Mainland policy-academic journal about Taiwan, this concession by the PRC seems quite within reach and could play an essential role within a US-China cooperation spiral regarding Taiwan.

Washington's move 2 on Taiwan: The United States should reveal the full extent of its defense ties with Taiwan and should close the office of its military representative at the American Institute in Taiwan. Many of the recommendations in this book suggest that Beijing needs to improve its record on transparency, but here is an instance where Washington should be more forthcoming with information. In particular, the review of Chinese literature in the preceding section demonstrated a clear Chinese concern regarding the extent and nature of US defense ties with Taiwan. The allegation is that these defense ties are both broader and deeper than has been publicly revealed. A transparent accounting of these initiatives—including, for example, the training of Taiwan armed forces personnel—would add considerably to the process of building trust and confidence across the Taiwan Strait. An important symbol of US-Taiwan defense ties is the US military representative at the American Institute of Taiwan's office in Taipei. This position did not exist until President George W. Bush's administration created it as part of a general effort to ramp up US-Taiwan defense ties, after the administration said that the United States would do "whatever it takes" to defend Taiwan against the Mainland in the spring of 2001. Perhaps such a hard-line policy could then be rationalized in the face of ever-deepening cross-Strait tensions, but that time has passed. The increasingly positive relations across the Strait in support of peace and stability since 2008 should be rewarded by removing this symbolic irritant, which was never consistent with the Shanghai Communiqué and other key foundations of US-China relations.

Beijing's move 2 on Taiwan: China should remove its short-range ballistic and cruise missiles from within a radius of 1,000 kilometers from Taiwan. Mainland China's short-range missile forces are often cited as the most severe threat that the PLA wields against Taiwan. Indeed, such missiles were tested during the 1996 crisis, and their numbers have grown considerably since then. Like the sword of Damocles, these weapons threaten not only "shock and awe" but also the possibility of knocking out Taiwan's air and naval forces in a devastating first strike, not to mention the very real possibility of decapitating Taiwan's military and/or civilian leadership. Antimissile defenses such as the Patriot are very far from adequate to the threat, because those systems could quite easily be overwhelmed by the sheer weight of large missile salvoes. Moreover, PLA cruise missiles are now ranging around Taiwan in ever-increasing numbers and, though easier to shoot down, the cumulative threat of greater numbers of weapons will naturally be much higher. Confronting this very "clear and present danger," the citizens of Taiwan have naturally become unnerved. And this reaction has generally resulted in closer defense relations between Washington and Taipei—quite contrary to Beijing's goals. Thus, the Mainland will find it politically useful to actually lay this potent capability aside for the time being. This is not—at least at this early stage—a pledge not to use force. Rather, this is largely a symbolic move (because the weapons could quickly be redeployed closer to Taiwan) for political effect, aimed at showing goodwill and increasing confidence across the Strait and also between Washington and Beijing on this crucial, contentious issue.[55]

Washington's move 3 on Taiwan: The United States should endorse and actively push for final status negotiations. The Taiwan issue is a legacy of the Cold War, and specifically of the Chinese Civil War. As the review of Cold War history in the early part of this chapter reveals, the prevailing view in the US government during the 1940s was that Taiwan is a part of China, as codified in the Cairo

Agreement, and, as US secretary of state Dean Acheson argued at that time, attempts to prevent unification would only stir up the potent ire of Chinese nationalism against the United States. More than half a century after Acheson's prescient analysis, this ire remains focused on the United States and may even be intensifying, in step with Beijing's growing power and Washington's seeming attempts to constrain it. A close reading of history, given President Truman's judgment favoring Acheson's evaluation, reveals that Taiwan would be little different than Hainan Island (which was taken by the PLA in 1950) if the Korean War had not erupted. Confronted by what appeared from Washington to be the outbreak of World War III, Truman's reversal of Acheson's judgment was logical, given that time's particularly alarming global context. But the legacy that remains has plagued US-China relations and is unlikely to go away without fundamental changes in US policy. Of course, this must be a gradual step-by-step process, and the result of certain Chinese confidence-building measures both within and also external to the Taiwan process (see the concluding chapter 12). Up to this point, Washington has taken the position that "people on both sides of the Taiwan Strait recognize there is but one China," but this policy needs to change from this passive, rather diffident position to one that endorses and actively facilitates a long-term negotiation that accepts the "one country, two systems" approach within a Chinese confederation. At this stage in the cooperation spiral, an endorsement of the goal and process should suffice—though more active measures may follow in Washington's move 5, which is elaborated below.

Beijing's move 3 on Taiwan: China should institutionalize a system for developing an expanded international presence for Taiwan. Among Taiwan's many admired achievements is the creation of its extraordinarily open and cosmopolitan society. Undoubtedly, this disposition has partly resulted from its existence on the periphery of China, as well as its lengthy and intense exposure to both the Western powers and Japan. Taiwan will never be just another Chinese province, and Beijing has accepted this through its endorsement of the one country, two systems approach. It is well known that Beijing and Taipei have competed for decades in the international realm (mostly for diplomatic recognition), but this competition has generally wasted resources in odd corners of the world, and it is now recognized that Beijing has won the contest to limit Taiwan's international status. Still, Beijing has demonstrated some flexibility in the past—for example, by accepting Taiwan as a full-fledged member of the World Trade Organization and as an observer at the World Health Organization. Similarly, the compromise worked out for the Olympic Games, whereby Taiwan sends a team under the name "Chinese Taipei," has seemed to work out fine and is not an onerous humiliation for Taiwan's athletes. But to build Taipei's confidence in the cooperation spiral, it will be essential for Beijing to move beyond ad hoc solutions to address the issue of Taiwan's international contacts—the loss of which remains a major concern for the future of Taiwan. This could involve, for example, special branch offices at all Chinese embassies that are staffed completely by Taipei. Most important would be China's broader acceptance of the need for Taiwan's leaders and representatives to travel abroad for official visits and to actively participate in key international organizations on a regular and widespread basis. A new red line might reasonably be drawn by Beijing regarding Taiwan's participation in defense and security organizations, for example, but generally the Mainland must accept an enlarged Taiwanese international presence in the process of enhancing cooperation between Beijing, Taipei, and Washington.

Washington's move 4 on Taiwan: The United States should halt the sale of new types of weapons systems. This concession is not recommended lightly, but Steinberg and O'Hanlon seem to call for similar adjustments in US policy in exchange for a reduced Mainland military posture targeting Taiwan.[56] As true as it may be that Taiwan has had the confidence to enter into negotiations because of its military relationship with the United States, it is just as certain, if not more so, that Taiwan may continue to resist serious negotiations regarding its political status vis-à-vis the Mainland as long as defense ties to the United States remain robust. The notion that the United States can indefinitely maintain such a close security relationship with a claimed island off the coast of a nuclear-armed, rising superpower is simply absurd and defies all the "natural laws" of international relations. Seeking for a point of comparison, one might think of the position of Berlin during the Cold War, and yet the USSR did not claim Berlin as its own "sacred territory." Imagine, instead, if the United States had sought to hold Crimea or some such territory against Moscow's will. Such a position would have been strategically untenable and risky in the extreme. Even in present circumstances, Washington has refused to take any military steps to counter Russia's 2014 annexation of Crimea. Military analysts knowledgeable about the cross-Strait "balance" fully recognize that there is no balance at all. China's military modernization has steadily outstripped Taiwan's armed forces, to the point where Taiwan's armed forces are now outclassed in practically every domain of warfare. With ballistic and cruise missile saturation, Beijing, if it so chooses, can effectively eviscerate Taiwan's air force (and navy), claim air superiority, and then successfully conduct amphibious operations. Thus, arms sales have for some time taken on a purely symbolic meaning. This is well understood on Taiwan—hence, the reluctance to spend large sums on big-ticket weapons systems. In effect, the Obama administration has recognized the necessity to limit arms sales to Taiwan by agreeing to upgrade existing aircraft, rather than selling F-16C/D aircraft. Indeed, this policy is actually consistent with the 1982 US commitment not to sell Taiwan advanced military hardware. Regarding that particular agreement, Nathan and Scobell suggest that Washington has been duplicitous in the past: "Once the agreement was in place, the Americans proceeded to use legalistic reasoning to empty it of all meaning."[57] It is worth stating, moreover, that Taiwan may well seek military hardware from other states, such as those in Europe or even Russia. But the value to global security of stability in US-China relations has long outweighed any marginal gain that Taipei gains in negotiations from these weapons sales.

Beijing's move 4 on Taiwan: China should restrict the building of its amphibious fleet. Having secured major new commitments by Washington to restrict arms sales and to help facilitate an accord regarding Taiwan's final status, Beijing must respond with concrete and measurable new limits on its own ability to strike at Taiwan. Although somewhat improbable, amphibious invasion still ranks near the top of Taipei's fears regarding the Mainland, especially as the Chinese Navy makes continual forward strides. More than Beijing's initial testing of an aircraft carrier in 2012, the Type 071 amphibious assault ship, which carries one marine battalion plus fifteen to twenty armored vehicles, is a platform that especially concerns Taiwan. The vessel is nearly on par with Western equivalents, and has the special capability to launch high-speed large hovercraft, which amounts to a rapid, over-the-horizon strike capability with the potential to overturn traditional calculations regarding the feasibility of an amphibious attack across the Strait.[58] As of 2014, three Type 071s had been launched, but another may be under construction.[59] In addition, all signs point to an air assault complimentary capability, known as the Type 081, that will be capable of deploying dozens of large helicopters—also quite ideal for a modern amphibious assault. Moreover, a 2014 exercise sought to demonstrate that new Chinese Z-10 attack helicopters, which had previously only been associated with the ground forces, could be operated from Chinese naval vessels of various types.[60] Such innovative capabilities, deployed on a large scale, could gravely threaten Taiwan. Although missile and aerial bombardments, of course, are massively threatening to Taiwan, the threat of amphibious assault nevertheless causes the most anxiety naturally, as it holds out the possibility of an all-out and appallingly bloody campaign to completely subjugate Taiwan. If China builds a dozen large amphibious attack vessels (either 071s or 081s), it will have the premier amphibious attack capability in the world, especially as state-of-the-art attack helicopters are added into the mix in extensive numbers. Anything above that number of amphibious attack vessels (in combination with other assets, including low-technology transports) would give China the ability to invade Taiwan outright. Undoubtedly, these multimission platforms can provide China with important new capabilities for exerting global power—including giving humanitarian relief, evacuating Chinese nationals from a conflict situation, and even pursuing open ocean antisubmarine warfare. Nevertheless, a dozen of these large, amphibious attack vessels should be more than adequate for implementing China's newly ambitious foreign and defense policies. An explicit commitment to cap the PLA Navy's amphibious capabilities would offer Taiwan (and other neighboring island states) the additional assurance that Beijing has no need for colossal capabilities for an amphibious attack. Such military restraint would play an important role in a China-US cooperation spiral for Taiwan.

Washington's move 5 on Taiwan: The United States should cease all arms transfers to Taiwan. In halting arms shipments to Taipei, Washington can make a clean break with its involvement in the Chinese civil war. This involvement originally was an accident of history, when the United States found itself after World War II presiding over the entire Asia-Pacific region, and Washington, to its credit, tried hard to reconcile the Communists and Nationalists in the late 1940s for the greater good of the Chinese people. Whether or not this was warranted, or whether the Chinese people had to find their own way, is debatable, of course. But the record clearly shows that the United States intended to leave the island to communist rule, except when the Korean War briefly led Washington's decision makers to believe that a titanic World War III was in the immediate offing. Thankfully, it was not, but Taiwan by happenstance rather than by strategic design thereafter became an American protectorate. Most likely, the Taiwanese people and even the Mainland have to some extent benefited from this accident of history, but it is time to end this unnatural protectorate status, which would otherwise only intensify for the worse and fester like an infected wound under current global power trends. It is a wonder that such a situation persisted for so long—a condition that can only be explained by China's perennial weakness. The adjustment is not only an imperative for US foreign policy, but also for global security that demands effective US-China cooperation in the security domain, and all others as well. Gilley is quite correct in asserting that "Taipei's decision to chart a new course [in 2008] is a godsend for [the] . . . United States. . . . The overburdened giant should happily watch [the cross-Strait rapprochement] and focus on other pressing regional and global issues."[61] Also, according to Michael Swaine, "It is . . . extremely unlikely that Washington will significantly alter its balanced policy . . . [on] the Taiwan issue."[62] But he also concludes that "Washington . . . should consider negotiating directly with Beijing, in consultation with Taipei, a set of mutual assurances regarding PLA force levels and deployments on the one hand, and major US arms sales and defense assistance on the other hand that are linked to the opening of a cross-Strait political dialogue." That is precisely the process that is being advocated here. The arms sales cutoff will not significantly alter the military balance, which, as has been discussed above, is now largely symbolic. However, it will obviously alter the political calculus, focusing the minds of cross-Strait negotiators to press forward toward an agreement. Contrary to the dire predictions of American conservatives, such a policy would not destabilize the Strait, because the military options would remain arduous and incredibly destructive. Thus, both Taiwan and the Mainland could be expected to remain on the negotiating track.

Beijing's move 5 on Taiwan: China should renounce the use of force as part of a peace treaty process that joins Taiwan and the Mainland in a confederation. Beijing has long insisted that the threat of the use of force not only remains on the table but is absolutely critical to ensuring Beijing's eventual goal of unification, not to mention holding onto its other restive regions. However, the combination of ending US arms sales and the original US move to limit forces on Guam, when combined with a treaty process aimed at a kind of unification, should be adequate to sway Beijing on this final point. Within a confederation structure, Taiwan will assuredly be granted a generous arrangement amounting to very substantial autonomy. Indeed, this arrangement will be substantially more accommodating than that arranged with Hong Kong. For example, Hong Kong has a garrison of the PLA (albeit small and symbolic)—a provision that, for Taiwan, Beijing had already long ago taken off the table. Also off the table but not understood widely in the West, Beijing has said that no Chinese Communist Party personnel would be posted to the island. Some skeptics have decried the Hong Kong model for Taiwan, claiming that Hong Kong citizens' rights have been trampled, but the PRC's allegedly heavy-handed approach to the former British colony has long been overhyped in the West. As Richard Bush writes: "[The PRC] has not abused civil liberties [in Hong Kong]. . . . The PRC has by and large made good on its pledge in the 1984 joint declaration with Britain to give the territory a high degree of autonomy and to allow Hong Kong's people to govern Hong Kong."[63] True, there have been some concerning incidents of late—for example, the early 2014 attack on the journalist Kevin Lau Chun-to—but there is little evidence to suggest that Beijing is making systematic efforts to halt freedom of speech or assembly in Hong Kong. The 2014 democracy protests in Hong Kong have precipitated an important dialogue in that city, but also within China more widely about the meaning of democracy and its future prospects in China. Hong Kong authorities, in particular, are to be commended for acting with admirable restraint in delicate circumstances. And yet it is noteworthy that few if any commentators have anticipated that Beijing would resort to a use of force in this situation—demonstrating the considerable stability of the present arrangement. Although democracy is well established on Taiwan and is likely to remain so within a confederation including the Mainland and Taiwan, skeptics about unification have long neglected the trend pointing in the other direction: that Taiwan (and Hong Kong for that matter) will exercise a powerful liberalizing influence within a confederated China. Indeed, the soft power that these entities already enjoy on the Mainland could hardly be overestimated, ranging across the spectrum from fast food to pop singers to cinema directors and writers. The Mainland Chinese are certainly aware that the governing structures in Hong Kong and Taiwan, though admittedly somewhat unpredictable, at the same time clearly excel in facilitating innovation and sound management. Therefore, contrary to the predictions of doomsayers suggesting that unification would herald the end of democracy and deal a bitter blow to the cause of freedom in East Asia, such analysts underestimate the resilience of Taiwan's institutions and especially the island's potent soft power. As reviewed in the conclusion of this chapter's previous section, Kastner and Saunders's analysis shows the enormous potential of a momentous Beijing–Taipei peace treaty to have dramatic positive consequences for US foreign policy, East Asian security, and indeed global security and governance. Hugh White's recent conclusion is on the mark: "There is no reason for the United States to oppose the eventual, peaceful, consensual reunification of Taiwan with China, and every reason to encourage it."[64]

Conclusion

Contrary to almost all the other chapters in this book, this one is not nearly as pessimistic. Whereas China-Japan relations continue to be deeply troubled, and US-China rivalry has only intensified in Southeast Asia and on the Korean Peninsula, the Taiwan situation constitutes a remarkable and somewhat astonishing anomaly. Not only are cross-Strait links blossoming in all directions—including, as discussed above, in the security realm—but the dramatic changes since 2008 were also effectively ratified in the Taiwan election of 2012. This is certainly not to say that progress in cross-Strait relations is irreversible and that the situation could not unfortunately return to a crisis period for US-China relations like that of 1996–2006. Significant instability related to a new trade pact across the Strait, witnessed by Taiwan students opposing further cross-Strait integration by taking over Taiwan's Legislative Yuan in March 2014. John Garver aptly summed up the contemporary political situation on Taiwan: "The speed and breadth of the development of cross-Strait relations under Ma's policies are impressive. However, Ma has not established an adequate consensus-building process because of the political difficulty in doing so."[65] These difficulties became even more plain as the KMT took a fierce drubbing in the December 2014 local elections in Taiwan, prompting major questions about the way forward in the presidential election year of 2016. Some backsliding in cross-Strait relations may be inevitable, as within any major policy redirection, but the trend of integration is likely to persist, since the alternative of returning to estrangement would not benefit anyone. Despite such tribulations, it is nevertheless vital to see the larger picture and appreciate that since 2008 "peace is breaking out" across the Taiwan Strait.

Given Taiwan's historical development, the warming trend across the Strait is all the more remarkable and is potentially crucial to the future of US-China relations. Readers familiar with the relevant Cold War history will know well that Taiwan has long been the most acute point of tension in US-China relations, and was also the focus of the delicate negotiations that finally brought the nations together for a far-reaching rapprochement during the 1970s. Westerners claiming that "unification" is an issue that should be decided by the Taiwanese alone lack an objective view of history, culture, and identity. Richard Bush, hardly a Beijing apologist, writes in his classic book on Taiwan: "The people involved are socially and culturally the same. The population of Taiwan is made up of two major groups, both of which came from China."[66] Few Westerners realize that the Taiwan dialect is called "Minnan Hua," which literally means "speech of those south of the Min River." But the Min River is located not on Taiwan but in Fujian Province. The cultural bonds across the Strait may not have been so strong four hundred years ago when Coxinga (Zheng Chenggong) battled the Qing Dynasty along with the Dutch, but that is simply no longer the case, and has not been for centuries. As Chas Freeman quite correctly points out, "Perhaps the United States should try to create circumstances that promote the settlement of the Taiwan problem rather than its perpetuation."[67]

Two plausible objections may be discussed briefly at this point, though each is dealt with more comprehensively in chapter 12, the book's conclusion. A first objection concerns the oft-made argument that any concession to Beijing represents "appeasement" that will only invite greater aggression. For those making this argument, Taiwan is the "ultimate prize" for Beijing, and thus would raise China's confidence to unacceptably high levels. A related argument concerning the fate of US alliances in the Asia-Pacific region is made that any kind of reunification between the Mainland and Taiwan would signal a "death blow" to the US-Japan Alliance, and other allies would also be dubious of the US commitment to the region's security. However, both arguments turn out to be specious—having been built on crude and simplistic assumptions. A clear view of history shows plainly that Beijing approaches the Taiwan issue quite differently than other issues, and so the expectation that China, following unification, would immediately seek to apply its hubris to other issues only stretches the imagination. The "Munich" appeasement argument also seems to be ignorant of geography, neglecting the fact that Taiwan's defense is not feasible over the long term. White quite correctly concludes: "America can no longer defend Taiwan from China, and a policy towards Taiwan that presumes that it can is unsustainable."[68] Even putting military capabilities aside, as Nathan and Scobell relate, "Beijing is convinced that it enjoys an asymmetry of motivation over the United States with respect to Taiwan."[69]

Moreover, a Washington policy premised on Munich-type fears also ignores the fact that Mainland China has reasonable expectations for its security. As for the US alliance structure, this book is advocating major changes in that structure, in the hope that it would evolve toward something lighter and more defensive. Credibility is logically questioned when commitments exceed genuine US national interests. If US commitments in the Asia-Pacific region are constrained to cover only the clearest threats to US national security (thus excluding Taiwan, in addition to various rocks and reefs along China's maritime periphery), those alliance relationships will actually be strengthened. Thus, it is well known that many South Koreans, Japanese, and others in the region have been reasonably concerned that their states, quite against their will, might be pulled by treaty commitments into the vortex of a Taiwan scenario. Having alleviated such alliance strains, chiefly caused by unreasonable war-fighting requirements, these alliances will actually benefit from enhanced and increasingly stable Taiwan–Mainland integration.

Although Washington and Beijing have increasingly taken one another as rivals in recent years, Taiwan and the Mainland have been taking concrete and frequently difficult steps toward peace. As one Mainland visitor to Taiwan recently said: "I really want more mainland people to come and see Taiwan, and then they will understand [that] . . . it's not like what they see on the TV. . . . This impression will gradually let Mainland people, especially my generation, think: 'Oh, Taiwan is so good, why do we want to conquer them? It's not necessary. We should learn from them.'" This comment illustrates the strength of interdependence in action.[70] Given unpredictable electoral politics in Taipei, some Western commentators are already predicting Chinese "sabre-rattling" and a new cross-Strait crisis just over the horizon, but astute diplomacy in Washington, Beijing, and Taipei can help to mitigate the impact of these foreseeable difficulties.[71] History, geography, culture, and economics are all compelling the cross-Strait rapprochement. Instead of attempting to counter this trend, US strategy should seize upon this opportunity to achieve the breakthrough that will be imperative to US-China cooperation in the twenty-first century.

Notes

1. Chas W. Freeman Jr., *Interesting Times: China, America and the Shifting Balance of Prestige* (Charlottesville, VA: Just World Books, 2012), 155.
2. Richard Bush and Michael O'Hanlon, *A War Like No Other: The Truth about China's Challenge to America* (New York: John A. Wiley & Sons, 2007).
3. Alan Wachman, *Why Taiwan? Geostrategic Rationales for China's Territorial Integrity* (Stanford, CA: Stanford University Press, 2007), 162–63.
4. Tonio Andrade, *Lost Colony: The Untold Story of China's First Great Victory over the West* (Princeton, NJ: Princeton University Press, 2011), 99.
5. Ibid., 100, 125.
6. Ibid., 138.
7. Wachman, *Why Taiwan?* 56.
8. Ibid., 64.
9. Author's visit to historical museum in Weihai, Shandong, PRC, spring 2009.
10. 张迎来 [Zhang Yinglai], "日据时期台籍日本兵研究" [A Study of Taiwanese Imperial Servicemen during Japanese Colonial Rule], 现代台湾研究 [Modern Taiwan Studies], April 2012, 59–60.
11. See, e.g., 邓明忠 [Deng Mingzhong], "台湾抗日老兵及后代来渝'寻找抗日足迹" [Old Taiwan Soldiers Who Fought the Japanese Return to

Chongqing to "Seek Out the Tracks of the Anti-Japanese Forces"], 两岸关系 [Cross-Strait Relations], July 2012, 48–49.

12. Alan Wachman, *Taiwan: National Identity and Democratization* (New York: M. E. Sharpe, 1994).

13. Dean Acheson, "Memorandum for the President," December 30, 1949, quoted by Thomas J. Christensen, *Useful Adversaries: Grand Strategy, Domestic Mobilization, and Sino-American Conflict, 1947–1958* (Princeton, NJ: Princeton University Press, 1996), 108.

14. See, e.g., 葛东升 [Ge Dongsheng], "人类共同的历史使命: 全面禁止彻底销毁核武器" [Mankind's Common Historical Mission: The Comprehensive Prohibition and Total Elimination of Nuclear Weapons], 中国军事科学 [China Military Science], January 2013, 33; 白纯, 申海良 [Bai Chun and Shen Hailiang], "抗美援朝战争与台湾问题关系研究述评" [A Review of Research concerning the Relationship between the War against US Aggression and Aiding Korea and the Taiwan Issue], 军事历史 [Military History], February 2013, 72–76.

15. See, e.g., 候中军 [Hou Zhongjun], "新中国控诉美国侵台背景下的台湾地位问题再探" [A Reexamination of the Status of Taiwan against the Backdrop of New China Condemning the American Occupation of Taiwan], 中共党史研究 [Research on Chinese Communist Party History], November 2011, 59–69.

16. He Di, "The Last Campaign to Unify China: The CCP's Unrealized Plan to Liberate Taiwan, 1949–1950," in *Chinese Warfighting: The PLA Experience since 1949*, ed. Mark Ryan, David Finkelstein, and Michael McDevitt (London: M. E. Sharpe, 2003), 84.

17. Niu Jun, "Chinese Decision Making in the Taiwan Strait," in *Managing Sino-American Crises: Case Studies and Analysis*, ed. Michael Swaine and Zhang Tuosheng (Washington, DC: Carnegie Endowment for International Peace, 2006), 310.

18. Robert L. Suettinger, "US 'Management' of Taiwan Straits 'Crises,'" in *Managing Sino-American Crises*, ed. Swaine and Zhang, 259.

19. [Wang Dong], "一九六二年台海危机与中美关系" [The Taiwan Strait Crisis of 1962 and US-China Relations], 中共党史研究 [Research on Chinese Communist Party History], July 2010, 60–69.

20. [Tao Wenzhao], "中美'上海公报'与台湾问题" [The China-US Shanghai Communique and the Taiwan Issue], 两岸关系 [Cross-Strait Relations], March 2012, 19.

21. Nathan and Scobell provide an interesting perspective on Chinese perceptions regarding the outcome of the negotiations surrounding the Shanghai

Communiqué. They discuss the idea that Washington only "acknowledged" but did not "recognize" China's claim over Taiwan. They write: "In retrospect, Chinese analysts came to believe that the Americans had taken advantage of Mao Zedong and Zhou Enlai, using a legalistic manipulation of the letter of an agreement to trap the Chinese, who naively put faith in the spirit of the agreement." Andrew Nathan and Andrew Scobell, *China's Search for Security* (New York: Columbia University Press, 2012), 102.

22. James Mann, *About Face: A History of America's Curious Relationship with China, from Nixon to Clinton* (New York: Vintage Books, 1998), 336.

23. Robert S. Ross, "The 1995–96 Taiwan Strait Confrontation: Coercion, Credibility, and the Use of Force," *International Security* 25, no. 2 (Fall 2000): 122.

24. Evan A. Feigenbaum, "China's Challenge to Pax Americana," *Washington Quarterly* 24 (2001): 31–43, http://muse.jhu.edu/journals/washington_quarterly/v024/24.3feigenbaum.html.

25. Sarah Mishkin, "Chinese Tourists Boost Taiwan's Economy," *Washington Post*, August 30, 2012, http://articles.washingtonpost.com/2012-08-30/world/35490771_1_chinese-tourists-taiwanese-society-mainland.

26. Daniel H. Rosen and Zhi Wang, *Deepening China-Taiwan Relations through the Economic Cooperation Framework Agreement*, Policy Brief PB10-16 (Washington, DC: Peterson Institute for International Economics, 2010), cited by Dong Wang, "ECFA and the Elections: Implications for Cross-Strait Relations," *China Brief* 12, no. 1 (January 6, 2012), www.jamestown.org/single/?no_cache=1&tx_ttnews%5Btt_news%5D=38855.

27. "ECFA One Year On," *Taiwan Review*, November 1, 2011, http://taiwanreview.nat.gov.tw/ct.asp?xItem=177522&CtNode=1337.

28. 单玉丽 [Dan Yuli], "ECFA 后的两岸经济形势与未来影响因素探析" [Analysis of the Cross-Strait Economic Situation after ECFA and Future Prospects], 现代台湾研究 [Modern Taiwan Studies], October 2011, 37–42.

29. Lawrence Chung, "Breakthrough in Ties between DPP and Beijing," *South China Morning Post*, November 10, 2012, www.scmp.com/news/china/article/1079014/breakthrough-ties-between-dpp-and-beijing.

30. [Pan Linfeng], "台湾2012年'大选'综合分析" [A Comprehensive Analysis of the 2012 Taiwan General Elections], 现代台湾研究 [Modern Taiwan Studies], December 2011, 29–32.

31. [Xin Qi], "和平发展大道之行" [Walking the Great Path of Peaceful Development], 两岸关系 [Cross-Strait Relations], February 2012, 20.

32. [Lu Yang], "从'民族'塑造到'国家'建构" [Molding a "Nation" into a "State"], 现代台湾研究 [Modern Taiwan Studies], no. 3 (2011): 9–14.

33. [Zhang Shirong], "基于国际经验构建中国反分裂战略体系的几点思考" [Some Reflections on China's Construction of Its Anti-Secession Strategy

System on the Basis of International Experience], 国际关系学院学报 [Journal of the University of International Relations], no. 6 (2011): 25–29.

34. 白纯 [Bai Chun], "美台对台军售目的弱化台军独立作战能力" [US Arms Sales to Taiwan Revealing Its Purpose of Weakening Taiwan's Independent Combat Capability], 现代台湾研究 [Modern Taiwan Studies], October 2011, 64–65.

35. 陈虎 Chen Hu, "美国对台军售'王牌'已成鸡肋" [The US Arms Sales "Trump Card" on Taiwan Already Has Little Value], 当代海军 [Modern Navy], September 13, 2011, 4.

36. [Liu Guofen], "重返亚洲战略下的美国与台海两岸关系之探讨" [A Discussion of US Policy toward Cross-Strait Relations under Its "Return to Asia" Strategy], 现代台湾研究 [Modern Taiwan Studies], December 2011, 12–16.

37. "Mainland, Taiwan to Hold Joint Exercises," Xinhua, August 31, 2012, www .chinamedia.com/2012/08/31/mainland-taiwan-to-hold-joint-exercises/.

38. [Shi Xiaodong], "结束战争理论视野下的两岸建立军事安全互信机制问题探讨" [Analysis of the Problem of Building the Cross-Strait Military and Security Mutual Trust Mechanism from the Perspective of War Termination Theory], 台湾研究 [Taiwan Studies], no. 1 (2012): 1–7.

39. 袁鹏 [Yuan Peng], "警惕台湾的战略焦虑症并发" [Be Vigilant against the Ailment of Taiwan's Strategic Anxieties], 台湾研究 [Taiwan Studies], January 2014, 6–7.

40. 刘飞涛 [Liu Feitao], "美国涉台政策辩论及对台军售政策走势" [Debates on US Policy toward Taiwan and Trends in Arms Sale Policies], 国际问题研究 [International Issues Research], no. 4 (2012): 51–65.

41. Bill Owens (admiral, US Navy, ret.), "The US Must Start Treating China as a Friend," *Financial Times*, November 17, 2009.

42. Bruce Gilley, "Not So Dire Straits: How the Finlandization of Taiwan Benefits US Security," *Foreign Affairs*, January–February 2010, 49.

43. Charles Glaser, "Will China's Rise Lead to War? Why Realism Does Not Mean Pessimism," *Foreign Affairs*, March–April 2011, 87–88.

44. See, e.g., the recommendations of *A Way Ahead with China: Steering the Right Course with the Middle Kingdom* (Charlottesville: Miller Center for Strategic and International Studies at the University of Virginia, 2011), http://miller center.org/policy/chinaroundtable.

45. Nancy B. Tucker and Bonnie Glaser, "Should the United States Abandon Taiwan?" *Washington Quarterly* 34 (Fall 2011): 25.

46. Ibid., 26, 29.

47. Daniel Blumenthal, "Rethinking US Policy towards Taiwan," *Foreign Policy*, March 2 2011, http://shadow.foreignpolicy.com/posts/2011/03/02/rethinking us_foreign_policy_towards_taiwan.

48. James Holmes and Toshi Yoshihara, *Defending the Strait: The Taiwan Naval Strategy in the 21st Century* (Washington, DC: Jamestown Foundation, 2011), www.jamestown.org/programs/recentreports/single/?tx_ttnews%5BbackPid%5D=7&tx_ttnews%5Btt_news%5D=38201&cHash=a3b42979832fb62c1b8c1156a873fd99.

49. L. C. Russell Hsiao and Mark Stokes, "Taiwan's Role in Air–Sea Battle," Project 2049 Asia Eye, April 16, 2012.

50. Philip Saunders and Scott Kastner, "Bridge over Troubled Waters: Envisioning a China-Taiwan Peace Agreement," *International Security* 33 (Spring 2009): 91.

51. Ibid., 114.

52. Shirley Kahn, *Guam: US Defense Deployments*, CRS Report for Congress RS22570 (Washington, DC: Congressional Research Service, 2012), 1.

53. Some examples of this extensive literature include 天天 [Tian tian], "美军关岛建航母母港" [The US Military Is Building a Berthing Dock for Aircraft Carriers at Guam], 中国国防报道 [China National Defense Report], August 13, 2013, 5; 夏效生, 张家齐 [Xia Xiaosheng and Zhang Jiaqi], "美新型轰炸机欲落户关岛" [New Type American Bombers Are Planned to Base at Guam], 中国国防报 [China National Defense Report], June 21, 2011, 4; 曹琳琳, 王运祥 [Cao Linlin, PLA Navy, and Wang Yunxiang], "美国加强关岛军事基地建设的战略解读" [A Strategic Analysis of the Accelerated US Buildup of the Military Base on the Island of Guam], 广东外语外贸大学学报 [Journal of Guangdong University of Foreign Studies], January 2010, 55–58; and 韩江波 [Han Jiangbo], "关岛: 美军控制西太平洋作战体系的纲" [The Island of Guam: The Key Link for the US Military's Combat System to Control the Western Pacific], 当代海军 [Modern Navy], December 2006, 30–34.

54. See, e.g., 鞠海龙 [Ju Hailong], "当代南海问题的函数解析: 兼论两岸关系对我国和平解决南海问题的影响" [A Functional Analysis of the Contemporary South China Sea Issue: The Influence of Cross-Strait Relations on the Peaceful Settlement of the South China Sea Issue], 东南亚研究 [Southeast Asian Studies], June 2009, 41–45; 郭健青 [Guo Jianqing], "两岸应携手维护南海主权" [Editorial: Both Sides Should Join Hands to Defend Sovereignty over the South China Sea], 现代台湾研究 [Modern Taiwan Studies], no. 2 (2012): preface; and 张文生 [Zhang Wensheng], "南海为权, 两岸能否合作" [Supporting Rights in the South China Sea May Depend on Whether the Two Sides of the Strait Can Cooperate], 两岸关系 [Relations across the Strait], August 2012, 21–22.

55. However, it is certainly true that the weapons could rather quickly be moved back into firing positions. It is significant that such a movement would require

at least 12 to 24 hours. That, admittedly, small amount of time could allow civilians to enter shelters, etc., and generally mitigate the worst effects of a "bolt from the blue" attack.

56. James Steinberg and Michael E. O'Hanlon, *Strategic Reassurance and Resolve: US-China Relations in the Twenty-First Century* (Princeton, NJ: Princeton University Press, 2014), 209.

57. Nathan and Scobell, *China's Search*, 105. Bader's conclusion is similar. Jeffrey A. Bader, *Obama and China's Rise: An Insider's Account of America's Asia Strategy* (Washington, DC: Brookings Institution Press, 2012), 19; on the Obama administration's calculations with respect to Taiwan arms sales, see 71–77. This position is difficult to discern, for Bader argues that such sales are necessary to (1) defend against Chinese attack, (2) signal Washington's enduring commitment to Taiwan's security, and (3) demonstrate US credibility to allies (p. 71). However, he then relates that he emphasized to China's ambassador "what [sales] were not authorized" (pp. 73–74). In the end, Bader explains, the Obama administration made clear to Beijing that "any discussion touching on the Taiwan Strait could not take US arms sales as their focus" (p. 77).

58. According to this Chinese analysis, air-cushion craft quadruple the amount of possible feasible landing areas on Taiwan. See 气垫登陆艇: 对中国海军的意义" [The Significance of Air-Cushioned Landing Craft for the Chinese Navy], 现代舰船 [Modern Ships], March 2008, 9.

59. Ridzwan Rahmat, "Images Suggest Fourth Chinese Type 071 Is in Build," *Jane's*, October 21, 2014, http://www.janes.com/article/44857/images-suggest -fourth-chinese-type-071-lpd-is-in-build.

60. 伊鸣 [Yi Ming], "武装直升机如何上舰?" [How Does an Attack Helicopter Go Aboard Ship?], 兵工科技 [Ordnance Science and Technology], no. 9 (2014): 15–17.

61. Gilley, "Not So Dire Straits," 58.

62. Michael D. Swaine, *America's Challenge: Engaging a Rising China in the Twenty-First Century* (Washington, DC: Carnegie Endowment for International Peace, 2011), 91.

63. Richard Bush, *Untying the Knot: Making Peace in the Taiwan Strait* (Washington, DC: Brookings Institution Press, 2005), 92.

64. Hugh White, *The China Choice: Why We Should Share Power* (New York: Oxford University Press, 2013), 100.

65. Andrew Windsor, "An Interview with John Garver: Sunflower Movement Questions Future Direction of Cross-Strait Relations," National Bureau of Asian Research, June 18, 2014, www.nbr.org/downloads/pdfs/psa/Garver_ interview_061814.pdf.

66. White, *China Choice*, 3.
67. Freeman, *Interesting Times*, 162.
68. White, *China Choice*, 100.
69. Nathan and Scobell, *China's Search*, 308.
70. Quoted by Mishkin, "Chinese Tourists."
71. Robert Manning, "Forget the South China Sea: Taiwan Could Be Asia's Next Big Security Nightmare," *National Interest*, December 5, 2014, http://nationalinterest .org/feature/forget-the-south-china-sea-taiwan-could-be-asias-next-big-11790.

4

MUTUALLY ASSURED DEPENDENCE
Economic Aspects of US-China Relations

The Chinese "economic miracle" since 1978 is not the focus of this book, but it does serve as fundamental bedrock for the argument made here. Indeed, there would be no special urgency to fully understand US-China relations if the Chinese economy were not all but certain to exceed that of the United States in aggregate size during the present decade. These impressive resources will endow Chinese leaders with the opportunity, and some might say even the responsibility, to act on the world's stage as never before. However, as enumerated in the preceding chapter regarding Taiwan, and in many chapters to follow, this clear and stark change in the balance of global power obviously carries attendant risks, as well as opportunities.

Many observers, including many Chinese, would be loathe to characterize China's current economic status as "miraculous." The Chinese will immediately point out the shockingly putrid air quality in most Chinese cities and the horribly unsafe working conditions pervasive in various sectors, such as mining, not to mention the truly difficult lives of the millions who constitute the so-called "floating population" that exists and survives unofficially (and quite without legal protections) on the margins of Chinese urban society. Investors and economists alike opine about the many obvious imbalances that continue to characterize the Chinese economy. This unease spans the gamut from concerns regarding transparency and quality control to those accusing China of practicing mercantilist or "beggar-thy-neighbor" policies by manipulating the value of the renminbi (RMB). A broad consensus, which now encouragingly includes the top Chinese leadership, holds that growth should slow down, and that the economy needs to be "rebalanced" away from infrastructure investment as the primary driver toward an economy that has a much larger service sector and is driven primarily by domestic consumption.

The arguments of skeptics—for example, Michael Pettis of Qinghua University in Beijing—have merit and are discussed in turn over the course of this chapter.[1] However, if China's rapid economic ascendancy is taken as an objective fact, given average annual gross domestic product (GDP) growth of 9.9 percent for the thirty years between 1979 and 2009, then it is appropriate to examine a variety of scenarios for China's economy that could have an enormous impact on global order and the prospects for peace. A number of these scenarios are positive, including the hardly farfetched possibility that sustainable Chinese growth will lead in the future to a China that is not only increasingly globalized and enmeshed in the world trading system (and all related behavioral norms) but is also generally satisfied that China benefits from protecting the international status quo. In this rosy picture, economic factors are crucial to encouraging Beijing to become a genuinely "responsible stakeholder." Unfortunately, there are a number of scenarios in which China's economic growth develops as a highly destabilizing factor: through increasing instability at home precipitated by rapid social change, traditional competition between states for natural resources, and tensions arising over fair trade practices, not to mention the possibility of a Chinese "crisis of expectations." In other words, China's impressive new strength could well lead it to adopt new and uncompromising geopolitical ambitions—to seek for its "place in the sun."

For the US-China relationship, the long-running debate regarding the pacifying effects of growing economic interdependence is hardly only of academic interest. Now with staggering annual bilateral trade of close to $600 billion—one of the largest such trading relationships in the world—many reasonable thinkers on both sides of the Pacific are inclined to agree with Niall Ferguson's notion of "Chimerica," in which the two titans are so thoroughly linked that they could never lock horns.[2] And yet it is widely understood, at least among scholars of international relations, that Europe also enjoyed high levels of economic interdependence during the years before World War I[3] and that America was Japan's leading trading partner in the years before Pearl Harbor. Of late, it seems that economic tensions are actually at the core of anxieties on both sides of the Pacific. As is demonstrated in this chapter, the Chinese are concerned that Americans are seeking to constrain or even derail China's path toward prosperity and leadership. Meanwhile, Americans are deeply concerned about ceding economic leadership, and they even fear that the US economy has been hollowed out by unfair Chinese trading practices. Ultimately, this chapter, like the others in this book, seeks concrete steps to reduce the significant strains that have arisen specifically within US-China economic relations. These tensions, if left unchecked, could pose major challenges for global order and prosperity.

Background

China's economic success before the nineteenth century is not generally in dispute. As Fairbank explains, beginning in the Tang Dynasty (the eighth century AD), "China [was] . . . the world's most advanced society, [producing] . . . a series of startling inventions—printed books, the abacus, paper money and credit instruments, gunpowder explosives, water pumps, canal locks, water-tight bulkheads and the compass for seafaring, to say nothing of earlier creations like ceramics and 'Chinaware,' lacquer, silk, and cotton textiles."[4] It is estimated, for example, that China contributed almost one-third of global manufacturing output in 1750.[5] Kissinger cites the seventeenth-century French Jesuit Jean-Baptiste Du Halde, who relates his observations from 1736: "The riches peculiar to each province, and the facility of conveying merchandise, by means of rivers and canals, have rendered the domestic trade of the empire always very flourishing. . . . The inland trade of China is so great that the commerce of all Europe is not to be compared therewith; the provinces being like so many kingdoms."[6]

The next obvious question regarding Chinese economic history concerns what the Peking University economist Justin Yifu Lin terms "Needham's Puzzle." As Lin writes: "[Joseph Needham] . . . noted the lag between China and Europe. Before the fifteenth and sixteenth centuries, technology flows were one way, from East to West. . . . After the middle of the eighteenth century, the flow again was all one way, from West to East."[7] There are numerous explanations for China's precipitous decline beginning with the Opium War, such as the paucity of external competition, the pervasive "Middle Kingdom" complex that clouded any sense of reality, the excess of labor inhibiting incentives to develop technology, and the low social prestige for either merchants or warriors (groups that led technological innovation in the West). For Lin, the imperial examination system that was the key to China's success as a civilization came to form an "institutional trap" because it did not allow China's elite to adequately embrace the scientific revolution wrought by the shift from human experience to controlled experiments.[8] Interestingly, a recent Chinese scholarly study examines global "currency geopolitics" (币缘政治) and concludes that the failure to recognize the importance of China's system of currency played a significant role in the downfall of both the Ming and Qing dynasties.[9]

After the chaos of World War II, followed almost immediately by the Chinese Civil War and the Korean War, the economy of the new Communist China could not help but improve, and there were broad increases in living standards and productivity during the mid-1950s. However, as detailed in chapter 2, the "left deviation" led by Mao Zedong after 1957 resulted in widespread economic disasters, from which China only really recovered in the 1980s. Some Chinese intellectuals now very openly state in the Chinese press that this "left deviation" cost China dearly, by isolating it from global capitalism and related technological trends.[10] Lin observes, moreover, that "average living standards scarcely improved between 1952 and 1978. . . . Clearly, heavy industry, the atomic bomb, and the satellite took priority over people's well-being."[11]

The successes of Deng Xiaoping's economic reform program are widely accepted and understood. No wonder one may see his visage still gracing placards quite commonly in contemporary China, whereas Mao is rarely pictured. Deng's focus on agriculture and establishing special economic zones, and his emphasis on light manufacturing, initiated the Chinese economic miracle, though critics may well suggest that his principal contribution was to get the Chinese state to stop inhibiting the great entrepreneurial spirit and energy of the Chinese people. Above all, his contribution was to favor practical solutions over grandiloquent ideology. More controversial, certainly in the West, was his deliberate choice to undertake economic reforms while keeping a tight lid on political reform. Comparing his reformist legacy with that of Mikhail Gorbachev, it is tempting to suggest that Deng's phased approach favoring economic reform has been much more successful. Still, it is worth noting that China enjoyed certain natural advantages over the USSR, including the fact that its larger agricultural sector was more easily reformed than Soviet heavy industry. Perhaps most decisive in judging the success of Chinese economic reforms against those undertaken in Russia a decade later is that the extreme failures of Mao's leftist policies were so starkly evident that Deng presided over a relatively strong national consensus favoring reform, whereas the Soviet legacy was more ambiguous and therefore many constituencies in the Russian context urgently resisted the process of reforms.

Deng's strong revolutionary credentials also gave him credibility when it came to trimming Chinese state power—for example, when he placed military modernization conspicuously last among the four modernizations. If the People's Republic of China had previously sacrificed "butter for guns," the balance was radically reversed under Deng, with good results. The fact that Deng had lived abroad in France during his youth gave him a very different perspective than Mao, but his later travels to Singapore, Japan, and the United States no doubt spurred his determination to preserve China's "reform and opening up"—a development trajectory for China that seemed to be at risk after the Tiananmen Square Massacre of 1989 but was subsequently solidified with Deng's Southern Tour in 1992. Jiang Zemin, Deng's successor, also deserves substantial credit for preserving the economic reform momentum. Among the major achievements of his tenure, one may note fiscal and tax reforms, removing the Chinese military from business, and, crucially, the challenging reform of large state-owned enterprises. Moreover, Beijing certainly gained regional prestige with its adroit actions during the Asian Financial Crisis of 1997–98. Although other major economies in the region, such as that of South Korea, were viewed as deeply troubled, China stepped up with several significant loans to smaller countries and also crucially did not seek to further lower the value of the RMB—in effect, allowing itself to take a hit from its neighbors so that their economies could be stabilized. This episode may be viewed as China's "coming out party" on the global financial stage.

A key step in China's economic reform effort was its accession to the World Trade Organization (WTO), which ultimately took place in 2001. The critical negotiations involved difficult bargaining with Washington during the years 1998–99. A Qinghua University professor, Wang Qingxin, recently published a fascinating English-language scholarly account of these negotiations from a Chinese perspective. This account reveals major inhibitions on the Chinese side that were eventually countered by the "language of neoclassical economics," as applied especially by Chinese premier Zhu Rongji and several influential liberal economists in Beijing. He writes that these economists looked at the Asian Financial Crisis of the late 1990s and concluded that "the East Asian Model of the developmental state was inferior to the Western laissez-faire market system and further strengthened their belief about the applicability of neoclassical economics to [state-owned enterprise] reform in China."[12] China's WTO accession also enabled an even higher level of dynamic exchange between the two mammoth economies. For example, a new scholarly study of

US private equity practices in Asia finds that, "with US ownership, Chinese capital, and a preponderance of Chinese private equity executives, the RMB funds that US private equity firms have launched in China also exemplify complex interdependent relationships."[13]

Even as China was grappling with the impact of fully opening to the world at the turn of the millennium, as amply demonstrated by Wang, the world began to feel the full force of China's explosive economic growth, with similarly turbulent results. These "tremors" were brilliantly revealed in the introduction to a recent book by James Kynge, a former China correspondent for the *Financial Times*: "As Chinese demand drove up the price of scrap metal to record levels, thieves almost everywhere had the same idea. . . . More than 150 covers disappeared during one month in Chicago. Scotland's 'great drain' robbery saw more than a hundred vanish in a few days."[14] Indeed, the consequences of China's quest for markets and resources appeared rather suddenly to be having an impact on geopolitical quandaries around the globe, from East Africa (see chapter 6) to the Persian Gulf (see chapter 7) to Central Asia (see chapter 11) to even the world's polar regions. China's naval expansion—the subject of much speculation and anxiety in recent years—has been linked to the dragon's insatiable appetite for fossil fuels, whether in the form of newly explored undersea fields in the South China Sea (see chapter 10) or the imperative to protect related sea lanes crossing the Indian Ocean (see chapter 11).

The economic tensions between Washington and Beijing, already quite visible in the 1990s, reached full flower during the first decade of the new century. A potent symbol of these new tensions was the 2006 rejection of a Chinese attempt to acquire the US energy firm UNOCAL. Congress weighed in and judged that it was too risky for China to take a major stake in the US energy infrastructure. Thus, the issue was viewed as a national security concern in Washington. However, the circumstances of the UNOCAL episode further poisoned what were already tense economic relations. American leaders and economists decried the lack of Chinese investment in the United States, especially when compared with American investments in China, yet Beijing claimed that Chinese capital was being deliberately excluded from opportunities, for noneconomic reasons.

On worsening transpacific economic tensions, Charles Freeman III wrote in 2009: "It is tempting to equate closing a US factory with the decline of US power, and perhaps even the transfer of that power to a potential rival like China." However, he concludes: "If [American] jobs are being lost to China, there seems to have been relatively little macroeconomic effect that can be measured in a zero-sum way." In this piece Freeman criticizes then-candidate Hillary Clinton for resorting to populism, blaming "Chinese . . . malfeasance [and] rapacious financiers . . . [seeking to] satisfy the urges of a nervous . . . [American] public."[15] These tensions were undoubtedly exaggerated by the onset of the global financial and economic crisis in 2008.

Clinton was hardly alone in wielding the economic cudgel against China in election season. A remarkable political advertisement appeared on US televisions beginning in 2010. The most interesting thing about this particular ad was that its lengthy dialogue was given entirely in Mandarin Chinese. The ad showed a lecture hall in a Chinese university set some years in the future, with a Chinese professor explaining how the precipitous decline of the United States occurred as a result of financial irresponsibility. Although the ad was not overtly anti-Chinese, the clear subtext was that the Chinese are giddy with pleasure at US economic difficulties and are themselves girding to replace the United States as the world's most powerful state.[16] Perceptions of acute economic tension in US-China relations were not restricted to the popular media and election campaigns, however. For example, the prestigious journal *International Security* published an article in 2009 titled "Assessing China's Financial Strength in Great Power Politics."[17] This article concluded that "China has translated its large capital surplus into minor but not major foreign policy gains." The author, Daniel Drezner, also pointed to the analogy with nuclear deterrence, suggesting that the US-China "'balance of financial terror' implies a more peaceful coexistence, but at the same time it is a relatively nervous coexistence."

In his January 2011 State of the Union Address, President Obama also sought to play on this wider sentiment among Americans. Pointing to Chinese achievements in developing "the world's fastest computer" and the "world's largest private solar research facility," Obama called upon Americans to realize another "Sputnik moment," by rising to compete more effectively with China's increasing power.[18] During the 2012 presidential election, a strange feature of the several final debates between Mitt Romney and Obama was the fact that China was a major and almost dominating issue of the "domestic policy" debate but only came up for a short time in the "foreign policy debate," because most of the latter was spent discussing general US policies toward Iran and the Middle East. This interesting "miscategorization" of the China issue as a "domestic policy issue" may demonstrate the salience of economic and even "bread and butter" issues within the larger bilateral relationship, but that salience, and particularly the seeming crossover between economic and national security issues, could also increase the volatility of the wider relationship.

As noted above, there is now a wide consensus that China's economy must be rebalanced, and this may indeed relieve (to a degree) certain sources of economic tension in US-China relations. Justin Yifu Lin, for example, describes the "three excessives" that have emerged in the Chinese economy over the last decade: excessive investment and insufficient consumption, an excessive supply of credit, and an excessive trade surplus.[19] Pettis, for example, writes alarmingly: "By 2005 household consumption in China had declined to around 40 percent of GDP. With the exception of a few very special and unique cases, this level is unprecedented in modern economic history. . . . By 2010, the last year for which we have complete statistics as of this writing, household consumption declined to an astonishing 34 percent of GDP. This level is almost surreal."[20] However, against many doomsayers' predictions, an extremely detailed survey in *The Economist* of the Chinese economy in mid-2012 proved quite unexpectedly bullish, revealing that "China's economy will not crash; . . . the contribution of foreign demand to China's growth has always been exaggerated, and it is now shrinking."[21] The same survey noted China's shrinking overall current account (trade surplus) and also that the RMB has risen in value by 27 percent since mid-2005, when measured by the real effective exchange rate.[22] As part of the broader effort to increase both living standards and consumption, the survey also notes approvingly that Beijing has started to put in place both a rural pension scheme and a much broader health insurance system.[23] The overall report concludes that in the all-important economic domain, "China does face significant problems, but nothing it cannot handle."[24] At this writing in late 2014, *The Economist* forecasts remain relatively bullish: "China's economy slowed to 7.3% year-on-year growth in the third quarter, slipping below the official target of 7.5%. For most countries, growth above 7% would be a rare triumph. For China, it is the economy's weakest performance since the depths of the global financial crisis in early 2009. This should not be cause for alarm. The economy is 50% bigger than it was five years ago, so some deceleration is natural."[25]

It is now conventional wisdom that the US economy will be surpassed in the near future (if not already) in aggregate size by the Chinese economy. Meanwhile, the economist Arvind Subramanian of the respected Peterson Institute of International Economics has seemingly toppled what passed for conventional wisdom with his book *Eclipse: Living in the Shadow of Economic*

Dominance, which employs the latest economic forecasting methods as well as reasonable assumptions. He concludes quite emphatically: "China's economic dominance is imminent (if not already at hand), likely to be broad in scope, and substantial in magnitude. . . . These basic trends are quite robust. Mindful of false positive predictions of the past. . . . I am conservative in my growth and trade projections for China. The basic picture of dominance does not require China to grow at anything close to current rates."[26] This economist sees "a picture by 2030 not of relative American decline leading to a multipolar world, but of a near-unipolar world with Chinese economic hegemony," because China's economy in 2030 is likely to be twice the size of that of the United States (in purchasing-power-parity dollars).[27]

As noted above, some economists are much more skeptical regarding China's growth prospects. Pettis, for example, predicts: "As a consensus about the need for a radical transformation of the growth model develops, and China begins adjusting over the next two or three years, the impact of the global crisis will probably manifest itself in the form of a 'lost' decade or longer for China of much slower growth and soaring government debt."[28] Another skeptic regarding the Chinese economy, the economist Patrick Chovanec also of Qinghua University, warns Washington not to try to emulate Beijing's state-led economic model. Referring to China's much-touted government support for high-speed rail and also green energy, Chovanec concludes: "In fact, Beijing's mandarins are no better at picking winners, and just as prone to blow money on boondoggles, as their Beltway counterparts."[29] However, even Pettis is not wholly pessimistic regarding China's prospects. He concludes: "Will slower growth be a disaster for China, and lead to social instability? Not necessarily. If the rebalancing is well managed, by definition household income and consumption will grow faster than GDP."[30]

Among Subramanian's boldest predictions is that the RMB may supersede the dollar as the world's primary reserve currency in the coming decades. He concludes: "The economic fundamentals are in place to sustain a rapid bolstering of the reserve currency status for the renminbi. . . . It is . . . misleading . . . to think that the fate of the dollar or economic dominance more broadly is in the hands of the United States rather than China." However, he is hardly uncritical of Chinese economic practice and its distinct weaknesses, describing its heretofore monetary practices as unabashedly "mercantilist," and even suggesting that the RMB's hypothetical new status as a major global reserve currency could amount to a "poison chalice," albeit a prestigious one.[31] But his analysis is refreshing in its value-free analysis of current and historical economic data. The near certainty of the emergence of a much stronger China in coming decades undergirds the basic argument of this book.

Chinese Perspectives on the Chinese Economy and Related Trade Tensions

The section above has sought to lay out the parameters of understanding regarding China's economy from the English-language discussion of the subject, with the caveat that a truly comprehensive survey would require several volumes rather than a mere section of a chapter. The next section may be more unique as it seeks to gauge the tenor of Chinese-language discussions and debates regarding Chinese economic development and the nature of China's economic interactions with the wider world. The discussion of Chinese language sources naturally mirrors that in the West to some degree, focusing on the near-term imperative to "rebalance" China's economy. However, this literature also illustrates the strident nationalism that is increasing among Chinese observers of economic affairs. There is also a clear sense of awareness regarding the so-called financial balance of terror in US-China economic relations and the vital importance of trade in the overall relationship. Recall that the discussion of Chinese sources here does *not* imply an endorsement of these assessments, but they are discussed in order to fully explain Chinese perspectives.

Illustrative of its overall import in China's economic future, 人民日报 (*People's Daily*) carried a front-page story in May 2013 under the headline "Service Sector Enters Period of Rapid Growth." Now constituting 47.8 percent of GDP, the service sector was said to exceed the construction sector for the first time ever. As observed in this article, developed state economies often have in excess of 70 percent of GDP made up of the service sector, so "there is tremendous room for future expansion in [China's] service sector."[32] A recent Chinese scholarly article also demonstrates China's determination to fully understand the challenge it confronts in rebalancing its economy by encouraging domestic consumption. This article uses statistical and survey analytical tools to suggest that the Chinese government has long underestimated consumption and overestimated levels of investment. The former problem is blamed on the phenomenon of 怕露富 (fear of showing wealth), among other factors.[33] Another potential area for energizing further growth in China's economy is a geographical approach, namely, one that looks to regions that have yet to reach their full potential. The success of economic development along the Chinese coast, and spreading out from the special economic zones, has also inspired efforts during the last decade to promote growth in the poorer western region, as well as the "rust belt" north. A new and related concept recently promoted in the Chinese press is that of the Golden Central Triangle, which would encompass the interior southern provinces of Hubei, Hunan, and Jiangxi.[34] Even with substantial rebalancing to new domestic markets, however, the Chinese economy will remain tightly linked to the global market, and hence there is a need in China for objective forecasts regarding the global economic situation. Such a scholarly survey of the global economic landscape in 2012 noted reassuringly that there will be no "second great recession" and viewed the central uncertainties surrounding the crisis in Europe, the slow recovery in the United States, and continuing instability in the Middle East as the major risk factors. The article was careful to note that China does not in any way welcome paralysis and decline regarding the concept of European integration, but it also suggested—conversely, and perhaps somewhat triumphantly—that the world economy now exhibits 两速发展, 南高北低 (two-speed development, with the South outpacing the North), and that this trend is predicted to be durable.[35]

Undoubtedly, a strong current of economic nationalism is evident in contemporary Chinese analyses. A 2011 scholarly article, the lead article in a rather prestigious Chinese academic journal, on currency geopolitics was rather skeptical about the prospects for the US economy, and it suggested that "it is not hard for people to see . . . the crisis in the financial system based on the US dollar is sowing doubts about free markets and the free market economic system, and this crisis is undermining the openness of the global trading system." It notes the "not insignificant tremor" set off by Hu Jintao's January 2011 statement that "the international currency system was a legacy of the past and that the current system had certain fraudulent practices, and was not appropriate for economic and financial global development." The author is careful to suggest that China has "limited goals" with respect to the financial system and does not seek a "thoroughgoing breakup" of the dollar-based financial system, but also concludes that a general move away from using the dollar on the Eurasian continent is a 'real nightmare' for the United States."[36]

A 2012 Chinese scholarly article warns of the danger that the United States is seeking to cause China to 美国化 (Americanize) with respect to its values, politics, and type of economic and lifestyle model, in order "to realize its strategic objectives" with respect to China. It is argued that as US-China economic interaction has increased, China's independent space for economic decision making has been curtailed. China's industrial policy and its policies against unfair competition and labor and environmental standards are all said to have suffered from the influence of US investment. In addition, this scholar argues that the relevant international treaties and agreements were by and large created under US direction and thus mainly serve US interests.[37] A detailed Chinese survey of Western appraisals of China's entry into the WTO arrives at a somewhat similar conclusion. This survey faithfully reports on the "huge challenges confronting the Chinese Communist Party," that the positive impact of entering the WTO should not be exaggerated, and that many countries have been exasperated by China's trade policies. The study concludes that many Western demands go well beyond the parameters of the WTO and reflect a desire to impel China to "walk the same route as Western countries."[38] With respect to the crucial and controversial issue of intellectual property protection, there may be some grounds to think that China has turned a corner in this domain, but there may also be somewhat of a backlash among Chinese scholars. For example, a detailed Chinese scholarly article recently examined the many distinctions between European and American intellectual property rights standards and suggests, moreover, that many errors had occurred in Chinese law as a result of tendencies to simply replicate foreign laws and because of "foreign pressures."[39]

Chinese economic nationalism is not simply the province of scholars, however. For example, a vice director of the Bank of China, Chen Siqing, wrote a quite scathing critique of US economic and trade practices in the progressive and influential magazine 财经 (*Finance and Economics*) in February 2013. Though recognizing the singular importance of US-China trading relations, he also suggests that these relations are tense, with new conflicts arising "on a daily basis." He emphasizes that this trade has greatly favored the United States, furnishing the example of the Apple iPad, wherein just a tiny proportion of the value added comes from China. He complains of a US double standard on trade, and says that the Trans-Pacific Partnership (TPP) trade pact promoted by Washington will certainly try to exclude China. He also suggests that irresponsible US debt has become a burden on the entire global economy. He ultimately calls for China to search out and exploit new markets in its competition with the United States. Moreover, he asserts that nations all over the world urgently need a new and important currency for global economic transactions, so he recommends that Beijing accelerate the process of RMB internationalization.[40]

Even more troubling is the tendency of economic tensions to pervade the larger relationship. It is hardly difficult to find areas where these tensions are aggravating the already-strained military relationship. A piece published by a People's Liberation Army Air Force general, Qiao Gen, who is now a professor at China National Defense University in Beijing, illustrates this troubling tendency. Demonstrating his evident contempt for the United States, General Qiao states emphatically: "Today, no matter how many internal problems we have to face, we can hardly be indifferent that externally our country confronts a mighty opponent—the United States, which strives always to impede [掣肘] us." The focus of Qiao's concerns lies primarily in the economic domain. Instead of praising the US-China trading relationship, he rails against it: "We [Chinese] have sent a huge amount of wealth to the United States. . . . To satisfy the US market, we exploited our own resources and destroyed our environment. Was this in the nation's interest?" He asserts that the United States has fought four wars in the last twenty years to preserve the "financial imperialism" of the dollar. Moreover, he claims that "without the hegemony of the US dollar, there would be no more US hegemony."[41] The reasoning of this Chinese flag officer and professor at an important educational institution in Beijing strongly suggests that tensions in US-China economic relations may be pervading the broader relationship, and this same tendency can be found among national security thinkers in the United States. Of course, such tendencies contradict the hopes of the interdependence advocates, who have argued that dynamic US-China trade precludes the possibility of rivalry or military conflict.

Nevertheless, Chinese scholars (and also leaders) as a whole are hardly oblivious to the stark implications of mutual economic interdependence. For example, an article in the leading Chinese academic journal 当代亚太 (*Journal of Contemporary Asia-Pacific Studies*) analyzes the so-called 金融恐怖平衡 (balance of financial terror) in considerable detail and confirms its existence. This analysis actually finds that China's vulnerability within this relationship is much greater than that of the United States—a view actually quite in line with that of Pettis.[42] These authors note that China's dependence on the dollar, what they term a 美元陷阱 (dollar trap), has both helped and hindered China's economy.[43] They recommend that Beijing speed up its effort to make the RMB fully convertible and also that China continue its rebalancing away from the dependence on foreign trade. The same mutual vulnerability is implied in a recent Chinese newspaper article noting that "China will suffer huge losses in the event of . . . US dollar depreciation."[44]

The fact that the TPP trading bloc is a major plank of the US "rebalancing" to Asia is undoubtedly rather unnerving for Chinese strategists and economists alike, as, for example, was illustrated in the piece by Chen Siqing discussed above. But even more nationalist publications, such as 环球时报 (*Global Times*), editorialize in favor of patience and the rational pursuit of "win–win." It is observed that the Western growth model relied on imperialism, "but China cannot do that."[45] In order to cope with China's myriad challenges in the domain of international trade, Chinese researchers are studying the Japanese example for both positive and negative lessons. They believe, for example, that Japan's stagnation during the 1990s was partially the result of the yen's appreciation, which resulted from a 1985 agreement with the United States. They also note that Japan has frequently used the WTO to successfully resist US trade pressures. Comparing Japan's successes at the WTO with the troubled outlook for China, which confronts cases brought by a panoply of nations, the authors recommend learning from Japan's approach that united scholars, industry leaders, and officials in the search for solutions.[46] It is certain that Chinese analysts were extremely concerned by the accusations leveled at China throughout the 2012 US presidential campaign, including the charge that millions of US jobs in vital sectors, such as automobile parts, have fallen victim to unfair competition. Moreover, they have duly noted the increased activity of US trade negotiators at the WTO under the Obama administration.[47]

Despite ongoing trade tensions, numerous Chinese scholars are maintaining an open mind with regard to TPP and its meaning for China. One scholar from the prestigious Fudan University argued in the spring of 2013 that TPP is not necessarily in direct competition with the Regional Comprehensive Economic Partnership that China has generally favored to unite the region in a free trade bloc. Although an "obvious intention to surround China" is said to be apparent in the US rebalancing and also the TPP initiative, it is thought that both the regional partnership and TPP both have worthy goals, so that the RCEP and TPP might serve to complement one another.[48] Another Fudan professor went even further to suggest that "Asia needs America," and that if Vietnam and the Philippines do not fear the high standards for commercial practices in the TPP, then why should China fear to enter the TPP?[49] Indeed, a statement by a senior official at the US Treasury Department that the United States would welcome China's participation in the TPP qualified as big news in China's financial metropolis, Shanghai, in May 2013.[50]

It is hardly surprising that China has its own economic hawks with respect to US-China relations. As demonstrated above, it is not difficult to find Chinese economic nationalists who believe that China has not been adequately rewarded for its unceasing labors and environmental degradation. Many of them see the West, led by the United States, as jealous of China's recent success and desperate to halt its rise. However, it is also clear that many Chinese experts are aware of the benefits that have accrued to China from vastly increased economic interaction and interdependence. A recent article in the influential Beijing academic journal 国际政治 (*International Politics*) demonstrates the pervasiveness of this thinking. For decades, Chinese scholars have criticized "US hegemony" as a malevolent force in world affairs. In this paper, by contrast, the argument is made that declining US hegemony poses a major threat for the fate of the world economy. Among the key factors that an effective hegemon must possess, the article explains, is the "willingness to shoulder international responsibility," as well as a "willingness to serve the system and its members."[51] Interestingly, the author refrains from suggesting that China should take up these responsibilities. However, it is undoubtedly encouraging to see that Chinese scholars are reevaluating the role that the United States has played in the international system over the last century. Moreover, they are clearly probing the essential question of what kind of global leadership will be required to maintain a stable, growing, and sustainable world economy in the twenty-first century. The subsequent section elaborates how the US-China economic partnership can reach its full potential to create a solid basis for international order and peace in the twenty-first century (figure 4.1).

Cooperation Spiral for US-China Economic Relations

Washington's move 1 in the economic relationship: The United States must reform its process for evaluating Chinese investment projects. As noted previously in this chapter, the example of CNOOC's failed 2005 bid to acquire UNOCAL has become a symbol of US skittishness regarding Chinese investment. James Dorn explains in his comprehensive evaluation of the circumstances of that episode: "The increasingly confrontational approach Congress is taking toward China is leading to 'creeping protectionism,' often in the guise of protecting US national security."[52] A smaller but still high-profile case arose in late September 2012, when President Obama took the highly unusual step of exercising a presidential veto over a business transaction involving a Chinese company installing wind turbines near a naval base in Oregon. The proximity of this announcement to the presidential elections raises the unsavory possibility that this decision could well be attributed to the seeming popularity of "China-bashing." There is a formal, institutionalized process for review of

Figure 4.1 Cooperation Spiral: Economic Relations   合作螺旋: 经济关系

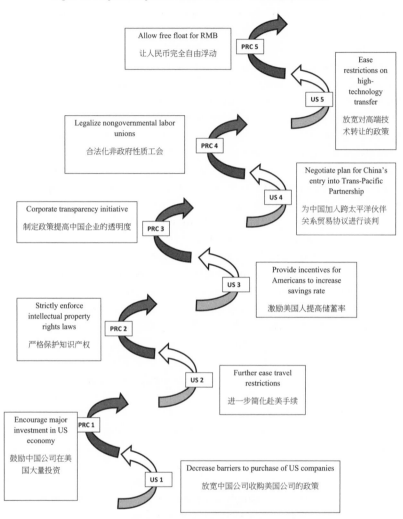

Allow free float for RMB
让人民币完全自由浮动

PRC 5

US 5

Ease restrictions on high-technology transfer
放宽对高端技术转让的政策

Legalize nongovernmental labor unions
合法化非政府性质工会

PRC 4

US 4

Negotiate plan for China's entry into Trans-Pacific Partnership
为中国加入跨太平洋伙伴关系贸易协议进行谈判

Corporate transparency initiative
制定政策提高中国企业的透明度

PRC 3

US 3

Provide incentives for Americans to increase savings rate
激励美国人提高储蓄率

Strictly enforce intellectual property rights laws
严格保护知识产权

PRC 2

US 2

Further ease travel restrictions
进一步简化赴美手续

Encourage major investment in US economy
鼓励中国公司在美国大量投资

PRC 1

US 1

Decrease barriers to purchase of US companies
放宽中国公司收购美国公司的政策

such cases called the Committee on Foreign Investment in the United States (CFIUS), and it is chaired by the Treasury Department. But given the results outlined above, one may doubt that this process is working effectively. Indeed, a recent acquisition by a Chinese company of the world's largest pork producer, Smithfield Foods, will apparently trigger a CFIUS case. As the *New York Times* reported, "[The US] food supply chain is not specifically mentioned in [the CFIUS] mandate, but the panel's jurisdiction is considered broad."[53] Could not the alleged risk of potential spying by a Chinese wind farm company have been mitigated rather simply by occasional spot inspections by the relevant agency? Americans interested in attracting investment and jobs to their communities in the twenty-first century should question the appropriateness of current procedures.

Beijing's move 1 in the economic relationship: China should promote major investment projects in the United States. There are numerous reasons for China to boost investment in the United States. Most of these reasons involve pure self-interest, including a desire to learn from US technology and business practices, but more particularly the need to unload huge amounts of US dollars into assets that are less likely to depreciate than the currency itself. A more magnanimous reason is likely also at work: the perceived imperative to "rebalance" the economic relationship, which has previously seen enormous amounts of US capital flowing into China, but little going the other direction. Symptomatic of the urgency of this issue from China's perspective was the cover of the influential and progressive magazine 财经 (*Finance and Economics*), which devoted a special December 2012 issue to the topic of boosting Chinese investment in the United States. According to a summary of this report: "[Chinese investment in the United States] is likely to experience explosive growth in the next 5–10 years. . . . [But a] . . . consensus between the two sides is that if the misunderstandings and current obstacles cannot be overcome, a major opportunity for both sides will be squandered."[54] Former Treasury secretary Henry Paulson was undoubtedly correct when he argued in mid-2012 that "we would benefit . . . from more investment from China. . . . Where US investment once flowed principally to China, we now need investment to flow from China—and in a way that creates good jobs for American workers, farmers, and ranchers. We should want our dollars back."[55] Naturally, China must be prudent in its investment practices—avoiding negative perceptions. An obvious model is to follow the approach of various Japanese corporations that were once much maligned but have now become a fully integrated and accepted part of the US commercial landscape, to the great benefit of both countries. Positive momentum in economic relations was developed at the November 2014 Obama-Xi summit, where an important agreement on reducing tariffs was reached. But the presidents also agreed to aggressively pursue negotiations under way on a Bilateral Investment Treaty (BIT), which could be highly significant for the proposal made here. Increased Chinese investment in the United States can both accelerate the economic relationship and provide much-needed ballast for US-China relations more generally.

Washington's move 2 in the economic relationship: Washington should take the initiative to establish visa-free travel between China and the United States. Undoubtedly, economic relations between Beijing and Washington have already reached a high degree of development. When a relationship is not well developed, it is relatively simple to make changes that strongly increase marginal gains; but that becomes more difficult in a mature relationship. However, easing travel restrictions would be precisely such a measure that could substantially smooth US-China transactions across the board, enabling not only energized economic interactions but also the related, yet crucial, people-to-people cultural interactions that will form an essential component of dynamic interdependence. The visa agreement reached between Xi and Obama at the APEC summit that will extend visas to five- and ten-year time frames amounts to major progress on this front. But it does not go far enough. Indeed, a paradox of the notion of extending visas for longer periods may be that the new procedures could inadvertently make the visas harder to get. One could imagine bureaucrats on both sides of the Pacific fretting about making requirements more stringent before granting a foreign citizen up to ten years of travel privileges. Hopefully, this will not be the case, but there is a danger that an already difficult process could become more burdensome, especially for one-time travelers. Fees for visa and passport processing are truly onerous, limiting business and tourist opportunities to big corporations and wealthy travelers. Two decades ago, such travel restrictions may have made some sense. The wealth gap between the nations was so wide that Chinese were literally dying to come to America, as when a ship carrying illegal Chinese immigrants ran aground in New York Harbor in June 1993. Estimates by the US Department of Homeland Security, however, show a steady decline in illegal immigration from China, suggesting that economic development has all but solved this particular issue.[56] The espionage threat is also not very relevant to this calculation, because China gains more from "cybertheft" than it does from classical cloak-and-dagger espionage. Moreover, the steady homeland security improvements since the September, 11, 2001, terrorist attacks suggest that the United States could handle the somewhat increased monitoring and surveillance tasks that upgraded interaction may require. In this case the potential gains of accelerating trade and investment far outweigh the small risks. One essential bridging community that will certainly benefit from such reforms will be the well over 100,000 Americans now living in China, who include President Obama's half brother. A truly dynamic twenty-first-century economic and cultural relationship between China and the United States requires that the red tape involved in the most basic transactions be dramatically reduced. Longer visa time frames as agreed in Beijing in late 2014 may form a vital interim step, but we must also consider the massive gains that could follow from eliminating the cumbersome visa process altogether. That system will continue to regrettably weigh down bilateral commercial, cultural, and government interaction under current arrangements.

Beijing's move 2 in the economic relationship: China must follow through on its new commitments to enforce protections of intellectual property rights (IPR). Impressive strides have been made by China in this crucial area of US-China economic relations. More than 87,000 civil lawsuits related to IPR were filed in Chinese courts during 2012, up 44.1 percent from the previous year. In that year, more than 60,000 suspects were detained in China for IPR infringement.[57] This apparent spike in activity follows the 2011 decision by the State Council to create a permanent "leading small group" to coordinate the Chinese government's response to the country's enormous IPR problem.[58] Continuing to build this momentum should not be especially difficult for China, because the steps taken to date reflect an earnest desire to move away from a "copycat" economy and toward a genuine "innovation economy" that rewards creative pioneers, whom China does not lack.[59] Moreover, there seems to be a clear recognition that many Chinese individuals and corporations have themselves been the victim of IPR fraud. Nevertheless, the future challenge cannot be minimized. If IPR fraud cases are growing exponentially in China, that is a good sign, but no one should be under any illusions that the legal authorities have the necessary experience and judicial propriety to suddenly handle this booming case load in a fair, consistent, and efficient manner. Given proper enforcement, it may take decades for China's legal reforms in this area to take root and alter the "Wild East" culture that has heretofore prevailed in Chinese markets. New evaluation criteria and new watchdog institutions will likely be needed on a bilateral basis to police IPR protection in the digital age.

Washington's move 3 in the economic relationship: The United States must take steps to increase its national savings rate. Even as China takes steps to rebalance its economy toward greater consumption and reduced personal savings, the United States must do the opposite, in order to stabilize its own finances and indeed to support the global economy and continued expansion of the vibrant US-China trading relationship. In a hypothetical zero-sum world, where China pursues reckless mercantilist policies, the status quo may be perceived as beneficial to Beijing insofar as Americans continue to spend massively at Walmart, Target, and so on, and the United States becomes ever more in debt to China.

Pettis, for example, notes that China (and also Japan) will suffer if and when the United States can succeed in reigning in its reckless "overconsumption."[60] However, it is widely agreed, even in China, that the current model is deeply unsustainable and that an uncomfortable correction is all but inevitable unless steady progress is made to reduce these obvious imbalances, which are in turn driving other obvious imbalances—the United States' trade deficit with China foremost among them. In April 2013 *The Economist* pointed out the disturbing fact that Americans' saving rate had returned to its habitual declining trend after a brief flirtation with more cautionary spending after the 2009 recession.[61] Even as Washington is learning to live within its means again by shutting down two expensive wars and even resorting to sequestration, more steps are required to rebalance US household finances. The most obvious measure to achieve this change will be to gradually increase interest rates, which have remained near zero for far too long, creating numerous distortions in the national economy, but also distorting the bilateral trade relationship. Since the 2009 recession, the worst examples of irresponsible credit instruments have been curbed by regulation, but financial responsibility in the United States dictates that credit card and other debts be reduced. Given that China is now a major "stakeholder" in the US economy, it is hardly surprising that Beijing has been actively calling for such measures for several years now.[62]

Beijing's move 3 in the economic relationship: China should radically increase the transparency of its major corporations. As with many of the measures suggested here, this step is less an actual concession than a natural part of the economic reform process that is well under way within China. Indeed, transparency seems to be an inevitable trend within Chinese society more broadly, as the society becomes both better educated and also more technologically savvy. Chinese scholars are themselves calling for increased transparency as a core plank of a more refined and civilized Chinese economic foreign policy.[63] In addition, the use of cellphone cameras to capture corrupt practices is now all the rage in China, and muckraking reporters are enjoying a high level of popularity. Nevertheless, the lack of transparency is widely recognized as a continuing roadblock to China's ascendance in the economic realm. It is perhaps the chief explanation for the rather stunted growth of its various stock indexes. After all, the bedrock concept that undergirds a stock market is the fundamental norm that the public has access to basic information regarding the management and business practices of all relevant companies so that accurate investment decisions can be made. One report, for example, observes that the New York Stock Exchange and NASDAQ indexes had to investigate twenty different Chinese companies during the first half of 2011 and eventually had to delist five because of irregularities.[64] The Qinghua University economist Patrick Chovanec wrote of a developing accounting crisis in US-China relations during late 2012: "With dozens of Chinese stocks traded on US exchanges dragged down by fraud allegations, costing investors billions of dollars in losses, the [American] Securities and Exchange Commission had to act."[65] Another sign that the Chinese economy is not quite realizing its potential is the lack of globally successful distinctly Chinese brands. Thus, Walmart and Nike rely heavily on Chinese suppliers, but they are hardly Chinese brands. Perhaps the success of the computer maker Lenovo will herald a new era of global success for Chinese companies, but it seems that Lenovo has generally adapted to Western business practices that help to explain its success.[66] Greater Chinese corporate transparency will not only help Chinese business practices but will also play a key role in decreasing suspicions regarding China's role in global markets, including that of the United States.

Washington's move 4 in the economic relationship: The United States must encourage and then negotiate China's entry into the Trans-Pacific Partnership. The TPP has unwittingly taken center stage in the geopolitical, and indeed geo-economic, rivalry now unfolding between Beijing and Washington. The reasons for this are threefold: First, Washington has been anxious to show that the rebalancing is not primarily a military initiative, and therefore has emphasized the TPP as the leading edge of its "pivot" to the Asia-Pacific. Second, the TPP accomplishes a highly symbolic union within American domestic politics among economic nationalists, human rights advocates, and environmentalists, together with geopolitical hawks, who can unite around a view of China's challenge as unfair, unjust, and dangerous all at the same time. A final pertinent reason to consider the TPP is that discussion of this trade bloc as part of the US rebalancing strategy has had a very deep and negative impact on the view of US-China relations as seen from Beijing. This is because, though American military deployments to places such as Australia and Singapore do register some concern, such moves are generally regarded as symbolic and without great impact on the bilateral relationship. However, the TPP is viewed as a potentially grave threat to Chinese economic development, insofar as that development has been largely premised to date on radically dynamic trading relationships. In other words, the TPP is a cudgel that may strike China where it truly hurts. Advocates of a zero-sum rivalry and all that it entails may delight at an instrument that makes bureaucrats in Beijing truly nervous, but those favoring a cooperative bilateral future will see major dangers lurking in this growing economic rivalry. The literature cited above shows that at least some Chinese thinkers are open to adopting a positive approach to the TPP—viewing the institution quite akin to the WTO breakthrough that began in the late 1990s—as an opportunity to further drive reforms within China. If Washington could take steps to show that it might see the TPP in a similar light, that might enable a process of further dynamic economic cooperation to unfold between the United States and China.

Beijing's move 4 in the economic relationship: Beijing should legalize trade unions independent of the Chinese Communist Party (CCP) apparatus. The horrific June 2013 fire in a Jilin poultry plant that killed 119 reminds the world of the frequently atrocious working conditions that still characterize Chinese capitalism. Coming directly after similarly gruesome tragedies in Bangladesh, the Jilin tragedy may suggest that, at least in certain sectors, China may unfortunately still resemble a very backward country with poorly enforced regulatory norms and no labor movement to speak of. It is hardly novel to reflect on the deep irony of an officially Communist country that lacks legitimate labor representation. Labor strikes have been one segment of growing Chinese civic activism attributable to positive trends, such as the rise of social media on the internet, and a simple tightening of the country's labor market, especially along its eastern seaboard.[67] Traditionally, the CCP has been wary of any alternative power centers, and official CCP labor unions have sought to stifle and redirect worker frustrations. Some strike activities have apparently been given the green light, especially when Japanese companies, or even companies in Taiwan, are the target of the strike. However, the problem has hardly been defused, and labor difficulties will continually plague China as it progresses to higher-level manufacturing unless a more stable, institutionalized pattern can be established. Here is an opportunity for the CCP to gradually, and in a controlled way (perhaps first through experimentation), allow genuinely independent unions and thus to defuse internal tensions, but also to improve China's reputation abroad. Indeed, China's poor record on labor relations is a major source of complaints abroad that argue quite reasonably that there can be no fair trade and competition with China as long as its workers are so disenfranchised. Such a step by Beijing would go a long way toward stabilizing and accelerating US-China economic interactions for the long run.

Washington's move 5 in the economic relationship: The United States should ease transfers on high technology to China, and specifically repeal the arms embargo that has been in place since 1989. China has long requested that the United States ease the sale of high technologies to China. There is no question that easing such barriers could help to correct the major imbalances that currently plague the relationship. The agreement on lowering high technology tariffs that emerged from the November 2014 Obama-Xi Summit is suggestive of the major gains that can accrue from progress in this area.[68] The arms embargo, moreover, in particular has become a symbol in China of Washington's alleged long-term intention of containing and constraining China's rise. Immediately after the devastating earthquake in Sichuan in 2008, Chinese national security leaders were especially galled that they could not purchase the necessary spare parts for the Blackhawk helicopters that had been bought back in the 1980s and were still among China's most capable helicopters for the required dangerous, high-altitude mountain flying. Of course, there are grounds for legitimate concerns from a national security perspective in sharing technologies with China. However, three factors suggest that this particular threat has been exaggerated, to the detriment of US national interests. First, China has found a variety of workaround methods to secure advanced technologies for developing weaponry, both by turning to alternative suppliers (e.g., Russia, Israel), through a careful study of US weapons development processes, and by devoting massive indigenous resources to the effort. Second, leading US companies have not been active in the Chinese market as a consequence of national security concerns, with the predictable result that they have lost major market share to European competitors, because China has generally formed one of the world's most dynamic markets in the last two decades. Third and finally, though it is true that the US arms embargo has seemed to fail to constrain Chinese military development, it may be the case that a narrow and very targeted effort that focused on five to ten special sectors (e.g., laser weaponry, submarine acoustics) rather than a broad net where all sales are suspect could be much more effective. Reformed export technology processes would not only be more consistent with the realities of globalization and the very low probability of US-China conflict, but the sale of the type briefly promoted by President Obama in 2010 (C130 cargo aircraft) also could have major benefits for both US manufacturers and the broader bilateral relationship.[69]

Beijing's move 5 in the economic relationship: China must finalize the convertibility and free market determination of the renminbi. With all the myriad difficulties in US-China economic relations, one may retain a certain optimism if one examines the issue of the value of China's currency. This has long been the "holy grail" of US-China economic tensions, and for good reason. Any person traveling between the United States and China could immediately feel the vast difference of the value between the two currencies and thus sense that a change in this value could be critical to rebalancing the troubled economic relationship. In this case the pressure on China has seemed to work, in the sense that the value of the RMB has seen a creeping but unmistakable upward trend. In the spring of 2008, $1 was worth RMB 7 for the first time. And three years later, $1 broke the RMB 6.5 barrier. In late 2013, $1 almost broke the RMB 6 barrier before retreating slightly through 2014. This overall trend of progress on this issue of critical importance in the economic relationship may eventually form a case study in US-China relations—in which China yielded, but yet succeeded in saving face. Paulson's, and later Geithner's approach of pushing, but not too hard, seems to have been quite successful. As Subramanian concludes: "There is no mistaking China's plans, reflected above all in its actions. It is seeking a dominant role for its currency and working gradually but consistently toward it."[70] In April 2013, full convertibility was announced for the RMB with the Australian dollar, marking "good news for Australian exporters—especially small and medium-sized enterprises."[71] No one should be under any illusions that a trend of increasing RMB value against the dollar will erase the trade deficit altogether or even dent it seriously. It may indeed have very little impact, because much of China's comparative advantage derives from the flexibility and adaptability of its disciplined workforce.[72] Still, Chinese productivity has been increasing relative to that of American workers, so the RMB still needs to rise in value significantly to reflect that reality, according to Pettis.[73] Moreover, charges of mercantilism will be reduced, and American companies will also greatly benefit from the newly liberalized capital markets that will accompany full convertibility. Chinese will also benefit substantially from these moves, which will not only assist in the process of rebalancing China's economy but also significantly raise Chinese incomes, for example, by dramatically reducing the costs of energy and natural resources.[74] Like the other recommendations made in this book, these policy reforms are profoundly in the interest of the country making the reform, which will make the interactive process of accommodation that much easier to realize.

Conclusion

Skeptics abound with respect to the Chinese economy, and this group certainly includes many Chinese. They cite growing inequality, stark regional differences, a skewed labor market and underemployment, excessive investment, a rapidly aging population, cautious consumers, environmental disasters, corruption, bad loans, political instability, and a general lack of transparency—to cite a few of the often-named problems. And yet those who have walked the back streets of China's tier-two cities—such as Dalian, Xiamen, Taiyuan, and Hangzhou—know well that China's economy is not a hallucination or a fantastical mirage. Some insight into modern Chinese capitalism was offered by a reporter who recently visited a frigid factory floor in Zhejiang. The reporter asked why people were working on a holiday and was told that "money never sleeps."[75] In other words, quite a bit of China's success since 1978 is attributable to good old-fashioned hard work and sacrifice.

The purpose of this chapter, however, is not to make grand predictions regarding the Chinese economy. Will it indeed surpass the US economy in the near term? Or will there be a hard landing, as Beijing's effort to rebalance its economy goes off the rails? Such predictions are of significant importance, but quite beyond the scope of this effort. This chapter has simply made the point that the dynamic US-China trading relationship has been and should continue to be the crucial ballast that keeps US-China relations stable and productive. Yet in the last decade, major contradictions arising from these interactions have actually injected significant tensions into the broader relationship. Such geo-economic tensions were intense enough so that a serious strategist at one of Washington's most prestigious think tanks published an academic book in 2012 that actually openly advocates for policies to "impede China's economic growth, and in sufficient degree to preserve a tolerable balance of power."[76] This suggestion is profoundly cynical and inflammatory, and that dark and illiberal approach is rejected here. However, that strain of argumentation may serve to demonstrate the current close interlinking of geo-economics and geo-political rivalry. The emerging US-China rivalry is everywhere in evidence, and is detailed extensively in the following chapters.

Transactions in the course of trade are driven by mutual benefit from interaction. A superb example of such an exchange relationship in US-China relations was recently fully described in James Fallows's *China Airborne*, which richly details how the Boeing Corporation has played an extraordinary role in vastly improving China's civil air safety record from the 1990s through the present.[77] This particular interaction has changed Chinese society, saved innumerable lives, and garnered handsome profits for companies in both countries—win–win on a massive scale. As argued above, many more such collaborative endeavors are within reach if US-China relations are able to realize their potential through a series of cooperative steps toward mutual accommodation in the economic and other realms.

Notes

1. For an informed and quite skeptical view of the current Chinese economy, see Michael Pettis, *The Great Rebalancing: Trade, Conflict, and the Perilous Road Ahead for the World Economy* (Princeton, NJ: Princeton University Press, 2013).

2. This figure is given by Wayne Morrison, *China-US Trade Issues*, CRS Report for Congress RL33536 (Washington, DC: Congressional Research Service, 2013), www.fas.org/sgp/crs/row/RL33536.pdf.

3. A recent and rather detailed Chinese scholarly discussion of the role of economic interdependence in European diplomacy in the years prior to the outbreak of the First World War is 梅然 [Mei Ran] "经济追求, 相互依赖与德国在 1914 年的战争决定"[Economic Needs, Interdependence, and Germany's War Decision in 1914] 国际政治研究 [International Politics Quarterly], no. 2 (2013), pp. 128-153.

4. John King Fairbank, *The United States and China, Fourth Edition* (Cambridge, MA: Harvard University Press, 2009), 30.

5. Paul Bairoch, "International Industrial Levels from 1750 to 1980," *Journal of European Economic History* 11, no. 2 (1982): 269–34; cited by David Kang, *China Rising: Peace, Power, and Order in East Asia* (New York: Columbia University Press, 2007), 29.

6. Henry Kissinger, *On China* (New York: Penguin Press, 2011), 12.

7. Justin Yifu Lin, *Demystifying the Chinese Economy* (Cambridge: Cambridge University Press, 2012), 31.

8. Ibid., 52.

9. 王湘穗 [Wang Xiangsui], "币缘政治: 世界格局的变化与未来" [Currency Geopolitics: Change and Future Prospects for the World Situation], 国际政治 [International Politics], July 2011, 4.

10. 马国川 [Ma Guochuan], "何方: 中苏同盟的历史启示" [He Fang: Revelations Concerning the History of the Sino-Soviet Alliance], 财经 [Finance and Economics], April 1, 2013, 96–100.

11. Lin, *Demystifying the Chinese Economy*, 101.

12. Qingxin Wang, "The Rise of Neoclassical Economics and China's WTO Agreement with the United States in 1999," *Journal of Contemporary China* 20 (May 2010): 460.

13. Justin Lee Robertson, "New Capitalist Processes, Interdependence, and the Asia-US Private Equity Relationship," *Pacific Review* 25, no. 2 (2012): 652.

14. James Kynge, *China Shakes the World* (Boston: Houghton Mifflin, 2006), xii–xiii.

15. Charles W. Freeman III, "Remember the Magnequench: An Object Lesson in Globalization," *Washington Quarterly*, January 2009, 63–65.

16. See "Chinese Professor," YouTube, www.youtube.com/watch?v=OTSQozWP-rM.

17. Daniel Drezner, "Bad Debts: Assessing China's Financial Influence in Great Power Politics," *International Security* 34 (Fall 2009): 8, 44.

18. Chris McNeal, "State of the Union Address: US Must Seize 'Sputnik Moment'; President Appeals to Republicans for Co-operation to 'Win the Future' and Warns That Rise of China Is Threat to US Influence," *The Guardian*, January 26, 2011, www.guardian.co.uk/world/2011/jan/26/state-of-the-union -address-obama-sputnik-moment.

19. Lin, *Demystifying the Chinese Economy*, 247.

20. Pettis, *Great Rebalancing*, 75–77.

21. "Pedalling Prosperity," *The Economist*, May 26, 2012, 4–5.

22. "The Retreat of the Monster Surplus," *The Economist*, May 26, 2012, 5–6.

23. "Dipping into the Kitty," *The Economist*, May 26, 2012, 16.

24. "Beyond Growth," *The Economist*, May 26, 2012, 18.

25. "China's Fast-but-Slow Economy," *The Economist*, October 21, 2014, http:// www.economist.com/blogs/graphicdetail/2014/10/daily-chart-13.

26. Arvind Subramanian, *Eclipse: Living in the Shadow of China's Economic Dominance* (Washington, DC: Peterson Institute for International Economics, 2011), 146–47.

27. Ibid., 83, 100–101.

28. Pettis, *Great Rebalancing*, 2.

29. Patrick Chovanec, "WSJ: China's Solyndra Economy," September 13, 2012, http://chovanec.wordpress.com/2012/09/13/wsj-chinas-solyndra-economy/.

30. Pettis, *Great Rebalancing*, 96.

31. Ibid., 115, 125. Regarding the "poison chalice," Pettis emphatically agrees; see ibid., 176.

32. "服务业进入快速增长周期" [Service Sector Enters Period of Rapid Growth], 人民日报 [Peoples Daily], May 19, 2013.

33. [Xu Xianchun], "准确理解中国的收入，消费和投资" [Accurately Understanding Income, Consumption, and Investment in China], 中国社会科学 [Social Sciences in China], February 2013, 4.

34. 奏尊文 [Zou Zunwen], "中三角：中国经济增长第四极" [The Central Triangle: China's Fourth Stage of Economic Growth], 环球时报 [Global Times], April 23, 2013.

35. 谷源洋 [Gu Yuanyang], "客观分析和判断我国面临的外部经济环境" [An Objective Analysis and Judgment of China's External Economic Environment], 亚非纵横 [Asia and Africa Survey], no. 2 (2012): 1–5.

36. 王湘穗 [Wang Xiangsui], "币缘政治：世界格局的变化与未来" [Currency Geopolitics: Change and Future Prospects for the World Situation], 国际政治 [International Politics], July 2011, 10–11.

37. 马方方 [Ma Fangfang], 美国对华民主输出战略对中国经济主权安全的影响 [The United States' Democracy Export Strategy and the Security of China's Economic Sovereignty], 国际关系学院学报 [Journal of the University of International Relations], January 2012, 87–88.

38. 巫云仙 [Wu Yunxian], "西方学者对中国'入世'十年的观察和研究述评" [Western Scholars' Observations and Research Review of China's Entry into the WTO for 10 Years], 中共党史研究 [Chinese Communist Party History Research], August 2012, 93–105.

39. 王迁 [Wang Wu], 著作权法借鉴国际条约与国外立法: 问题与对策 [Copyright Law as Drawn from International Treaties and Foreign Legal Systems: Problems and Responses], 中国法学 [China Legal Studies], March 2012, 28–38.

40. 陈四清 [Chen Siqing], "重塑中美经贸关系" [Reappraising China-US Economic and Trade Relations], 财经 [Finance and Economics], February 18, 2013, 118–20.

41. 乔良 [Qiao Gen, People's Liberation Army Air Force general], "大战略天平上的中国决择" [China's Decision in the Great Strategic Balance], 军事文摘 [Military Digest], March 2013, 14–17.

42. Pettis, *Great Rebalancing*, 193–94.

43. 项卫星, 王冠楠 [Xiang Weixing and Wang Guannan], "中美经济相互依赖中的敏感性和脆弱性: 基于'金融恐怖平衡'视角的分析" [The Sensitivity and Fragility of Economic Interdependence in China-US Relations: An Analysis Based on the "Balance of Financial Terror"], 当代亚太 [Journal of Contemporary Asia-Pacific Studies], no. 6 (2012): 90–111.

44. 崔建军 [Cui Jianjun], "中国货币超发隐忧重重" [China's Currency Allays Each Anxiety in Turn], 环球时报 [Global Times], May 3, 2013.

45. "中国经济升级版的舞台连着世界" [Global Links Form the Stage for China's Economic Springboards], 环球时报 [Global Times], April 26, 2013.

46. 戴龙 [Dai Long], "日本应对国际贸易摩擦的经验和教训及其对中国的启示" [Japan's Experience and Lessons Dealing with Trade Frictions and Lessons for China], 当代亚太 [Journal of Contemporary Asia-Pacific Studies], no. 4 (2011): 79, 89.

47. 左璇, 王宁 [Zuo Xuan and Wang Ning], "谈看中美贸易摩擦" [A Brief Discussion regarding Tensions in China-US Trade], 财经 [Finance and Economics], March 12, 2012, 42–43. The author thanks James "Austin" Whittaker of Brown University, who capably translated this article.

48. 贺平 [He Ping], "RCEP 与TPP 并行不悖" [RCEP and TPP Are Actually Not at Odds], 东方早报 [Oriental Morning Post], May 9, 2013.

49. 张建新 [Zhang Jianxin], "东亚需要高水平的自贸区" [East Asia Needs a High-Level Free Trade Area], 东方早报 [Oriental Morning Post], May 14, 2013.

50. "美高官称欢迎中国加入TPP" [US Senior Official Says China Welcome to Enter TPP], 东方早报 [Oriental Morning Post], May 18, 2013.

51. 沈本秋 [Shen Benqiu], "美国霸权式微: 国际贸易公共产品供给的视角" [The Decline of US-Style Hegemony: An International Trade and Public Goods Perspective], 国际政治 [International Politics], August 2011, 4.

52. James Dorn, *US-China Relations in the Wake of CNOOC*, Cato Policy Analysis 553 (Washington, DC: Cato Institute, 2005), www.cato.org/sites/cato.org/files/pubs/pdf/pa553.pdf.

53. Michael J. De La Merced and David Barboza, "Needing Pork, China Is to Buy US Supplier," *New York Times*, May 29, 2013, http://dealbook.nytimes.com/2013/05/29/smithfield-to-be-sold-to-shuanghui-group-of-china/.

54. [Wang Yanchun], "提速对美投资" [Increasing the Pace of Investment in the United States], 财经 [Finance and Economics], December 17, 2012, 58–60, 160.

55. Henry M. Paulson Jr., *A New Framework for US-China Economic Relations*, Issue Brief (Washington, DC: Atlantic Council, 2012), 2, www.atlanticcouncil.org/images/files/publication_pdfs/403/Paulson_0.pdf.

56. Michael Hoefer, Nancy Rytina, and Bryan C. Baker, *Estimates of the Unauthorized Immigrant Population Residing in the United States: January 2010* (Washington, DC: US Department of Homeland Security, 2011), 4.

57. Wang Zhenhua, "Nation's IPR Suits See Spike in 2012," *China Daily*, April 23, 2013.

58. Li Jiabao, "China Regrets US Charges of Inadequate IPR Protection," *China Daily*, May 3, 2013.

59. On the sensitive subject of Chinese innovation prospects and Chinese competitiveness, see, e.g., 黄亚生 [Huang Yasheng], "中美印国家竞争力分析" [Analysis of the Competitiveness of China, the US, and India], 财经 [Finance and Economics], April 14, 2014, 98–101. Huang is an economist at the Massachusetts Institute of Technology.

60. Pettis, *Great Rebalancing*, 186.

61. "Too Thin a Cushion," *The Economist*, April 2, 2013, www.economist.com/blogs/freeexchange/2013/04/saving.

62. Michael Wines, Keith Bradsher, and Mark Landler, "Chinese Leader Says He Is 'Worried' over US Treasuries," *New York Times*, March 13, 2009, www.nytimes.com/2009/03/14/world/asia/14china.html?_r=0.

63. 张晓通 [Zhang Xiaotong], "中国经济外交理论构建: 一项初步的尝试" [Constructing a Chinese Theory of Economic Diplomacy: A Preliminary Effort], 中国外交 [Chinese Foreign Policy], May 2014, 46.

64. Nathaniel Flannery, "The Great Wall: How Transparency Problems and Governance Risk Are Shaking Investor Confidence in Chinese Companies," *Forbes*,

June 16, 2011, www.forbes.com/sites/nathanielparishflannery/2011/06/17/the-great-wall-how-transparency-problems-and-governance-risk-are-shaking-investor-confidence-in-chinese-companies/.

65. Patrick Chovanec, "Foreign Policy: Clash of Balance Sheets," December 10, 2012, http://chovanec.wordpress.com/2012/12/12/foreign-policy-clash-of-the-balance-sheets/.

66. "From Guard Shack to Global Giant: How Did Lenovo Become the World's Biggest Computer Company?" *The Economist*, January 12, 2013, www.economist.com/news/business/21569398-how-did-lenovo-become-worlds-biggest-computer-company-guard-shack-global-giant.

67. Pettis describes "lagging wage growth" as one major component of the Japanese growth model, which promotes "underconsumption" to favor investment. Pettis, *Great Rebalancing*, 43.

68. Adam Behsudi, "US, China Reach Tech Trade Breakthrough," *Politico*, November 14, 2014, http://www.politico.com/story/2014/11/us-china-reach-ita-breakthrough-112768.html.

69. Bill Gertz, "Obama Loosens Sanctions on C130s to China," *Washington Times*, October 11, 2010, www.washingtontimes.com/news/2010/oct/11/obama-loosens-sanctions-on-c-130s-to-china/?page=all.

70. Subramanian, *Eclipse*, 112.

71. Tim Harcourt, "Australia Taking Yuan Step at a Time," *China Daily*, April 24, 2013.

72. See, e.g., Charles Duhigg and Keith Bradsher, "How the US Lost Out on I-phone Work," *New York Times*, January 21, 2012, www.nytimes.com/2012/01/22/business/apple-america-and-a-squeezed-middle-class.html?pagewanted=all&_r=0.

73. Pettis, *Great Rebalancing*, 67.

74. Pettis notes that the undervalued Chinese currency has functioned as a tax on Chinese importers. Ibid., 84.

75. "Let a Million Flowers Bloom," *The Economist*, March 10, 2011, www.economist.com/node/18330120.

76. Edward N. Luttwak, *The Rise of China vs. the Logic of Strategy* (Cambridge, MA: Harvard University Press, 2012), 267.

77. James Fallows, *China Airborne* (New York: Pantheon, 2012), 72–80.

5

TOXIC EMBRACE
The Environment and US-China Relations

During the summer of 2010, Americans were consumed by an unfolding tragedy in the Gulf of Mexico. As polluting crude oil gushed from the deep sea floor in vast quantities, millions of citizens in the surrounding affected states pondered how their lives might be impacted by the disaster. Although the Gulf tragedy in 2010 was eventually brought under control, the BP spill dramatically illustrated the inherent environmental dangers of the ongoing global hunt for fossil fuels. On the other side of the world, Beijing was actually coping with an oil spill crisis of its own during that same summer. In fact, the July 2010 spill in Dalian threatened to despoil the reputation of one of the country's greenest cities. By the admission of Chinese specialists themselves, that crisis demonstrated the weakness of China's maritime pollution emergency response system.[1]

The specter of China and the United States each confronting major environmental disasters of a similar nature at the same time is hardly surprising. The world's two largest economies are both haunted by the reality of their intense dependence on fossil fuels. This fundamental similarity between the two nations has and should continue to bring them together—to some extent geopolitically and also geo-economically, as argued in chapters 4, 7, and 11— but the environmental perspective may be the most significant of all. Whereas many of the issue areas discussed in this book have illustrated the development of steadily worsening tensions between Washington and Beijing, the environment is one of the few domains where tangible, large-scale cooperative measures are under way. A historic agreement was reached between Xi and Obama to address the daunting challenge of climate change at their summit in Beijing in November 2014. This agreement, which has problems to be sure, does nevertheless point to the promise of US-China cooperation to confront environmental challenges. This chapter reviews some of these cooperative steps, surveying the current status of US-China cooperation in "green energy"—where the central thrust has been made in recent years. As in the other chapters of this book, a plethora of Chinese sources help to enrich the reader's understanding of relevant perspectives, but once more the reader is cautioned that the use of Chinese sources here does not imply an endorsement of those perspectives. The chapter additionally does not overlook the immense environmental challenges now facing both states, but that are particularly acute for China. As the severe effects of global warming become ever clearer, the truly interdependent nature of US-China environmental policies comes into stark relief. Centuries in the future, citizens may well regard the environmental dimension of the US-China relationship to have been the most significant aspect of this most important relationship in the twenty-first century.

Background

Americans are justly proud of the enormous progress that has been made in the environmental sphere in the last four decades. Indeed, few readers would seriously consider any kind of environmental comparison between the United States and China at present, especially given the salient differences in each context, for example, the vibrant community of nongovernmental organizations that has been at the forefront of environmental progress in the United States. And yet American perceptions of Chinese environmental challenges certainly seem to have a rather ahistorical perspective, ignoring generally long periods in American history when the environment was severely degraded. Nor does one have to search very hard to find such evidence. Many New Englanders will know that the now–incredibly picturesque White Mountains of New Hampshire a hundred years ago had been clear-cut so badly as to resemble a moonscape. Offshore, New England's fisheries remain a case study of the depletion of natural resources.

While studiously avoiding the common practice of "wagging fingers," it is widely agreed, not least among most Chinese observers, that objective reality in China today yields the profoundly desperate plight of the environment. Scholars have analyzed the degree to which Chinese culture may itself be responsible for this tragic state of affairs. The picture is mixed, but it is also apparent that some of China's environmental degradation does predate the communist era. Thus, Elizabeth Economy notes, for instance, that "economic development during the Qing was an environmental disaster. There was a dramatic population increase, excessive cultivation of land, overherding, over-fishing, and overcutting."[2]

Mao Zedong's leadership was highly destructive to the Chinese environment. According to Judith Shapiro, "the modernization ethos received its starkest expression during the Maoist period . . . [that] led to endless human suffering and destruction of wetlands and rainforests, and cast nature as an enemy to be humbled and punished."[3] Mao promoted the unbridled growth of China's population for strategic reasons that cost China dearly in its drive for modernization. His various campaigns not only wreaked havoc on Chinese society but also despoiled the Chinese environment, for instance, when forests were cut down to fuel "backyard steel furnaces," which in the end produced little actual steel during the catastrophic Great Leap Forward. Environmental protection could hardly rank as a priority for such an impoverished country.

However, under Deng Xiaoping's rapid economic modernization policies, the Chinese natural environment suffered to an even greater degree. Although China's "one-child policy" was enacted in 1978 to contain this aspect of resource depletion, the entrepreneurial instinct was unleashed in China without any serious consideration for environmental protection. Describing the dark side of Deng's "economic miracle," Economy explains: "The small-scale town and village enterprises (TVEs) that have fueled so much of China's growth have proved difficult to monitor and regulate. . . . By 2000, these TVEs were estimated to be responsible for 50 percent of all pollutants nationally."[4] Another driver of China's rapid economic growth, foreign investment, could also be said to have had negative repercussions as China gained the "status as a destination of choice for the world's most polluting industries."[5] When Beijing acceded to the Montreal Protocol to ban ozone-depleting chemicals in 1991, this step marked China's debut on the world stage of global environmental agreements. Ann Kent's research on China's efforts to comply with the Montreal Protocol is modestly optimistic that as the Chinese become more and more exposed to environmental ideas and develop their own indigenous environmental research capacity, they will take effective measures to curb pollutants.[6] Economy's powerful description of the 1994 scene on the banks of the desecrated Huai River, where responsible government official were forced to literally drink a bitter glass from the fouled waterway, gives a sense of both the epic challenge within China, but also of the hope that a threshold had been reached that might prompt dramatic action to reverse the stark trends.[7]

In 1998 Beijing took the landmark environmental step of banning logging in most parts of China. At the same time noteworthy measures were adopted to conserve China's depleted marine fisheries. We will return in detail to each of these crucial domains of China's environmental crisis later in this chapter, but these efforts did represent important first steps in a positive direction. Nevertheless, the general trend apparent in the first decade after 2000 illustrated the reality that China's environmental crisis was becoming even more acute. The 2003 SARS epidemic put a spotlight on quality practices in Chinese agriculture and also hygienic issues in China's crowded cities. These issues returned with a vengeance just a few years later, with the tragic child deaths from contaminated milk powder. Demonstrating the high potential of environmental issues to spill across borders, a 2005 incident witnessed the inadvertent release of poisons into the Songhua River, which went unreported until Russia protested the contamination of its waters downstream. This event created new bitterness along an already-tense, but also long and vitally important, border. China got high marks for its execution of the 2008 Summer Olympic Games, of course, but that event also showcased the wretched air quality prevalent in China's cities. Despite dramatic efforts to curb air pollution in Beijing in advance of the games, international athletes were reportedly so anxious about this issue that many would fly in only for their event and avoid a longer stay in China.[8] In the second decade of the new century, China's significant achievements in "greening" its economy threatened to be marred by dogged questions regarding quality, for example, those related to the awful high-speed rail accident in 2011, and also about exporting environmental travails, for example, those concerning the many hydroelectric projects that China has under way in Southeast Asia.

The connection of US-China relations to the environmental situations in each country may seem to be somewhat indirect and nebulous. One interesting example of such a connection is the air-quality sampling data provided on the Web site of the US Embassy in Beijing. These data have apparently become quite popular in Beijing as a more credible source for gauging the capital's response to air pollution. Setting an example for one another and even shaming the other power into greener policies within a competitive framework can clearly achieve some good as well, but this chapter also considers the panoply of environmental areas that could see improvement for both countries if Washington and Beijing were to grasp the opportunity for robust, green cooperation.

The Dimensions and Spillover Dangers of China's Environmental Crisis

While US and Chinese diplomats deserve ample credit for achieving the climate change accord announced at the Beijing summit in November 2014, one should not forget that very significant tensions in US-China relations related to climate change policy came out of the previous international summits in Copenhagen (2009) and Durban (2011). Illustrative of major tensions in this area, one Chinese expert reviewing results of the Copenhagen conference, concluded that "the US uses climate change and energy cooperation opportunities to reinforce its technical and competitive advantage, limiting China's rise and perpetuating [the US] system of international leadership."[9] In the wake of the Durban Summit, Chinese climate change analysts despaired that this meeting was notable, in that it was the first time that the principle of "common but differentiated responsibilities" was not endorsed by the collective.[10] Even as this book promotes the notion that positive progress in the environmental domain can be a useful model for other, more difficult aspects of US-China relations, it is unfortunately true that the reverse phenomenon remains a real danger. In other words, the negative dynamics in the broader relationship regrettably still threaten to undermine substantial prospects for progress in this crucial area of US-China relations.

It is appropriate to first consider the energy dimension of China's environmental challenge because energy and environmental issues are so closely linked and also because the connection to US-China relations is quite tangible. China became the world's largest emitter of carbon in 2009, surpassing the United States for that dubious distinction. The two countries are bound to be the world leaders in emissions for decades to come because of the sizes of their economies, and also because of their common dependence on coal. According to a recent survey of US-China clean energy cooperation by Merritt Cooke, "Among fossil fuels, coal is particularly problematic for the environment. It has a higher carbon-to-hydrogen ratio than oil [or] natural gas; . . . more carbon is . . . release[ed] into the environment. . . . But chemistry is not the only issue at play. The other issue is prevalence. Coal currently supplies almost half the electric power generated in the United States. In China, coal supplies more than 70 percent of electric power generation. These 'facts on the ground' are unlikely to change."[11]

The costs of hydrocarbon emissions, moreover, go well beyond warming the atmosphere to causing acid rain and related ocean acidification, along with precipitating respiratory problems throughout China and well beyond. Shapiro notes, for example, that "particulate air pollution from China is regularly measured in California, Oregon, and Washington State; . . . and China is a major source of mercury deposition in the Western United States, providing a striking reminder that a nation's environmental problems do not respect political boundaries.[12]

Also, as has been well documented, coal extraction has a nefarious safety record that has left far too many widows and broken families in the United States, and also especially in contemporary China. The author's own visit to China's coal country in Shanxi Province in the fall of 2011 powerfully demonstrated for me both the pervasive and also destructive quality of this resource for China's future.

Although China has been making admirable efforts in renewable energy that are discussed in detail in the next section of this chapter, the current reality is daunting: Wind power accounts for just 0.8 percent of electric power generation in China, and solar power—about which much has been said in the newspapers—amounts to just 0.006 percent of the total.[13] Hydroelectric power, also a green energy source, at least in terms of emissions, has much greater significance for China's current energy mix, at 15.1 percent—more than double that of the United States. With the recent completion of the Three Gorges Dam along the Yangtze River, China could take pride in completing an engineering achievement first envisioned by Sun Yatsen well before the People's Republic of China had even been created. Despite much criticism from environmentalists, among others, the dam could be said to have certain positive effects beyond the massive emission-free generation of electric power to include flood control and increasing the navigability of China's most important inland waterway. The latter fact, moreover, suggests added environmental benefits, because moving goods by ship is considerably more fuel efficient than relying on trucks. Yet environmentalists and strategists are extremely concerned about the possible impact of China's wave of dam building, particularly for vulnerable downstream populations and ecosystems.[14]

If China far outpaces the United States in hydroelectric power, the opposite is true with respect to nuclear power, wherein China has been a relative latecomer. Compared with 19.8 percent of power generation in the United States, nuclear currently makes up just 1.9 percent of China's energy mix.[15] Beijing's enormously ambitious approach to advancing nuclear energy has been slowed in the wake of the Fukushima plant disaster in Japan. But plans remain on track to triple China's production of nuclear power in the coming years.[16] Critiques of this policy are more and more open. Thus, the Qinghua University professor Lu Feng wrote in the fall 2012: "Nuclear power experts will say that nuclear power can resolve the carbon emissions problem—that it is clean energy. But the nuclear waste issue is difficult to deal with . . . and presents a danger for our posterity."[17]

It is clear that despite major advances in promoting clean energy, China will remain highly dependent on fossil fuels for the foreseeable future. Noting this tendency, Ma Xiaojun, a professor at the Communist Party Central Party School, lists numerous concerns with respect to China's energy security: the possibility of major shortfalls in imports after 2020; the so-called Malacca Dilemma, whereby other powers or terrorists could inhibit China's importing of needed energy supplies; and the inadequacy of China's current strategic petroleum reserves. In a chilling reminder of how geopolitical competition may constrain environmental and energy cooperation, Ma observes: "As the United States controls the world's most important strategic energy transport routes, there is a long-term, real, and yet hidden danger to China's strategic energy transport." Nevertheless Ma concludes that virtually all US-China conflicts in the energy domain can be resolved through negotiations. To ensure the provision of "public goods" within a climate change regime, he notes, it will be necessary for sovereign states to break through the constraints of both sovereignty and ideology. He also emphatically lauds the ongoing cooperative projects between the United States and China in the energy and climate change sectors.[18]

Another Chinese climate change expert, Yu Hongyuan, of the Shanghai Institute for International Studies, is considerably more pessimistic. Yu believes that US leadership on climate change has been "continuously declining." He holds that one of America's objectives in climate change negotiations is to "weaken China's competitiveness." He further notes that Obama's efforts at emissions reductions have been stifled by a divided government and by Congress's unwillingness to confront the huge costs of carbon emissions reductions. However, there has been some notable progress in Obama's second term, particularly since the June 2014 Supreme Court affirmation that the US Environmental Protection Agency could act against major carbon emitters without any new legislation.[19] But with very considerable suspicion, Yu charges that

Washington is seeking to "limit China's emissions at an early point, before its economy is truly immense. With China still lacking the necessary funds or technologies to realize lower emissions, the United States will thus contain China's rise."[20] Regarding the crucial issue of transparency with respect to verification for a potentially more robust international climate regime, Yu is particularly skeptical, suggesting that the United States is using this concept to "destroy the principle of national sovereignty," and that China should vigorously oppose US "borrowing from the model of nuclear inspections to lower carbon emissions and thus interfering in every country's internal affairs."[21] Yu sees Washington joining with its allies to isolate and pressure Beijing into altering its climate change policies.[22] Depressing as such mistrustful sentiments may be from an American perspective, there are still many other Chinese ecologists who are calling for major change at home. Thus, Lu contends that China must actively reduce its consumption in order to realize lower emissions, and he thus directly challenges the current Chinese ethos of "scientific development" by suggesting that China must "forsake scientific determinism, transcend materialism, and build the socialist civilization of ecology."[23] In announcing that China would cap its carbon emissions "around 2030" at the Obama-Xi Summit in November 2014, Beijing has taken a major step forward in asserting the imperative to prioritize ecological goals.

Though carbon emissions, air pollution, and climate change together form the most important nexus of China's environmental crisis vis-à-vis US-China relations, it is essential to realize that today China's environmental predicament goes well beyond carbon emissions. Deforestation, for example, remains a severe challenge for Beijing, despite the 1998 ban on logging in most parts of China. According to Economy, China's forest cover amounts to just 16.6 percent, which is well behind the United States, at 24.7 percent, and the world average of 27 percent.[24] When the journalist Jonathan Watts recently went to northeastern China to explore China's "Green Great Wall," he concluded that, unfortunately, China's "Great Northern Wilderness was becoming the land of dead rivers and hollow forests." As one of his interviewees explained, it is true that Chinese have been planting many trees; "but the trouble is they tend to be monoculture plantations. They are not places where birds want to live."[25] Watts explains, for example, that 1.5 billion poplars have been planted in China over the last five years, but the tree may be an appropriate symbol of Beijing's heavy-handed and largely ineffective approach to restoring its environment, because poplar "hybrids grow fast, [but] they are sickly plants, vulnerable to disease and unable to reproduce."[26] Agriculture has also suffered from a similar tendency toward conformity and a lack of consumer protection. It is not surprising, therefore, that "Chinese farmers use twice as much fertilizer and insecticide per hectare as their American counterparts."[27]

Waste disposal has also become an issue of greater environmental significance in China. Indeed, Chinese have long alleged that China had become the dumping ground for the rest of the world. Watts describes the sad example of Guangdong Province's city of Guiyu, the "world's computer graveyard, . . . [where] studies reveal . . . the amount of lead in the blood of children . . . is 50 percent higher than limits set by the US Centers for Disease Control." He notes, moreover, that "American companies often falsely claim to be recycling domestically while actually shipping e-waste to China."[28] Shapiro observes that "China has already surpassed the United States in overall production of household garbage." She also notes that China has a new "NIMBY-ism of the middle class, which is often heralded as a form of environmental awakening."[29] A major protest erupted in Hangzhou in May 2014 over a planned incinerator that involved dozens of injuries to police and protesters.[30]

The Chinese media has been surprisingly open in its coverage of this new environmental activism. In a country where mass activism has not been lauded since the Cultural Revolution, it is interesting to see an article, for example, in a prominent magazine celebrating the environmental activists in Qidong (near Shanghai), where a paper mill wastewater pipeline was suspended in July 2012. The article describes in detail the achievements of the so-called antipollution volunteers (反污志愿者) and also discusses the difficult dilemma of whether to dispose of industrial pollutants into the Yangtze River or alternatively into the ocean, where local fishermen were bound to be affected. But, as the article observes, "Actually, the practice of dumping in the ocean has been around for well over one hundred years."[31]

Ample evidence suggests that China's proximate marine environments have suffered intensive degradation from both excessive dumping and overfishing. A 2011 Chinese study found that pollution was a significant reason that Bohai fish production is now just 20 percent of the level it was as recently as the 1980s.[32] The available data reveal similarly near catastrophic declines in the Beibu Gulf (Gulf of Tonkin).[33] Nor is it clear that the stocks can be rebuilt, because a recent study from Guangdong shows that four of five critical species show no improvement under current fishing regulations.[34] Another recent Chinese study is similarly pessimistic: "Fishing methods in thirty-two [Chinese] fishing ports [reveal] . . . trawling intensity greatly exceeds the reproduction capacity of fishery resources, and the fishing yields are of low value and immaturity, subsistence fishing and commercial fishing show . . . prominent contradictions, . . . [but] mesh size . . . and net mouths are getting bigger."[35] As with dams and river pollution, and also air pollution, the potential for environmental crises, such as in the area of marine fisheries, to straddle across borders and have an impact on key international relationships is high. The opposite conclusion, however, also holds true: that international cooperation will be the key to coping with many of China's environmental problems. Moreover, as many environmentalists are concluding, the world has no choice but to work with China to mitigate the environmental impact of its rise.

From Crisis to Opportunity

Although a broad consensus holds that China's rapid economic growth has spawned enormous environmental costs and challenges, a variety of hints suggest convincingly that China has turned a corner in its environmental crisis, not least Xi Jinping's recent announcement that China will seek to cap its carbon emissions within fifteen years. The end goal of a genuinely "green dragon" is not yet in plain view; but one might, nevertheless, at least surmise that China has reached the "end of the beginning" in its struggle to balance development and new ecological imperatives. Foreign countries, and the United States in particular, have and must continue to play an important role in this process.

Before returning to the all-important issue of how to alleviate global warming and the critical role of US-China cooperation in that effort, let us briefly touch on the health of the oceans, which was mentioned at the conclusion of the preceding section. Even as headlines have emphasized the difficult tensions in East Asia as countries compete over reefs and dwindling fish stocks (see chapters 9 and 10), a more complete look at Beijing's evolving approach to fisheries has been widely neglected. China began major reforms to its fisheries practices during the late 1990s, with the inauguration of the summer fishing ban in the Yellow Sea and East China Sea in 1995, the adoption of an explicit policy to favor aquaculture while "stabilizing" marine fisheries in 1996, and new fisheries agreements with Japan in 1997 and South Korea in 1998. The most important step in this reform process, however, appears to have been the zero-growth plan to control fishing capacity adopted in 1999, along with a measure to spread the summer fishing bans to both the Bohai and also the South China Sea. Other achievements of this period of reform included a fisheries agreement with Vietnam, the extension of fishing bans to parts of the

Yangtze River, and also an ambitious effort to create marine protected areas.[36] Enforcement of these promising regulations remains a problem, as with so many other aspects of Chinese environmental policy, but improvements are also becoming visible. According to recent official Chinese fisheries data, the zero growth plan has effectively controlled the growth of fishing capacity in such key fishing provinces as Guangdong and Shandong, while the distant water fishing fleet has also been reduced.[37]

In fact, Beijing and Washington have a record of fisheries cooperation going back almost two decades. In 1993 a memorandum of understanding was reached between the countries to jointly act against driftnet fishing in the North Pacific, a practice prohibited by the United Nations. The memo established the innovative concept of posting a Chinese fisheries enforcement officer aboard a US Coast Guard cutter in order to give the American ship the necessary jurisdiction to enforce the UN prohibition effectively. China Fisheries Law Enforcement Command (FLEC) personnel and related specialists have also visited various US fisheries enforcement training centers in Alaska and elsewhere. In the future, however, a more robust FLEC (now integrated into the larger China Coast Guard) may become a more equal partner in this kind of cooperation, regularly dispatching one or more high-endurance cutters to patrol the waters of the North Pacific. Some may criticize these efforts as more symbolic than substantive, but that is not at all how such efforts are presented in Mandarin-language (i.e., for Chinese audiences) official reports, wherein international exchanges and cooperation are actually prioritized.[38] This is consistent with provincial-level FLEC reports that also highlight the benefits of close cooperation with the US Coast Guard.[39] This example illustrates how US-China environmental cooperation can and must be enlarged to cover the gamut of global environmental challenges.

There is now wide skepticism in the United States regarding China's environmental situation and future intentions. In Watts's important book, *When a Billion Chinese Jump: How China Will Save Mankind—or Destroy It*, many observers, both Chinese and foreigners, will quite justifiably focus on the latter possibility highlighted in Watts's clever title, and indeed the dimensions of China's environmental crisis were detailed in the preceding section. However, what is also compelling about Watts's survey of the environmental situation is that it details a very wide scope of effort that is under way in China to address the environmental crisis. In Guangzhou, for instance, he reports on a company that claims to be the first to mass produce plug-in hybrid cars and also describes the "seventy-one-story solar and wind-powered Pearl River Tower

. . . [that is] the world's most energy efficient super skyscraper."[40] In discussing another major city not often associated with environmental consciousness, Shenyang—industrial powerhouse of the northeast—the description is quite surprising and altogether encouraging:

> Today . . . Shenyang boasts one of the most improved environments in China. . . . That such a notoriously dirty industrial center could clean up its act gave hope to a nation. . . . The improvement in air quality has been achieved largely through a mass dechimneyfication campaign. From 2003, the authorities began tearing down smokestacks at the rate of three per day. . . . The Hun and Pu rivers no longer run black and their banks are lined with trees thanks to a municipal greening campaign. In the north of the city, the Shenbei district has been developed with leafy streets and high rises topped with solar panels. Nearby, another eco-city is being designed by Tongji University students and US architects.[41]

In the city of Linfen, purported to be China's most polluted, Watts encounters a local environmental official who explains how China has turned a corner: "'We have more power than before. . . . The mayor says we can sacrifice economic growth in order to improve air quality. That used to be unthinkable.'" Indeed, Watts further explains that new "green targets" are shifting bureaucratic self-interest, which had previously focused only on ever more rapid economic growth.[42] Likewise, Shapiro is not altogether pessimistic: "Will China pursue the same level of wasteful consumption that Western powers have enjoyed? . . . Or is there a possibility that by 'leapfrogging,' using clean technologies, . . . creating sustainable cities and clean transportation networks, . . . [that] China can show the world a gentler, less destructive way of achieving high living standards and human development?"[43]

Of course, another reason for optimism is that some major steps have been taken within the context of US-China relations to address the environmental challenges that both nations face. At the Obama–Hu summit in 2009, it was agreed that the two countries would initiate large-scale cooperation in the domain of clean energy, which has resulted in the setting up in each country of three Clean Energy Research Centers, each of which has a collaborating partner in the other country. In the United States, these centers are an effort dedicated to studying and developing electric vehicles at the University of Michigan; an initiative to study clean coal technology at the University of West Virginia; and, finally, a project to enhance the energy efficiency of buildings that is focused at the University of California, Berkeley, near San Francisco. Although there are complex hurdles in this kind of scientific-technological collaboration, such as ensuring intellectual property rights, these directed collaborative efforts are already beginning to yield some results. According to a recent report by Merritt Cooke of the Woodrow Wilson International Center for Scholars, the Berkeley–Qinghua partnership focused on building efficiency is now developing research in six areas: advanced monitoring and simulation; building envelope technologies; building equipment; cool roofing materials; whole-building efficiency; and windows and day-lighting technology.[44] With 16 percent of total global emissions tracing back to buildings in either the United States or China, the potential for making a major positive impact on global warming is huge. Another area where collaboration is moving toward successful results is in developing facilities for testing carbon capture and sequestration. The initial setting up is rapidly being done in China, but "with American researchers, American companies, and American investors as innovation leaders."[45]

To be sure, there are real tensions in the US-China relationship with respect to green technologies. For example, China has seemingly employed protectionist measures in order to further develop its own wind turbine manufacturing. The net result is that foreign companies were gradually squeezed out of the lucrative Chinese wind market. By the time the United States brought an effective case before the World Trade Organization and forced the Chinese to settle the case in mid-2011, however, the "horse was already out of the barn," as Cooke explains.[46] And yet US companies have and will continue to benefit from US-China green energy initiatives. GE, for example, has done more than 1,000 turbine installations in China, whereas Chinese companies have hardly done any in the United States. Apparently undaunted by trade irregularities in the past, GE acted in 2010 to form a partnership with Harbin Electrical Machinery to position itself for future opportunities in the Chinese wind market.[47] Given the wide array of other joint projects—including a shale gas initiative; smart grid cooperation; and US corporate involvement in setting up new nuclear power stations in China—it seems that the benefits of collaboration will be quite evident enough to outweigh the various objections and concerns. Suggesting that each nation may contribute to mitigating the current environmental crisis by drawing on its unique strengths, Cooke concludes that US-China clean energy cooperation will continue to make progress, "steered by US innovation but powered by the twin engines of Chinese scale and speed."[48]

Skeptics are likely to make the counterargument that a major turnaround in China's environmental situation will only come about as a result of major changes in China's current political system. However, it is worth noting briefly that some keen observers of environmental politics, such as Thomas Friedman, have actually argued the opposite point—suggesting that a Chinese government more insulated from populism and short-term economic interests could be more capable of creating and implementing green reforms.[49] Still, there is little doubt that a fundamental weakness of China's environmental policies has been the paucity of civil society. In other words, China has lagged in environmental protection because it lacks dynamic and successful green nongovernmental organizations, not to mention a free press to keep all parties honest. But interesting movement is now quite visible on this front, as the phenomenon of environmental protest movements, often inspired by local misdeeds, is catching fire in China, enabled by new social media technologies. What is just as intriguing and significant is that these protests are receiving quite extensive and favorable coverage in the Chinese press. For example, the August 2012 edition of 财经 (*Finance and Economics*) magazine carried an extremely detailed analysis of such green protests and concluded: "Enormous public opinion pressure, will garner the attention of the government and its officials, leading to a resolution of the problem." Notably, the article adds that such resolutions may actually not be informed by scientific debate. Also interesting is the fact that the article discusses in detail the gradual development of the environmental protest movement in the United States.[50] Shapiro also emphasizes the increasingly positive role that China's journalists are playing in highlighting environmental causes, suggesting that, in combination with the "growing public clamor" that is now under way, a "'green hurricane' is cleaning up China."[51]

This public clamor may partly explain why China and the United States were able to reach a climate accord in Beijing during November 2014. Far from a "done deal," the accord faces many skeptics on both sides of the Pacific. One informed critic makes the important point that the "agreement" is not so much a "deal" as a joint announcement of separate national goals.[52] Predictably, conservatives have been much more critical. The *Wall Street Journal* editorialized that Obama had to turn to a dictatorship to support his "anti-carbon ambitions," since democracies are not amenable.[53] Charles Krauthammer interprets the agreement in stark, zero-sum terms and concludes: "we cut, they cruise." But Krauthammer's critique does raise some vital questions regarding the credibility of Chinese promises outside of a verifiable, legally-binding agreement.[54] The crucial issues are discussed in greater detail within the proposed cooperation spiral below. In any aspect of contemporary Chinese society, it is now not difficult to see a blossoming environmental consciousness. The rest of the chapter focuses on concrete steps that can be taken within the context of US-China relations to improve the global environment. The chapter began with a discussion of the impact both countries are having on the health of the oceans. Because China is a major force on the world's waterways—with the largest merchant fleet, largest fishing fleet, and largest ports—its environmental impact on the seas will only grow more profound. It is encouraging, for example, to see that China, as the world's largest shipbuilder, is actively investigating how to fabricate "green ships,"[55] and also looking to curb the emissions of its gigantic riverine transportation fleet, along with its ports—the latter taking a US port as its low emissions model.[56] Given, moreover, that China and the United States are themselves separated by a gigantic ocean, the stewardship of which is inherently a joint responsibility, it is again appropriate to start to accelerate green cooperation in the shared blue maritime domain.

A US-China Cooperation Spiral for the Global Environment

Washington's move 1 on the environment: The United States should focus on maritime spill mitigation in enhancing environmental and civil maritime cooperation with China (figure 5.1). This chapter began with the assertion that it is not simply coincidental that China suffered a giant oil spill in the midst of the "green city" of Dalian at the same time (summer 2010) as the United States was engaged in the BP crisis and the resulting vast cleanup of spilled oil in the Gulf of Mexico. Insofar as oil and natural gas will continue to play vital roles in both these economies for the foreseeable future, it is imperative that these fossil fuels are extracted from the sea floor in the safest manner and using the most ecologically sensible safeguards. In this area US technology and practices will be of huge interest to the relevant Chinese agencies and companies. At the same time, and given the regrettably common occurrence of spills in Chinese waters, US practitioners will also gain from having access to China's widening experience in this area, for example, through the use of extensive case studies. Moreover, as undersea drilling expands to previously inaccessible areas (e.g., the Arctic) and sensitive domains (e.g., the South China Sea), it will be especially important to have developed integrated and interdependent commercial and official networks that can ease mistrust and enhance cooperation

Figure 5.1 Cooperation Spiral: Environment and Climate Change   合作螺旋：环境保护与 气候变化

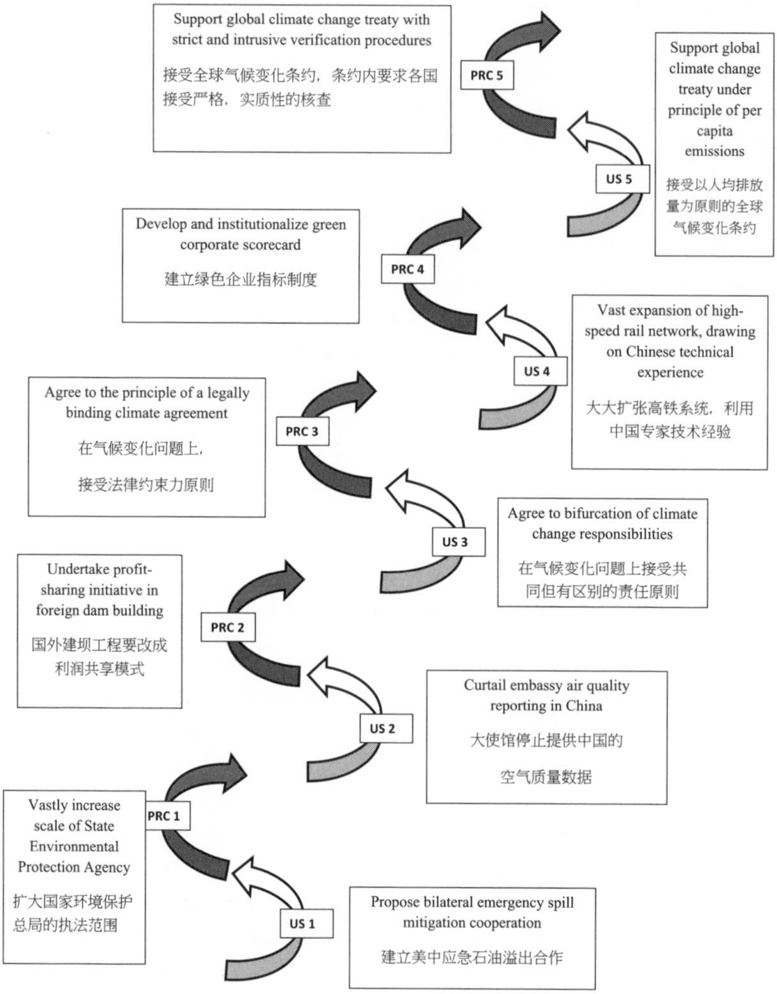

Support global climate change treaty with strict and intrusive verification procedures

接受全球气候变化条约，条约内要求各国接受严格，实质性的核查

PRC 5

Support global climate change treaty under principle of per capita emissions

接受以人均排放量为原则的全球气候变化条约

US 5

Develop and institutionalize green corporate scorecard

建立绿色企业指标制度

PRC 4

Vast expansion of high-speed rail network, drawing on Chinese technical experience

大大扩张高铁系统，利用中国专家技术经验

US 4

Agree to the principle of a legally binding climate agreement

在气候变化问题上，

接受法律约束力原则

PRC 3

Agree to bifurcation of climate change responsibilities

在气候变化问题上接受共同但有区别的责任原则

US 3

Undertake profit-sharing initiative in foreign dam building

国外建坝工程要改成利润共享模式

PRC 2

Curtail embassy air quality reporting in China

大使馆停止提供中国的空气质量数据

US 2

Vastly increase scale of State Environmental Protection Agency

扩大国家环境保护总局的执法范围

PRC 1

Propose bilateral emergency spill mitigation cooperation

建立美中应急石油溢出合作

US 1

to benefit the world's endangered oceans in a new era of technology-enabled exploitation of its resources.

Beijing's move 1 on the environment: China should vastly expand the State Environmental Protection Agency (SEPA). It is widely accepted that implementation is the Achilles heel of China's efforts to gain control over the deteriorating environmental situation. Shapiro writes, for example, that "China deserves tremendous credit for trying to integrate environmental concerns into its plans, laws, and policies, . . . [but] there is a tremendous implementation gap."[57] Since its inception, SEPA has been severely underresourced. As an example, Economy observes that the agency only had about 100 personnel as recently as a decade ago. She draws an important comparison between the staffing of local branches of the US Environmental Protection Agency and local branches of SEPA that yields the fact that SEPA needs to be upgraded so that it is more comparable in its profile to other powerful ministries, for example, the influential Ministry of Transport. When SEPA is resourced appropriately, Chinese environmental governance should be substantially improved. It is not the role of the US government to improve SEPA, of course, but an improved SEPA will both serve US national interests and serve as a key enabler to long-run smooth US-China cooperation in the environmental domain.

Washington's move 2 on the environment: The United States should curtail reporting on air quality by the US Embassy in Beijing. Though many, including not a few residents of Beijing, might protest this small measure, in the last few years the US Embassy air-quality monitor has been the source of substantial bilateral friction.[58] As Ann Kent demonstrates in her pioneering study of Chinese attitudes toward ozone-depleting chemicals, it was essential that the environmental issues be grounded in science—and preferably in Chinese science. In other words, the Chinese are much less likely to choose cooperation if the perception is that an agenda is being forced on China. The existence of the embassy air-quality monitoring is justified as a protection for embassy personnel. However, the less-than-subtle subtext to Chinese also seems to be that the air pollution situation in the Chinese capital remains atrocious, and Chinese government environmental data are suspect. When one adds the recent tendency of dissidents to escape into the US Embassy, many Chinese may begin to suspect that the air-quality monitoring program is part of a coordinated effort to bring about regime change. It is certainly true that the air-quality monitoring by the US Embassy has played a useful role and may have even been critical for athletes visiting during the Olympics. But that time is past, and now Beijing has reacted by setting up a comprehensive air-quality monitoring network for the city. Although the US State Department could tactfully claim a success and now lay the groundwork for increased trust in environmental cooperation by ceasing this activity, it is instead creating a more confrontational atmosphere by initiating such monitoring from its consulates in other Chinese cities. The argument for such activities would be considerably stronger if other US embassies around the globe engaged in the same practice, but that does not appear to be the case, even though reports suggest that Beijing is no longer the most polluted major capital.[59]

Beijing's move 2 on the environment: China should develop a standard profit-sharing plan, in addition to transparent practices, in reaching dam-building agreements with foreign nations. Chinese dam-building practices are coming in for ever closer scrutiny around the globe. Beijing's reach in the hydroelectric world market is now extremely wide, with an enormous quantity of projects located on nearly every continent. According to Brahma Chellaney, "Thirty-seven Chinese financial and corporate entities are involved in more than 100 major dam projects in the developing world."[60] Moreover, these projects are having a significant impact on China's relations with key neighboring countries, such as Laos and Cambodia. In addition, these projects and their related political effects are actually becoming a significant irritant in US-China relations, particularly in the sensitive region of Southeast Asia. Thus, dam politics in Myanmar, for example, seem to have become an integral part of the great power contest to entice Naypyidaw. Preliminary evidence suggests that the Chinese are quite aware of the role that dam politics have played in that particular situation, and are realizing that Beijing needs to increase transparency and court public opinion in such countries.[61] As part of a reform of China's approach to dam building in foreign countries, certain norms should be institutionalized throughout the industry. However, the Chinese government must play an active and supervisory role—producing a "white paper" at a minimum to show that practices are being reformed. A core component of a new best practices approach might incorporate an innovation from Canada that could be termed "profit sharing," whereby, after decades of rampant dam building, the aboriginal First Nation people have started to be paid an income from hydropower revenue.[62] Universal opposition to all Chinese dam building in the developing world is hardly feasible or warranted. Although the costs to the environment (e.g., fish populations) are very considerable, the benefits are also quite significant, including obviously emissions-free electrification in many poor countries. Therefore, the objective needs to be enhanced cooperation in mitigating the impact of these dam projects and improving the process of decision making and implementation. Ultimately, China will likely view such reforms as in its economic and strategic interest.

Washington's move 3 on the environment: The United States should agree to the principle of bifurcation of negotiations into general categories of developing states and developed states. Within the Kyoto Protocol process, this bifurcation was highly objectionable, and Washington rightly opposed it. At that time, the developed states were asked to make economic sacrifices, and the developing states did not need to make any commitments. Moreover, they were to enjoy the benefits of a generous aid program to help restructure their economies to exploit green technologies and reduce emissions. In other words, Americans were justly skeptical and considered China among other states as the likely beneficiaries, while the United States would see significant costs. But the ground has shifted considerably and that earlier understanding is now quite obsolete. Although not obligated by Kyoto, Beijing has "seen the writing on the wall," partly due to external pressure but more likely attributable to rising environmental awareness within China and among Chinese scientists. Therefore, the US concern that China would merely "free ride" within a global carbon emissions reduction framework is no longer valid, especially given the US-China climate accord reached in November 2014. It is important to realize that US flexibility on this point will also help with the major difficulty to persuade other major developing countries as well, primarily India, Brazil, and South Africa. The key point for negotiators here will be that acceptance of the principle of differentiated responsibilities does not leave China (or India) outside the framework of lowering emissions—quite the contrary. In effect, by allowing that China could have additional time to increase its emissions (until about 2030), Washington has informally accepted that different countries should be allowed to respond differently to the climate change challenge. And yet a formal commitment, which would necessarily entail some buy-in from the US Congress, would go much further toward allaying Chinese concerns, and thus encourage further positive movement by China, including even the major leap into a legal accord. The way to split the difference effectively here is for Washington to agree to the principle of financial and technical support for poor countries as part of the climate change negotiations, with the vital caveat that no US funds will go to China for that purpose. That is a simple caveat that both Beijing and Washington can live with.

Beijing's move 3 on the environment: China should agree in climate change talks to the principle of an internationally legally binding agreement. A significant controversy ensued at the Durban Summit in December 2011, when the Chinese representative, Xie Zhenhua, appeared to signal a major change in Beijing's approach by agreeing to a legally binding agreement. However, this change in China's policy appeared actually not to be a significant change after all.[63] The confusion likely could be put down to a "lost in translation" moment. Under the Chinese conception, therefore, "legally binding" would refer to the fact that China would be bound by its own laws to reach various reduction targets. Indeed, the November 2014 bilateral climate accord reached between Obama and Xi is notable in that it does not broach the difficult issue of a legally binding agreement. Perhaps that is the only viable approach at present? However, the strong economic interests in both the United States and China that are arrayed against slashing emissions suggests that a legally binding accord could be critical to making genuine progress. Thus, it is not at all surprising that American conservatives are already suggesting that China has duped a naïve American president. In other words, they will be unalterably opposed to cuts to American emissions without concrete agreements from China that they will carry through on their promises. Defining the scope of that regime, including the penalties against states that are noncompliant, is beyond the scope of this study, but China's role as a responsible great power requires that Beijing participate and even lead with respect to the international climate change regime.

Washington's move 4 on the environment: The United States should vastly expand its high-speed rail (HSR) network, drawing on China's positive experience in recent years and its affordable technology. By 2012 China had built more HSR than all other nations of the world put together, with forty-two major lines covering over 13,000 kilometers. With a high density of urban concentrations in relatively close proximity over a large, flat geographic plain,[64] HSR made sense for China, just as it does for the United States.[65] Although Americans have traditionally preferred automobile travel out of habit and for convenience, the "car culture" has made for traffic congestion and is also contributing massively to unsustainable carbon dioxide emissions. Though some projects are currently in development, much more ambitious plans are warranted. For example, the well-traveled Northeast corridor has the Acela, but this service operates at less than half the average speed of Chinese HSR. Huge, untapped economic potential can be realized in creating new linkages among cities that are reasonably close, for example, between Boston and Montreal. As HSR in California moves forward, there have been some serious discussions about extensive Chinese involvement, to the point where negotiations proceeded to include 80 percent of manufactured components, which were to be made in the United States, as was the more labor-intensive final assembly of train cars.[66] Such an ambitious project will require partners from all over the world, but China's experience over the last decade in this period is unmatched, and they are hardly daunted by large projects. Moreover, Chinese companies are likely to be more affordable than Japanese or European competitors. Just as American companies have played an enormous role in building China's airlines and air transportation industry, China can now reciprocate by advancing US HSR in support of a common green agenda.

Beijing's move 4 on the environment: China should develop a green scorecard program for its major companies, including especially companies with extensive overseas operations. In the new century Chinese companies have aggressively sought out untapped markets and at the same time have built up some of the largest and most successful companies in the world. And yet there is a wide global perception that Chinese companies are not conforming to global norms, especially with respect to the environment. This problem will likely persist, in part due to the structural conditions related to China's comparative advantage and particularly its late entrance into many international markets. Its condition as a latecomer does suggest that Chinese companies will continue to work in poorer countries, providing technical and management skills for comparatively dirty and resource-intensive enterprises. There has been some progress in recent years. For example, Chinese fishing boats operating off the African coast have been accused of illegal practices and shady deals, and also of displacing local subsistence fishermen by draining the African coasts of low-priced species. But it is apparent that Beijing is concerned about this reputation and has taken steps to more effectively license and monitor the practices of its distant water fishing fleet.[67] Nevertheless, such piecemeal steps will inevitably fall short, given the massive scale of China's economic interaction with the world in the coming century. In particular, what is needed is for the Chinese government to work with major Chinese companies to develop a credible green scorecard system to monitor their practices on a wide scale. As with comparable processes that have been developed in the West, the system would rely not on formal penalties but rather on a process of "public shaming." One such scoring of US and global companies evaluates corporate environmental impact, environmental management, and also environmental disclosure to develop "green rankings."[68] Although Chinese journalism will be challenged by this task, Beijing may assume a constructive role by contributing resources to the effort and by developing consistent and objective standards.

Washington's move 5 on the environment: The United States should join a global climate change agreement with an acceptance of the per capita emissions principle as the guiding standard for dividing up respective responsibilities within the agreement. Having taken the interim step of accepting differentiated responsibilities among developed and developing nations, an international climate change treaty will certainly require a much more difficult commitment by Washington, because of the fundamental need to commit to specific emissions targets. To its credit, the United States has agreed at the November 2014 Beijing Summit, in principle (not law), to seek reductions of emissions of 26 percent from 2005 emission levels by 2025. The stricter EPA regulations, which were most recently affirmed by a Supreme Court ruling, now make these commitments more credible. Adopting a per capita principle will take these laudable steps further, by codifying a recognition by Washington that populations in developing countries (including China) are entitled to living standards (and consequent carbon emissions) approximating, if not on par with, those of Americans. An obvious argument against the per capita principle would be the critique that countries that have not attempted to control explosive population growth will be at an advantage. Given Beijing's aggressive one-child policy since 1978, this critique can hardly be applied to China, but it could be grounds for skepticism regarding India's and Brazil's claims for justice on the grounds of a per capita principle for future emissions targets. President Obama has taken the brave step in Beijing in November 2014 of granting China some "running room"—a necessary but likely unpopular concession. But this was a vital step toward eventually bringing China into an agreement, so the United States has to swallow this unappealing medicine. According to Bader's description of the 2009 Copenhagen negotiations, President Obama appears to have accepted that per capita emissions will be a key metric for developing the outlines of a final global climate change treaty.[69]

Beijing's move 5 on the environment: China should join a global climate change agreement with the acceptance of a strict and intrusive verification mechanism. In the last several years, Beijing has made progress in reorienting away from massive carbon emissions and in striving for a greener economy. In part, this newly aggressive stance with respect to climate change reflects China's natural discomfort with being the globe's largest emitter. However, it also seems to reflect the increasing green consciousness of China's population, which has been confronted by a full-blown ecological crisis of severe air and water pollution, along with other challenges, as detailed above. These changes, along with the various US efforts to both control emissions and also make accommodations, as described above, in this "cooperation spiral" may enable Beijing to make the largest leap of all: into a global climate change treaty regime. The tremendous urgency of bringing Beijing into an effective climate regime was underlined by a May 2014 report, which concluded that China's dependency on coal could be the largest single factor in determining if the world can stay below the 2 degrees Celsius of threatened increase.[70] That report recommends that the Chinese use of coal be "capped" by 2020. Of course, the Beijing Summit climate accord of November 2014 gives China ten additional years to increase emissions and so, unfortunately, that may doom the 2 degrees target. But this might have been a necessary interim step in order to achieve a more far-reaching global and legally binding agreement that goes beyond China and includes other major emitters like India and Brazil as well. To get there would additionally require such stringent requirements as verification. For China, the notion of intrusive verification mechanisms is distasteful not only from the point of view of national sovereignty, but also following the somewhat dubious precedents of observing verification principles in a succession of non-proliferation crises from Iraq to North Korea to Iran, that have left Chinese diplomats extremely cautious and generally wary of such diplomatic tools. It is quite clear that the issue of verification was the issue that most starkly divided Washington and Beijing at Copenhagen, according to Bader's account.[71] In order to mitigate Chinese inhibitions regarding verification, it will be essential to develop a scientific, broad, and inclusive process in the development of the verification regime that will accompany a global climate change treaty that could have the support of both China and the United States.

Conclusion

It is ironic that perceived failures at the Copenhagen summit to realize US-China cooperation on global warming seem to have played a role in Washington's tougher posture toward China, which has emerged since 2010.[72] True enough, climate change negotiations did not prove easy; but did anyone really expect Washington and Beijing, coming at this problem from completely divergent starting positions and respective governing philosophies, would rapidly come to an agreement? Involving the most serious considerations—the wealth and livelihoods of respective populations—these negotiations will be inherently difficult, and both states will inevitably pursue their national interests, perhaps even through a "strategic lens." And yet a long-term, broad perspective yields the result that major progress has been accomplished across a variety of fronts and in the domain of clean energy research, in particular. Close observers of Chinese politics and society have detected a major change in public attitudes toward the environment, and these attitudes are percolating upward through the Chinese system. Not surprisingly, the new environmental consciousness that is evident in China evinces intense admiration for the environmental movement in the West and its important successes. Building on this admiration, and also on a seemingly new appreciation of the dangers of global warming in the United States, there could be a basis for substantial forward movement in US-China environmental cooperation, over and above the substantial efforts already under way. The November 2014 bilateral climate accord gives us hope that key diplomats on both sides of the Pacific do understand the enormous stakes. Such progress reflects a mounting awareness among specialists in US-China relations that environmental cooperation is no longer just one segment of this complicated relationship but is increasingly the most important aspect of all.

Notes

1. 赵远哲, 王海潮 [Zhao Yuanzhe and Wang Haichao], "'7.16'事故: 我国水域污染应急体系建设亟待加强" [The 7.16 Accident: The Urgent Requirement to Strengthen the Emergency Response System for Coping with Pollution in Our Nation's Waters], *中国海事* [China Maritime Affairs], August 2010, 5–8. Illustrative of possible future, bilateral, cooperative synergies, Chinese specialists are clearly interested in the lessons of the 2010 Gulf of Mexico spill, as demonstrated by this article: 雷海 [Lei Hai], "回顾: 墨西哥湾溢油的教训和启示" [Review: The Lessons Learned and Enlightenment from the Oil Spill Incident in the Gulf of Mexico], *中国海事* [China Maritime Affairs], September 2011, 11–12.

2. Elizabeth Economy, *The River Runs Black: The Environmental Challenge to China's Future* (Ithaca, NY: Cornell University Press, 2004), 41.

3. Judith Shapiro, *China's Environmental Challenges* (Malden, MA: Polity Press, 2012), 89.

4. Economy, *River Runs Black*, 63.

5. Ibid.

6. Ann Kent, *Beyond Compliance: China, International Organizations, and Global Security* (Stanford, CA: Stanford University Press, 2007).

7. Economy, *River Runs Black*, 4.

8. Shapiro, *China's Environmental Challenges*, 52.

9. 于宏源 [Yu Hongyuan], "哥本哈根谈判进程和中美碳外交的发展" [The Process of the Copenhagen Negotiations and the Development of US-China Carbon Diplomacy], *当代亚太* [Asia-Pacific Studies], no. 3 (2010): 98.

10. 薄燕, 高翔 [Bo Yan and Gao Xiang], "原则与规则: 全球气候变化治理机制的变迁" [Principles and Rules: The Transformation of the Global Climate

Change Regime], 世界经济与政治 [World Economics and Politics], February 2014, 58.

11. Merritt T. Cooke, *Sustaining US-China Cooperation in Clean Energy* (Washington, DC: Woodrow Wilson International Center for Scholars, 2012), 50–51.

12. Shapiro, *China's Environmental Challenges*, 3.

13. Cooke, *Sustaining US-China Cooperation*, 54. These data are supported by the official report "China," updated February 2, 2014, US Energy Information Administration (EIA) at http://www.eia.gov/countries/cab.cfm?fips=CH.

14. See, e.g., "Banyan: One Dam Thing after Another," *The Economist*, November 11, 2011, www.economist.com/node/21538158.

15. Cooke, *Sustaining US-China Cooperation*, 54. Also see US Energy Information Administration, "China," February 2, 2014, www.eia.gov/countries/cab .cfm?fips=CH.

16. Keith Bradsher, "China Slows Development of Nuclear Power Plants," *New York Times*, October 24, 2012, www.nytimes.com/2012/10/25/business global/china-reduces-target-for-construction-nuclear-power-plants.html?_r=0.

17. 卢风 [Lu Feng], "整体主义环境哲学对现代性的挑战 [The Environmental Philosophy of Holism and Its Challenges to Modernity], 中国社会科学 [Social Sciences in China], September 2012, 59.

18. 马小军 [Ma Xiaojun], 国际战略视野下的能源与环境问题 [Energy and Environmental Issues in the View of International Strategy], 中国外交 [Chinese Foreign Policy], no. 3 (2012): 13–16.

19. Adam Liptak, "Justices Uphold Emissions Limits on Big Industry," *New York Times*, June 23, 2014, www.nytimes.com/2014/06/24/us/justices-with -limits-let-epa-curb-power-plant-gases.html?_r=0.

20. Yu, "Process," 101.

21. Ibid., 102.

22. 于宏源 [Yu Hongyuan], "体制与能力：试析美国气候外交的二元影响因" [An Analysis of the Dualistic Effects of Institutions and Power on US Climate Diplomacy], 当代亚太 [Asia-Pacific Studies], no. 4 (2012): 128–29.

23. Lu, "Environmental Philosophy," 207.

24. Economy, *River Runs Black*, 64.

25. Jonathan Watts, *When a Billion Chinese Jump: How China Will Save Mankind—or Destroy It* (New York: Charles Scribner's Sons, 2010), 283–84.

26. Ibid., 254.

27. Ibid., 256.

28. Ibid., 88–90.

29. Shapiro, *China's Environmental Challenges*, 140.

30. Austin Ramzy, "Police Pursue Arrests after Clash over Incinerator," *New York Times*, May 12, 2014, http://sinosphere.blogs.nytimes.com/2014/05/12/police-pursue-arrests-after-clash-over-waste-incinerator/?_php=true&_type=blogs&ref=world&_r=0.

31. 焉建彪, 贺涛 [Yan Jianbiao and He Tao], "启东启示" [Qidong's Inspiration], 财经 [Finance and Economics], August 13, 2012, 117.

32. 张显良 [Zhang Xianliang, ed.], 中国现代渔业体系建设关键技术发展战略研究 [Strategic Research on the Key Technologies and Development of China's Contemporary Fishing System] (Beijing: China Ocean Press, 2011), 66.

33. Yunjun Yu and Yongtong Mu, "The New Institutional Arrangement for Fisheries Management in the Beibu Gulf," *Marine Policy* 30 (2006): 251.

34. 候秀琼 [Hou Xiuqiong et al.], "2007–8年伏季渔深圳市海域鱼类资源调查研究" [Research on the Fisheries Resources of the Shenzhou Sea Area during the Hot Season Moratoriums of 2007–8], 海洋开发与管理 [Ocean Development and Management] 21, no. 6 (January 2009): 111.

35. 孙中之 [Sun Zhongzhi et al.], "黄渤海区拖网渔具综合定性调查及特点分析" [Investigation and Analysis of Trawl Gears in the Yellow Sea and the Bohai Sea Area], 渔业科学进展 [Progress in Fishery Science] 32, no. 5 (October 2011): 127.

36. 2009中国渔业年鉴 [2009 China Fisheries Yearbook], 4–5. On China's marine protected areas, see Wanfei Qiu, Bin Wang, Peter J. S. Jones, and Jan C. Axmacher, "Challenges in Developing China's Marine Protected Area System," *Marine Policy* 33 (2009): 599–609.

37. 2009中国渔业年鉴 [2009 China Fisheries Yearbook], 7, 208.

38. Ibid., 118–22.

39. 执法为民 浙江省查处北太非法流网工作简报 [Faithful to the Law, Enforcement Serves the People: Short Report of Work Concerning the Investigation of Illegal Drift Nets in the North Pacific] (Hangzhou: Zhejiang Province Fisheries Law Enforcement Command, 2009).

40. Watts, *When a Billion Chinese Jump*, 95.

41. Ibid., 235.

42. Ibid., 178.

43. Shapiro, *China's Environmental Challenges*, 20.

44. Cooke, *Sustaining US-China Cooperation*, 112–13.

45. Ibid., 124.

46. Ibid., 159–60.

47. Ibid., 61–62.

48. Ibid., 125.

49. Friedman, quoted by Watts, *When a Billion Chinese Jump*, 271.

50. 谭翊飞, 贺涛 [Tan Yifei and He Tao], "求解环境群体事件" [The Occurrence of Mass Events to Resolve Environmental Problems], 财经 [Finance and Economics], August 27, 2012, 102.

51. Shapiro, *China's Environmental Challenges*, 58, 67.

52. Elizabeth Economy, "Obama's Big China Win at APEC: Not What You Think: The Climate Deal Was Not Insignificant, But It is Not the Real Takeaway from APEC," *The Diplomat*, November 13, 2014, http://thediplomat.com/2014/11/obamas-big-china-win-at-apec-not-what-you-think/.

53. "Green Leap Forward," *Wall Street Journal*, November 12, 2014, http://online.wsj.com/articles/green-leap-forward-1415838404.

54. Charles Krauthammer, "The Climate Pact Swindle," *Washington Post*, November 20, 2014, http://www.washingtonpost.com/opinions/charles-krauthammer-the-climate-pact-swindle/2014/11/20/f78f6474-70e9-11e4-8808-afaa1e3a33ef_story.html.

55. [Cui Yan], "船舶技术的绿色创新" ["Green Innovation for Ship Technology], 中国船检 [China Ship Survey], July 2012, 56–59.

56. 魏昕, 徐建豪 [Wei Xin and Xu Jianhao], 船舶节能减排思考 [Consideration of Energy Efficiency and Emission Reduction for Ships], 中国海事 [China Maritime Safety], 38.

57. Shapiro, *China's Environmental Challenges*, 58.

58. Susan Shirk and Steven Oliver, "Beijing Has No Good Answer to the US Embassy Pollution Monitoring," *The Atlantic*, June 13, 2012, www.theatlantic.com/international/archive/2012/06/china-has-no-good-answer-to-the-us-embassy-pollution-monitoring/258447/.

59. Heather Timmons, "New Delhi, Now More Polluted Than Beijing," *New York Times*, November 21, 2011, http://india.blogs.nytimes.com/2011/11/21/new-delhi-now-more-polluted-than-beijing/.

60. Brahma Chellaney, "China's Dam Frenzy," *Project Syndicate*, December 2, 2011, www.project-syndicate.org/commentary/china-s-dam-frenzy.

61. 王冲 [Wang Chong], "缅甸非政府组织反坝运动刍议" [Analysis of the Anti-Dam Movement of Myanmar's NGOs], 东南亚研究 [Southeast Asian Studies], April 2012, 81.

62. Simon Marks, "Chinese Dam Project in Cambodia Raises Environmental Concerns," *New York Times*, January 16, 2012, www.nytimes.com/2012/01/17/business/global/17iht-rbog-cam17.html?pagewanted=all&_r=0.

63. Chris Holly, "US Sees No Change in China's Stance on Binding Emissions Cuts," *Energy Daily*, December 6, 2011, www.theenergydaily.com/unclimatechangeconf/12-6-11/.

64. "World Bank Report Commends China's Development of High-Speed Rail," World Bank Press Release, July 27, 2010, www.worldbank.org/en/news/2010/07/27/world-bank-report-commends-chinas-development-high-speed-rail.

65. For a skeptical view on Chinese high-speed rail, see Tom Zoellner, "High-Speed Empire: The Bullet Train," *Foreign Policy*, March–April 2014, 44–51. Zoellner points to economic, safety, and management concerns. However, the analysis may underestimate the macroeconomic effects of a system that is now moving 1.3 million riders a day and can expeditiously carry a business executive 320 miles "to reach an early morning appointment" (p. 46).

66. Keith Bradsher, "China Is Eager to Bring High-Speed Rail Expertise to the US," *New York Times*, April 7, 2010, www.nytimes.com/2010/04/08/business/global/08rail.html?pagewanted=all.

67. Guifang (Julia) Xue, "China's Distant Water Fisheries and Its Response to Flag State Responsibilities," *Marine Policy* 30 (2006): 653.

68. See "Green Rankings 2012: Full Methodology," *Newsweek*, October 22, 2012, www.thedailybeas.t.com/newsweek/2012/10/22/newsweek-green-rankings-2012-full-methodology.html.

69. Jeffrey A . Bader, *Obama and China's Rise: An Insider Account of America's Asia Strategy* (Washington, DC: Brookings Institution Press, 2012), 62.

70. Michael Forsythe, "China's Coal Dependency Threatens Efforts to Curb Warming," *New York Times*, May 12, 2014, http://sinosphere.blogs.nytimes.com/2014/05/12/chinas-coal-dependency-threatens-efforts-to-curb-warming/.

71. Bader, *Obama*, 62.

72. See, e.g., Cooke, *Sustaining US-China Cooperation*, 11.

6

"SOUTH–SOUTH" PIVOT
The Developing World and US-China Relations

The tragic Ebola Crisis developing in West Africa during 2014 provided at least one silver lining: the spectacle of the two superpowers' militaries working side-by-side in extremely arduous and even unprecedented circumstances to try to stem the tide of disaster. US special envoy to the UN Samantha Power, traveling in the afflicted region during late October 2014, was said to have tweeted that "it was heartening to see US soldiers and Liberians working together with Chinese to unload [the China Air Cargo] plane."[1] Indeed, Beijing has sent over $100 million to aid the crisis response and has now committed several hundred specially trained military personnel as well. Despite certain tendencies toward superpower rivalry in the developing world, this crisis might stand as an example of US-China strategic cooperation in the developing world.

A year before the Ebola Crisis, Obama made a trip to Africa and he visited both Tanzania and South Africa, countries that had each been visited by Chinese president Xi Jinping on his first trip abroad just three months earlier. This substantial overlap in the foreign policy agendas of the world's two most powerful leaders might suggest two contradictory conclusions. With the Obama trip coming fresh on the heels of Xi's swing through America's backyard—which took him to Costa Rica, Trinidad, and Tobago, as well as Mexico—one interpretation is that geopolitical competition between the two superpowers is intensifying around the globe and especially within the developing world, with the possibility for destabilizing outcomes and even conflict. Two scholars from the US Air War College, for example, concluded in a detailed analysis of minerals exploitation in Southern Africa in mid-2013 that, "given the rising levels of Chinese demand for resources, . . . the probability exists of friction and eventual conflict between China and the United States."[2]

Yet another interpretation of Obama's 2013 trip might note optimistically that the overlap in destinations could suggest a certain similarity of interests among the two superpowers in fostering sustainable development, while at the same time searching out new market opportunities. In other words, the zero-sum competitive model in which certain states are in the Chinese orbit and others are pro-Western has limited explanatory power, even if it cannot be dismissed altogether. Although controversial in many respects, Beijing's vigorous pursuit of trade and investment opportunities appears to have had a genuine impact on growth trajectories throughout the developing world. Duly noting some of the negative aspects of China's increasing influence, not least some tendencies toward troubling geopolitical competition, this chapter concludes by highlighting impressive examples of US-China cooperation in the developing world—for example, in the recent Ebola Crisis—and suggests further steps to deepen cooperation and dampen competitive impulses. Given that other chapters in this book examine in detail US-China interaction in the Greater Middle East (chapter 7), Southeast Asia (chapter 10), and South Asia (chapter 11), this chapter focuses on Sub-Saharan Africa and to a lesser extent on Latin America.

Background

Unlike the other regions discussed in this book, China's substantial ancient power and cultural influence did not leave major imprints on either Africa or Latin America. The visits of Zheng He's massive fleets to East Africa likely occasioned substantial hand-wringing among the awed local populations, but they are mostly discussed today in relation to the giraffe that was brought back to amuse the Chinese emperor and his court. The book *1421: The Year China Discovered the World*, which posits, among other extraordinary claims, that Chinese fleets also had extensive interaction with peoples in Latin America in the Premodern Era, has been compared by one academic historian to "close encounters with alien hamsters," or, put more diplomatically, as pop-history, and will thus not be treated seriously here, though that book is widely read.[3] It is an interesting fact of history that comparatively tiny states, such as Belgium and especially Portugal, have had a much more important historical impact on Africa and also Latin America.

However, Western analysts are also wrong to ridicule the historical factor in evaluating China's interactions with the developing world. It is common, for example, to point out wide discrepancies between China's spoken commitment to communist, egalitarian principles and the activities of Chinese companies that appear to prioritize profit above principle. Another line of critique holds that China's noninterference principles were evidently put aside during the Cold War, when China supported numerous revolutionary movements in the developing world, fostering instability and protracted underdevelopment. One need only recall that Mao Zedong severely criticized Nikita Khrushchev for cowardice in backing down during the Cuban Missile Crisis in 1962 to realize that Chinese foreign policy in that period inclined toward the bombastic and irresponsible. As one recent review of Chinese foreign policy in the middle of the Cold War concludes, "Throughout the 1960s China expressed support for . . . Latin American countries that confronted the United States."[4] When the Cold War became more complex against the background of the Sino-Soviet dispute, moreover, the result was somewhat bizarre and ironic, as, for example, in Angola, where Beijing ended up backing the same faction (UNITA) as South Africa and the United States—an inconvenient fact that likely "delayed establishment of official diplomatic ties between Angola and China."[5]

Despite such strange twists of geopolitics, the underlying theme of sincere kinship borne of the common experience of domination by the West still provides a rather robust ideological and experiential foundation for the development of dynamic ties. To be sure, there are major symbols of this cooperation, such as the well-known Tanzania–Zambia Railway Authority (TAZARA), which sought to connect Zambian mines with Tanzania so these states could decrease their dependence on then-apartheid South Africa. Built in just five years, with the assistance at its peak of 16,000 Chinese technicians, this immensely challenging project involved building 10 kilometers of tunnels and 300 bridges.[6] Not all of China's assistance was so glamorous, however. As one African account of this period relates, "[During the 1960s], . . . Tanzania went through considerable primary industrialization, which included, among other things, textiles, farm implements, large-scale rice farming and coal, and steel mining. Most of this was undertaken with Chinese capital and technical assistance. It was probably the only time in Tanzania's history that such a high level of industrial employment has been reached."[7] To be sure, there were costly excesses related to such policies, including overenchantment with the Chinese model in Tanzania, but also definitely rather extravagant and indeed imprudent levels of foreign aid (reaching 5 percent of total government expenditures) that China could not hope to sustain.[8] Deborah Brautigam, a scholar who has studied Chinese influence in Africa for decades, relates her impression from field research in Africa during the 1980s: "In interview after interview, people told me that the Chinese working in their countries spent almost no effort trying to convince people to adopt their model." In that respect, she notes that TAZARA and other major Chinese aid programs followed the disaster of the Great Leap Forward, which likely mellowed the ideological zeal of Chinese aid workers. But she also relates how the work ethic of Chinese aid workers could be contagious: "A local farmer told me how he was inspired to follow the example of the Chinese, who worked in the paddy fields by lantern late into the night." On this basis, she concludes that "China's increased visibility in Africa today should be seen in this context: *China never left,* we just stopped looking" (emphasis added).[9]

The explosive growth of trade between China and Africa has been widely covered elsewhere. Here, it is enough to simply relate that trade reached an impressive $198.5 billion in 2012, up 19.8 percent from 2011 and an astounding ten times the figure a decade ago.[10] The often-skeptical *Economist* was fulsome in praising the ever-more-dynamic Africa-China relationship in March 2013: "Sino-African links have broadened in the past few years. The relationship is now almost as diverse as Africa itself." This detailed report hails diversifying trade that goes well beyond minerals and also notes that Africans are generally not just being steamrolled by polished Chinese bureaucrats in making various business deals, citing, for example, an instance in which Congo had sent "rogue [Chinese] commodities traders" packing. The long-standing critique of China—that it protects and enables human rights violators, such as Zimbabwe's Robert Mugabe—is at least somewhat mitigated by the fact that it has also reached out to the most promising alternative to Mugabe by inviting Morgan Tsvangirai to Beijing. According to *The Economist*: "China has occasionally played peacemaker. . . . Sudan and South Sudan are both big Chinese trade partners. When they hovered on the brink of war last year [in 2012], China intervened diplomatically along with other powers."[11] A recent detailed case study of the vibrant China-Angola relationship reveals some aspects of the resource curse—including corruption, to be sure—but also many positive aspects of the bilateral interaction, including, for example, the following: "Civil engineers and architects note that buildings and infrastructure built by Chinese firms are of good quality, low cost, and oftentimes are completed in less than half the time that such projects would usually take in Angola."[12]

One of the most promising aspects of China's approach to the developing world concerns the growth of its involvement in international peacekeeping efforts. A rather remarkable event transpired during the course of a tragedy, when US and Chinese peacekeepers actually patrolled in tandem after the devastating earthquake in Haiti in January 2010. But it is in Africa where Beijing's UN "blue helmet diplomacy" has been most visible, with China playing a significant role in six of seven UN peacekeeping operations. In June 2013 it was announced that China would contribute combat and other troops to UN forces in a new Mali operation. China's growing commitment to UN peacekeeping reflects not only Beijing's sense that it must "undertake more responsibilities" (更大责任) but also, more pragmatically, the reality that it should protect its own overseas interests.[13] As the Sudan case amply demonstrated, Beijing has much to lose if regional tensions spiral out of control into protracted armed conflict.

China's trade with Latin America reached a similarly astounding figure of $255.5 billion in 2012, growing by a slower but still impressive clip of 8 percent from a year earlier.[14] A complicating feature of certain relationships in Latin America is that China has more often been a fierce trade competitor rather than a major partner. The most glaring example of this competition has been with Mexico, the region's second-largest economy. President Xi's June 2013 trip to Mexico attempted to "reset" that troubled relationship with Mexico's newly elected president by especially focusing on the yawning trade deficit between the two countries. China has long cultivated its relationship with Brazil, which still has not been immune from certain controversies similar to the Mexican case. Still, it was no small sign of change in the region when China surpassed the United States as Brazil's leading trade partner. China has also gained the pole position in trade with Chile, one of Latin America's most successful economies. Two scholars examining growing Chinese economic influence in Latin America have found that part of Beijing's success derives from the fact that "Chinese companies have the capacity to complement their mining projects with significant projects in infrastructure, which places them in a strong position when competing with other investors." It was also noted that "[Chinese companies] . . . rely only partially on stock markets and shareholders, which gives them more freedom to concentrate on medium- to long-term profit making."[15]

As noted above, China's rapid emergence as an important political and even more important economic force in the developing world has not only fed the "decline" debate that is ongoing in the United States and in the West more generally, but more particularly, it has also spawned serious academic and policy discussions regarding the potential for geopolitical and military conflict between the superpowers in the developing world. One analysis, published in the prestigious *China Quarterly* in 2012, surveys the phenomena of "hegemonic challenge" in Latin America, and though rather optimistic with respect to US-China relations, does warn that "at the core of the relations between Nazi Germany and Latin American countries was trade; . . . for four decades . . . the perception of a German threat in Latin America was crucial in shaping US foreign policy."[16] Although not approaching the level of tensions witnessed recently in flashpoints, such as the South China Sea, there are nonetheless signs of growing strategic competition. One Western analysis, for example, recently asserted: "It's an open secret [that] AFRICOM [the US Africa Command] was created [in 2007] to counter the growing presence of China in Africa."[17] That may indeed be an overstatement, but the salience of the relationship between AFRICOM and growing Chinese influence is also suggested by a slew of publications on the subject in US military journals, for example.[18] Among the challenges that the United States and China will confront in the decades ahead, some will undoubtedly arise from the thicket of complex intersecting and sometimes clashing interests in the developing world. Before addressing some compromises to avert such tensions, the next section takes a closer look at China's analyses of its own growing role in the affairs of the developing world. However, the reader is once again cautioned that the use of Chinese sources here does not imply an endorsement of these assessments.

Chinese Analyses Explore China's Prospects in Africa and Latin America

Though this section concentrates on China's relationship with Africa, one particularly significant journal article regarding Latin America warrants close attention and may have deep significance for US-China relations. This Chinese analysis probes "America's Rise and Its Policies toward Latin America," noting explicitly in the title that this case study should be mined for lessons regarding China's rise. Not surprisingly, the article dwells on the impact of the Monroe Doctrine (罗门宣言), observing that Monroe's policy was more rhetoric than reality, given that the naval balance vis-à-vis the great European powers remained extremely unfavorable for the United States. Interestingly, it is also emphasized that the Monroe Doctrine was warmly welcomed by the countries of Latin America, even as it laid the foundations for subsequent US expansion in the region. The analysis notes that in the War with Mexico of 1846–48, Washington employed all the tools of statecraft, though force was the most vital tool in "seizing more than half of Mexico's territory (about 55 percent), including California." It is observed that the United States' reputation needed to be repaired after that historical episode, but that Washington's success resulted from its ability to "ingeniously use contradictions among the European powers," as well as its moderation, flexibility, and the fact that it "did not lose sight of principle" in pursuit of its strategy. It is noted that in the course of its rise, the United States faced numerous external challenges, above all from Great Britain. Here, the interesting and encouraging lesson is drawn that the United States "did not give up any opportunity to improve its relations with Britain" and pursue cooperation.[19] This rendering seems quite remarkable, in that it is not ideologically predisposed against US hegemony in Latin America, but rather sees much to emulate in America's rise to power in the Western Hemisphere. Of course, this article may be more relevant to understanding Chinese foreign policy in Asia than to its actual policies in Latin America. A somewhat troubling trend in that respect is that though Chinese arms sales to Latin America have been minor to this point, Chinese arms industry analysts, however, see major opportunities in increasing defense budgets in Latin America, whether in "suppressing armed rebellion" (打击叛乱) or in combating full spectrum air and naval threats.[20] Historically, arms sales to Latin America by other powers have been a major factor in raising Washington's ire, so clearly that it is one domain of China-Latin America relations that bears close watching in the coming decades.[21]

On the occasion of President Xi's visit to Africa in the spring of 2013, the Chinese press was full of florid descriptions of China-Africa cooperative progress in development. There was an unmistakably triumphalist tone to the articles—for example, one appearing in 人民日报 (*People's Daily*)—that highlighted the truly impressive trade figure of $200 billion achieved in 2012. That paper reminded readers that "even when China was extremely weak and facing the most difficult circumstances, it still rendered steadfast support for African liberation movements," and also suggests that many Western countries are "anxious" regarding the success of China-African relations.[22] A raft of new infrastructure projects—for example, upgrading African port facilities—may give Chinese businesses a commanding presence on the continent in the future.[23] However, another article in *People's Daily* noted that though Africa could be entering a "golden era," it would likely also be one of rising contradictions in the African context. It emphasized the imperative of breaking with the "pessimistic theory of African economics" but also underlined the necessity of avoiding the pattern of "growth without development."[24] Such has been the clamor in Chinese intellectual circles regarding "Africa rising" that in influential forums some have even advocated "a great transformation in Chinese diplomacy" that would emphasize the importance of the developing world. One such scholar noted that African countries' gross domestic product has continued to average about 6 percent growth in spite of the global recession, and it also notes that cumulative trade between China and the developing world (Africa, Latin America, Southeast Asia, and the Middle East) actually exceeds China's trade with Europe and the United States. At the same time, the analysis suggests that China must also recognize itself as a "different type of developing country"—a distinction with significant implications, of course.[25] Driving home the same point, another Chinese scholar, Liu Hongwu, the director of African studies at Zhejiang Normal University, argues even more explicitly that a Chinese pivot to Africa should be the essential component of China's overall "global rebalancing strategy." He argues that confronted by the US "rebalancing to Asia," China must escape the strategic encirclement by "expanding its scope for strategic maneuver" in seeking "new-type South–South relations."[26] Undoubtedly, these ideas articulated in early 2013 fit extremely well with the "New Silk Road Strategy" that was unveiled at the end of 2013. This strategy, which perhaps is rightly interpreted as an explicit attempt to favor relations with developing countries, is certain to favorably impact China's growing relations with Africa. This new strategic direction is discussed further in the next chapter (7), which focuses on China's relationship with the greater Middle East.

A late 2012 article in the magazine 财经 (*Finance and Economics*), moreover, suggests that the expanding relations are not simply good propaganda but also represent very real investment opportunities. Although noting that further growth is "not smooth sailing by any stretch" and that Chinese investors have suffered major losses on occasion (as in Libya), the article highlights that Chinese investment may represent the core of future economic interaction. It makes the interesting observation, from the Chinese perspective, that today's Africa resembles in many respects the situation of China at the start of its reforms in the late 1970s.[27] Interestingly, this article does cite an interview with a World Bank Africa expert, suggesting that such global financial institutions are given some weight among Chinese analysts. However, a recent scholarly article is quite revealing regarding the obvious tensions between the World Bank and China over African development. Such tensions surfaced openly in 2006, for example, when World Bank president Paul Wolfowitz publicly excoriated Beijing for its lending practices.[28] Thus, a Chinese scholar, writing in the prestigious journal 国际政治研究 (*International Politics Quarterly*) in 2012, offers a sharp critique of World Bank lending practices. The critique begins with the statement that the "East Asian economic miracle" was in no way the result of World Bank policies. It deplores the pressure put on developing nations, and it contends that such external interference has often pushed for reforms that were not feasible and led to negative outcomes. This critique suggests that the World Bank's emphasis on "good governance" (良治) since the 1990s has created evaluation criteria that are "very easily politicized." The tendency of Bank practices to support the "realization of US strategic interests" is also noted. Observing the potential of "emerging donors," the author concludes by calling for the diversification (多元化) of development theories and models.[29]

Despite such stark disagreements, there seems to be little appetite among Chinese analysts for Cold War–style geopolitical competition in Africa. To broach one such sensitive issue briefly touched on in the previous section of this chapter, the breakup of Sudan into two separate states in 2011 could well have turned into an international crisis of major proportions. If Beijing followed the troubling model of the Kremlin during the Cold War, the crisis might have witnessed a lightning intervention by Chinese expeditionary forces to secure all-important energy supplies. But Beijing is quite disinclined to follow that dubious, militarized model, and it has instead played a constructive role in the crisis. Indeed, a timely Chinese scholarly analysis immediately following the creation of South Sudan in mid-2011 is impressively even-handed and objective, noting that the stark results of the independence referendum resulted from a history of political, economic, religious, and cultural repression of the South by the North in Sudan. Moreover, the UN Security Council is praised for pressuring both sides to undertake negotiations in order to prevent a major armed conflict.[30] In addition, it is noteworthy that Premier Li Keqiang's May 2014 visit to Africa included a Beijing commitment to pursue an East Africa rail network that will link South Sudan (along with Uganda, Burundi, and Rwanda) to the sea for the first time via a route to the Kenyan port of Mombasa.[31]

Likewise, a systematic Chinese survey of "security incidents" in Africa from 2006 to 2012 does note the dangers confronting the estimated 1 million Chinese reported to be presently working and living in Africa. This survey groups risks to Chinese citizens among several different categories, including (1) political risks, (2) social security risks, (3) risks caused by unlawful activities of Chinese citizens themselves, (4) pandemic diseases, (5) terrorist incidents, (6) piracy, (7) traffic accidents, (8) financial fraud, and (9) natural disasters. Significantly, this detailed and methodical study, which entailed visits by the Chinese author to eighteen different African countries in mid-2012, makes hardly any mention of the use of the Chinese armed forces and refrains entirely from recommending expanded deployments.[32]

Still, one can observe increased Chinese strategic attention to Africa, as demonstrated simply by a clear increase in discussions regarding African security issues in the Chinese military and military-related publications. Indeed, the leading Chinese naval journal 舰船知识 (*Naval and Merchant Ships*) ran a special issue devoted to Africa in October 2012 that featured five separate, rather detailed articles. Among these articles is an extremely detailed description of the organization and activities of Washington's new Africa Command, or AFRICOM, which notes, among other features, the existence of a rapid reaction force on 72-hour alert for deployment that is the largest concentration of US ground forces based in Europe south of the Alps.[33] Another of the articles begins by observing that on Secretary of State Hillary Clinton's July 2012 trip to Africa, the two major themes that she discussed were terrorism and increasing Chinese influence. In that article it is suggested that the United States employed the "excuse" of terrorism to set up AFRICOM in 2007 as part of an effort to contain new, rising powers, including China.[34] Moreover, an article also appearing in 2012 in the prestigious international relations journal 国际政治 (*International Politics*) illustrated how AFRICOM is not just a concern for Chinese military strategists. The author asserts that "over the last few years, . . . the United States has continually increased its deployments and operations in Africa." It goes on to suggest that "with respect to military affairs, . . . many African countries have expressed doubts about US intentions, and are anxious regarding a new imperialist effort."[35]

A 2013 Chinese analysis also points to increasing US-China tensions in Africa. The analysis begins by suggesting that the "US is extremely suspicious of China-Africa cooperation, unceasingly seeks to blacken China-Africa cooperative relations, and strives to throw up obstacles to China-Africa development relations." Noting that the United States has a major influence on

African citizens, public opinion, the press, and political leaders, the article cites concerns about African negative opinions regarding Chinese products, merchants, and businesses. "'Playing the China card' in the midst of elections in certain African countries has caused some cooperation projects to be terminated for no reason and even Chinese citizens to be attacked." But though the article recognizes that many Chinese are, as a result of these "anti-Chinese" policies, extremely suspicious, the author strongly advocates converting the heretofore "negative . . . African factor," into a positive factor in US-China relations. According to this analysis, Beijing and Washington have a wide variety of shared interests in Africa, including (1) safeguarding African peace and security, (2) accelerating African development, (3) protecting the security of investments in Africa, and (4) encouraging the further development of reformed economic conditions and market structures. Above all, the author warns that armed conflict in Africa has caused huge catastrophes in the past and that the United States and China have a shared ethical responsibility to uphold peace and stability. By contrast, "the expansion of bilateral contradictions could bring about devastating consequences."[36] In this spirit, the final section of this chapter proposes a number of concrete steps toward building substantive US-China cooperation in the developing world.

Cooperation Spiral for US-China Relations in the Developing World

Washington's move 1 in the developing world: The United States should propose enlarged US-China military engagement in the sphere of military medicine with a focus on Africa (figure 6.1). The current Ebola Crisis powerfully demonstrates the imperative for greater global engagement in Africa's health situation, as well as the potential for Washington and Beijing to spearhead these efforts. Both the United States and China have large and well-developed military medical establishments. In each country, these military medical institutions enjoy high prestige for professionalism, high-quality care, and the unique ability to offer large-scale care in extremely austere conditions when called upon to do so, as they have each demonstrated in the 2014 Ebola Crisis. Both nations deploy military medical units around the world, and especially in the developing world, to offer medical aid. Undoubtedly, both Washington and Beijing likely have ulterior motives beyond altruism, not least competing for "hearts and minds" to outperform the other superpower in the grand game to increase their respective influence. The United States has engaged in such a

Figure 6.1 Cooperation Spiral: The Developing World   合作螺旋: 与发展中国家的关系

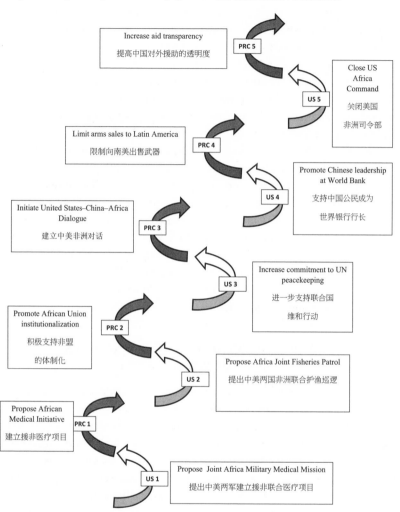

form of military medical diplomacy for decades, and undoubtedly much good has been done, though the effort has not been entirely without missteps.[37] Africa is a natural focal point of such efforts.[38] China has radically increased its capabilities in this arena during the last decade. With the only purpose-built naval hospital ship in the world, Beijing has dispatched this unique vessel recently to both Africa and Latin America to deliver medical aid to needy countries. Arguably, a competitive approach to delivering aid between the two superpowers could actually benefit the developing world. However, a more cooperative approach would have the benefit of integrating the efforts, preventing redundancies, allowing for specialization, and generally offering the developing world the prospect that the two superpowers could work toward the common objectives of development and better health, as suggested by the example given at the start of this chapter. A joint patrol by hospital ships from the Chinese and US navies along the African coast could have immense symbolic importance for the bilateral relationship more generally. Indeed, the two navies have already engaged in regular educational exchanges between hospital ship personnel. In the current Ebola Crisis, the two hospital ships could work in tandem off the coast of West Africa to form a proximate safe haven for infected medical aid workers—a step that could plausibly boost the morale of those risking their lives on the front lines of the crisis. Whether or not American and Chinese hospital ships are deployed in the present crisis, it is certain that the US and Chinese militaries have certain capabilities that make them uniquely well-suited for such challenging operations. For example, they each have a wealth of heavy transport aircraft that are so critical for keeping supplies flowing into impacted crisis zone. In addition, they have expeditionary capabilities, including the ability to move heavy equipment, but also each practice routines for nuclear, chemical, and biological warfare—skills that are quite similar to coping with pandemic outbreaks. It is hoped that this proposal might prompt the superpowers to look beyond the current Ebola Crisis to see where further military medical cooperation could make an impact on enhancing African development in the health domain. Military medical cooperation between the United States and China in the developing world, moreover, could also help to strengthen the larger foundation for US-China military engagement.

Beijing's move 1 in the developing world: China should promote a major bilateral medical initiative in Africa. Of course, the possible synergies for US-China medical cooperation in the developing world go well beyond the military sphere and the latest pandemic outbreak. China has been especially active in building medical facilities in Africa—a fact highlighted recently when President Xi attended the opening ceremony of the China-Congo Friendship Hospital in Brazzaville in March 2013. As noted above, Chinese building projects have been praised for high quality, low cost, and rapid completion.[39] The Brazzaville hospital is just one of thirty major hospitals that China committed to building during the landmark 2006 Beijing meeting of the Forum on

China-Africa Cooperation. Not surprisingly, the Sierra-Leone China Friendship Hospital on the outskirts of Freetown has become a significant center in that country's struggle against Ebola and also a focal point of China's aid effort. A significant initiative is under way, moreover, to send "container hospitals" and "container clinics," which have the virtues of easy set up and maintenance as well as scalability, to many parts of Africa.[40] Of course, Washington also has major achievements to its credit when considering the provision of health care in Africa, including especially the widely praised President's Emergency Plan for AIDS Relief that was inaugurated in 2004. But rather than proceeding entirely in parallel, it will be useful to join US-China medical initiatives to some degree. Again, there is the possibility of capitalizing on the positive momentum from cooperation developed in the 2014 Ebola Crisis. One possibility would be for Beijing to fund one or two guest American doctors to serve on fellowships at each of the new hospitals built by China in Africa. Though such a program would be expensive, this would represent a very clear signal that not only is China interested in cooperating with the United States to further African development, but also that it is truly committed to the ongoing provision of health care in the relevant communities.

Washington's move 2 in the developing world: The United States should propose a joint US-China fisheries enforcement patrol for African waters. African waters are now in crisis. Where other fishing grounds off Europe and North America have been systematically depleted over the course of centuries, the African littoral now beckons. But now that the world's distant water fleets are now all chasing Africa's last remaining fish, even these stocks are becoming severely depleted—a process that threatens the livelihood of millions of Africans. Indeed, it is hardly farfetched to suggest that rapacious fishing practices by external powers have caused the piracy crisis in the Gulf of Aden, because local subsistence fishermen could not compete with the factory ships coming from Europe and Asia. China has a large, distant-water fishing fleet. A Chinese source, for example, claimed a decade ago that as many as three hundred Chinese trawlers might be working in West African waters at one time.[41] For the most part, China's fishing activities are legal, in that they are undertaken after making agreements with local African states to fish in their exclusive economic zones. But there is also substantial illegal activity, including especially underreporting of catches. The US Coast Guard has already begun to operate sporadically in African waters to improve fisheries enforcement by local states. Moreover, the US Coast Guard has an excellent working relationship with Beijing's maritime enforcement agencies that has been built up over many years of step-by-step cooperation. From China's perspective, growth in the distant-water fishing fleet has been welcome, but there have also been ample concerns that its activities could offend locals and thus substantially embarrass China. Finally, the Chinese Coast Guard has been improving and integrating its capabilities and would likely welcome a more international profile. Therefore, the conditions are ripe for expanded multilateral fisheries cooperation, taking the US Coast Guard and the Chinese Coast Guard as the core organizing elements, in support of enhanced fisheries enforcement in African waters. It is also likely that such cooperation would additionally generate new pressure on Beijing to take the much-needed step of becoming more transparent regarding the nature of its fisheries agreements with African countries.

Beijing's move 2 in the developing world: China must put substance behind its support of the African Union (AU). In developing close relations with Africa, Chinese foreign policy leaders have recognized the importance of creating a strong relationship with the AU. In June 2013 the AU's fiftieth-anniversary celebrations were held in its gleaming new $200 million headquarters building constructed by China in Addis Ababa.[42] One reason clearly recognized in Beijing for why that relationship is so essential is the widespread, negative perception that China's evolving relationship with many if not most African states is starkly asymmetrical, both with respect to economic leverage and to negotiating expertise. The notion that China is using these asymmetrical advantages to leverage deals that are not in the broader interests of Africans more generally is quite widely held in Africa and among US leaders.[43] To reduce this perceived imbalance, Beijing needs to add substance to its efforts to collaborate closely with the AU's on efforts that go well beyond leadership dialogues and glitzy buildings. One obvious way to redress such concerns will be to place a priority on transnational rail and road infrastructure, such as the Lagos–Mombasa highway project to connect West and East Africa, that will benefit long-term continental trade and development. A second and potentially more difficult move for Beijing would be to support continent-wide labor and environmental norms, as monitored and reported at the AU. Both these efforts may run counter to the preference of Chinese diplomats to emphasize bilateral relationships, but reinvigorating China-AU ties with substantive agendas will serve to mitigate legitimate African and American concerns about Chinese practices.

Washington's move 3 in the developing world: The United States should make a commitment to participate actively in traditional "blue helmet" United Nations peacekeeping activities. Americans, in general, have been extremely frustrated with the United Nations, and particularly with the limits and failures of its peacekeeping activities. Since the end of the Cold War, Washington's perspective on UN peacekeeping has seemed to go from bad to worse, particularly when the UN has failed to help to resolve various intractable conflict situations—in the Balkans, then later in Afghanistan and Iraq, and most recently in Syria. The logic of the American approach amounted to a concept, whereby the United States would take on very difficult and pressing challenges, while the UN could tackle less urgent tasks. This bifurcation has not worked well for the United States, for the UN, or for the developing world. In short, US-led operations have lacked legitimacy and have been plagued by excessive reliance on military instruments to solve difficult political problems. UN peacekeeping operations, by contrast, have suffered from poor organization and training, along with inadequate resources. As of mid-2013 the United States had 115 soldiers serving in UN peacekeeping operations, though Bangladesh had 8,836 and China contributed 1,645.[44] US president Franklin Delano Roosevelt's vision of the UN was not one in which weak and poor countries like Bangladesh assumed the primary role of providing security forces to UN efforts. Rather, FDR's concept relied on the competence and vast military resources of the "five policeman" to maintain world order by resolving conflicts when necessary. The good news is that Beijing has for all intents and purposes embraced FDR's concept of world order. If the United States were to recommit itself to this founder's vision of the UN, then military interventions would be less common, to be sure, but they would also be less bloody, more widely accepted both internally and externally, and hence more successful. FDR's legacy provides the tools to manage great power conflict and competition in the developing world, and returning sincerely to his original vision should be a major step toward resolving the dilemmas of US-China global rivalry.

Beijing's move 3 in the developing world: China should initiate a quiet but formalized bilateral dialogue focused on Africa. It has been widely noted that the US-China relationship has a plethora of dialogues but is still lacking in basic trust, despite all these exchanges. In light of this critique, this book has (with only a very few exceptions) refrained from proposing the creation of new dialogues. The subject of Africa—given its quite new, delicate, and yet dynamic role between the new superpowers—may constitute an exception, and a regular dialogue among informed experts on both sides is now clearly needed. A variety of think tanks and foundations have already filled in the gap—generally with trilateral efforts involving nongovernmental experts from the United States, China, and Africa.[45] However, this dialogue would be something rather different: bilateral rather than trilateral, closed to the media rather than open, and emphasizing the role of diplomatic and senior military officials (perhaps at the assistant secretary level) and their staffs rather than nongovernmental experts (though such experts may be invited to participate occasionally to present research, etc.). In fact a model for this effort seems to be available, from the "US-China dialogue on Latin America," which began in 2006 and has continued into the Obama administration. According to one scholarly review of this "extraordinary" dialogue, the "content [of the dialogue] is still largely unknown," but from interviews, researcher Gonzalo Sebastian Paz could glean that the "central intention . . . was to make clear to the other party their own interests and policy, to increase transparency and avoid miscalculation." For Beijing the dialogue represents an opportunity to "reassure the United States," whereas, for Washington, it is seen as "a mechanism to shape . . . China's role in the region." Not surprisingly, Paz also found some significant concerns regarding a "Group of Two" (commonly referred to as the "G-2") among Latin American diplomats, who considered this dialogue to be "against their own countries' sovereignty."[46] But the imperative to prevent geopolitical rivalry and the associated dangers of conflict should trump diplomatic niceties in this case.

Washington's move 4 in the developing world: The United States should promote a Chinese president for the World Bank. After a string of twelve American presidents of the World Bank, this step might seem to be an extraordinary concession by Washington. However, it is well worth asking if the World Bank has been well served to have such a uniform set of leaders, including, notably, two rather discredited leaders from the Defense Department, Robert McNamara and later Paul Wolfowitz. In the immediate aftermath of World War II, such American commercial leadership made eminent sense; but this leadership tradition is now an anachronism in need of reform. As a seeming nod to East Asia's rising economic preeminence, the current World Bank president is an American citizen of Korean ancestry. But Beijing's case for leadership of the World Bank is very strong, indeed: China will soon have the world's largest economy, its rather low gross domestic product per capita suggests that it has the perspective of a developing country, its economic rise has been extraordinarily consistent and rapid, and this rise has had positive ripple effects throughout the developing world. Objections will surely follow from adherents to the so-called Washington Consensus, which favors free markets, over adherents to the "Beijing Consensus," which instead supposedly favors a statist capitalist model. This grand dichotomy, though intellectually interesting, does not really serve the interests of developing countries, and it may even prove dangerously destabilizing if permitted to become a central feature of geopolitical rivalry between the superpowers in the developing world. The fact that Justin Yifu Lin, a University of Chicago–trained Chinese economist, recently served as chief economist of the World Bank suggests that the possibility of Chinese leadership at the World Bank is not such a distant prospect. This not-insignificant concession by Washington would go a long way toward building a bridge between the United States and China in the developing world. It would also be likely to result in China adopting a more global and responsible outlook on its activities in the developing world, as it naturally begins to shoulder a greater burden of leadership.

Beijing's move 4 in the developing world: China should agree to caps on its arms sales to Latin America. Geopolitical rivalry can hopefully be mitigated by the measures outlined in this book, but some anxieties related to emerging threats, whether genuine or just perceived, cannot be entirely extinguished. Rather than wishing them away or ignoring them, the approach advocated here takes them seriously. Just as Beijing has legitimate security concerns in its neighborhood, the same holds true for Latin America. Of course, Washington will be closely scrutinizing the defense relationship that evolves between China and various Latin American countries. Logically, "for the United States one of the main concerns was China's relations with Chavez's Venezuela."[47] The Cuban Missile Crisis, but also tensions with Germany in Latin America going back more than a century, amply illustrate that arms transfers can become a lightning rod for geopolitical rivalry in the developing world. That is undoubtedly because certain types of arms transfers have the potential to rapidly overturn the regional balance of power. Some evidence was discussed above suggesting that Chinese arms manufacturers see ample scope for growth in Chinese arms exports to Latin America. There is mounting evidence that Chinese arms exports to Latin America are becoming more sophisticated, such as a recent suggestion by China that it would sell antisubmarine helicopters to Venezuela.[48] The prospect of Argentina acquiring new fighter jets with accompanying antiship cruise missile weaponry from China may draw more attention in London than Washington, but the trend is illustrative of tensions that could lie ahead as China's defense industry makes further inroads in Latin America.[49] Up to this point, China has seemingly demonstrated little appetite to associate with anti-American sentiment in Latin America. Recognizing the dangers, moreover, Beijing has seemed to act with great caution in Latin America. Hence, the public announcement of such caps on Chinese arms sales in Latin America could ultimately prove unnecessary. Nevertheless, such voluntary limitations on arms sales—whether defined by weapons type, recipient, or market share—could prove to be a powerful inoculation against the concerns of the China skeptics in Washington, who may see Chinese shadows in Latin America as intolerably threatening.

Washington's move 5 in the developing world: The United States should shutter AFRICOM. The new AFRICOM should be shut down for many reasons completely unrelated to US-China relations, including, but not limited to, costs, widespread suspicions across the continent, the imperative of burden sharing by European allies with higher stakes in Africa, the marginalization of other more important US initiatives in Africa, and the simple fact that Africa is not and should not become a major US national security priority. Arguably, the chief benefit of AFRICOM has been to institutionalize regular engagement with African militaries that might increase their competence and professionalism and thus help the cause of good governance and democracy across the continent. This goal undeniably has some merit—as the recent, bloody terrorist attack against the West Gate Mall in Nairobi demonstrated that the incompetence of security forces in Africa may provide a "soft target" for terrorists. But there is also no denying that the world's most powerful armed forces have little in common with the generally small and weak militaries of Africa. Beyond basic marksmanship, African militaries are unlikely to gain much from US forces that are naturally focused on air mobility, tactical surprise, and battlefield surveillance. Where does awe at a superpower's boundless resources and capabilities end and jealous resentment begin? Then there is the problem that they may turn their newly studied surveillance and forced entry techniques against their own populations. The mantra of professionalism, that military officers should be "above politics," will ring hollow for armed forces in poor countries where some military involvement in politics is all but inevitable. The examples of both Egypt and Mali, to some extent, seem to illustrate the reality that military engagement can also turn antidemocratic, thus implicating the United States in the often-unfortunate power struggles that generally characterize civil/military struggles in the developing world. Indeed, one of the major sticking points of arranging in the late spring of 2014 for US combat forces to aid Nigerian security forces in the hunt for kidnapped schoolgirls was the complication that US law forbids security assistance to military units that are accused of human rights abuses. Nor does Africa Command appear to be of huge importance to the ongoing Ebola Crisis response, as the key institutional enabler in the US military appears to be the US Army

Medical Research and Material Command.[50] What does this have to do with US-China relations in the developing world? As noted above, there is a widely held perception, both in Africa and in China, that AFRICOM was set up with the unstated goal (among several) of countering Beijing's growing influence in Africa. Closing AFRICOM, therefore, will not only allay suspicions in Africa, send a signal to allies that they need to be more involved in African security, and allow the US military to focus on other regions of greater geopolitical import, but will also help to demilitarize the US approach to an essential region of the developing world and open up greater possibilities there for cooperation with China.

Beijing's move 5 in the developing world: China must not only conform with conventional norms regarding foreign aid but must also give a clear accounting of its investment projects. As with so many other recommendations in this book, the heavy lifting in this case is needed in the domain of transparency. A very common critique of China's activities in the developing world is that they are beyond scrutiny because the agreements are most often bilateral and generally are negotiated behind closed doors, with only the sparest of details made public. Unfortunately, and not surprisingly, allegations of bribery and corruption seem almost endemic to China's relations in the developing world today. China's significant history of offering generous amounts of foreign aid, particularly during the early years of the People's Republic of China and at the height of the Cold War, engendered a secretive approach to foreign aid that still seems to linger in Beijing's corridors of power and foreign policy. Moreover, there is the very significant problem that most of China's actual aid comes in the form of "investment," and therefore is not quite comparable to the aid programs offered by other external actors. But several trends point to the possibility for significant reform. First, China enjoys a "can do" reputation in the developing world for rapid, results-oriented projects. Such a reputation suggests that unsavory methods for securing deals are now quite unnecessary and may even be viewed as wasteful by Chinese managers and diplomats themselves. Another relevant trend, moreover, is the new focus within China regarding transparent government. To be sure, there are limits on this development, but Chinese "netizens" have become quite expert at ferreting out corruption, and they will not like to see the Chinese taxpayer's money wasted on lining the pockets of bureaucrats in the developing world. Finally and perhaps most important, Beijing has recently encountered a host of foreign policy setbacks (and lost investments) in countries such as Libya and especially Myanmar as a result of its secret deal making. Open covenants that are openly arrived at will be much more durable and secure investments for China. Recent scholarship suggests, moreover, that China will tend to conform with aid norms in the developing world in certain circumstances.[51] A White Paper on Foreign Aid published by Beijing in mid-2014 was viewed by one expert as "heavy on cumulative statistics, and light on country specifics," but clearly this is a step in the right direction.[52]

Conclusion

The incipient dangers of a Cold War–style geopolitical rivalry flaring and then burning out of control in the developing world should not be neglected. There are, of course, the choices represented by the contrast between the "Washington Consensus" and the "Beijing Consensus" with regard to development. In addition, there are strategic resources, such as rare minerals and oil, not to mention geopolitically salient transport corridors, such as maritime chokepoints, that are at stake. To this combustible brew, one might add the most obvious destabilizing factor: the inherently unpredictable and wobbly nature of political dynamics throughout most of the developing world. No wonder so many of the very worst crises and conflicts of the Cold War took place in the developing world.

To date, signs are quite encouraging that US-China relations are up to the challenge of managing difficult issues in the developing world. Beyond some level of coordination in the ongoing Ebola Crisis discussed at the outset of the present chapter, Chinese and US diplomats appear to have collaborated with some effectiveness in at least avoiding the very worst outcomes of the unfolding Sudan crisis in 2011–12. Another encouraging sign is that a high-level, bilateral dialogue on Latin America has been functioning since 2006 and seems to have played a role in easing superpower tensions in an important region. Yet another good sign for this challenging relationship appeared in a mid-2013 issue of the prestigious American magazine *Foreign Policy*. In a survey of Africa experts from the West, who were polled on a wide variety of issues, a decisive 85 percent of experts said that "China's growing involvement in Africa . . . [is] . . . a good thing," whereas just 8 percent said it was a "bad thing."[53] Such numbers may suggest that building a consensus behind active US-China cooperation in the developing world may not be so difficult after all.

Notes

1. Megha Rajagopalan, "China to Send Elite Army Unit to Help Fight Ebola in Liberia," Reuters, October 31, 2014, http://www.reuters.com/article/2014/10/31/us-health-ebola-china-idUSKBN0IK0N020141031.

2. Stephen Burgess and Janet Beilstein, "This Means War? Scramble for Minerals and Resources Nationalism in Southern Africa," *Contemporary Security Policy* 34 (Spring 2013): 120.

3. "Gavin Menzies: Mad as a Snake—or a Visionary?" *The Telegraph*, August 1, 2008, www.telegraph.co.uk/culture/books/3557568/Gavin-Menzies-mad-as-a-snake-or-a-visionary.html.

4. Jiang Shixue, "The Chinese Foreign Policy Perspective," in *China's Expansion into the Western Hemisphere*, ed. Riordan Roett and Guadalupe Paz (Washington, DC: Brookings Institution Press, 2008), 29.

5. Lucy Corkin, "All's Fair in Loans and War: The Development of China-Angola Relations," in *Crouching Tiger, Hidden Dragon: Africa and China*, ed. Kweku Ampiah and Sanusha Naidu (Scottsville, South Africa: University of KwaZulu Press, 2008), 109.

6. Deborah Brautigam, *The Dragon's Gift: The Real Story of China in Africa* (New York: Oxford University Press, 2009), 39.

7. Mwesiga Baregu, "The Three Faces of the Dragon: Tanzania-China Relations in Historical Perspective," in *Crouching Tiger, Hidden Dragon*, ed. Ampiah and Naidu, 154.

8. Brautigam, *Dragon's Gift*, 41.

9. Ibid., 33, 38–39, 54.

10. Moran Zhang, "China's Yuan Internationalization: Africa Eyeing Dim Sum Bond Market" *International Business Times*, April 10, 2013, www.ibtimes.com/chinas-yuan-internationalization-africa-eyeing-dim-sum-bond-market-1182383.

11. "More Than Minerals: China's Trade with Africa Keeps Growing—Fears of Neo-Colonialism Are Overdone," *The Economist*, March 22, 2013, www.economist.com/news/middle-east-and-africa/21574012-chinese-trade-africa-keeps-growing-fears-neocolonialism-are-overdone-more. China's rather helpful role in the complex Sudan situation is also revealed in this scholarly treatment: Daniel Large, "China's Sudan Engagement: Changing Northern and Southern Political Trajectories in Peace and War," *China Quarterly* 199 (September 2009): 610–26.

12. Sigfrido Burgos and Sophal Ear, "China's Oil Hunger in Angola: History and Perspective," *Journal of Contemporary China* 21 (March 2012): 358–59.

13. Pang Zhongying, "Issues in the Transformation of China's Engagement with International Peacekeeping," in *Not Congruent, but Quite Complementary: American and Chinese Approaches to Nontraditional Security*, China Maritime Studies 9, ed. Lyle Goldstein (Newport: Naval War College Press, 2012), 53.

14. "China/Latam Trade Expanded 8% in 2012 and Region's Deficit Jumped to 6.6bn," *MercoPress*, May 22, 2013, http://en.mercopress.com/2013/05/22/china-latam-trade-expanded-8-in-2012-and-region-s-deficit-jumped-to-6.6bn.

15. Ariel Armony and Julia Strauss, "From Going Out (Zou Chuqu) to Arriving In (Desembarco): Constructing a New Field of Inquiry in China-Latin America Interactions," *China Quarterly* 209 (March 2012), 9.

16. Gonzalo Sebastian Paz, "China, the United States and Hegemonic Challenge in Latin America: An Overview and Some Lessons from Previous Instances of Hegemonic Challenge in the Region," *China Quarterly* 209 (March 2012): 28–29.

17. Andrei Akulov, "Confronting China: US Boosts Military Presence in Africa," March 28, 2013, 4, www.globalresearch.ca/confronting-china-us-boots-military-presence-in-africa/5328676.

18. See, e.g., Drew Petry, "Using AFRICOM to Counter China's Aggressive African Policies," *Airman Scholar*, Fall 2011, 25–30, www.dtic.mil/cgi-bin/GetTRDoc?AD=ADA559095; and Commander Todd Hofstedt (US Navy), "China in Africa: An AFRICOM Response," *Naval War College Review* 62 (Summer 2009): 82–100, www.usnwc.edu/getattachment/52b59501-ad3e-4d14-a797-5e1351d6bce0/China-in-Africa--An-AFRICOM-Response---Todd-A--Hof.aspx.

19. 陈积敏 [Chen Jimin], "从国家独立到西半球霸权：美国崛起过程中的拉美政策—兼论对中国崛起的启示" [From National Independence to Hegemon of the Western Hemisphere: America's Rise and Its Policies toward Latin America—A Concurrent Discussion of Lessons for China's Rise] 和平与发展 [Peace and Development], August 2012, 56–62.

20. 尚希, 司晓 [Shang Xi and Si Xiao], "成长中的拉美防务市场" [The Maturing Market for Defense in Latin America], 国防科技工业 [National Defense Science and Technology Industry], May 2013, 63; and 姚琛 [Yao Chen], "2013巴西防务展上的中国军工" [Brazil's 2013 Military Industry Development for Defense], 国防科技工业 [National Defense Science and Technology Industry], May 2013, 64.

21. Paz, "China," 28.

22. 钟声 [Zhong Sheng], "中非从来都是命运共同体" [The Destinies of China and Africa Have Always Been Shared], 人民日报 [People's Daily], May 27, 2013.

23. See, e.g., 王超 [Wang Chao et al.], "西非港口发展现状及趋势分析" [Analysis of the Development Situation and Trends for West African Port Development], 中国港口 [China Ports], February 2014, 61–63.

24. 怨基荣, 张建波, 倪涛 [Yuan Jirong, Zhang Jianbo, and Ni Tao], "非洲发展迎来黄金期和矛盾凸显期" [African Development Ushers in a Golden Era, but Also One of Emerging Contradictions], 人民日报 [People's Daily], June 3, 2013.

25. 刘明昊 [Liu Minghao], "为什么中国仍然要重视发展中国家" [Why China Should Still Emphasize the Developing World], 东方早报 [Oriental Morning Post], March 12, 2013.

26. 刘鸿武 [Liu Hongwu], "非洲机遇'与中国的'全球再平衡战略" [The "African Opportunity" and China's "Global Rebalancing"], 东方早报 [Oriental Morning Post], March 27, 2013.

27. 胡维佳 [Hu Weijia], "非洲投资新局" [The New Situation in African Investments], 财经 [Finance and Economics], September 24, 2012, 76–79.

28. Françoise Crouigneau and Richard Hiault, "Wolfowitz Slams China Banks on Africa Lending," *Financial Times*, October 24, 2006, www.ft.com/intl/cms/s/0/45e594e0-62fc-11db-8faa-0000779e2340.html#axzz2XteGyH00.

29. 徐佳君 [Xu Jiajun], "新型的援助附加条件: 评析世界银行绩校导向的援助分配政策" [The New Assistance with Aid Conditionality: An Evaluation of the World Bank's Policy of Performance-Based Allocation], 国际政治研究 [International Politics Quarterly], March 2012, 24–36.

30. 杨勉, 翟亚非 [Yang Mian and Zhai Yafei], "苏丹分裂的原因与南苏丹独立面临的问题" [The Causes of Sudan's Disintegration and the Problems Faced by the Independent Sudan], 亚非纵横 [Asia and Africa Review], no. 4 (2011): 15, 18.

31. Amy Copley and Amoudu Sy, "Chinese Premier Li Keqiang's Visit to Africa: A (Rail)road to Success in Sino-African Relations?" *Brookings Africa in Focus*, May 14, 2014, www.brookings.edu/blogs/africa-in-focus/posts/2014/05/14-li-keqiang-africa-china-sy.

32. 夏莉萍 [Xia Liping], "中非涉非领事保护分析" [An Analysis of China's Consular Protection Practice in Africa], 西亚非洲 [West Asia and Africa], January 2013, 20–35.

33. 黄凯, 曹晓光 [Huang Kai, Cao Xiaoguang], "美国非洲司令部" [United States Africa Command], 舰船知识 [Naval and Merchant Ships], October 2012, 67.

34. 刘兵 [Liu Bing], "非洲: 被大国关注的大陆" [Africa: A Continent Attracting the Attention of the Great Powers], 舰船知识 [Naval and Merchant Ships], October 2012, 59–62.

35. 罗会钧 [Luo Huijun], "中美对非战略的对比与启示" [The Strategies of China and the US toward Africa: Contrast and Revelation], 国际政治 [International Politics], no. 6 (2012): 128, 130.

36. 王洪一 [Wang Hongyi], "寻求中美在非洲的合作之道" [Exploring the Path of China-US Cooperation in Africa], 国际问题研究 [International Relations Studies], no. 2 (2013): 88, 95–97.

37. One obvious critique of such military medical missions has been a perceived deleterious impact on local medical practitioners. E.g., a dentist trying to make a living in a developing world community may see their business totally undermined by the visit of an external medical team. Though there could be obvious short-term benefits from providing free, high-quality care, the long-term sustainability of health care in poor areas remains in doubt.

38. See, e.g., Jefferey Hernandez, "Africa Partnership Station Brings Medical Practitioners Together," April 9, 2013, www.africom.mil/Newsroom/Article/10637/africa-partnership-station-brings-medical-practitioners-together.

39. Burgos and Ear, "China's Oil Hunger," 359.

40. "Chinese 'Container Hospitals' Ready to Deploy to Africa," *GhanaVisions*, June 15, 2013, www.ghanavisions.com/latest-news/49392-chinese-container-hospitals-ready-to-deploy-in-africa.html.

41. This source is cited in Lyle J. Goldstein, "Strategic Implications of Chinese Fisheries Development," *Jamestown China Brief*, August 5, 2009, 12n13.

42. "Chinese-Built Headquarters Towers over African Union Summit," Voice of America, June 3, 2013, http://blogs.voanews.com/state-department-news/2013/06/03/chinese-built-headquarters-towers-over-african-union-summit/.

43. David Smith, "Hillary Clinton Launches African Tour with Veiled Attack on China," *The Guardian*, August 1, 2012, www.guardian.co.uk/world/2012/aug/01/hillary-clinton-africa-china.

44. "Contributors to United Nations Peacekeeping Operations," www.un.org/en/peacekeeping/contributors/2013/may13_1.pdf.

45. See, e.g., "The US, China, and Africa: Pursuing Trilateral Dialogue and Action," Brookings Institution, May 13, 2013, www.brookings.edu/events/2013/05/13-us-china-africa-trilateral.

46. Paz, "China," 23–24.

47. Ibid., 23.

48. "委海军购买中国直升机反潜" [Venezuelan Navy to Buy Chinese Helicopters for Antisubmarine Warfare], 舰船知识 [Naval and Merchant Ships], October 2012, 4.

49. Richard Fisher, "Argentine Officials Confirm Joint-Production Talks over China's FC-1 Fighter," *Janes Defense Weekly*, June 23, 2013, www.janes.com

/article/23497/argentine-officials-confirm-joint-production-talks-over-china-s-fc-1-fighter?from_rss=1.

50. Nick Minecci, "Logistics Mission for Ebola 'Intense' and Highly Coordinated," December 6, 2014, https://mrmc.amedd.army.mil/index.cfm?pageid=media_resources.articles.ebola_mission_intense_and_highly_coordinated.

51. James Reilly, "A Norm-Taker or a Norm-Maker? Chinese Aid in Southeast Asia," *Journal of Contemporary China* 21 (January 2012): 80–81.

52. Philippa Brant, "China's Foreign Aid White Paper: A Quick Overview," July 14, 2014, http://www.lowyinterpreter.org/post/2014/07/10/China-Foreign-Aid-White-Paper-overview.aspx?COLLCC=740177664&.

53. Margaret Slattery, "Africa Rising?" *Foreign Policy*, July–August 2013, 88.

7

PERSIAN SPRING
The Middle East and US-China Relations

The ever-increasing turmoil in the Middle East suggests the possibility that this region could be an especially fruitful region for US-China cooperation. Any US ambition to transform the troubled region since the September 11, 2001, terrorist attacks has been severely curtailed in the wake of the costly Iraq War. The Arab Spring—which began in such a promising light on the principle of nonviolent protest, carried along by new social media in such countries as Tunisia and Egypt—has certainly entailed very severe human hardship in the ensuing civil wars in both Libya and Syria. The tragic loss of American diplomats in Benghazi during the summer of 2012, the bloody conflict between Israel and Gaza in mid-2014, the emergence of new extremist elements in Iraq and Syria and related US-led air strikes that began in September 2014, as well as the troubling human rights situation unfolding in Egypt and Bahrain, home of the US Fifth Fleet in the Persian Gulf—all suggest that US foreign policy has yet to find an effective framework to help guide the region to a more stable and prosperous future. And yet the election of Hassan Rouhani as the new president in Iran in mid-2013 still holds out the possibility that peacemaking may yet have a future in this deeply troubled region.

Chinese analysts have long considered the Middle East to be "the graveyard of the superpowers," yet Beijing is now also inexorably being drawn into the vortex. Most obviously, this trend is dictated by China's enormous appetite for oil and gas to fuel its ongoing rapid economic development. As the trend of

Chinese fossil fuel imports has continued to accelerate since the early 1990s, Chinese diplomats have accorded the Middle East more and more attention. And yet it would be a significant oversimplification to suggest that China's interest in the Middle East only concerns fossil fuels. In that light, a recent article in the *Economist* reveals that "Dragon Mart [in Dubai] is the biggest Chinese shopping mall outside the Chinese Mainland, . . . [and] Dragon Marts [are] springing up across the Middle East." This insightful glimpse into China's expanding engagement with the Middle East warns against "mak[ing] fun of Dragon Mart. It sells some of the most hideous things devised by man—polyester Persian carpets, [etc.]." But the trend is much more profound for global capitalism, because it demonstrates the link between "thousands of independent bamboo capitalists" and "the world's most exciting group of consumers, . . . the emerging middle-class . . . people who cannot afford to shop in the Mall of the Emirates." It is nothing less than the "rebirth of one of the world's oldest trading routes: the Silk Road, . . . albeit with a stress on plastic."[1]

Over the course of 2013–14, Beijing has rolled out a new foreign policy orientation: the so-called New Silk Road Strategy. The first component was announced by Xi Jinping in Kazakhstan in September 2013 and is intended to build up China's economic and transport links with Central Asia, while the second component was announced a month later in Indonesia and will comprise the "Maritime Silk Road."[2] This orientation toward the western flank appears to be a strategic response to the American "rebalance to the Asia-Pacific" in that it purposefully seeks to redirect China's energies away from direct zones of conflict with the United States and its allies, particularly in troubled Northeast Asia. While Central Asia and South Asia may receive the most immediate impact from this strategic reorientation by Beijing, there is little doubt that the Middle East figures prominently in China's larger strategic calculations. As in other regions, therefore, China' s approach is by and large commercial in nature, but there are strategic undercurrents and implications, to be sure. On the positive side, China's diplomacy in the region reflects the imperative for China to "step up" as a "responsible global power." As such, China has sent naval patrols to the Gulf of Aden, and it dispatched a warship to cover the withdrawal of its refugees from the Libyan conflict in 2011. In late 2013, moreover, the Chinese Navy sent a warship to escort the forces working to remove chemical weapons from Syria. A potentially darker side of Beijing's regional strategy may be suggested by the gradually accelerating ties between China and Iran. Although Beijing has demonstrably reined in the impulse to work more closely with Tehran on various occasions and has never seriously entertained the possibility of a formal military–political alliance, a strain of Chinese strategic thinking clearly seeks to empower Iran for the purpose of offsetting perceived Western hegemony in this critical region. In September 2014, Chinese warships made a first-ever port call in Iran. Giving front page coverage to this unprecedented event, one Chinese newspaper quoted an expert as saying that China has "broken America's blockade . . . [America] comes to our near seas to stir up problems, so then we will go to the Persian Gulf which [the US] considers important and undertake joint exercises with Iran." Thankfully, that theme is not the major thrust of the article, which stresses Beijing's caution in developing military ties with Iran. Still, this quote implies that ties between Beijing and Tehran could assume a more strategic role in the future under certain circumstances.[3]

To encourage China to pursue the former and not the latter approach outlined above, it will be important to draw China into a cooperative framework, and in keeping with the pattern of this book, a possible cooperation spiral for the Middle East is proposed at the conclusion of this chapter. This particular spiral is premised in part on the realist perception that, at least since the end of the Cold War, Middle Eastern international relations have actually not benefited from the region's extreme imbalance of power favoring Western interests. Actually, this imbalance has fueled extremism and with it terrorism, grave insecurity, and nuclear proliferation, along with conservative policies that have excessively delayed needed reforms. But if the Middle East were instead guided in part by multipolar interests with an enhanced, much-needed Chinese role, that would go some distance toward helping to restore much-needed balance, thus offering the requisite ballast to improve security in what has been one of the world's most volatile regions.

Background

China's trade links with the Middle East go back several millennia. Porcelain pots of Chinese origin found in Oman date back more than four thousand years.[4] China's interactions with the people of the Middle East have by and large been peaceful, mitigated by distance and the forbidding terrain that divides the two geographic regions. In one exceptional instance, at the battle of Talas in 751 CE, Arab armies defeated those of the Tang Dynasty, limiting China's reach into the Middle East. Still, the iconic Tang Horse came from the Fergana Valley in present-day Uzbekistan, and West Turkestan was for some time paying tribute to the Dragon Throne at the height of the Qing Dynasty's power in the mid–eighteenth century. A plausible theory concerning Admiral Zheng He's grand expeditions of the early fifteenth century holds that the effort was undertaken in part to balance the threat posed by Tamerlane, the Central Asian conqueror who dominated the Middle East at that time. The Chinese admiral, himself a Muslim, did undertake the pilgrimage to Mecca during one of his many journeys to the region. True, Zheng He's fleets were massive and also well armed, but this show of strength was exceptional and certainly did not amount to a Chinese attempt to establish colonies, much less some kind of Chinese hegemony in the Middle East.

In the modern era, China and the Middle East did not have a high level of engagement, in part because the West dominated the sea lanes that replaced the ancient Silk Road. And yet, China and the peoples of the Middle East were drawn together by the common experience of subjugation. As John Garver relates in his seminal book *China and Iran: Ancient Partners in the Post-Imperial World*: "Western Powers penetrated ever more deeply into the Persian and Chinese empires, . . . lands of both the Persian and Chinese empires were stripped away, [and] . . . in both Persia and China deepening foreign penetration stirred popular resistance."[5]

In the early part of the twentieth century, geostrategic and geo-economic linkages between East Asia and the Middle East had been all but curtailed by Western dominance. Without a doubt, the Allied conferences in Cairo and Tehran had profound implications for China (and the Taiwan question in particular), but these epic meetings simply reflected the fact that the Middle East was a secure location for a meeting in the midst of a global war rather than a key geopolitical influence on global politics. Another potential linkage between the regions surfaced in the 1950s, when Mao Zedong stated that China's shelling of the offshore islands occupied by the Kuomintang was actually a response to the US military intervention in Lebanon. Historians have not taken Mao's explanation very seriously, but he did take an active interest in global political developments outside East Asia. During the early Cold War, Beijing's rather minor role in the Middle East was to lend support to various "national liberation" causes.

Following closely the larger global realignments occurring after the Sino-Soviet split in the late 1960s, two Iranian princesses, the daughters of the Shah, arrived in Beijing during the spring of 1971 shortly after the US ping-pong team. In that same spring, Kuwait became the first of the Gulf monarchies to establish diplomatic relations with Beijing. In the decades to follow, Kuwait would become an important source of loans for Beijing as major economic reforms got under way at the end of the decade. In a bizarre twist of fate, China-Iran relations achieved major progress just before the Iranian Revolution in 1979. Indeed, the completely unprecedented visit of the Chinese leader Hua Guofeng to Iran's capital just as Tehran was becoming enveloped in revolutionary chaos remained a source of major embarrassment for Beijing and even required a formal apology to rectify bilateral ties in the 1980s.[6]

During the 1980s Beijing's relations with the region were dominated by arms sales. Most important, China played a crucial role in bolstering Iran's strategic position in the long and bloody Iran-Iraq War. Interestingly, most of these sales were "off the books," because they were frequently undertaken through intermediaries in third countries. China has been accused of great cynicism for providing arms to both sides of this conflict, but the US policy of supporting and encouraging Saddam Hussein during this period also appears rather dubious in light of subsequent developments. Beijing was plainly seeking to increase exports and gain hard currency during this period, and thus arms sales to Saudi Arabia, including a controversial sale of fifty or more intermediate-range ballistic missiles, also formed a part of this effort. However, it is additionally noteworthy that weaponry was also flowing in the opposite direction, as this decade featured the blossoming of an arms sales relationship between Israel and China, whereby Beijing was seeking to import high-technology matériel that it could not access elsewhere—a situation that was only intensified after most Western countries imposed an arms embargo on China in 1989.

A recent, very detailed Chinese military analysis of the US Navy's Operation Praying Mantis of 1988 observes that this secret operation destroyed almost all the Iranian Navy's significant fighting platforms, in no small part because "Iran's fast boats had no ability to cope with the airborne threat." This historical treatment concludes that "after [this operation], the yardstick for US naval intervention grew ever larger, causing Iran to believe that the United States was firmly on Saddam's side in seeking to overthrow the newly constituted Islamic regime in Iran."[7] Another set of events from this period, however, had a much more lasting impact on US-China relations. In July 1993 the Chinese ship *Yin He* left Dalian en route to Bandar Abbas. US intelligence concluded that the ship was carrying precursors for chemical weapons to Iran, but after a long and bitter diplomatic standoff, the ship was found not to be carrying the suspected chemicals. According to Garver, "Chinese officials and public opinion were outraged by the *Yin He* episode. . . . From the Chinese perspective, . . . this was the sort of arrogance at the core of hegemonism."[8] Recent Chinese accounts of that incident confirm Garver's earlier conclusion. For instance, a mariner's perspective on that event recently appeared in a Chinese publication related to the shipbuilding and maritime transportation sector. This account relates how the *Yin He*'s crew recognized from an early point that this event would "seriously impact the struggle for national political sovereign rights," and so the *Yin He*'s captain "righteously and in the strongest terms" refused supplies of food and water from an escorting American warship as supplies ran short on the suspect ship while its fate was determined by American and Chinese diplomats.[9] A detailed Chinese account of the related diplomatic negotiations was also recently published. This rendering places the incident in the context of the early Bill Clinton administration, which was determined to "bring pressure" on Beijing, especially with respect to the proliferation issue, and thus seized upon the *Yin He* intelligence as an "excuse" to force matters to a head. Although this account pulls no punches in suggesting that China's reputation suffered from the "groundless accusations," along with suffering considerable economic losses as a result of the disruption in its maritime trade, the author nevertheless concludes that the incident's ultimate resolution, when the ship was searched and no chemical weapons precursors were found, actually helped to swing the Clinton administration toward a more cooperative approach to the US-China bilateral relationship.[10]

As the US role in Persian Gulf security expanded during the 1990s, China's interest in the Middle East was also growing rapidly because Beijing had begun a major expansion of oil imports from that region during this period. For example, Chinese oil imports from Iran over the period 1995–2003 expanded at an average annual rate of 45 percent.[11] During the years after the Persian Gulf War, US foreign policy focused on the proliferation threat, and major pressure was directed at Beijing to curtail, or at least strictly limit, its large-scale nuclear and conventional arms cooperation agreements with Tehran. These efforts by Washington were reasonably successful because a considerable policy change was made by Beijing during the years 1996–97. For example, China announced at that time that it was suspending a project to build a 300-megawatt reactor in Iran, and it pledged not to sell Tehran either a uranium hexafluoride plant or a heavy-water production plant.[12] A deal for the transfer of advanced C-802 cruise missiles was also frozen under US pressure (although half the order, seventy-five weapons, had already been shipped).[13] Among possible motives that may be ascribed to Beijing are a desire to avoid isolation in the international community and appear as a "responsible stakeholder"; the perceived imperative to improve US-China relations after the Taiwan Crisis in 1996, and obviously to avoid the threatened sanctions; and a genuinely new conviction that nuclear and missile proliferation also posed a threat to China itself.

At the turn of the millennium, Beijing could take pride in its steadily growing network of relationships in the Middle East, and also some concrete achievements, for example, the opening of the first section of the Chinese-engineered Tehran Metro in 2000. As a sign of a blossoming relationship, Beijing was chosen to build Tehran's new fleet of very large crude carriers, producing the first of these giant ships in 2002, and it was also awarded major upstream oil and natural gas contracts in Iran during 2004. By that year, China was already importing an impressive 40 percent of all Omani crude oil exports, and it also opened the remarkable Dragon Mart (discussed in the introduction to this chapter) in Dubai, which covers 87 square miles.[14] In 2000 China also inaugurated the policy of 西部大开发 (Actively Promote the Development of the Western Regions), which naturally sought to reduce the isolation of the interior parts of China by promoting greater contact with South and Central Asia, as well as the Middle East more generally, not least because of common cultures and a shared religious heritage.

After the 9/11 attacks China's response was, indeed, shaped in large part by instability and concern over persistent violence in the largely Muslim province of Xinjiang, a concern that has arisen anew with several large-scale attacks occurring in the years 2013–14. The Chinese government had growing apprehension about a pattern of terrorist attacks emanating from discontent in this region and also cast a wary eye on the Taliban government in Afghanistan and its shadowy connections to radical groups in Xinjiang. Given this background, it is rather easy to see why Beijing, at least initially, would line up relatively strongly behind the US "war on terrorism," voting in the UN Security Council to support American military action both in Afghanistan in 2001 and also in Iraq two years later. However, China elicited a price for giving its support in the latter case (not unlike the case a decade earlier before Operation Desert Storm in Iraq). Undoubtedly, there is no coincidence in the fact that the United States placed the East Turkestan Independence Movement on its official list of terrorist organizations at about the same time that Beijing opted not to veto the UN resolution authorizing the use of force in early 2003.

However, the US-China common perspective on the Middle East did not last, if indeed it ever existed at all. Beijing became increasingly suspicious and critical of Washington's policies in the Middle East. A strong current of unofficial opinion in China held that the Second Iraq War amounted to an attempt to ensure US control over the fossil fuel riches of the Middle East.[15] By 2011 Saudi Arabia had become the largest exporter of oil to China, while Iran occupied the third spot, behind Angola. Just over half of Chinese oil imports came from the Middle East.[16] Reflecting the primary importance of Saudi Arabia, Hu Jintao made two visits to the desert kingdom, first in 2006 and then in 2009. However, it is the China-Iran nexus that has been in the news so often for the last few years, because Beijing's reluctance to sanction Iran has seemed to save Tehran from near-total isolation. Erica Downs and Suzanne Maloney wrote in 2011 that "the US political climate has turned more rancorous toward both Iran and China," but they recommended stepped-up cooperation with Beijing, because "China is the only major player still active in the Iranian oil patch."[17] Of this vital relationship for the twenty-first century, Garver concludes in his comprehensive treatment of the multifaceted relationship that "a sense of Sino-Iranian civilizational solidarity [does] infuse China-Iran relations." He also makes the important observation that among the various Asian powers (e.g., India, Japan, Russia, and Indonesia), "Iran promises to be more comfortable with great Chinese power than does any other major Asian state."[18]

Contemporary Chinese Analyses of the Middle East, and Particularly of the Iran Dilemma

Relatively little is known about Chinese perceptions and strategy regarding the Middle East. Garver's path-breaking work on the subject draws on numerous Chinese sources, but many of these were published in the 1990s, so an update is badly needed because China's role in the Middle East has been rapidly evolving. Although a very useful survey of Chinese writings would focus on Chinese perspectives regarding the origins and consequences of the Arab Spring, as well as the burning civil wars in Syria and Iraq, this effort only touches lightly on these crucial issues. Because the focus of this book is on the most important and most problematic issues in US-China relations, this section focuses largely on Chinese analyses of the Iran questions, especially the nuclear issue. Recall that extensive use of Chinese sources here does not imply endorsement of these viewpoints. Rather, they are presented to better explain these alternative perspectives.

Still, it is useful to offer some discussion of China's appraisal of the transformative Arab Spring that swept away the ruling regimes in Tunisia, Egypt, and Libya, and roiled several others, including Bahrain and Yemen. One such analysis was published in 西亚非洲 (*West Asia and Africa*) by the Shanghai scholar Li Weijian in late 2012. Interestingly, Li suggests that "most Chinese scholars have been very conservative" in analyzing the Arab Spring, and he criticizes their inclination to either overemphasize international factors or alternatively link the Arab Spring to Chinese internal reform possibilities. By contrast, he states emphatically that the political and social transformation of the Arab world is "extremely necessary." At the same time, he scoffs at the Western notion that democracy would easily push aside more than a thousand years of traditional and social principles. This specialist suggests that the fate of transformation in the Middle East will be determined by three sets of conflicts: between religious and secular advocates, between adherents of Sunni and of Shiite Islam, and finally between the regional powers, among which Li sees Turkey as now ascendant. Ultimately, he recommends that Chinese readers should not "hastily react to Western hegemonic discourse," nor should China "passively hide behind other countries or care too much about the opinions of other countries." But Li also argues for innovative Chinese policies in the Middle East—recognizing, for example, that China suffered major economic losses in the recent Libyan War—and he concludes with a reference to Hu Jintao's 2009 assertion that ethics should play a greater role in Chinese foreign policy in the Middle East.[19]

Chinese coverage of ongoing tensions involving Iran has been widespread, reflecting Beijing's growing role in the Middle East, and has also been relatively objective. There is substantial concern about the trajectory of the Iranian nuclear crisis, though the analyses generally conclude that a US military strike against Iran is quite unlikely. In this literature there is little if any discernible questioning of Beijing's ongoing strong relationship with Tehran, but there is a general awareness of new peace overtures from the West, of Iran's growing military capabilities and likely nuclear weapons potential, and of the bellicose rhetoric and risky behavior in which Tehran had engaged under its previous president.

It is evident from Chinese military and defense publications that Chinese defense specialists not only observe Iranian military development very closely but have clearly also played an important role in this development process. One Chinese naval expert at the Jiangnan Shipbuilding Corporation, for example, describes a visit he had made to Iran a few years ago to work on collaborative shipbuilding projects. He found "backward fabrication capabilities, poor management practices, and . . . low productivity." No wonder, he comments, that it required Iran eight whole years to construct its first relatively small (1,400-ton) surface combatant, which was launched in 2010. Although conceding that Iran has made progress in certain areas of defense capabilities, especially missiles, he concludes that Tehran's 2011 threat to block the Strait of Hormuz lacks credibility, explaining that "Iran's ability to 'play with fire' is hardly great."[20] A survey of Iranian missile capabilities in a Chinese military periodical from late 2011 reveals a force of more than 1,500 missiles, and finds that Iran's missile forces are achieving longer ranges and moving toward solid fuel engines. The article notes that Western sanctions have made it harder for Iran to import missile technologies, but also makes the interesting point that North Korean rocketry is too backward to have been of any serious help to Iran's effort. A serious recent setback in the program—an explosion during a test that killed many Iranian missile specialists—is also noted in the article.[21]

Chinese military analyses of the Persian Gulf situation do not openly discuss the role of Chinese arms or defense technologies in the overall balance. For instance, a very detailed rendering of the missile strike against the Israeli corvette *Hanit*, published in a Chinese unofficial naval journal in late 2006, simply noted that the missile was an Iranian fabrication of a Chinese-designed C802, but there was no elaboration on how the missile (and related training) was acquired by Hezbollah, nor any due reflection regarding the possibility that there might be a deleterious impact from the proliferation of such advanced weaponry into the hands of radical nonstate groups. The analysis observes that the ship burned for hours, that the ship's internal systems were [largely] destroyed, and that the ship had to be towed back to an Israeli port. Undoubtedly, some Chinese missile engineers may view this battlefield success as confirmation of their weapon's prowess. However, the tone of this particular article is rather a reflection on how or why the crew failed to protect the ship—a shortfall largely blamed on poor intelligence.[22] Another article in the same journal appraises Iranian antiship missiles and observes that not much is known in the West about these programs. The article curtly notes the Western view that China's role has been considerable, but it is rather critical, noting the short range and low explosive yield of various Iranian systems, and yet it concludes that "concealing and defending aircraft carrier groups against antiship missiles in the Persian Gulf or Gulf of Oman would be extremely difficult."[23]

Regarding Iran's nuclear programs, Chinese analyses have not been oblivious to the rapid pace of Iranian advancement. Thus, a spring 2012 appraisal in the Chinese journal 国防科技工业 (*National Defense Science and Technology Industry*) takes note of both Iran's 3,000 centrifuges and its fourth-generation indigenous uranium separation technology. Like many Chinese articles on Iran's nuclear program, this description also emphatically states that the program was initiated in the 1950s with American assistance and, moreover, that Iranian leaders well before 1979 had argued that nuclear power generation could enable Iran to sell more oil and gas.[24] Another detailed article in an official Chinese military periodical candidly suggests that Iran has sufficient enriched uranium for five "nuclear warheads," but it also notes that Iran has not exceeded the boundaries of peaceful nuclear research, so Tehran has become "a state possessing the capability to build nuclear weaponry." The authors write: "It is plain that the US is exaggerating the possibility of using force in order to pressure Iran and extend its control in the Middle East," but they conclude that the wider situation in the Middle East is hardly propitious for a US attack and, moreover, "there is really no possibility for a 'Libyan model' with respect to Iran." Encouragingly, this article duly notes international sanctions that forbid countries from exporting tanks, fighter aircraft, warships, or nuclear and missile-related technologies. However, the authors also plainly state in the article's conclusion that China increased its oil imports from Iran in the first half of 2012—irrespective of tighter US sanctions against such oil importers—perhaps expecting Washington to inevitably take a hard line on Beijing because of the election.[25]

Chinese scholarly appraisals of the unfolding Iranian nuclear issue also tend to be rather skeptical about the possibility that Washington could resort to war. One 2012 analysis, for example, reaches that conclusion based on Iran's inherent strengths, the exceedingly high economic costs of such a conflict, and the lack of a global or regional consensus on the issue. Although an editor's introduction to this article offers the interesting caveat that "we [the Chinese] always underestimate Western force and determination," the article concludes that the Western use of force against Iran is all but impossible, given China's certain opposition in the UN Security Council, determined by, among other factors, China's increasing reliance on Iranian oil and the fact that the China-Iran-Pakistan oil pipeline is said to be of "critical significance" to China's energy security.[26] Another detailed scholarly analysis details the logic of Israel's acute anxieties with respect to Iran, noting the historical experience of the Holocaust and also Israel's small size in that regard. However, a strike against Iran is regarded as quite infeasible, given the multiple and dispersed sites at issue in Iran and also the apparent fact that Iran's "air defense is much stronger than were those of Iraq back in 1981." As in many Chinese analyses, the US Defense Department's appraisal that an attack would only delay Iran's nuclear ambitions by three years or so is taken to be quite credible. Though Chinese analyses indicate an awareness of Iranian domestic fissures, Chinese analysts believe a military strike against Iran would actually serve only to consolidate the ruling regime's hold on power. With respect to the economic costs of a conflict, this analysis observes that many countries, including China, would suffer from a blockage of the Strait of Hormuz. However, it is emphasized that Tehran is "not irrational" (非理性), as it is sometimes portrayed in Western appraisals, and that Iran would only seek to block the Strait in retaliation for a strike on its nuclear facilities. In this interpretation, the Strait is Tehran's "poker chip" (筹码).[27]

A rather alarming analysis of the Iranian issue was published in a scholarly journal by Wang Nan, senior editor at *People's Daily*, in late 2011. Like the analyses cited above, Wang suggests many reasons why a strike is quite unlikely, not least because "城门失火, 殃及池鱼" (when the city gates burn, calamity befalls the fish in the moat), meaning that most regional actors are unlikely to support a US attack on Iran. He also warns that Iran's strength and "secret fighting capabilities" should not be underestimated. According to him, a major reason for the Western strategic focus on Iran is the broader goal of constraining China's rise, and so the nuclear issue is simply a convenient "excuse" to subjugate Iran. He concludes that, ultimately, the United States and other Western countries may be willing to assume major risks and pay a large price "to protect the hegemonic position they have enjoyed on the world stage for hundreds of years," but he ominously adds that the resulting war "could spread to other global regions . . . and thus precipitate a third world war."[28]

A 2011 Chinese analysis grapples with the internal calculus of Tehran's nuclear decision making and concludes that the domestic political calculations of Iran's leadership with respect to the nuclear question are of paramount importance. That is why, the author explains, Iran's decisions in this sphere cannot be figured in terms of a simple cost/benefit calculation. Indeed, this Chinese author reckons that the costs to Iran's economic and social development have been "enormous" (巨大代价). For him, Iran sees itself on the "moral high ground," because Iranians think the West has "the real goal to contain Iran," in part because of the "different attitudes toward Israeli nuclear programs and toward Iranian nuclear programs." The analysis highlights the May 2010 agreement signed between Iran and Turkey for joint peaceful nuclear research as an illustration that some states may agree with certain aspects of Tehran's approach.[29] Indeed, Ankara's unique and significant approach to the Iranian nuclear issue was further analyzed in another Chinese scholarly piece covering the issue. The article notes impressive growth in trade between Iran and Turkey, Turkey's apparent desire for a nuclear-free Middle East, and Ankara's evident frustration that Washington will hardly even discuss Israel's nuclear weapons program, much less consider economic sanctions against it.[30]

A similar frustration pervades Chinese analyses of the Iranian nuclear issue. Wang Ning, for example, observes that Western countries have put no pressure whatsoever on Israel to submit to any kind of nuclear inspections regime, and he even suggests that Israel is also being offered a "nuclear security umbrella" by Washington. By contrast, most Middle Eastern countries have neither nuclear weapons nor nuclear security guarantees from the great powers, leading to what Wang calls an "extremely grave nuclear imbalance" (极其严重的核失衡).[31] Indeed, Chinese military analysts have noted Israel's progress toward fielding advanced nuclear forces, for example, submarine-fired nuclear-armed cruise missiles.[32] A 2012 article in an official Chinese military newspaper speculates about the possibility that Saudi Arabia will pursue nuclear weapons and says that the United States "turns a blind eye" to Israeli nuclear weapons, which, it is maintained, have planted the "seeds" (种子) of nuclear rivalry in the Middle East.[33]

It seems evident that many Chinese analysts are sympathetic to, or at least empathetic with, Tehran's alleged ambition to possess nuclear weaponry. But even Chinese scholars are somewhat amazed at the "striking process of change [to China's policies on nuclear nonproliferation], evolving from opposition to the norm of nonproliferation to partial acceptance, and later to strong support."[34] Moreover, there is substantial reason to believe that the recent unfortunate developments in North Korea may lead Beijing toward a more proactive approach to the Iranian nuclear issue, especially given the much-improved climate for negotiations since Rouhani's election in mid-2013. Although Chinese military strategists continue to worry about a worst case scenario of the United States' blockading the Strait of Hormuz to China-bound tankers, they are also cognizant that other states are also vulnerable at this maritime energy chokepoint and, moreover, that the threat posed by terrorism or even an accidental closure of this critical Strait could also pose a significant threat to China.[35] These points, by and large, suggest a potentially broad scope for US-China strategic cooperation in the Middle East.

An interesting scholarly article appeared in the journal 国际政治 [International Politics] in mid-2014 that appraises the effectiveness of Washington's sanctions against Tehran. The author observes that many countries "被迫" (were forced) to abandon cooperation with Iran. The author somewhat ambiguously places China among many Asian states, including Japan, South Korea, and India, that have "大幅减少" (severely curtailed) oil imports from Iran. At that point, the author departs somewhat from political correctness in China, where it is often held that sanctions are wholly detrimental, and the assessment is offered that the sanctions produced "一定冲击" (a certain shock) within Iranian domestic politics, causing the Iranian people to elect the moderate Rouhani. The author goes on to explicitly concede that the sanctions effort succeeded in bringing Iran back to the negotiating table. And yet the article also points out that Tehran has continued to move ahead aggressively with nuclear and missile programs. This analysis, like many other Chinese discussions of the Iran crisis in recent years, holds that the United States does not really have any other realistic means to employ against Iran other than sanctions and, moreover, that Tehran is prepared in case the talks fail. In the end, the author concludes somewhat pessimistically that the sanctions and related negotiations are unlikely to curb Iran's "地区野心" (wild regional ambitions) and that it is difficult to use economic tools to try to resolve security issues.[36]

At the time of this writing in late-2014, it is impossible to predict whether Tehran and Washington will achieve the diplomatic breakthrough that will make possible much-improved relations and even a new Middle Eastern political landscape. In theory such a development could be quite unnerving to Beijing. After all, it would lose its near monopoly on Iranian investment projects; and even more ominously, improved US-Iranian relations could free up the United States' strategic resources so that it could concentrate on its policy of "rebalancing" to the Asia-Pacific region. It is encouraging that such suspicious and even paranoid tendencies do not seem to characterize Chinese assessments. For example, a detailed survey of the prospects for such a US-Iran rapprochement published in early 2014 is completely devoid of such zero-sum sentiments. This rather sober analysis does not underestimate the difficulties for both sides, and it says unequivocally that "US-Iran relations will not reach the point of a 'Nixon to China' moment." Yet the analysis is extremely candid in underlining the severe toll that post-2011 sanctions have taken on the Iranian economy, and the analyst concludes that the Iranian economy urgently requires détente with Washington.[37] Although this Chinese analysis does not seriously broach the question of how China's interests would be at stake in a hypothetical Tehran–Washington rapprochement, the constructive and rather hopeful tone of the analysis does at least suggest the theoretical plausibility of exploring win–win–win scenarios. The cooperation spiral that follows makes such an attempt.

A US-China Cooperation Spiral for the Middle East

Washington's move 1 in the Middle East: The United States should offer to sell natural gas to China and should also share advanced exploration and fracking technology with China (figure 7.1). A major root of US-China tension in the Middle East concerns energy security. As noted above, Chinese strategists are extremely concerned that the United States could attempt to coerce China by severing its energy "lifeline," by blocking either the Strait of Hormuz or the Strait of Malacca. Moreover, Washington has thus far stifled Chinese attempts to acquire and further integrate with American energy firms, such as the infamous 2005 UNOCAL case (see chapter 4). US strategists are also concerned about China's growing ties with Middle Eastern oil exporters, including longtime US allies such as Saudi Arabia, and there is a generalized fear concerning an all-out scramble among the great powers to seize diminishing energy resources. As noted above, Chinese strategists have even contemplated a "doctrine of retaliation" to cope with the vulnerability of China's maritime energy transportation corridor. To ease these tensions in the domain of energy security, greater interdependence will help to build trust and goodwill. Since 2009 US production of natural gas has been growing by leaps and bounds.[38] The commodities expert Edward Morse reported in the spring of 2014 that "US natural gas production has risen by 25 percent since 2010. . . . Having already outstripped Russia as the world's largest gas producer, by the end of the decade, the United States will become one of the world's largest gas exporters, fundamentally changing pricing and trade patterns in global energy."[39] As a world leader in fracking technology, the United States may even explore selling this technology to China, especially because the Chinese use of gas is certainly preferable to dirty coal. The Chinese are now pushing very hard to convert the pertinent infrastructure to adapt to cleaner-burning natural gas. As with any policy choice, this one also has costs and concerns (fracking dangers chief among them), but the jobs and development that would flow from a series of liquefied natural gas plants on the US West Coast to serve East Asian demand, and that of China specifically, would make a strong start on easing US-China tension in the critical energy domain.

Figure 7.1 Cooperation Spiral: The Middle East   合作螺旋：中东问题

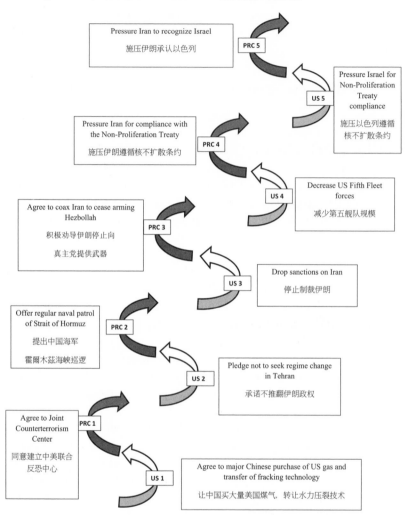

Beijing's move 1 in the Middle East: China should propose and (primarily) fund a bilateral counterterrorism center. China's concerns about terrorism have been growing during the past decade. There are persistent anxieties over restive areas of China—for example, Xinjiang, where bombs and other types of attacks have become regrettably routine. However, as Ely Ratner points out, this trend is also connected to globalization: "China's integration into the global economy has naturally meant a growing number of Chinese companies and expatriates in foreign lands—or in other words, an ever-expanding target set for those wishing to attack Chinese assets."[40] China's increasing interest in counterterrorism is easily documented, both in military and commercial trade journals, and has accelerated further since major attacks in the years 2013–14.[41] Although some limited antiterrorism cooperation between Washington and Beijing did take place after 9/11 and in preparation for the Beijing Olympics, much more could still be done. An established antiterrorism center with permanent bilateral staffing would be a powerful signal to both sides of a commitment to work together in this vital area. Given sensitivities on both sides, such a center would not be easy to set up in practice. And yet both sides could realize major benefits in terms of information awareness, socialization among security personnel, training, and the exchange of best practices. For obvious reasons, some of the center's activities would need to be kept secret, but unquestionably a major area of work and collaboration would concern those radical groups active in the Middle East that are threats to both nations' people and interests.

Washington's move 2 in the Middle East: The United States should explicitly renounce the objective of regime change for its Iran policy. Having worked on some of the foundational issues of increasing mutual trust and cooperation in the Middle East, the cooperation spiral must now evolve to cope with the hardest issue dividing the United States and China in the Middle East: Iran. As of late 2014, intense negotiations are now under way to try to resolve the long-lasting and dangerous stalemate over the Iranian nuclear issue. Appraising the state of negotiations between various Western powers, including the United States, with Tehran in early 2013, *The Economist* called for "juicier carrots." Indeed, the logic of this spiral rests on the idea that carrots will be more potent than sticks and, moreover, that Beijing can play a useful role in easing Tehran's anxieties about entering a deal to renounce nuclear weaponry once and for all.[42] The step of renouncing "regime change" would be difficult, but hardly out of the question. After all, Senator John Kerry suggested just such a move as the hallmark of the Obama administration's "new approach" to the Iran question back in May 2009, with the apparent hope that such a move would bring about gradual deescalation in the region.[43] Readers familiar with the 1953 seminal episode, when a plot by the US Central Intelligence Agency overthrew the elected leader of Iran, may realize why such an explicit policy, ideally codified in law, would be a major step toward both easing Tehran's march to acquire nuclear weapons and pacifying the whole region. In Beijing such steps would be welcomed as part of a larger process, in which it might play a larger role as a responsible great power helping to stabilize the volatile Middle East.

Beijing's move 2 in the Middle East: China should propose initiating its own semipermanent Hormuz Patrol squadron. Iran has long sought a closer security relationship with China, but Beijing has resisted so as to be free of foreign commitments and also to avoid the ire of the United States and other Middle Eastern powers. However, insofar as Iran's insecurity is at least a partial driver for the nuclear weapons program, an increased profile for China in the region could help to mitigate this security dilemma. It is quite true that China has long viewed the region as a "graveyard for superpowers," and moreover has supported the view that the Persian Gulf will be more secure if policed by local states rather than outside powers—a nod to Tehran in some respects, to be sure. However, Chinese security policy has changed to adapt to circumstances, and Beijing may well accept a larger role—particularly if it is low risk, low cost, lends further prestige to China's emerging role as a global power, and can contribute constructively to Middle Eastern peace. The patrol need not be large; perhaps, it could adopt the model of the antipiracy squadron in the Gulf of Aden, comprising just two warships and an oil tanker. This squadron would hardly be a threat to other powers, and it would simply underline Beijing's vital interest in maintaining unimpeded freedom of navigation through the Strait of Hormuz. In keeping with Beijing's policy of not developing foreign bases, it is nevertheless suggested that China's Hormuz squadron would make frequent stops at Iranian ports. As noted earlier in this chapter, the Chinese Navy made a first-ever visit to an Iranian port during September 2014, suggesting the further feasibility of this proposal. While mitigating Tehran's security anxiety by enhancing military engagement, the force would also serve the broader global interest and subtly warn Iran that closing the Strait under any circumstances would represent a grave threat to China.

Washington's move 3 in the Middle East: The United States should ease the sanctions regime against Tehran. As bilateral negotiations press forward during 2014 in Geneva, the likelihood of a significant easing of US economic sanctions may well come to fruition. Chinese observers had previously suggested that the Obama administration's policy on Iran looked almost identical to the Bush administration's policy.[44] Hard-liners will surely argue that Tehran is only coming to the table now because it has been coerced by the sanctions, and thus US pressure must continue. It is right and proper that US policy should employ both carrots and sticks. However, as noted above, it is essential that the carrots not be neglected, as they seem to have been in the past. Here, a recalibration of punishments and rewards could actually benefit from previously hard-line approaches. In the classic good cop / bad cop game, the interrogators shift between harder and softer approaches, and thus a new softer approach can appear to be a very juicy carrot, because the impact of ever-tighter sanctions has been illustrated over the last two years as causing significant if not devastating pain to the Iranian economy (inflation, etc.). The Chinese argument that sanctions are a problematic tool has at least some merit, because it places the target regime in the difficult position of caving to external pressure or, put in Chinese terms, of losing face. A significant easing of sanctions, well beyond the partial easing that occurred in early 2014, will be essential to building the will in both Tehran and critically also in Beijing to push for a major and durable compromise on the volatile nuclear issue. It may also be useful for Washington to assure Beijing that it will not seek to undermine China's existing oil and gas contracts with Iran, because one value of the sanctions regime for China has been that it has not faced competition from Western firms in seeking Iranian natural resources.

Beijing's move 3 in the Middle East: China should pressure Iran to halt its arms transfers to Hezbollah and other radical Middle Eastern groups. Given the extensive concessions made by the United States as proposed above, in addition to China's newly expanded security ties with Iran in the form of the Chinese Hormuz squadron, it is obviously time for Tehran to demonstrate its commitment to the process of deescalation by offering a major concession of its own. Undoubtedly, halting arms transfers to Hezbollah would constitute such a major concession for Iran, given that Hezbollah's military activities over the last five years have constituted one of Iran's few geopolitical successes, and it has clearly gained significant prestige in the region by creating a major security threat to Israel. It has also been suggested that Hezbollah's support (backed by Tehran) has been the crucial factor in maintaining the survival of the Assad regime in Damascus. Although Syria could form a likely backdrop for continuing US-Iran negotiations, Tehran will undoubtedly be reluctant to reduce its support for Hezbollah, so Beijing's pressure could be absolutely crucial at this juncture. Given its emerging role in the Syrian civil war and the newly unstable situation in Iraq, Tehran may be content to largely rein in its rivalry with Israel by limiting its ties with Hezbollah. There are numerous reasons to think that China could be successful in weaning Iran away from these destabilizing policies. Most obviously, as noted above, China has very substantial concerns about terrorism, both at home and increasingly abroad. Moreover, in the *Hanit* incident of 2006, when an Israeli corvette was nearly sunk by an Iranian-built missile of Chinese design that was fired by Hezbollah, Beijing must have been concerned that it might be blamed for the proliferation activities undertaken by Iran. Finally, it has been noted above that China has many other valued relationships in the region, especially with both Saudi Arabia and Israel, so such steps would help to ease the dilemmas now inherent to China's close ties with Iran. There is little doubt that China closely tracks Iran's relationships with such groups in the Middle East.[45] Nor can there be any doubt, given Beijing's enormous trading relationship with Tehran, that China has the requisite leverage if it can be convinced to deploy it at the crucial moment.

Washington's move 4 in the Middle East: The United States should shutter its Fifth Fleet base in Bahrain. Most Americans are unaware that the US military's footprint in the Persian Gulf is a relatively recent phenomenon, dating only from the 1980s. Unlike positions staked out after World War II (e.g., in Germany and South Korea), that military posture evolved in the wars with Saddam Hussein, but it was never part of a more coherent global strategy during the Cold War. At this point, this forward posture is not only a drain on resources but also a hardship post for military personnel, a major force protection issue, and, most important, a blot on the US commitment to human rights, because Bahrain witnessed major internal convulsions during the years 2011–12. These events included not only wholesale violations of human rights but also, more troublingly, a military intervention by forces from Saudi Arabia to preserve the ruling monarchy in Bahrain. Built on the former territory of the Royal Navy fleet base, the American presence sends all the wrong political signals, particularly in the uncertain era after the Arab Spring, when Washington should take care to avoid the perception that it is propping up authoritarian regimes in the Middle East to serve its own strategic interests. Judged even from a purely military perspective, the base itself has limited operational value, particularly in wartime, because it would very likely be a target for Iranian missiles during any military contingency. No wonder the fleet base has a large staff (and likely many force protection barriers) but very little actual combat power (e.g., ships, aircraft, or combat troops). For both Tehran and Beijing, removal of this base will serve as a powerful signal that Washington wants to seek a more stable region that respects legitimate Iranian and Chinese security interests, but will at the same time stress that US ships and aircraft will continue to play a role in Middle Eastern security as an "offshore balancer." In mid-2014, the lead article in an influential Chinese academic journal took up the possibility of Chinese military bases in the Middle East but concluded that China much prefers a "soft military presence" that emphasizes nontraditional security missions in support of generally economic (vice political) goals. It also clearly states that China would not challenge the leadership of other great powers.[46] Positive signals from Tehran in the 2013–2014 time frame should cause Washington to place all its cards on the table in order to realize the full strategic benefits from a truly comprehensive reduction of tensions in the crucial Iran-US relationship.

Beijing's move 4 in the Middle East: China should use its influence to pressure Iran into verifiable compliance with the Nuclear Non-Proliferation Treaty's safeguards. With a variety of concessions to pocket in advance, especially when combined with evidence of "new thinking" under President Rouhani, Tehran should feel adequately secure and also sufficiently confident to realize the benefits of a long-term agreement to reject nuclear weapons status. Up to this point in the cooperation spiral, Iran has gained formal assurances that the United States does not seek regime change, has been given alleviation from the harsh economic sanctions imposed during the past decade, and finally has been offered symbolic assurances from China that Beijing will take up a military security role in the Persian Gulf, if not as a formal treaty ally, then at least as a global power quite sympathetic to Iranian national interests. Of paramount importance, however, is the reality that Tehran can claim that its nuclear weapons research program was exchanged for a prize of at least equal value: the removal of the stinging presence of a major US fleet base located within the confines of the Persian Gulf. The reality is, of course, that US capabilities for power projection in the region will be almost entirely unaltered by this symbolic concession. However, accepting the Chinese analysis that Iranian nationalism is the preeminent explanatory value in the present crisis, the prior US concession will enable Tehran to fully relent on its nuclear weapons ambitions.[47] China can play a variety of key roles in enabling this crucial step in the cooperation cycle; most obviously, it could apply pressure and persuasion to support the Iranian leadership in surmounting its final hurdles. China might also play an important role in developing the proper verification procedures insofar as the Chinese are "trusted agents," which the International Atomic Energy Agency unfortunately may no longer be. One might imagine, for example, Chinese nuclear inspectors performing their requisite duties and then flying off to Tel Aviv or even Riyadh to offer evidence regarding Iranian compliance.

Washington's move 5 in the Middle East: The United States should exert pressure on Israel to disarm and join the regime for the Nuclear Non-Proliferation Treaty as a non–nuclear weapons state. Israeli nuclear weapons are the unseen and rarely discussed elephant in the room during any negotiations regarding either Iran's nuclear weapons capability or a lasting Middle East peace. Americans, by and large, are unaware that such weapons even exist, because they are rarely discussed or reported on by the conventional media. Israelis make the logical argument that such weapons are necessary for a state of such a small size that is surrounded by hostile neighbors. However, the most obvious argument for Israeli nuclear weaponry concerns the historical memory of the Holocaust and not rational, strategic calculation. Beyond this point it is additionally worth stating that Israel has by far the most potent conventional military forces in the region, not to mention strong backing from the world's most powerful military, the US armed forces. In other words, these forces exist for largely irrational reasons and represent extreme overkill when considered rationally. Although strategists may be tempted to suggest that they have no relevance at all, this survey of Chinese writings suggests that these weapons have a strong, deleterious impact: driving Iran's ambition to redress the perceived strategic imbalance in the region, and also seriously undermining the credibility of Western nuclear nonproliferation efforts, which are widely viewed in China and the Muslim world as hypocritical and biased. Just as Iran will likely retain the capabilities and expertise to "go nuclear" at some future point within this cooperation cycle, it may well be feasible for Israel to deactivate and warehouse its nuclear arsenal, so that it can rearm relatively quickly if circumstances warrant. Again, verification by neutral parties would be crucial, but that still leaves some room to creatively find a solution consistent with Israeli security requirements. The 2013–14 negotiations between Washington and Tehran in Geneva may show that negotiations can go forward on a rather narrow basis, focused primarily on the level of uranium enrichment that the United States can accept in Iran's nuclear program. However, a much more durable and stable peace may result from a lasting nuclear compromise, whereby Israeli nuclear capabilities are actually also on the table.

Beijing's move 5 in the Middle East: China should use its influence to pressure Iran to recognize Israel and initiate bilateral ties. A nuclear-free zone in the Middle East is profoundly in the interest of all the Middle Eastern states, including both Iran and Israel. Israel would gain substantially from the above cooperation spiral, because Tehran would agree not only to give up its ambitions for nuclear arms but also, critically, to stop arming terrorist groups and paramilitaries in the areas surrounding Israel. And yet a further part of a grand bargain between Israel and Iran, undertaken with substantial cajoling from the two superpowers, would involve Iran's official recognition of Israel, the exchange of embassies, and the related blossoming of social and economic relations that would inevitably follow. Such a future is not nearly as farfetched as is widely believed, given the current animosity between Iran and Israel. However, before 1979, Israel had rather close ties with Iran, and this reflected the historically important role that Jews have enjoyed in Persia. Indeed, the two countries' current animosities are much more an aberration than the continuation of a historical pattern. Moreover, Iran intensely admires China's development model, and thus it needs to recognize that one of the keys to Beijing's recent success is that a few decades after the Chinese Revolution, the resulting ideological zeal and ardor were put aside in order to prioritize pragmatic national interests. A similar process could well unfold in Tehran, where more than two decades after the Islamic Revolution, more pragmatic forces have become ascendant. It is even possible that a future Iranian regime could pursue economic legitimacy as the foundation for its evolving state in a way similar to what the Chinese regime has done since 1978. Under such a positive scenario, Iran's newly flexible diplomacy, and especially its revitalized trade relationships with both the West and Israel, would be critical for its further growth, prosperity, and security. Such a bright scenario may not be altogether fanciful under the new leadership in Tehran, though one must temper expectations, because the Persian Spring will likely face many harsh realities, just as the Arab Spring did.

Conclusion

Skeptics will rightly point out that the cooperation spiral outlined above has a low probability of success. China could well refuse to take up a larger strategic role in the Middle East. It has been extremely wary of employing its leverage to pressure its traditional partners, for fear of breaking relationships of high trust that have been painstakingly built up over time. Beijing also derides such coercive tactics as Western-style diplomacy that continuously infringes on the sovereignty of other states. Beijing's reluctance, moreover, may pale in comparison with the hurdles of seeking to work with the intransigent leaders in Tehran, in Jerusalem, and, yes, also in Washington.

However, few would assert, given present circumstances, that the Middle East is on a positive or even satisfactory trajectory. Warfare, whether interstate or internecine, is today endemic throughout the region. Terrorist attacks and assassinations are a daily occurrence, and the region is increasingly haunted by the specter of nuclear conflict. Meanwhile, crucial development initiatives are pushed aside by security issues and poverty remains acute. Evidently, the current structure of international relations prevailing in the Middle East is not optimal. Here, it is suggested that China's rise as a global power could help to rebalance the structure of power in the region, away from hegemony and toward a more fluid, flexible, and indeed progressive regional system. The odd circumstances surrounding the resolution of the Syrian chemical weapons crisis in September 2013 highlighted the troubled, but surprisingly still significant, role that Russia plays in the contemporary Middle East. However, the same set of rather awkward events point to the question of whether China's continued low-profile role—for example, on the difficult Syrian quandary— is beneficial and sustainable. Indeed, the preliminary evidence suggests that Chinese analysts were impressed by Russian president Vladimir Putin's adroit diplomacy to avert US military intervention in Syria during late 2013.[48] Perhaps, given the new opportunities afforded by the Persian Spring, China might be willing to step up and play a more active role, as suggested in the proposed cooperation spiral of this chapter. Given the developing break in US-Russia relations over the Ukraine crisis, moreover, China's increased role may be even more welcome.

Although Beijing could plausibly play a constructive role in other main regional issues—whether in North Africa, Syria, Iraq, or even in that most intractable of conflicts, the Israeli/Palestinian struggle—the focus of this chapter and of the cooperation spiral proposed above has been on the Iranian nuclear issue, given its salience both for global security and for US-China relations. However, a final vignette quite unrelated to the Iran question may suggest the future possibilities for the broader region: In 2003 China committed to send a significant number of peacekeeping soldiers to Lebanon. This was hardly an easy or glamorous mission. Indeed, a couple of Chinese soldiers were killed during fighting in the region in 2006, and Chinese president Hu Jintao attended the funerals. Although small in scale, this episode may point the way toward a more robust and active role for China in stabilizing the Middle East in cooperation with the United States—an imperative for both countries, as well as the region. As the United States confronts the strategic dilemmas related to the emergence of new extremists in Syria and Iraq, Washington may reflect on how a more multipolar system might allow it to act in concert with other great powers, especially including China, to build a more stable, just and prosperous Middle East.

Notes

1. "Mall of the Masses," Schumpeter Column, *The Economist*, April 14, 2011, 78.

2. On the New Silk Road Strategy, see, for example, Min Ye, "China's Views and Responses to Multilateral Talks in Pacific Asia," ASAN Forum, December 1, 2014, http://www.theasanforum.org/chinas-views-and-responses-to-multilateral-talks-in-pacific-asia/.

3. 郭孝伟, 马俊 [Guo Xiaowei and Ma Jun] "西方炒作我舰队进波斯湾" [The West Spins Story concerning Entrance of Our Fleet into the Persian Gulf] 环球时报 [Global Times], September 23, 2014, 1.

4. Geoffrey Kemp, *The East Moves West: India, China, and Asia's Growing Presence in the Middle East* (Washington, DC: Brookings Institution Press, 2010), 86.

5. John Garver, *China and Iran: Ancient Partners in the Post-Imperial World* (Seattle: University of Washington Press, 2006), 8.

6. Ibid., 57–64.

7. 仲光友, 龙永斌 [Zhong Guangyou and Long Yongbin], "两伊战争中美国对伊朗的海上秘战" [America's Secret Naval War against Iran during the Iran-Iraq War], 兵工科技 [Ordnance Industry Science and Technology], no. 19 (2012): 65–66.

8. Garver, *China and Iran*, 192–93.

9. 崔燕 [Cui Yan], "震惊世界的'银河' 号事件" [The "Yinhe' Vessel Incident That Shocked the World], 中国船检 [China Ship Survey], May 2010, 63.

10. 王巧荣 [Wang Qiaorong], "严重侵犯中国主权的'银河'号事件" [The "Yinhe" Vessel Incident That Seriously Violated China's Sovereignty], 党史文汇 [Party History Literature Collection], July 2009, 11–12, 14.

11. Garver, *China and Iran*, 265.

12. Ibid., 154.

13. Ibid., 183.

14. Kemp, *East Moves West*, 85–87.

15. See, e.g., Andrew Erickson and Lyle Goldstein, "Gunboats for China's New 'Grand Canals,'" *Naval War College Review* 62 (Spring 2009): 50, www.usnwc.edu/getattachment/f655705e-0ef3-4a21-af5a-93df77e527fa/Gunboats-for-China-s-New--Grand-Canals---Probing-t.

16. US Energy Information Administration, "China: Overview," www.eia.gov/countries/cab.cfm?fips=CH.

17. Erica Downs and Suzanne Maloney, "Getting China to Sanction Iran: The Chinese–Iranian Oil Connection," *Foreign Affairs* 90 (March–April 2011): 15.

18. Garver, *China and Iran*, 13, 301.

19. 李伟建 [Li Weijian], "中东政治转型及中国中东外交" [The Middle East Political Transformation and China's Middle East Diplomacy], 西亚非洲 [West Asia and Africa], no. 4 (2012): 4–14.

20. 风向标 [Feng Xiangbiao], "伊朗能封锁霍尔木兹海峡吗?" [Could Iran Blockade the Strait of Hormuz?] *舰船知识* [Naval and Merchant Ships], March 2012, foreword.

21. 吴涛 [Wu Tao], "伊朗导弹如多少?" [How Many Missiles Does Iran Have?], *人民海军* [People's Navy], December 20, 2011.

22. 社朝平 [She Chaoping], "喋血地中海: 以色列'哈尼特'号经型护卫舰遭重创内幕" [Mediterranean Bloodbath: The Inside Story of the Serious Wounding of the Israeli Frigate Hanit], *舰载武器* [Shipborne Weaponry], September 2006, 12–15.

23. 社朝平 [She Chaoping], "追风快剑: 扑朔迷离的伊朗反舰导弹" [Swift Sabre Following the Wind: The Mystery of Iran's Antiship Missiles], *舰载武器* [Shipborne Weaponry], September 2006, 15–18.

24. 伍浩松 [Wu Haosong], "伊朗核工业的'前世今生" [The Rebirth of Iran's Nuclear Industry], *国防科技工业* [Defense Science Technology and Industry], March 2012, 69–71.

25. 陈超, 赵华章, 陈宇 [Chen Chao, Zhao Huazhang, and Chen Yu], "波斯湾'裂变': 伊朗核问题走向" [Persian "Fission": Trend of the Iran Nuclear Issue], *当代海军* [Modern Navy], November 2012, 37–39.

26. 储昭根 [Chu Zhaogen], 对伊朗动武: 箭在弦上 [Using Force against Iran: Like and Arrow in the Bowstring], *国际政治* [International Politics], February 2012, 120–21.

27. 金良祥   [Jin Liangxiang],   美以武力解决伊核问题的合法性与可行性 [The Legitimacy and Feasibility of US and Israeli Military Action to Deal with the Iranian Nuclear Issue], *阿拉伯世界研究* [Arab World Studies], July 2012, 45–55.

28. 王南 [Wang Nan], "伊朗核问题摊牌在即" [The Iran Nuclear Crisis Comes to a Head], *亚非纵横* [Asia and Africa Review], no. 6 (2011): 28–32.

29. 刘慧[Liu Hui], "民族身份认同对伊朗核政策的影响" [The Effect of National Identity on Iran's Nuclear Decision Making], *阿拉伯世界研究* [Arab World Studies], July 2011, 33–39.

30. 郑东超 [Deng Dongchao], "共识与分歧: 美国和土耳其对伊朗核问题认识研究" [Common Understanding and Differences: A Study of the Iranian Nuclear Issue by the US and Turkey], *和平与发展* [Peace and Development], December 2011, 51.

31. 王南 [Wang Nan], "伊朗核问题摊牌在即" [The Iran Nuclear Crisis Comes to a Head], *亚非纵横* [Asia and Africa Review], no. 6 (2011): 29.

32. 社朝平 [She Chaoping], "海上铁骑: 称雄中东的以色列海军" [Maritime Cavalry: Israeli Navy Holding Sway over the Middle East Region], *舰载武器* [Shipborne Weaponry], September 2006, 21.

33. 华黎明 [Hua Liming], "中东会陷入核竞赛吗?" [Will the Middle East Sink into Nuclear Rivalry?], 人民海军 [People's Navy], February 7, 2012.

34. 刘建伟 [Liu Jianwei], "中国核不扩散政策和行为变化" [Changes in China's Nuclear Nonroliferation Policy and Behavior], 当代亚太 [Journal of Contemporary Asia-Pacific Studies], no. 4 (2011): 128.

35. 梁芳 [Liang Fang], 海上战略通道论 [On Maritime Strategic Access] (Beijing: Current Events Press, 2011), 224–25.

36. 王锦 [Wang Jin] "试析美国对伊朗制裁的有效性" [An Evaluation of the Effectiveness of U.S. Sanctions against Iran] 国际政治 [International Politics] (July 2014), 85–90.

37. 天文林 [Tian Wenlin], "美国与伊朗关系缓和: 神话还是现实?" [Detente between the US and Iran: Myth or Reality?], 国际政治 [International Politics], January 2014, 53, 55.

38. US Energy Information Administration, "US Natural Gas Marketed Production," www.eia.gov/dnav/ng/hist/n9050us2a.htm.

39. Edward Morse, "Welcome to the Revolution: Why Shale Is the Next Shale," *Foreign Affairs* 93 (May–June 2014), www.foreignaffairs.com/articles/141202/edward-l-morse/welcome-to-the-revolution.

40. Ely Ratner, "The Emergent Security Threats Reshaping China's Rise," *Washington Quarterly*, Winter 2011, 30.

41. See, e.g., 江记君, 蔡志强 [Jiang Jijun and Cai Zhiqiang], "打造反核化生恐怖袭击" [Building Capability to Counter a Surprise Nuclear, Chemical, or Biological Terrorist Attack], 解放军画报 [PLA Pictorial], November 2012, 86–87; and also the special issue devoted to the danger of terrorist aerial hijackings in the October 2012 edition of 航空知识 [Aerospace Knowledge].

42. "Nuclear Diplomacy and Iran: Where's the Deal?" *The Economist*, February 2, 2013, 36.

43. "US No Longer Wants Iranian 'Regime Change': Kerry," Agence France-Presse, May 6, 2009, www.google.com/hostednews/afp/article/ALeqM5gSGOBAtwiHUddAfMr4_rueIDqjkA.

44. [Deng Hongying], 困境与出路: 中东地区安全问题研究 [Predicament and Resolution: Research on Middle East Security Problems] (Wuhan: Hubei People's Press, 2011), 15.

45. See, e.g., 冀开运 [Ji Kaiyun], 伊朗与伊斯兰世界关系研究 [Research on Iran and Its Relations with the Islamic World] (Beijing: Current Affairs Press, 2012), 386–89.

46. 孙德刚 [Sun Degang] "论新时期中国在中东的柔性军事存在" [On China's Soft Military Presence in the Middle East in the New Era] 世界经济与政治 [World Economy and Politics] (August 2014), 4–29.

47. 刘慧 [Liu Hui] "民族身份认同对伊朗核政策的影响" [The Effect of National Identity on Iran's Nuclear Decision Making], *阿拉伯世界研究* [Arab World Studies], July 2011, 33–39.

48. 崔小西 [Cui Xiaoxi], "俄罗斯应对叙利亚危机的政策分析" [Analysis of Russia's Policy in the Syrian Crisis], *阿拉伯世界研究* [Arab World Studies], February 2014, 36.

8

BIPOLARITY RECONSIDERED
The Korean Peninsula and US-China Relations

In the wake of Pyongyang's third nuclear test in February 2013 and the generally ominous tensions prevailing on the Korean Peninsula since 2010, the "Korean question" would seem to stand as a stark illustration of the grave failure of US-China relations. Despite repeated assurances from both Washington and Beijing that both seek peace and stability rather than narrow national advantage, a tense and bleak bipolarity somewhat reminiscent of the 1950s once again pervades Northeast Asia. Even more disconcerting is the real possibility that the failure of US-China relations in this crucial case could have dire consequences for this most important of bilateral relationships and may at the same time pose the most fundamental of challenges to the global nuclear nonproliferation effort.

Reestablishing the path to Korean peace and stability will not only serve the US-China relationship and global nonproliferation norms but will also enable East Asia to more firmly grasp the success and prosperity promised in the so-called Asian Century by defusing the potentially apocalyptic tensions that lie dangerously close to its heart. Toward that end, this chapter, like the others in this book, presents many Chinese perspectives on the unfolding situation in Korea, but there is no implied endorsement of those perspectives by the author.

Most fundamentally, the process advocated here seeks both Chinese and American coequal leadership to bring about peace on the Korean Peninsula. The working of the "cooperation spiral" in this circumstance will require the recognition of three vital, albeit controversial, conclusions that may enable forward progress on the Korean question. First, it will be important to agree that North Korea's nuclear weapons program and volatile behavior are linked first and foremost to its severe weakness and its primary concern for regime survival. Second, a somewhat counterintuitive paradox is that in order to redress the issue of the first point, China must actually become significantly *more* involved in peninsular affairs. Finally, a close study of the modern history of Northeast Asia, and the last two decades in particular, reveals that the change of leadership in Pyongyang at the end of 2011, despite the raft of naysayers who have surfaced in the wake of the tensions in early 2013 and at the end of 2014, still provides a certain opening for Washington and Beijing to make significant progress in pacifying the troubled Korean Peninsula.

The complexity of the task in this case may be greater than any other challenge before American and Chinese diplomats, given the multiplicity and variety of actors and also the enormous stakes for all concerned. The millions of ghosts—Korean, Chinese, and American—from the ghastly conflict of 1950–53 may serve to implore those diplomats to seek to understand alternative perspectives, reach for new and creative solutions, and take the necessary risks for peace—and thus reject Korea's traditional role as the cockpit of great power competition.

Background

The continuous jockeying of the great powers for control of Korea is amply evident in the century preceding the Korean War. Indeed, the initial sparks for both the Sino-Japanese War of 1894–95 and the Russo-Japanese War of 1904–5 concerned the fate of Korea. Reaching back three centuries earlier, China's Ming Dynasty deployed forces to aid Korea's famous "turtle boats" at the battle of Noryang Point in 1597 that turned back the Japanese emperor Hideyoshi's invasion of Korea.

However, David Kang's scholarship on East Asian international relations preceding the Opium War raises questions regarding any assumption that Korea was simply the perennial battlefield for contesting outside powers. His research illustrates that from the time of Hideyoshi's invasion in the late sixteenth century up until the late nineteenth century, the Korean Peninsula was actually rather peaceful and devoid of great power geopolitical competition. He explains the logic of Chinese hegemony during that period: "With such a large central power in China, other nations did not wish to challenge

China, and China had no need to fight."[1] Explaining the complex relationship between Korea and China during this period, he quotes Gari Ledyard as follows: "China's 'control' was hardly absolute. While the Koreans had to play the hand they were dealt, they repeatedly prevailed in diplomacy and argument. . . . Korea often . . . convinced China to retreat from an aggressive position. . . . Chinese and Korean officialdom spoke from a common Confucian vocabulary; ... the relationship was equal, if not at times actually in Korea's favor."[2] Similarly fresh historical perspectives arise from a recent reappraisal of US diplomacy in East Asia at the dawn of the twentieth century that raises pertinent questions about the American role in Japan's acquisition of Korea after the Russo-Japanese War.[3]

Many contemporary American strategists seem disdainful of historical issues. Edward Luttwak, for example, condescendingly suggests that the continued focus of South Korean leaders on the "comfort women" issue renders them "unfit as active allies."[4] He seems not to recognize the degree to which history has an impact on identity and thus the formation of national interests. Revisionist history, in fact, sheds significant new light on the origins of the Korean War. In investigating the details of Kim Il-sung's emergence during the 1930s, the University of Chicago historian Bruce Cumings focuses on the exceedingly tight bonds uniting the Korean and Chinese communist parties from the earliest point. Kim Il-sung was fluent in Chinese and grew up in Manchuria because his father had fled the Japanese occupation of Korea. Confronted with the limitless brutality of Japan's "kill all—burn all—loot all" counterinsurgency campaign in Manchuria, Kim Il-sung had taken up arms against the Japanese in Manchuria as early as the spring of 1932. According to Cumings, "By February 1936 a formidable Sino-Korean army had emerged, with Kim commanding the Third Division and several Chinese regimental commanders under him."[5] Given this background, it is perhaps not surprising that "a majority of [North Korean] soldiers [during the Korean War] had [previously] fought in the Chinese Civil War."[6] The close intertwining of the Korean and Chinese communist movements from this early point helps to explain the fateful decision sixteen years later for China's military intervention—a decision that was not without controversy in Beijing. Although few Americans will accept Cumings's conclusion that Washington bears significant responsibility for the outbreak of hostilities on the peninsula in June 1950, his research on the US military occupation, particularly in the regions of Cholla and Cheju Island, gives ample food for thought regarding the conventional historical interpretation.[7]

Western scholarship has made a variety of other refinements to current understanding of the Korean War. Of special note were revelations in the 1990s regarding the substance of Kim Il-sung's attempts to persuade Joseph Stalin and Mao Zedong to support his ambitions to unify Korea, and it is now quite clear that Kim was the driving force behind the enterprise whereas both the Soviet and Chinese leaders were much more reluctant, but played along in the end. The scholarship of Yu Bin is revealing, for example, regarding the inhibitions among China's top generals preceding the conflict—they argued, for example, that the "firepower of an American division was perhaps ten to twenty times more powerful than its Chinese equivalent." This in-depth study is similarly deeply revealing regarding the extreme tensions that divided the Chinese commander, General Peng Dehuai, from Mao. He explains that the Chinese People's Volunteers (CPV) confronted "overwhelming UN firepower, . . . [and] Peng sensed that the CPV's earlier gains were slipping away. . . . In late February 1951, Peng hurried back to Beijing to tell Mao that the Korean War was entirely different from the Chinese Civil War."[8]

In contemporary China, the subject of the Korean War remains a theme of intense interest. Bookstores continue to supply an ample stock of memoirs and ever more detailed combat histories.[9] Articles on the Korean War also continue to be common in Chinese military magazines and military academic journals. As Peter Gries explains, "Pride in this Chinese 'victory' over America is an important psychological resource which builds self-confidence."[10] Indeed, conventional wisdom among Chinese continues to hold that the Chinese volunteers achieved triumph against the steepest odds. The author witnessed very extensive Chinese television coverage on the occasion of the sixtieth anniversary of the conflict.[11]

On the occasion of the sixtieth anniversary of China's intervention in the Korean War, then–vice president Xi Jinping made a speech that was subsequently published as the first in a volume of essays reexamining the war that was published in China during 2011. Xi stated, "We must actively study . . . the great patriotism and heroic, revolutionary spirit of the CPV." He asserts that the United States decided to intervene after the outbreak of the "Korean Civil War" (朝鲜内战) and "crossed the 38th Parallel despite repeated warnings from the Chinese government. Approaching the Yalu and Tyumen rivers on the border of the Chinese/Korean border, [the United States even] dispatched aircraft to bomb the cities and towns of our country's northeastern region, so that the flames of war burned the territory of our newly born People's Republic."[12] Aware of the odds confronting the Chinese volunteers, Xi observes that US forces "possessed all types of modern weaponry, and thus were able to seize both air superiority and also sea control, and relied on mechanized forces, while the CPV essentially relied on foot soldiers . . . with backward equipment."[13] Xi recognized the value of the battlefield experience in teaching the People's Liberation Army (PLA) "new tactics and new battle-field methods" and used the occasion of the speech to urge the continuation of China's contemporary efforts to "consolidate the building of mighty armed forces . . . not to seek hegemony . . . or threaten others . . . but to protect national sovereignty and also security."[14] According to Xi, "[This] wartime victory . . . placed the expansionist plans of the imperialists in disarray . . . and thus protected the peace of Asia and the world."[15] He concludes that "the Korean Peninsula and China are connected by mountains and rivers, and the peace and stability of the Korean Peninsula and the Northeast Asian region will impact the world's prospects for peace and stability."[16]

In the same Chinese volume commemorating the sixtieth anniversary is a detailed essay by the Chinese military scholar General Luo Yuan. Luo draws the linkage between the Taiwan and Korean situations, underlining that US president Harry Truman ordered the Seventh Fleet into the Taiwan Strait on the day after the war started in Korea (in June 1950), effectively "occupy-ing our territory of Taiwan."[17] He cites this development as one of several justifications for China's intervention in October 1950. He also lays out the traditional Chinese "buffer" argument for Beijing's supreme interest in North Korea, suggesting: "If the US-[South Korea] alliance were to extend to the Yalu River border, thus possessing our strategic, land attack corridor, [they could] at any time and on any excuse make war upon us." He further explains that China's steel output at the time of the Korean War was just 1/144 of that of the United States, and that 80 percent of the Chinese production in 1950 was based in Liaoning Province, right next to North Korea.[18] Employing an instructive analogy to illustrate China's motives in the Korean War, General Luo suggests that "if the Soviet Union had invaded Mexico, it would have been just five seconds before the United States dispatched its troops there."[19] With some evident pride, he suggests that Chinese troops in late 1950 inflicted the "most devastating military defeat on the United States since Pearl Harbor."[20] In placing the Korean War in the scope of China's modern history, General Luo draws upon the observation of General Peng, commander of the CPV in Korea, who said that "the era when the Western great powers could use big guns to force open China's coast, or when they could dispatch 20,000 soldiers from eight nations to occupy China's capital, is now hereby ended [with the

Korean War]."[21] Although this chapter cannot pretend to offer anything like a complete survey of Chinese writings on the Korean War—another worthy project, to be sure—it may at least suggest that Chinese leaders continue to consider the legacy of the Korean War as highly significant for Chinese security policy still today.

As Victor Cha points out, the contemporary North Korean regime continues to hark back to a "golden age" of the early Cold War. He writes: "Aid from the two Communist patrons, political turmoil in the South, and the American entanglement in Vietnam were all perceived as trends that favored Pyongyang." The legacy of colonial infrastructure built up by the Japanese, combined with aid and ideological zeal, enabled North Korea to outpace South Korea for decades, including on objective metrics, such as electrification. Cha points out the paradox, from today's vantage point, that during China's famine years in the late 1950s and early 1960s, the "Chinese . . . were migrating across the Yalu Border into . . . [North Korea] for sustenance."[22] A significant event to note from 1958, in addition to China's disastrous Great Leap Forward, was the complete withdrawal of Chinese troops from North Korea. Given the economic and military advantages that North Korea held over South Korea at that time, the move was perhaps not surprising; but this interesting asymmetry in the bipolar configuration of the balance of power on the peninsula, particularly in light of changes in the balance of capabilities between South Korea and North Korea, is discussed again below in the context of the chapter's recommendations for policy.

The Sino-Soviet conflict that developed in the early 1960s and escalated through the decade to armed conflict by its end had a dramatic impact on the Korean Peninsula. Jonathan Pollack points out that it is likely not coincidental that Moscow was pulling back from nuclear cooperation with Beijing at the very same time that it was lurching forward with the first major agreement for nuclear technology cooperation with Pyongyang. He writes: "Did the Russians fear that North Korea would turn to China if Moscow failed to provide meaningful assistance? . . . Khrushchev probably hoped to pull Kim more firmly into the Soviet camp."[23]

The 1960s began with North Korea skillfully playing China and Russia off against one another and gaining security pledges and military assistance from each. However, by the end of the decade, Pyongyang was decidedly "leaning to one side"—favoring Moscow. Kim was apparently criticized in Beijing as a "fat revisionist" and a "disciple of Khrushchev," while he confided to the Kremlin that Mao's Cultural Revolution was "mass lunacy" and later said that it amounted to "left opportunism."[24] At the same time, North Korea seemingly took advantage of Washington's difficulties in Vietnam with direct challenges, including no less than three attempted assassinations against South Korean president Park Chung-hee and the attack on the USS *Pueblo* in 1968, followed closely by the shooting down of an American reconnaissance aircraft in 1969. Though he suggests that incidents did occur along the China/ North Korean border during this volatile period, Pollack notes: "Unlike his risk-taking propensities with South Korea and the United States, Kim showed caution and avoided needlessly provoking Beijing."[25]

The US-China rapprochement naturally had major reverberations on the Korean Peninsula. Zhou Enlai visited Pyongyang shortly after Henry Kissinger's initial visit to Beijing in July 1971 to salve North Korea's natural discomfort with the new geopolitical reality. However, it was Seoul that seemed most perturbed by the resulting alteration of great power relationships, particularly as the United States acted at this time to undertake a significant withdrawal of US forces from the Korean Peninsula. Despite these initial inhibitions, the US-China rapprochement actually enabled the first ever high-level dialogue between North Korean and South Korean leaders, which took place in 1971–72. Unfortunately, numerous North Korean provocations broke this unprecedented positive pattern, including tunneling efforts apparently envisioned as invasion routes, and the barbaric killing of US soldiers in the Demilitarized Zone during 1976. However, it was the use of bombs against a senior South Korean delegation in Rangoon in 1983 that narrowly missed killing the South Korean president that caused another break in China-North Korea relations— this one of considerable duration. Pollack observes: "Deng allegedly concluded that Kim Jong-il was responsible for ordering the terrorist attack, resulting in a long estrangement between Deng and the younger Kim that never ended during Deng's years in power. Kim Jong-il's abiding suspicions of China did not dissipate in subsequent years, in particular as China pursued and consolidated relations with the United States and [South Korea]."[26] This break is persuasively suggested by the fact that Kim Jong-il did not visit China between 1983 and 2000, whereas his father, Kim Il-sung, had visited annually.[27] A grasp of Kim Jong-il's rough relationship with Beijing is integral to understanding the major instability that accompanied his reign as North Korea's leader, but may also suggest some potential for alternative futures for the Korean Peninsula.

In 1991 North Korea therefore confronted the quadruple jeopardy of (1) the collapse of the USSR, its primary patron; (2) elevated scrutiny for violation of nonproliferation norms by the increasingly dominant United States;

(3) continued alienation from China, even as Beijing sought to establish diplomatic ties with South Korea for the first time; and (4) perhaps most challenging, the question of succession, as the North Korean founder, Kim Il-sung, reached his final years. In the midst of these challenges, security on the peninsula reached a new level of volatility. Some positive momentum seems to have quite inadvertently started with the withdrawal of US tactical nuclear weapons from South Korea in late 1991, which was followed thereafter by the North–South Agreement on Reconciliation, Non-Aggression, and Exchanges and Cooperation. However, these positive steps were soon overshadowed by the 1993–94 North Korean nuclear crisis, which may be considered one of the most dangerous moments for East Asian security in the post–Cold War era.

An equally important factor intensifying North Korean insecurity was no doubt the heady afterglow of the first Persian Gulf War. A definite driver in the unfolding of that conflict with Iraq concerned Baghdad's efforts to acquire nuclear weapons, so that "counterproliferation" emerged as a major thrust of US diplomacy in the wake of that war. However, the Korean Peninsula was to prove a poor "test case" for the new policies to emerge from Desert Storm. Indeed, a recent scholarly review of Washington's diplomacy in the 1993–94 crisis revealed US policies to be "schizophrenic, . . . poorly coordinated, . . . [and] . . . 'disturbing, [in that] there appeared to be no one actually in charge of such a potentially explosive situation." In a conclusion that reinforces the general thrust of this book, the author concludes: "Compellant pressure absent assurances or conciliation of any kind not only failed to gain North Korean accession to required nuclear inspections but actually helped ignite the crisis."[28] The risk of "escalating to all-out war" on the Korean Peninsula was all too plain, as grocery stores were emptied in the South and the US State Department advised all US citizens to depart.[29]

The intervention of former US president Jimmy Carter, who met in person with Kim Jong-il in June 1994, "staved off the most acute security crisis in Northeast Asia since the Korean War."[30] The resulting Agreed Framework exchanged energy assistance, political normalization, and economic assistance for a freeze on, and the eventual dismantlement of, the North Korean nuclear weapons program. Noting that the elder Kim died three weeks after this crucial meeting with Carter, Pollack makes a number of key observations, including that "Carter's pledge that he would urge the Clinton administration to negotiate with Pyongyang was highly validating to Kim. The outcome represented an aged leader's final legacy," and, moreover, that the Agreed Framework "bore Kim Il-sung's personal imprimatur."[31] Presaging the volatile decade that would follow, however, the same analyst also points to US intelligence observations that the elder Kim was not comfortable with the younger Kim's handling of the crisis.[32]

It is beyond the scope of this study to detail or explain the long and winding road that ultimately led to the failure of the Agreed Framework. However, it suffices to say that "hawks" viewed this agreement as propping up the North Korean regime, but "doves" may suggest that its provisions were not executed properly, so that the agreement did not have a chance to prove its worth. The September 11, 2001, terrorist attacks on the United States appeared to reinforce Washington's determination to aggressively curb the proliferation of weapons of mass destruction. Indeed, it is likely that the George W. Bush administration hoped that making an example of Saddam Hussein's Iraq—in effect, "killing chickens to scare monkeys"—might convince other proliferators to cease and desist. Although some success with strategy could plausibly be claimed with regard to the case of Libya, on the Korean Peninsula events showed that Washington's aggressive approach in the Persian Gulf seemed to actually increase Pyongyang's determination to develop nuclear weapons.[33] Less than a year after President George W. Bush's famous "Axis of Evil" speech in January 2002, North Korean leaders declared the Agreed Framework terminated and announced they would withdraw from the Nuclear Non-Proliferation Treaty.

The Iraq War diverted "US attention from events on the peninsula, even as it concentrated the minds of leaders in Pyongyang."[34] An additional complexity of the unfolding situation on the peninsula was the dynamic in which Seoul under Kim Dae-jung and later Roh Mo-hyun promoted the so-called sunshine policy, which meant the provision by the South to the North of fertilizer, food, fuel, and even hard currency, amounting to almost $3 billion over the period 1998–2007.[35] The Bush administration undoubtedly objected to the conciliatory policies of the South Korean leadership, and there was also significant sparring over how US troops might be redeployed to reflect the "military transformation"—though in reality, this also seemed to reflect major tensions in the South Korea-US alliance.[36] In this volatile atmosphere—in which Pyongyang was newly anxious and defiant, while Seoul and Washington were at loggerheads over policy responses—Beijing stepped in to try to calm the precarious situation with the so-called Six-Party Talks beginning in mid-2003. However, on October 8, 2006, the initial North Korean nuclear bomb test shattered any illusion that the nuclear genie could be kept in a box on the Korean Peninsula.

Cha's recent book offers additional insight into the watershed events of the fall of 2006. A few weeks after the nuclear test, Cha, in his capacity as an administration adviser at the US National Security Council, accompanied national security adviser Condoleezza Rice on her trip to various Asian capitals, including Seoul and Beijing. He relates a testy exchange between South Korean president Roh and Rice as follows: "Roh said the United States must engage with North Korea to avoid more tests. I stared at my Foreign Ministry counterparts across the room with a 'You cannot be serious?' look. They were visibly uncomfortable with Roh's remarks. Rice's eyes sharpened. She was angry, but in a calm . . . tone responded that the United States would not succumb to this brinkmanship."[37] In Beijing Rice met with State Councilor Tang Jiaxuan. According to Cha,

> Tang had just returned from North Korea, where he had met with Kim Jong-il to deliver a stern message from President Hu. . . . [But] . . . we got an inspiring performance in classic Chinese 'muddling through.' . . . Tang made requisite statements about China's outrage at the test, but soon receded into a diplomatic defensive crouch, deflecting US demands to put more pressure on [North Korea]. . . . The Chinese, after much internal debate, once again chose the low-risk and low-commitment path, which was to call for the United States to be more flexible and more active in engaging with the North.[38]

Although Beijing's anger toward Pyongyang was palpable in some respects, it seems that China was wary of "unnecessarily aggravating North Korea, . . . [lest it] . . . run into the arms of the United States," and apparently the Chinese then began to prepare in earnest for "two worst case scenarios": the US use of force or internal upheaval in North Korea.[39] One Chinese strategist, reacting in late 2006 to the North Korean test, writes that Chinese interests had indeed suffered a major setback. This same analysis warned that Washington was likely to "fish in troubled waters" (混水摸鱼), and stated emphatically that "what is in the US interest is not in the Chinese interest." Concerned with the impact on Japan's defense posture and even the possibility that Japan might develop nuclear weapons, this strategist cautioned that with few weapons and no means of delivery, North Korea could not pose a genuine threat to its neighbors, especially if they do not threaten its "national survival."[40] Another Chinese analysis also reflects a tendency toward zero-sum thinking regarding the Korean Peninsula, at least from the vantage point of

US-China relations and rivalry. This study notes the simultaneous deepening of ties between the People's Republic of China (PRC) and South Korea, even as South Korea was swept by an "anti-American wave" (反美浪潮) during the first years of the new millennium that reflected South Korean sentiment that relations between the United States and South Korea were governed by "unequal treaties." While clearly stating that nuclear weapons developed by the North upset the military balance on the peninsula, the authors were concerned that South Korea could not be neutral in any US-China conflict and that Seoul increasingly viewed the United States as an important means to counter "Chinese pressure." The analysis remarked on the newly dynamic phase of the US-South Korea alliance after Lee Myung-bak became South Korean president in 2008, suggesting that the two sides now aimed to globalize the US-South Korean alliance following the pattern of Washington's alliances with both Britain and Australia.[41]

Ironically, US and South Korean politics have been significantly nonsynchronous over the last decade, so that South Korean or, alternatively, US overtures toward North Korea have been forthcoming amid more hawkish policies by the other member of the alliance. In this case, certain gestures during the last phases of the Bush administration—such as the visit of the New York Philharmonic to Pyongyang or the overture to remove North Korea from the list of state sponsors of terrorism, which both occurred in 2008—came just as the more conservative Lee came to power in Seoul with a promise to hold Pyongyang much more accountable for the aid that had been extended. President Obama's conciliatory notion of engaging pariah states like North Korea and extending a hand if they would only "unclench their fist" could hardly be revealed with respect to the peninsula when Northeast Asia was shaken by a second North Korean nuclear test in 2009 and then significantly traumatized by flagrant North Korean military attacks in 2010, first against a South Korean frigate, the *Cheonan*, and then a few weeks later against a South Korean island outpost—both of which caused significant South Korean fatalities.

Into the Dark and Murky Waters of the Yellow Sea

The sinking of the *Cheonan* stands out on the long list of incidents that have scarred the inter-Korean relationship. It marks the single largest loss of life among the various military clashes that have occurred periodically, but also had the potential to ignite a major war on the Korean Peninsula, insofar as North Korea had brazenly sought to destroy a high-value South Korean unit.

Forty-six South Korean sailors perished in the cold and dark waters not far from the contested Northern Limit Line that serves as the maritime frontier. "An emotional President Lee Myung-bak vowed Monday to find out why a South Korean naval ship sank and to 'deal resolutely' with whatever or whomever caused the sinking."[42] It is very likely, given the loss of life and national prestige, that the South Korean leadership carefully debated various responses, including the use of force against North Korea.[43] Thus it is not an exaggeration to suggest that 2010 witnessed the most dangerous period on the peninsula since the cessation of hostilities in 1953. Lee's restraint in this instance is not only laudable but also illustrates the relatively strong deterrent position that North Korea occupies, especially with its artillery trained on the metropolis of Seoul.

An international team investigated the sinking of the *Cheonan* and concluded that it had been perpetrated by a North Korean submarine. Much speculation has followed among military and political analysts to understand Pyongyang's motive behind the attack. Inter-Korean relations had been previously punctuated by a series of deadly naval skirmishes in 1996, 1999, 2002, and 2009, when North Korean forces frequently suffered higher casualties, so one interpretation of this attack is that it represented Pyongyang's attempt at revenge. One disciplined analysis concludes: "South Korean military vulnerabilities and Kim Jong-il's violent personality almost certainly played a role in the recent attacks. However, because these conditions were present for a long time, considering them does not add much to explaining the heightened aggressiveness." The study rather yields that this "aggressiveness originated from an extraordinary combination of militarism and frustration amid precarious leadership transition."[44]

After the *Cheonan*'s sinking, all eyes naturally turned to Beijing. But as Cha relates: "China remained conspicuously silent. It did not accept the results of the investigation; . . . nor would it accept high-level intelligence briefings on the incident offered by the United States." He also notes that South Korean president Lee was "infuriated" by China's token condolences over the "accident."[45] Beijing's apparent sympathy with Pyongyang in the *Cheonan* incident is evident in the writings of Chinese military analysts. For example, one detailed Chinese military analysis written shortly after the incident notes that the so-called Northern Limit Line was unilaterally demarcated by the United States in 1953 and never recognized by Pyongyang. The analysis emphasizes the preceding naval skirmishes in both the 1999 and 2002 incidents, when the North Korean Navy suffered extensive casualties. The article implies that the balance of power is beginning to shift again in and around the Korean Peninsula: "At the time of the Korean War, the US . . .controlled the air and also . . . had the advantage at sea. . . . Today, the US and [South Korean] superiority in naval and air forces has already declined." It is noted that employment of US Navy submarines in the Yellow Sea presents major difficulties because of their large size. The analysis ends rather optimistically, suggesting that, historically, China's strength is conducive to peace on the Korean Peninsula and also that China, Japan, and South Korea are all focused on common trade interests during the course of financial troubles in the West.[46]

Although Beijing has never officially endorsed the conclusion that Pyongyang perpetrated the sinking of the *Cheonan*—incurring the wrath of most South Koreans in the process—Chinese naval analysts in another article do conclude that "[North Korean] submarine technical personnel have quite a deep understanding with respect to submarine propulsion and operating technology."[47] A column written by Yan Baoxing, an Institute 701 researcher responsible for PLA Navy frigate design, appeared among several articles published in the June 2010 issue of a magazine affiliated with the Chinese Navy, just a couple months after the incident. Instead of criticizing the South Korean Navy for deficiencies in antisubmarine warfare, Yan emphasized the major difficulties for surface ships in confronting torpedo and mine threats. Prompted by the question of whether the South Korean Navy had been negligent, Yan responded by asserting that the situation on the Korean Peninsula demands extreme vigilance from all naval crews, even in peacetime. He concludes with praise for the South Korean Navy, betraying not a little admiration: "[South Korean] surface warships, after a long period of operations, have experienced accelerated building especially over the last twenty years, resulting in astonishing progress."[48]

Indeed, Chinese coverage of the South Korean armed forces generally has a tone of an objective admirer rather than that of a prospective adversary. This is seen, for example, in a survey of Chinese writings regarding South Korea's ambitious naval programs. There is a sense that the South Korean Navy has achieved rapid maritime capabilities that fully place it in the ranks of the world's middle powers. Chinese researchers seem to study the South Korean Navy not simply because it is a proximate state in a complicated neighborhood but also perhaps more particularly as a state quite like China with a dynamic shipbuilding industry that is undertaking rapid naval development—in other words, a model to emulate. Thus, an extremely detailed survey of South Korean fast-attack crafts concludes: "[South Korean] missile boats . . . are overwhelmingly superior to [North Korean] Navy missile boats. . . . Clearly, there is an enormous gap separating the two navies across the 38th Parallel."[49] Another similarly detailed article notes that Seoul may build its next-generation frigate at the brisk pace of two to three vessels per year through 2020, though it also describes certain possible limitations on South Korean surface fleet development, as well as various, unique characteristics of the challenge posed by Pyongyang, for example, its shore-based artillery.[50] In 2010 Chinese naval analysts pronounced the new South Korean Navy submarine as the most advanced diesel boat in the world.[51] The sense that the South Korean Navy faces similar challenges in its development as the Chinese Navy may partly explain the very detailed coverage afforded to the South Korean Navy in the Chinese military press. For example, in February 2012 人民海军 (*People's Navy*) carried a report on Seoul's intent to build a submarine headquarters.[52]

Though the coverage of the South Korean Navy is generally positive, Chinese military analysts have noted that the South Korean Navy is wrestling with certain issues. A *People's Navy* article, for example, in the spring of 2011 noted that the newest South Korean submarines were experiencing significant technical difficulties related to propulsion and that the force had been stood down until the problems were fixed.[53] A more in-depth analysis published in a Chinese military-related journal in early 2012 suggested that the South Korean Navy was in the midst of a major debate about whether to proceed with its "big ocean navy" plan or instead return to its traditional focus on the littoral threat. In addition to the Type 214 problems, the article also raises issues with both the new frigate building program and the current fast attack craft program. The analysis concludes: "At this moment, there are some not insignificant quality issues with the South Korean Navy's equipment. Although there are many management [contributing] factors, overreaching in the speed of development is undoubtedly an important factor."[54] It would not be a leap to suggest that such conclusions also may reflect some uncertainty regarding China's own Great Leap Forward in the naval domain. The broader implication of the above-noted survey of Chinese writings regarding the swiftly expanding South Korean fleet is that, in spite of the new tensions on the Korean Peninsula, Chinese military analysts do not seem unduly alarmed by South Korea's evolving military posture.

Conversely, there are signs that Chinese diplomats are perturbed by the new stark bipolarity on the peninsula, whereby the South Korea-US alliance has been strengthened but North Korea and China have also drawn closer. Returning to the lengthy Chinese foreign policy analysis from late 2011 discussed briefly above, the article views three factions contending in South Korean foreign policy: a pro-China faction, a faction advocating an independent course, and a pro-US faction. After the events of 2010, the analysis concludes, the pro-US faction has triumphed emphatically, bringing "an end to years of heated debates in [Seoul] diplomatic circles." The Chinese perceive that South Korea has reverted to seeing North Korea as its enemy, and that China is now viewed as a "hidden threat" to South Korea. They are disturbed by what they see as the tendency toward "Japanification" (日本化), suggesting that Beijing views Seoul as moving increasingly in lockstep with Washington on issues related to strategy. In what appears to be a subtle critique of China's 2010 diplomacy in the wake of the *Cheonan*'s sinking, they reference South Korean criticism of China's move toward an "irresponsible" foreign policy that may have an impact on South Korean–PRC relations "for the next hundred years."[55]

Two additional Chinese academic articles published in the Chinese journal 和平与发展 (*Peace and Development*) during the years 2010–11 also illustrate Chinese reactions to the evolving situation on the peninsula. As with the analysis described above, there is a hint of "self-criticism," as the article notes Obama's critique of Chinese foreign policy with respect to North Korea as turning a "blind eye" to North Korean provocations—reported in Chinese as acting with "one eye open and one eye closed" (睁一眼闭一眼). The same analysis, however, accuses the US high command of using the 2010 crisis to strengthen the US-South Korea alliance and also as "inciting [South Korea] to seek revenge against [North Korea]." The analysis concludes that the "rising tensions on the Korean Peninsula reflect the cold turn in US-China relations."[56] A second analysis in the same journal in early 2011 is darker still. It suggests that the root cause of North Korea's activation of its nuclear plans was the anxiety brought on by the Iraq War. Suggesting the US motive on the peninsula is to "contain China," this analysis proposes that Washington's ultimate objective for Northeast Asia is to draw South Korea into an "East Asian NATO" (东亚北约). It further suggests that Washington's effort to blame the situation on China is nonsensical and that US interests will suffer more damage than China from confrontational North Korean policies.[57]

Another Chinese analysis published in late 2011 in the academic journal 东北亚论坛 (*Northeast Asia Forum*) offers a hint of China's new strategy with respect to North Korea that is extremely focused on economic engagement. This analysis concludes: "A series of government pronouncements and measures adopted all suggest that the North Korean government is gradually stepping away from the issue of security through nuclear weaponry as the central focus to emphasize internal economic development and foreign trade cooperation." The analysis is not blind to the severe challenges that the North Korean economy continues to face, including underinvestment in agriculture and light industry, inflation, social instability, and the continuing need to import grain, not to mention the series of economic sanctions that have been imposed by the United States, Japan, and South Korea during the period 2006–10. Admitting that "it may be hard to judge whether North Korea has definitively embarked on economic reform," the analysis continues, "it is essential to note, however, that North Korea is now actively pushing China-North Korea economic cooperation." Trade statistics from this article suggest that PRC-North Korean trade exceeded $1 billion in 2003 and by 2010 was approaching $3.5 billion. A massive bridge spanning the Yalu River was apparently completed in 2013, and China is also developing a "mini–Hong Kong" in a special economic zone of North Korea. Trade is reported to be increasing at about 11 percent a year, with a staggering 86 percent of this trade occurring between China and North Korea, obviously reflecting the diminishing of inter-Korean trade.[58] China-North Korea trade is reported to have reached $5 billion in 2011.[59] These numbers are significant, to be sure, but events in 2012–13 interrupted these trends. It was reported that growth in bilateral China-North Korea trade slowed sharply in 2012 and remained slow in 2013—a situation that the Chinese press linked directly to regional tensions flowing from the third nuclear test.[60] Whether this development is an anomaly or a new pattern may become a key determinant of the peninsula's future trajectory.

Even before the third nuclear test in February 2013, Beijing was clearly uncomfortable with the direction of the Korean Peninsula. During the spring of 2012, tensions surrounding the major North Korean missile test to celebrate the one-hundredth anniversary of Kim Il-sung's birth, Chinese commentators said that the test baldly violated UN Security Council Resolution 1718, and welcomed consultations with the United States on the matter. But they also seemed resigned to the fact that no matter what actions North Korea took, Beijing would continue to provide Pyongyang with aid, and thus the negative impact of the test on China-North Korean ties would be very short term.[61] A summer 2012 Chinese analysis of North Korea's nuclear and missile capabilities accepted South Korean and US estimates that North Korea may possess between six and ten nuclear weapons, but also pointed out the small yields of the North Korean tests in 2006 and 2009. The same analysis also pointed to the inaccuracy of North Korean missiles and their vulnerability to South Korean and US air strikes.[62]

The third North Korean nuclear test in early 2013 elicited relatively strong negative reactions from Beijing. Speaking at the Boao Forum for Asia conference on Hainan Island in April 2013, Xi Jinping stated: "No one should be allowed to throw a region and even the whole world into chaos for selfish gains."[63] Likewise, Premier Li Keqiang was said to have likened North Korea's behavior to "picking up a stone and dropping it on one's own foot."[64] If these messages were somewhat indirect, an unsigned editorial in 环球时报 (*Global Times*) was rather blunt—daring the leadership in Beijing, it seems, to take a strong stand against Pyongyang. The article hints at fears in certain quarters of Beijing that current developments could prompt a total breakdown in the China-North Korea relationship akin to the belligerence that characterized China-USSR relations in the late 1960s. This choice of analogy is stark, indeed, because it will be recalled that the two communist giants stood on the brink of (nuclear) war at that time. However, the editorial continues that such fears result from a lack of confidence in Beijing and a tendency to exaggerate Pyongyang's irrational impulses. A key principle, according to the editorial, must prevail: that China does not fear North Korea. Moreover, "If China lacks the determination to insist [on opposing North Korean nuclearization], then we have no place in aspiring to be a great power." The editorial also warns against exaggeration of US-China tensions in East Asia.[65] Illustrating the grave tensions prevailing on the peninsula, however, *Global Times* also published a poll of several thousand residents of Liaoning and Jilin provinces and found high anxiety among their residents regarding the crisis because more than one-third feared that war would break out on the Korean Peninsula during that crisis. Zhu Feng of Peking University was quoted briefly at the end of this article: "Now, not just the US, but the whole world is watching China. We must tell the world that we are against [nuclear proliferation]."[66]

Nevertheless, more conservative opinions were also discernible in the Chinese media. A glimpse into prevailing military thinking regarding the situation on the peninsula just before the early 2013 crisis hinted at a very dark, Cold War–type mood. Thus, a magazine affiliated with the Chinese Navy ran a series of articles in August 2012 that evaluated the possible role of US tactical nuclear weaponry that may be deployed to the Korean Peninsula as a part of new and evolving Air–Sea Battle doctrine. Such deployments, the article concludes, constitute a "huge threat" to China's capital, as well as northeastern industrial centers and naval bases.[67] Opinion within the Chinese military regarding Pyongyang's third nuclear test remains a mystery, but one small hint is offered by a short article published in April 2013 by Colonel Du Wenlong of the influential Beijing Academy of Military Sciences. The article focuses primarily on the developing facts of the situation, observing "significant progress" since the first test in 2006 and also that Pyongyang was now "有弹无枪" (possessing a bullet without a gun). The article makes no criticism of North Korea whatsoever, and it concludes with a seemingly revealing sentence: "US Secretary of Defense Panetta is obviously already feeling the pressure from North Korea's nuclear, ballistic missile."[68] An article by the Fudan University strategist Shen Dingli reveals a somewhat similar disposition among various scholars. Although generally more critical of Pyongyang, the piece does show some sympathy for North Korea, in that he compares North Korea's striving for stability through nuclear weapons with that of China during the 1960s. Shen supports united steps to pressure Pyongyang, but he implies that US-China trust may not be sufficient for the task.[69]

Unquestionably, however, a rising tide of opinion in China has been calling for a reevaluation of Beijing's stance toward North Korea. This current of thinking is amply demonstrated by the lead article in the *Northeast Asia Forum* that followed immediately in the wake of the third nuclear test. In this paper the author, a professor at the Beijing Central Party School, laments that China's policy has placed "stability" ahead of "denuclearization," under the principle of "不战不乱不垮" (no fighting, no chaos, no collapse). The author is emphatically critical both of those Chinese who argue that a North Korean nuclear weapon has no relationship to Chinese security and those who believe that North Korean nuclear capability is "not a bad thing." Instead, the author decries Pyongyang's success in playing on great power rivalry and maintains that if "Korean denuclearization is destroyed, China will be the biggest loser," not least because such a capability would gravely threaten Northeast China, including the capital region.[70]

The execution of Jang Song Taek, Kim Jong-un's powerful uncle, in December 2013 was interpreted by many analysts to signal a new break between Pyongyang and Beijing. After all, Jang had been viewed as a key go-between for China and North Korea. When Jang visited China in August 2012, he was accorded "exceptional treatment" and met with both Wen Jiabao and Hu Jintao. Nevertheless, since his execution, little evidence has emerged to support the thesis of a major break. A significant special economic zone project had just been inaugurated on the China–North Korean border weeks before Jang's downfall. Moreover, bilateral trade growth of 10.4 percent in 2013 was reasonably high and seems not to have been affected too severely by the tensions surrounding Pyongyang's third nuclear test in early 2013. In 2014 the Chinese magazine 财经 (*Finance and Economics*) saw certain risks to foreign investors flowing from the leadership shuffle in Pyongyang, but also pointed out some possible advantages for investors.[71] According to a South Korean expert, "China's economic cooperation with North Korea has been moving beyond the previous policy of trade in goods to one emphasizing infrastructure and special economic zones in the border region." Whatever the exact motive for Kim Jong-un's move against his uncle, Beijing has quite clearly opted to limit any damage, as it took the unusual move to publicly urge a visit by Kim Jong-un to China in the near future during December 2013.[72]

A special issue in 2014 of 美国研究 (*Chinese Journal of American Studies*) was dedicated to the North Korean question. Consistent with the above interpretation, the articles take a relatively conservative approach and do not seem to reflect "new thinking" on Beijing's approach to Pyongyang and the nuclear question. One of these articles examines US food aid to North Korea. The researcher notes that US food aid is often interrupted due to "the long-lasting ideology of viewing North Korea as an enemy" in the United States. One especially interesting insight from this Chinese analysis is the observation that both the Bush and Obama administrations strenuously asked Chinese interlocutors for data on Chinese food aid to North Korea. According to this analysis, "Without any way to receive this data, the US understanding of the North Korean economy and its food shortfalls is not very clear."[73] Another broader paper on the Korean situation in the same issue singles out conservative South Korean president Lee (2008–12) for special blame for the deterioration of the security situation on the Korean Peninsula. The author's hostile and defensive tone is not too subtle in his discussion of US Navy deployments in the wake of the *Cheonan* sinking: "In the eyes of the Chinese people, . . . a US aircraft carrier group in the Yellow Sea area . . . could not help but remind them of the outbreak of the Opium War and the Sino-Japanese War." The author concludes quite pessimistically that North Korea will not give up its nuclear weaponry, but will instead employ this "asymmetric deterrent" to prevent "吞并统" (gobbling up unification).[74]

Nevertheless, it is still worthwhile to note that Chinese specialists are not completely pessimistic and oblivious to the goal of Korean unification. A unique 2011 study published in 国际政治 (*International Politics*) makes a variety of interesting comparisons between the process of German unification and the prospects for Korean unification—noting, for example, that though many countries are divided by ethnic nationalist strife, both Germany and Korea form distinct nations divided by boundaries. The analysis yields the interesting conclusion that Moscow was able to accept German unification because it was confident that a united Germany would not become either a threat or a proxy for American interests. In the end, the analysis calls emphatically for embracing Korean unification as a historical necessity and welcomes a united and mighty Korean nation.[75] Although many analysts judge that China is extremely wary of the prospect of unification, this piece nevertheless suggests that Chinese analysts are not completely insensitive to this aspiration for change.

A US-China Cooperation Spiral for the Korean Peninsula

Washington's move 1 on the Korean Peninsula: The United States should propose a military history project bringing together the Chinese and US militaries to jointly study the Korean War (figure 8.1). The last time that China and the United States engaged in armed hostilities was during the Korean War. This conflict, albeit occurring in a unique historical context, has much to teach current and future US and Chinese military leaders. Most critically, the two powers squared off in Korea inadvertently in a military conflict that neither sought directly. The costs were immense on both sides, moreover, and instructively, there was no decisive winner; the contest of two titans was fought to a draw. The process of joint study by a diverse group of scholars, veterans, policy experts, and most of all active-duty senior military leadership would have numerous benefits, not least some due reflection regarding misperception, escalation, and the role of third parties in drawing the great powers into disputes. Military exchanges between the United States and China are frequently symbolic and stilted—and almost uniformly lacking in substance. Insofar as most military professionals take a deep interest in both military history and tactical proficiency, the larger group would have much to discuss—and need not be weighed down by contemporary political issues. The project might adopt an annual pattern of a one-week "staff ride" that visited one or two Korean battlefields on an annual basis and that was attended ideally by the US senior military official in South Korea and the Chinese commander of the Shenyang Military Region. The proposal would undoubtedly benefit from the trend in Chinese historical studies toward much greater objectivity and correspondingly less ideology. Such a creative attempt by Washington to engage with Beijing on the Korean security issue could initiate the long-overdue

Figure 8.1 Cooperation Spiral: The Korean Peninsula   合作螺旋：朝鲜半岛

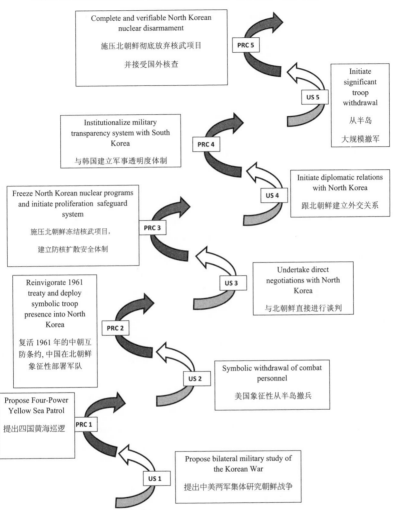

process of active US-China strategic cooperation on the peninsula, as well as benefiting the US-China security relationship more broadly.

Beijing's move 1 on the Korean Peninsula: China should propose the formation of a "Four-Power Yellow Sea Patrol." Maritime disputes lie at the very heart of security tensions on the Korean Peninsula. Most of the armed incidents between North Korea and South Korea have occurred in the maritime domain, including the notorious sinking of the *Cheonan*, discussed at length above. But China and the United States have also witnessed tensions in these same waters in recent years. In particular, the fall 2010 warning from China that US Navy carrier groups should not operate in the Yellow Sea caused quite profound disquiet in the Pentagon, grating as it did against the US Navy's core principle of freedom of navigation.[76] Chinese and South Korean maritime forces also have a somewhat uneasy relationship in the Yellow Sea, especially including interactions between Chinese fishermen and the South Korean Coast Guard, which have occasionally turned violent.[77] All these strains imply the immediate imperative to initiate substantive confidence-building measures in the Yellow Sea area. A four-power arrangement would immediately confer legitimacy on all parties operating naval and maritime forces in the area and decrease tensions around the volatile Northern Limit Line. For US-China relations, the acknowledgment of the appropriateness of US Navy patrols in the area could profoundly increase US trust with respect to partnering with China in order to enhance stability on the Korean Peninsula. For inter-Korean relations, the notion of a maritime partnership—even on a small scale—could be an important breakthrough. A logical area in which the four maritime forces could initiate cooperation would be in the domain of fisheries enforcement. But even this area could be tricky given the high economic stakes for the respective parties. An even more promising area could be the domain of sea mine clearance. A logical model for international efforts to clean up historically mined waters can be found in the example of the Baltic Sea, where a variety of navies have worked together for years to make the seas safer for all parties. Still another vital area that could be taken up by this Four Power Yellow Sea Patrol would be search and rescue (SAR). The tragic loss of the South Korean ferry in April 2014 serves as a powerful reminder of the importance of improving SAR capabilities in East Asia.

Washington's move 2 on the Korean Peninsula: The United States should make a symbolic withdrawal of forces to show goodwill. The United States has already engaged in numerous force reductions on the Korean Peninsula over the last several decades, and most recently during the George W. Bush administration, when additional ground forces were needed in the Middle East and in response to Defense Secretary Donald Rumsfeld's initiative to "transform" the force. Major reductions of US forces had already occurred under presidents Richard Nixon and Jimmy Carter. In the past, these reductions (combined with enhanced US-China cooperation) have resulted in progress in inter-Korean negotiations.[78] Recent efforts at withdrawals have focused on the widening gap between South Korea's military capabilities and those of North Korea. According to one mid-2012 assessment, "Director of National Intelligence Dennis Blair said the gap between North and South Korean power had become 'overwhelmingly great' and 'prospects for reversal' remote. Blair's successor as director of national intelligence, James Clapper, gave similar testimony last year."[79] At this stage, a purely symbolic withdrawal—of perhaps 1,000 to 2,000 personnel—would be appropriate, given China's promotion of a four-power naval patrol, as noted above. Previous US troop withdrawals have been "demand centric" (e.g., the pull of Iraq or Afghanistan) and have not been coordinated effectively with Beijing and Pyongyang in order to gain reciprocal concessions. As a carefully planned step in a process of step-by-step compromise, such a symbolic effort would have a substantial chance of success.

Beijing's move 2 on the Korean Peninsula: China should reinvigorate the 1961 Sino–North Korean Defense Treaty and also commit to a symbolic troop presence in North Korea. It may seem counterintuitive to invigorate a somewhat moribund defense treaty in order to deescalate tensions on the peninsula, but this move by Beijing would be extremely critical to subsequent cooperative steps. The move rests on the assumption—widely supported by the academic literature on nuclear proliferation, but also by common sense—that proliferation is generally motivated by acute insecurity. The reasons for North Korean insecurity are plain enough. If the collapse of the USSR was not enough, coupled with the end of Moscow's aid, not to mention the "Axis of Evil" concern regarding US intentions, Pyongyang's anxieties have no doubt been severe, given the rapidly shifting balance of conventional military capabilities in light of economic realities on the peninsula and all the talk of "regime collapse." To make possible a more stable peninsula, it is necessary that North Korea become substantially more secure—the more so to preclude the need to take radical steps, such as violently lashing out in order to demonstrate its will to fight. A token presence of Chinese troops in North Korea would hardly alter the military balance, but would indicate Beijing's new willingness to take responsibility for upholding security and stability on the peninsula. Following the course of this logic might entail a larger Chinese military presence, suggesting even that Mao's withdrawal of Chinese troops in 1958 might have constituted the "original sin" that set off the spiral of instability that continues to this day. The central difficulty of this move, beyond breaking with Beijing's major reluctance to station military forces abroad, would be the maturity and restraint required by both Seoul and Washington to realize that to get to a better place will require their acquiescence to shoring up North Korean security. It is envisioned that PRC military forces, deployed as a kind of "trip wire" into the territory of North Korea, would likely need to stay in place for a lengthy period of time—until full resolution of the nuclear crisis, at least.

Washington's move 3 on the Korean Peninsula: The United States should open direct and continuous negotiations with North Korea. The United States has had intermittent direct contact with North Korea, but in order to make the next leap in cooperation, a further gesture will be required from Washington. The Chinese have long advocated such direct negotiations. This step need not imply the failure of the Six-Party Talks process, which has had its uses for all sides. However, there is no arguing with the fact that the major epicenter of antagonism is between Pyongyang and Washington, so this step may begin to refocus negotiations on substance vice process. Nor is this step so dramatic for Washington. Given the various visits of high-level diplomats up to and including two former presidents and a secretary of state, this concession is appropriately moderate.[80] Conversely, the initial setup of institutionalized representation for North Korea in Washington and vice versa as a prelude to diplomatic relations will accord Pyongyang the necessary prestige to approach subsequent hard steps toward disarmament, with confidence that a normal and indeed rewarding relationship with Washington will be established in the near or medium term. This outreach will, moreover, have greater salience and effectiveness because the stronger China-North Korean relationship is bound to cause Pyongyang to seek additional great power friends in order to balance China's influence.

Beijing's move 3 on the Korean Peninsula: China should take the lead in ensuring North Korean compliance with nonproliferation norms. Having initiated the cooperation spiral, encouraged four-power cooperation, and accepted Beijing's long-held view that direct negotiations between North Korea and the United States would be most productive, it will now be time for China to truly step up. Indeed, this is the crucial step, whereby Beijing would achieve two critical interim steps toward a permanently stabilizing answer to the Korean question. As the now-recognized guarantor of North Korean security, China would supervise (1) a freeze on its nuclear programs, including an accounting of its arsenal; and (2) a system of checks to ensure that proliferation to other states is not occurring. Note that this step would not mean the dismantling of the current North Korean weapons stockpile of a dozen or so weapons. The key enablers for this policy would be the prior cooperative steps that decreased

North Korean insecurity by increasing its legitimacy, as well as Beijing's prior deployment of troops to North Korean defense as a further sign of commitment. However, what would make this step much more feasible than current proposals under discussion is that Beijing (with enhanced influence over Pyongyang) would also be the sole executor of this step to bring North Korea into conformity with the minimum nonproliferation goals. Pyongyang will be much more amenable if verification is undertaken by Beijing rather than by inspectors from the International Atomic Energy Agency (IAEA) or representatives from the United States, South Korea, or Japan.

Washington's move 4 on the Korean Peninsula: The United States should inaugurate diplomatic relations with North Korea. This major concession by the United States will be a logical reward for North Korea's taking concrete steps under Chinese supervision to come into conformity with nonproliferation norms. Nevertheless, it will be a highly controversial step, given North Korea's atrocious human rights record. And yet, the United States has diplomatic relations with many other countries with poor human rights records, among them Saudi Arabia, Pakistan, Vietnam, and China itself. Indeed, diplomatic relations will enable enhanced engagement—for example, by American corporations, which can help to influence the human rights situation in North Korea in a positive direction. From Pyongyang's point of view, this step has been long sought after and may be touted as a major achievement by the North Korean regime. True, it may ultimately serve to delay the cause of unification by adding further legitimacy to the "two-state" solution; but even South Koreans are wary of any near-term unification and legitimacy (and security), for North Korea will be a major part of the price for stability and demilitarization on the peninsula. Robust US engagement will confer numerous advantages, not least from a commercial point of view, but will also provide a natural check on China's extensive influence over North Korea.

Beijing's move 4 on the Korean Peninsula: China should institutionalize a military transparency mechanism with South Korea. Peace will only come to the peninsula in a durable way if Beijing and Seoul can return to the high levels of trust that were beginning to form before 2010. Indeed, it was posited during the early 2000s that for cultural, historical, and commercial reasons, South Korea and China were destined to grow ever closer. As has been explained above, in 2010 this vital relationship took a sudden plunge into the abyss with the *Cheonan's* sinking and the artillery attack against Yeonpyeong Island. It is worth considering the fact that Chinese diplomats may have done much more behind the scenes to pacify the peninsula than in public, but very significant damage was clearly done.[81] To repair that damage will be difficult, but Beijing has demonstrated its commitment with another successful Xi-Park summit in June 2014 and by reaching a free trade agreement with Seoul that was announced at the November 2014 APEC meeting. Another major step forward for Beijing to allay Seoul's broader security concerns will be to design an engagement and transparency program directed specifically at South Korea. Such an initiative would not only include an intensified pattern of exercises and exchanges but also, more particularly, would mean annual visits to major PLA bases in northeastern China, and even the permanent posting of a South Korean military representative at the Shenyang Military Region's headquarters. It is plain that South Korea may be unnerved by several of the steps outlined in this China-US cooperation spiral, so Beijing's outreach to Seoul will be extremely critical, and the importance of this particular step is plain. Some American strategists—for example, Luttwak—have been extremely critical of a prospective close relationship between Seoul and Beijing, but this is shortsighted and wholly contrary to genuine US national interests.[82] White's assessment is closer to the mark: "Washington can do little to help Seoul deal with Pyongyang because the only means of influence it has over the North is military coercion. . . . Beijing, by contrast, has many more effective ways to influence North Korea."[83]

Washington's move 5 on the Korean Peninsula: The United States should make a substantive withdrawal of forces from South Korea, maintaining but altering the US-South Korean alliance. A premise of this book has been that the United States must alter its Cold War–era alliance structure to adapt to new conditions. The decades following the collapse of the USSR and the so-called unipolar moment created major new power vacuums that were often proximate to new and potent agglomerations of power. On the Korean Peninsula, the sole superpower acting in concert with the now wealthy, strong, and increasingly vigorous South Korea—and backed up, to boot, by a robust Japan—simply formed a concentration of power that could not be matched in any way. The result has been a stark asymmetry of power in Northeast Asia, with predictably destabilizing results. As discussed above, South Korean superiority over North Korea in conventional capabilities is quite sufficient to enable major reductions in US forces, which have taken place intermittently for decades. This final step will help solidify North Korea's commitment to nuclear disarmament and to ensure that Beijing does not revert to a zero-sum approach. The

US troop presence should fall well below 5,000 troops—meaning the withdrawal of the two remaining brigades of combat troops, so that the remainder would be made up mostly of headquarters, logistics, and training personnel. Naval and air assets would continue to rotate through South Korean bases on a regular basis to ensure continuity of the alliance in order to support deterrence goals. Ironically, US-South Korea relations will actually be enhanced by this transformation, because many tensions are attributable to basing issues (e.g., noise, land ownership). A spring 2013 study by a RAND Corporation researcher calls into question the current ground force reductions in the US armed forces, asserting that the worst case scenario on the Korean Peninsula would require between 100,000 and 250,000 US troops. But even this rather pessimistic analysis puts a high premium on cooperation with Beijing, and even it concludes that "theoretically, coordination with China, preceded by consultation and operational agreements, could . . . reduce US [ground force] requirements."[84]

Beijing's move 5 on the Korean Peninsula: China should oversee North Korea's complete and verified nuclear disarmament. Denuclearization is the priority goal that both China and the United States are working toward in this cooperation spiral. The major steps outlined above will enable this possibility, including a closer defense relationship between Beijing and Pyongyang, but also, vitally, the carrots from Washington that grant diplomatic recognition and also withdraw the majority of US troops from the peninsula. As discussed above, a major factor enabling such concessions is the very strong position that Seoul occupies, whether viewed from a political, economic, or military perspective. This proposal might be different than most efforts to denuclearize the peninsula, in that it places China in the key oversight position, vice the IAEA or representatives of the Six-Party Talks. This difference is quite deliberate, and it is estimated that the arrangement favoring Beijing in the oversight role would have a much higher possibility of success. Given how far North Korea has progressed with nuclear weaponry, it seems that to change this course will require extraordinary incentives and also new approaches. Because a return to the IAEA process is likely to be too humiliating and awkward, an approach in which China leads the disarmament process is viewed as presenting the best possibility in present conditions. To be sure, such an arrangement will be less than ideal from Washington's point of view. However, China would have both the requisite expertise and the genuine incentive to assist North Korea with the process of denuclearization. Obviously, the other participants in the Six-Party Talks—including the United States, South Korea, Japan, and Russia—would want continuous reporting on the details of this process, and the success of the entire cooperation spiral would rest on the success of China's supervisory role here and on Beijing's credibility in overseeing and accomplishing this lofty goal.

Conclusion

Many Americans are eagerly anticipating the collapse of North Korea. The late 2014 only slightly comical "Sony Crisis" with North Korea seemed only to underscore how deeply Americans, as a whole, revile the regime in Pyongyang. Such a position may be consistent with human rights norms, as well as a general yearning for the "natural" reunification of a divided nation—akin to the surprisingly rapid and smooth process that occurred in Germany during 1989–90. Cha, a former Bush administration adviser, in his 2012 book calls North Korea "the impossible state." For him, the violence in 2010 and the awkward transition to a youthful leader with no experience were harbingers of imminent collapse. Buoyed by the Arab Spring, the US government also seems to be holding its breath and waiting for demonstrations in Pyongyang that might match those that brought down tyrants across the Middle East, but perhaps the failure of democracy to take root in that region provides a basis for sober reflections.

It is widely understood that China will not allow North Korea to collapse and is not holding its breath. Instead, trade figures suggest that Beijing is promoting North Korea's economic revival as a viable alternative to its collapse. Cha has criticized China as exploiting North Korea's resources for its own ends and also of attempting to effectively convert North Korea into another Chinese province. From Cha's perspective, increasing Chinese influence and money will only forestall its inevitable collapse.

The approach advocated in this book is quite different, and thus departs from many traditional US perspectives. Here, the most salient problem is viewed as North Korea's stark vulnerability and insecurity, which have led it to consistently and aggressively pursue nuclear weapons, along with other deterrent strategies, including "active deterrence." Under this logic, what is needed is not more and more pressure, or a stronger and stronger South Korea-US alliance. South Korea is plenty strong, and the alliance is also abundantly effective. Rather, to achieve disarmament, North Korea must be made more secure; and China has the means and incentive to aid in this endeavor. A more robust effort to focus US-China strategic cooperation within a series of step-by-step confidence-building measures will help to bring about a much more stable and peaceful Korean Peninsula for the twenty-first century. And once a modicum of stability and security is reached on the peninsula, one may begin to chart a safer path to unification.

Notes

1. David Kang, *China Rising: Peace, Power, and Order in East Asia* (New York: Columbia University Press, 2007), 41.
2. Ibid., 44.
3. James Bradley, *Imperial Cruise: A Secret History of Empire and War* (Boston: Little, Brown, 2009), 312–13.
4. Edward N. Luttwak, *The Rise of China vs. the Logic of Strategy* (Cambridge, MA: Harvard University Press, 2012), 179.
5. Bruce Cumings, *The Korean War: A History* (New York: Modern Library, 2011), 49, 52.
6. Ibid., 81.
7. Ibid., 113–39.
8. Yu Bin, "What China Learned from Its Forgotten War," in *Chinese Warfighting: The PLA Experience since 1949*, ed. Mark Ryan, David Finkelstein, and Michael McDevitt (London: M. E. Sharpe, 2003), 124, 133.
9. 宁伟 [Ning Wei], 难忘一九五: 中国人民志愿军入朝参战60周年图文实录 [Unforgettable 1950: A Record of the Chinese Peoples Volunteer Army Entering North Korea for the 60th Anniversary] (Beijing: Xinhua Press, 2010); 齐德学 [Qi Dexue], 巨人的较量: 抗美援朝高层决策 [Giants Wrestling: High-Level Decisions in the War to Resist America and Rescue North Korea] (Shenyang: Liaoning People's Press, 2010).
10. Peter Gries, *China's New Nationalism: Pride, Politics, and Diplomacy* (Berkeley: University of California Press, 2004), p. 57.
11. Author's personal observations, Dalian, China, October 2010.
12. [Xi Jinping], "在纪念中国人民志愿军抗美援朝出国作战60周年座谈会上的讲话" [A Speech Commemorating 60 Years since the Chinese People's Volunteers Went Off to Fight in the War to Resist America and Rescue North Korea], in 抗美援朝60年后的回眸 [A Glance Back at the War to Resist America and Rescue North Korea after 60 Years], ed. 张星星 [Zhang Xingxing] (Beijing: Contemporary China Publishing House, 2011), i–vi.
13. Ibid., ii.
14. Ibid., iv–v.

15. Ibid., iii.
16. Ibid., v.
17. [Luo Yuan, PLA General], "伟大的抗美援朝精神万岁" [Long Live the Great Spirit of the War to Resist America and Rescue North Korea], in 抗美援朝60年后的回眸 [A Glance Back at the War to Resist America and Support North Korea after 60 Years], 48.
18. Ibid., 57.
19. Ibid., 51.
20. Ibid., 53.
21. Ibid., 59.
22. Victor Cha, *The Impossible State: North Korea, Past and Future* (New York: HarperCollins, 2012), 21–26.
23. Jonathan Pollack, *No Exit: North Korea, Nuclear Weapons and International Security* (London: Routledge, 2011), 57.
24. Cha, *Impossible State*, 29–30; Pollack, *No Exit*, 67–68.
25. Pollack, *No Exit*, 68.
26. Ibid., 90.
27. Ibid.
28. Van Jackson, "Making Diplomacy Work: Coercion and Conciliation in the First North Korean Nuclear Crisis," *Comparative Strategy* 31 (April 2012): 176–77.
29. Cha, *Impossible State*, 253.
30. Pollack, *No Exit*, 117.
31. Ibid., 117.
32. Ibid., 115.
33. See, e.g., Michael Gordon, "Giving Up Those Weapons: After Libya, Who Is Next?" *New York Times*, January 1, 2004, www.nytimes.com/2004/01/01/world/giving-up-those-weapons-after-libya-who-is-next.html.
34. Pollack, *No Exit*, 140.
35. Dong Sun Lee, "Causes of North Korean Belligerence," *Australian Journal of International Affairs* 66 (April 2012): 109.
36. On these tensions, see Chang-hee Nam, "Relocating the US Forces in South Korea: Strained Alliance, Emerging Partnership in the Changing Defense Posture," *Asian Survey* 46 (July–August 2006): 615–31.
37. Cha, *Impossible State*, 333.
38. Ibid., 333.
39. Report of the CCP International Department, quoted by Pollack, *No Exit*, 150.

40. [Wang Wei], "大国之略: 写在朝鲜核试之后" [Among the Great Powers: What Comes to Mind after the North Korean Nuclear Test], 舰载武器 [Shipborne Weaponry], December 2006, 21–22.

41. 汪伟民, 李辛 [Wang Weimin and Li Xin], "美国同盟再定义与韩国的战略选择: 进程与争论" [The Redefinition of the US-ROK Alliance and the ROK's Strategic Choice: Developments and Debates], 国际政治 [International Politics], December 2011, 61, 63, 65–66.

42. "S. Korean President Vows Action over Sunken Warship," CNN, April 19, 2010, http://articles.cnn.com/2010-04-19/world/south.korea.president.ship_1 _yellow-sea-korean-myung-bak?_s=pm:world.

43. Luttwak excoriates Seoul for not engaging in "prompt, convincing and proportionate retaliation"; Luttwak, *Rise of China*, 172. In doing so, he seems to show a stunning indifference to the millions of lives that might be lost in an inter-Korean war that resulted from an escalation spiral. It seems obvious that if he or his relatives lived in Seoul, he might well perceive this crisis in rather different terms. On the contrary, the administration of Lee Myung-bak should be commended in the strongest terms (in this particular instance) for exhibiting extraordinary restraint and a more mature appreciation of the situation's potential risks and costs. Strategic bargaining in a situation in which one side has much more to lose than the other is much more complex than Luttwak and others seem to appreciate.

44. Dong Sung Lee, "Causes of North Korean Belligerence," *Australian Journal of International Affairs* 66 (April 2012): 104.

45. Cha, *Impossible State*, 334.

46. No author, "天安'号事件与中国周边安全" [The Cheonan Incident and Security Around China's Periphery], 舰船知识 [Naval and Merchant Ships], July 2010, 22–25.

47. No author, "浅析朝鲜小型潜艇技术" [Brief Analysis of DPRK Small Submarine Technology], 舰船知识 [Naval and Merchant Ships], July 2010, 27.

48. 严宝兴 [Yan Baoxing], "韩国'天安'号护卫舰沉没: 引发的思考" [Sinking of the ROK's Frigate Cheonan: Initial Reflections], 现代舰船 [Modern Ships], June 2010, 23.

49. No author, "欲速不达: 韩国海军攻击快艇简史" [Haste Does Not Bring Success: A Brief History of the ROK Navy's Fast Attack Craft], 舰载武器 [Shipborne Weapons], December 2010, 70.

50. 曾晓光,吴伟 [Zeng Xiaoguang and Wu Wei], "韩国海军FFX护卫舰研制实录" [A Record of the Research and Development for the ROK Navy's FFX Frigate], 舰载武器 [Shipborne Weapons], October 2010, 47, 50–51.

51. No author, "韩国最先进AIP动力潜艇'安重根'服役" [South Korea's Most Advanced AIP Propulsion Submarine "Anzhonggen" Enters Service], 当代海军 [Modern Navy], January 2010, 4.

52. "韩国拟造潜艇司令部" [South Korea Draws Up Plans for a Submarine Command], 人民海军 [People's Navy], February 28, 2012, 4.

53. No author, "韩国三艘最新型214级潜艇因螺丝问题被禁航" [The Three ROK Most Adanced Type 214 Submarines Are Not Permitted to Sail Because of Problems Related to Their Screws], 人民海军 [People's Navy], May 24, 2011, 4.

54. [Li Hongjun], "韩国'大洋海军'之困" [Difficulties with South Korea's Big Ocean Navy], 军事世界 [Military World], January 2012, 49.

55. 汪伟民, 李辛 [Wang Weimin and Li Xin], "美国同盟再定义与韩国的战略选择: 进程与争论" [The Redefinition of the US-ROK Alliance and the ROK's Strategic Choice: Developments and Debates], 国际政治 [International Politics], December 2011, 67–69.

56. "2010年的中国周边安全形式" [The Security Situation in China's Neighboring Areas in 2010], 和平与发展 [Peace and Development], February 2011, 39.

57. 卞庆祖 [Bian Qingzu], "对2010年中美两国博弈的思考" [Reflecting on the Gambling in US-China Relations during 2010], 和平与发展 [Peace and Development], April 2011, 23.

58. 张慧智 [Zhang Huizhi], "朝鲜经济发展方式探析" [An Exploration of the DPRK's Economic Development Mode], 东北亚论坛 [Northeast Asia Forum], no. 6 (2011): 3–9.

59. Peter M. Beck, "North Korea in 2011: The Next Kim Takes the Helm," *Asian Survey* 52, no. 1 (2012): 68. For another perspective on increasing China-North Korea trade, see Balazs Szalontai and Changyong Choi, "China's Controversial Role in North Korea's Economic Transformation: The Dilemmas of Dependency," *Asian Survey* 53 (March–April 2013): 269–91.

60. "North Korea's Trade Growth with China Slowed Sharply in 2012," Reuters, March 6, 2013, www.reuters.com/article/2013/03/07/us-korea-north-trade-idUSBRE92605A20130307. See also 梁晨 [Liang Chen], "半岛变局令中朝经贸放慢脚步" [The Altered Situation on the Peninsula Causes China-North Korea Trade and Finance to Advance at Slower Pace], 环球时报 [Global Times], July 16, 2013, 7.

61. 蔡婷贻 [Cai Tingyi], "朝核问题重归旧路" [The North Korean Nuclear Issue Significantly Returns to the Old Pattern], 财经 [Finance and Economics], March 26, 2012, 36–37.

62. 洋志成, 孟巧凤 [Yang Zhicheng and Meng Qiaofeng], "朝鲜核与弹道导弹能力透视" [A Look at North Korean Nuclear and Missile Capabilities], *现代兵器* [Modern Weaponry], July 2012, 23–26.

63. This is as reported by Celia Hatton, "Is China Ready to Abandon North Korea?" BBC, April 12, 2013, www.bbc.co.uk/news/world-asia-china-22062589.

64. This is as reported by 沈丁立 [Shen Dingli], "朝鲜以退为进拥核不变" [North Korea Retreats in Order to Advance: It Does Not Alter Its Stance on Possessing Nuclear Weapons], *东方早报* [Oriental Morning Post], June 19, 2013.

65. "中国珍惜中朝友好, 朝鲜需珍惜" [China Treasures China-North Korea Friendship, North Korea Should Also], *环球时报* [Global Times], February 26, 2013.

66. 邱永峥 [Qiu Yongzheng], "中朝边境居民最担心半岛开战" [Citizens Living Near the China-North Korean Border Are Most Concerned about the Possibility of War Breaking Out], *环球时报* [Global Times], April 13, 2013.

67. 戴艳丽 [Dai Yanli], "B61-12配戴F-35: 针对中国, 朝鲜" [F-35 Armed with the B61-12: Aimed at China or North Korea?], *舰船知识* [Naval and Merchant Ships], August 2012, 28.

68. 杜文龙 [Du Wenlong, PLA Colonel], "核云笼罩的朝鲜" [A Nuclear Cloud Envelops North Korea], *兵器* [Ordnance], April 2013, 74–75.

69. 沈丁立 [Shen Dingli], "朝鲜以退为进拥核不变" [North Korea Retreats in Order to Advance: It Does Not Alter Its Stance on Possessing Nuclear Weapons], 15.

70. 张琏瑰 [Zhang Liangui], "维护朝鲜半岛无核化处于成败关键期" [The Critical Period for the Success or Failure of Korean Denuclearization], *东北亚论坛* [Northeast Asia Forum], March 2013, 17, 19, 21.

71. 蔡婷贻 [Cai Tingyi], "朝鲜人事巨变之后" [After the Major Personnel Shuffle in North Korea], *财经* [Finance and Economics], January 20, 2014, 35.

72. This paragraph is drawn entirely from Dong Wook Won, "Will Jang's Execution Affect Bejing's Economic Ties with Pyongyang?" *Global Asia*, Spring 2014, 31–32, 36.

73. 李 Nan [Li Nan], "美国对朝鲜粮食援助策的演变与评估" [Evolution and Assessment of US Food Aid to the DPRK], *美国研究* [Chinese Journal of American Studies], 28 (January 2014): 24–25.

74. 朴建一 [Piao Jianyi], "冷战后朝鲜半岛局势演变的基本特征" [The Evolution of the Situation on the Korean Peninsula since the End of the Cold War], *美国研究* [Chinese Journal of American Studies] 28 (January 2014): 27, 30, 44.

75. 王一 [Wang Yi], "朝鲜半岛的未来之路" [The Future Path for the Korean Peninsula], 国际政治 [International Politics], December 2011, 130–32.

76. Regarding Obama administration decision making and the Yellow Sea deployment, see Jeffrey A. Bader, *Obama and China's Rise: An Insider's Account of America's Asia Strategy* (Washington, DC: Brookings Institution Press, 2012), 89.

77. Choe Sang-hun, "Chinese Fisherman Kills South Korean Coast Guardsman," *New York Times*, December 12, 2011, www.nytimes.com/2011/12/13/world/asia/chinese-fisherman-kills-south-korean-coast-guardsman.html.

78. See, e.g., Pollack, *No Exit*, 72–79.

79. Richard Halloran, "The Rising East: US Seeks to Trim Armed Forces Posted in South Korea," *Honolulu Civil Beat*, July 2, 2012, www.civilbeat.com/articles/2012/07/02/16213-the-rising-east-us-seeks-to-trim-armed-forces-posted-in-south-korea/.

80. On the depth of antagonism toward any shift away from Washington's confrontational approach to Pyongyang, see Bader's discussion of his distaste for candidate Obama's assertion during the Democratic primaries that he was willing to meet with adversary leaders, including Kim Jong-il. Bader notes that he was "uncomfortable with the statement," and says with evident satisfaction: "During my time in office, I never heard the statement reiterated in any form." Bader, *Obama*, 29–31. Similarly, when former president Bill Clinton went to North Korea in early 2009, Bader relates with pride that his colleague Kurt Campbell had told the former president to "channel his inner Dick Cheney" (p. 36), despite the fact that the original Agreed Framework of the mid-1990s had resulted from the controversial visit of another former US president to North Korea.

81. Comments by a senior US diplomat, as reported secondhand to the author in the spring of 2011.

82. See, e.g., Luttwak, *Rise of China*, 175.

83. Hugh White, *The China Choice: Why We Should Share Power* (New York: Oxford University Press, 2013), 94.

84. David C. Gompert, "North Korea: Preparing for the End," *IISS Survival* 55 (June–July 2013): 39.

9

KEYSTONE
Japan and US-China Relations

Hollywood, which is perennially looking for apocalyptic scenarios, may want to examine contemporary Japan-China relations in order to develop next summer's big blockbuster. Japan-China relations have been in a virtual death spiral since at least 2010, if not before. Perhaps this spiral has been arrested finally by "cooler heads" as Presidents Xi and Abe were able to meet and even shake hands at the APEC Summit in Beijing in November 2014. But if the leaders' antagonistic facial expressions were not enough to cast doubt on prospects for a diplomatic thaw, commentators on all sides of the Asia-Pacific remain pessimistic.[1]

To be sure, the bilateral trade statistics are quite extraordinary to behold, but a combination of persistent security concerns, internal identity crises, and the perennial history question have embittered the vital Japan-China relationship to a disconcerting extent. An authoritative US government study of this relationship concluded in 2007 that "Sino-Japanese relations were close to a post–Cold War low," but that ominous report actually predated the Diaoyu/Senkaku crisis of the fall of 2010 that set off a whole new round of bitter recriminations.[2] The crisis in the East China Sea escalated still further during the fall of 2012, and the tension has hardly dissipated. Indeed, an article published in mid-2013 by a magazine affiliated with the Chinese Navy said Japan-China relations had now reached a new nadir and, illustrating the very dangerous escalating dynamic of this relationship, quoted a senior Japanese admiral's recommendation that Tokyo "must prepare for the possibility of the worst case."[3] Given such severe strains, it is no wonder that the study on the US-Japan-China triangle published by the high-profile Carnegie Endowment for International Peace in 2013 concludes starkly that "the status quo is likely to prove unsustainable."[4] As in many other chapters of this book, close attention is paid here to Chinese sources for the purpose of giving the reader a more complete understanding of Beijing's perspective. Obviously, a more comprehensive treatment of the China-Japan-United States triangle would require parallel attention to Japanese sources. But Tokyo's perspectives are already quite well understood and well represented in the West. Again, extensive use of Chinese sources does not imply endorsement of their viewpoints.

This chapter operates from two fundamental premises regarding the critical China-Japan relationship. First, the divisive issues between Tokyo and Beijing are to a large extent "imagined." For Japan, the major concerns are not generally related to current Chinese policies. Rather, Tokyo frets about an immensely powerful, militaristic, and nationalistic China that could hypothetically emerge at some point in the distant future to threaten Japan's sea lanes and other vital interests. It is not helpful, moreover, that US analysts have tended to exaggerate the condition of Japan's national security problem.[5] Beijing is also "shadow-boxing" in large part, considering how cautiously and sparingly Japan has been in deploying its armed might since 1945. Since World War II, Japan has operated only "self-defense forces" under its peace constitution, which was written by the US occupying forces after the war. Chinese historical grievances from that catastrophic conflict are wholly legitimate and demand redress, but this process must be channeled in support of a positive dynamic that upholds regional peace. On the most crucial issues confronting leaders in the twenty-first century—from energy security to environmental protection to nuclear nonproliferation and preventing terrorism—Beijing and Tokyo in fact share surprisingly similar outlooks. What is remarkable to consider regarding China-Japan relations is how a number of comparatively simple steps, often of a merely symbolic character, could radically improve the situation and thus yield massive economic and security gains.

A second premise of the chapter is that Washington has a major role to play in this process. Conventional wisdom frequently defaults to the contrary position. The 2007 report cited above, for example, concludes: "The United States . . . cannot deliver better relations between Tokyo and Beijing. Indeed, it would be foolhardy to try."[6] A so-called hands-off approach, however, is no longer warranted, because it significantly understates US diplomatic prestige and Americans' unique ability to broker difficult compromises. If US diplomats spent even a fraction of the time and energy accorded to the various, divisive conflicts in the Middle East on this foremost problem in East Asia, a new and positive regional dynamic might well result. A few cynical realists may contend that Washington benefits from the tension between Tokyo and Beijing, but this view is shortsighted in the extreme and is not seriously entertained in this chapter. Most obviously, the hands-off approach that has characterized US policy over the last decade has yielded few results. Washington has been altogether too passive in observing the growing chasm between China and Japan, which could well result in catastrophic consequences, including for the United States.

Background

Although the "history issue" is frequently cited as an insurmountable barrier to improved Japan-China relations, it is essential to note that history prior to the mid–nineteenth century is actually extremely favorable to close relations between China and Japan. In contrast to the millennia of violent struggles that overshadow Muslims and Christians in the Mediterranean region or even the centuries of belligerence that divided France and Great Britain, such premodern animosities are simply not relevant to the China-Japan relationship, suggesting that history may actually undergird this relationship and not poison it. A passing familiarity with the Japanese written language—of which nearly half is derived from traditional Chinese characters—is suggestive of the intense cultural interaction that has bound China and Japan together for thousands of years. Finding common roots for their shared essential artistic and literary heritage is the norm and hardly the exception.[7]

If there is a puzzle within the deep historical interaction between China and Japan, it is explaining the apparent paucity of violence in the relationship. Indeed, the most rapacious episode—which featured the world's largest amphibious attack, undertaken against the shores of Kyushu in the late thirteenth century—was perpetrated by the Mongols and not by the Chinese.[8] There has never been a Chinese invasion of Japan, and this single instance forms the closest approximation. Though undoubtedly important to the Japanese character—it was the divine wind (*kamikaze*) that ultimately destroyed the Mongol invasion fleet—the Song Dynasty had felt the lash of Mongol aggression much more severely. The only major clash between Chinese and Japanese armed forces came in Korea during the late sixteenth century, but this episode is the exception that proves the rule of generally harmonious relations.

Japan's self-conception as having a "unique racial and cultural purity," combined with the conviction borne of crisis, led Japanese leaders in the mid–nineteenth century to the conclusion: "If we take the initiative, we can dominate; if we do not, we will be dominated."[9] Thus, beginning in the 1870s, Japan began to follow in the footsteps of the many other imperialist powers, rapidly reaching the front ranks of those countries engaging in predatory activities in China. Regrettably, it seems that certain American diplomats played a significant role in goading the Japanese to undertake to "bring the whole of Asia from its barbarous and primate stage to the civilized stage," especially as regarded the fate of Taiwan.[10] If it had not been for the Triple Intervention, Tokyo would have absorbed most of Manchuria in 1895, but it had to be satisfied with merely acquiring Taiwan, "a [concession] that grated at the dignity of a proud society," and still does.[11] The Sino-Japanese War of 1894–95 witnessed significant Japanese atrocities, including the apparent practice of executing Chinese prisoners of war.[12] A recent Chinese survey of China-Japan relations notes that Japan's armed forces formed the core of the eight-nation assault on Beijing during the Boxer uprising in 1900.[13] The role of Japanese imperialism in developing Chinese nationalism is well accepted among China specialists, who point to both the May 4 movement following Tokyo's demand for Shandong Province at the Versailles Treaty in 1919 and also the 1936 "Xian Incident" as pivotal steps in the formation of a more cohesive Chinese national identity. The latter episode witnessed the kidnapping of Chinese leader, Generalissimo Chiang Kai-shek, by his own generals in an attempt to force him into fighting against the Japanese more aggressively.

During the period 1937–41, Japan's aggression in China reached a new stage, with an effort by Tokyo to destroy Chiang Kai-shek's Kuomintang (Nationalist) regime. After a major battle in Shanghai, Japanese forces marched on the Kuomintang capital of Nanjing in the hopes that vanquishing the enemy capital would result in the final conquest of China. The result was the infamous Nanjing Massacre, one of the most shameful atrocities of the modern era, in which 260,000 to 350,000 Chinese were killed and 20,000 to 80,000 women were raped. However, it is well worth considering that "we will never know everything that happened in the many cities and small villages that found themselves prostrate beneath the boot of [the Japanese Army]. . . . Ironically, we do know the story of Nanking because some foreigners witnessed the horror and sent word to the outside world at that time."[14] Chinese sources put the total military and civilian death toll at 35 million during the period 1937–45.[15]

A 2013 encyclopedic history of the war by the Oxford historian Rana Mitter sheds some considerable new light on this controversial history. Mitter's estimate of total Chinese war dead is 14 million, suggesting a discrepancy from the official Chinese figure cited above, but he notes that his number is "conservative," and he, moreover, emphasizes that the total number of Chinese war dead far outstrips those of either the United States or Great Britain by a factor of more than thirty times and more closely approximates the losses suffered by the Soviet Union.[16] It is noteworthy that Mitter does not challenge the official Chinese estimate of 300,000 massacred at Nanjing in 1937, and even presents some evidence from American diplomatic archives suggesting that this figure could be too low.[17] His only specific comment on the debate surrounding that figure is that "this dispute should not obscure the fact that a very large number died as the out-of-control Imperial Army exacted revenge on a population that had stood in the way of its advance."[18] Mitter also suggests a point that bears repeating: "Nanjing was just one, albeit the most prominent, of a series of atrocities carried out by the Japanese during their invasion of Eastern China."[19] One can certainly read Mitter as a plea for "justice" within the intellectual vacuum precipitated by toxic politics, especially during the early Cold War, when "Japan and China traded places in American and British affections."[20]

No doubt this high death toll reflects the relative poverty of China at that time and its comparatively backward armed forces. But there is little doubt that Japan must bear primary responsibility for what can only be objectively termed a war of aggression. Unfortunately, American and other Western scholars seem to dismiss these historical truths, whether out of ideological spite for the current regime in Beijing or out of concern that a full discussion of this crucial history could damage the US-Japan alliance.[21] The tendency to delegitimize Chinese perspectives on the basis that they are merely "seeking advantage" is unseemly and quite as ridiculous as suggesting that remembrances of the Holocaust or the Turkish brutality against the Armenians may be dismissed because they serve various political agendas. Western scholars, claiming that "enough is enough" when it comes to Tokyo's culpability for such atrocities themselves, do damage to China-Japan relations and demonstrate extraordinary insensitivity when comparing the "contrition chic" of adulterous presidents with responsibility for vast and horrific war crimes.[22] A spring 2013 commentary in a British magazine perceptively comments with respect to the infamous Yasukuni Shrine issue: "Imagine . . . if Angela Merkel were to get up one morning, put on her best togs, and make a state visit to a

German shrine that venerates Hitler. The world's outrage would be as nothing compared to the horrified reaction from Germans."[23]

The Cold War obscured these historical issues to a large extent. China was either in the chaos of Civil War or, two decades later, in the chaos of Mao Zedong's Cultural Revolution, so China was largely incapable of taking a coherent position with respect to war crimes and reparations. As Peter Gries explains: "Under Mao, there was little research on the history of Japanese aggression."[24] In between, the Korean War ensured that Beijing was totally estranged from the United States, the principal occupying power of Japan, and at the same time caused Washington to take a more lenient approach to Tokyo's historical responsibility in order to strengthen Tokyo's emergent role as a bastion of anticommunism in East Asia. Investigating the details of the US occupation of Japan, a 2011 study by a Chinese researcher concludes: "The Tokyo War Crimes Tribunal process . . . was at its core focused on the Pacific War, and [almost] completely neglected the facts of Japan's invasion of China, Korea, and other Asian neighboring states."[25]

According to a recent study of the Japan-China-US triangle by June Dreyer, Tokyo had originally sought to recognize the People's Republic of China (PRC) back in the early 1950s, but only agreed under pressure from US secretary of state John Foster Dulles to give sole recognition to the Republic of China on Taiwan. She observes: "Since Taiwan had been a successful colony of the Japanese empire, and Chiang Kai-shek an admirer of many aspects of Japanese society, the relationship between the two states [*sic*] was a comfortable one."[26] It is also interesting to note that even during the period of maximum estrangement during the Cold War, Tokyo and Beijing were still able to reach agreements, albeit informal, on issues of practical importance, such as those concerning fisheries.[27]

Tokyo was not pleased about the secretive nature of the Nixon–Kissinger overtures toward Beijing in the early 1970s, but Japan's opening to China followed very swiftly after the American example. On this news, "The Tokyo stock market leapt to record highs, . . . and there was much talk of a Sino-Japanese-US entente that would ensure the peace and stability of Asia."[28] It seems odd from the present vantage point, but the major sticking point of the landmark 1978 Treaty of Friendship was neither historical issues nor technology transfer, but rather concerned the Chinese preference that the treaty have wording regarding a common "anti-hegemony" position—a clause that Tokyo believed might unduly alarm Moscow. Ezra Vogel describes Deng Xiaoping's October 1978 visit to Japan as a seminal moment in the Sino-Japanese relationship. He writes: "[Deng] was . . . the first [Chinese leader] to meet the emperor of Japan. When Deng said that despite an unfortunate period during the twentieth century, the countries had enjoyed two millennia of good relations; . . . it touched the Japanese who know how much the Chinese had suffered from Japanese aggression and who deeply wanted to express their sorrow. . . . Many felt that at last the healing, some three decades after World War II, had begun."[29] For Deng, Japan represented such an essential partner because it could be a beacon of modernization and also a wellspring of ideas and investment to reform the troubled Chinese economy. As Paul Smith observes: "Beijing . . . enjoyed Tokyo's munificence in the form of overseas development assistance (ODA). Between 1979 and mid-2005, Tokyo disbursed more than $26.6 billion in loan aid, $1.23 billion in grant aid, and $1.23 billion in technical cooperation aid to the PRC."[30] With respect to Japanese ODA, Marie Söderberg explains that when Japan began to place political restrictions on ODA during the 1990s, this caused intense resentment, because the aid was viewed "partly as compensation for the war reparations that were never paid."[31]

During the 1980s, the Japan-China relationship witnessed impressive stability, but the initial construct of the revitalized relationship became unhinged during the 1990s, and major tensions were evident by the middle of the decade. The 1989 Tiananmen Square incident isolated China diplomatically, while the collapse of the Soviet Union in 1991 and the Persian Gulf War fueled additional anxiety in Beijing. It was the 1995–96 Taiwan Crisis, however, that seems to have made a major, chilling impact on China-Japan relations. From Tokyo's perspective, as one scholar related, "Japan has regarded Taiwan as the friendliest political entity toward Japan in Asia, if not in the world."[32] Japan also views Taiwan as located strategically astride its most crucial sea lanes. Conversely, it is also worth observing that some voices in Tokyo were deeply concerned by the possibility of "entrapment"—and not for the first time—the possibility that Japan could be pulled into an unwanted military conflict by its alliance with Washington.[33] For Beijing, the major concern was that the US-Japan alliance would be strengthened with the possibility of an enhanced role in any hypothetical Taiwan scenario. Tom Christensen observes, "By spring 1996, the Nye initiative [to strengthen and clarify the US-Japan alliance] had led to harsh reactions in China. . . . [Beijing now] feared that the United States would encourage Japan to adopt new military roles and develop new military capabilities."[34]

Tensions also surfaced concerning the Diaoyu/Senkaku Islands during the summer and fall of 1996, especially as groups of protesters from Hong Kong and Taiwan attempted to land on the Japan-administered islets. However, evidence suggests that in this case "China's leaders sought to quash expressions of anti-Japanese sentiment for fear that they would damage Sino-Japanese economic relations and might turn into antigovernment protests."[35] Just a couple of years later, Jiang Zemin's visit to Japan in 1998 did not go well, because "Prime Minister Keizo Obuchi refused to offer an apology to Jiang . . . that used the same contrite wording as the rather forthright apology Japan offered to South Korea earlier in the year."[36]

The tenure of Junichiro Koizumi as prime minister (2001–6) marked a new nadir for Japan-China relations. Koizumi was operating in a totally new political landscape. On one hand, the Japan Socialist Party had virtually imploded during the 1990s, removing the traditional pacifist bloc in Japanese politics.[37] On the other hand, the terrorist attacks of September 11, 2001, seemed to call Japan to take more visible action to support its stricken ally, the United States. Koizumi's initiatives to dispatch Japan Maritime Self-Defense Forces to the Arabian Gulf and also to send Japanese troops to Iraq raised suspicions in Beijing that Tokyo's support for the global war on terrorism might be used to alter Japanese constitutional restraints on the use of force abroad. However, it was Koizumi's repeated visits to the Yasukuni Shrine—where fourteen war criminals are also honored—that caused the most damage to the bilateral relationship. Meanwhile, the Taiwan issue continued to boil, with Tokyo dispatching a military attaché to Taipei in 2003, Diet members forming a "committee for the defense of Taiwan" in 2004, and US and Japanese officials jointly announcing in 2005 that Taiwan represented a "common defense concern."[38] As China began to drill for hydrocarbons on its side of the median line in the East China Sea during 2003, Japan shortly thereafter created a military plan to retake the Senkaku/Diaoyu Islands if seized by China.[39] The April 2005 anti-Japanese riots that occurred in several Chinese cities demonstrated the low point that had been reached in the bilateral relationship.

From Bad to Worse: China-Japan Relations on the Brink

From the vantage point of the tense relations prevailing in 2013–14, it is ironic that when Shinzo Abe replaced Koizumi as prime minister in 2006, this change appeared to herald a new era in China-Japan relations. In a somewhat remarkable symbolic act, Abe went to Beijing as his first trip abroad. Before Abe's trip in October 2006, the last China-Japan bilateral summit had occurred back in 2001. As one commentator reflected at that time: "[Abe's] election has brought the hope of a regional rapprochement."[40] This breakthrough was perhaps overshadowed a few days later by North Korea's first ever nuclear test, but that event only seemed to underline the importance of closer regional cooperation between East Asia's foremost powers. The possibilities for a genuine rapprochement between Tokyo and Beijing seemed especially ripe after a decade of skyrocketing commercial exchange, as bilateral trade increased by 239 percent during the period 1996–2006, compared with just 12 percent in US-Japan trade during the same period.[41] In 2007 Chinese visitors to Japan exceeded those from the United States to Japan for the first time.[42]

Abe's visit was not just symbolic and focused on the Korean Peninsula crisis, but also began to tackle some of the most difficult issues in China-Japan relations, including the sensitive history issue. Picking up on an earlier initiative for a trilateral historical study effort from a few years earlier, Chinese and Japanese leaders agreed to a bilateral process involving history scholars from both countries that met intermittently until 2010—a process that Western scholars appear to have ignored.[43] A recent Chinese scholarly study of the process initiated during the Abe visit concludes hopefully that some progress was achieved. This study also concludes that a significant difference between Japanese approaches to history and that of Chinese scholars concerns a Japanese tendency to focus on microscopic issues, while the Chinese tend to favor macroscopic issues. Very substantial differences of interpretation remain, of course—concerning, for example, whether the Nanjing Massacre was more a product of chance (偶然性) or rather inevitable (必然性) and the result of calculated plans. Learning from the French/German case, it is recommended that the textbook issue can be ameliorated if historians restrict themselves to presenting facts and allow students themselves to form their own opinions regarding the significance of those facts. Of particular importance for this book, it is germane to note that this Chinese scholar's very first statement suggests that Washington is partly responsible for the present problems in Sino-Japanese relations because "for the sake of controlling the Far East, the United States guided Japan's rise without a complete reckoning of its war responsibilities."[44]

According to research by James Reilly, the Chinese government had taken proactive steps to halt the slide into crisis for China-Japan relations: "They began by restraining negative media coverage of Japan, blocking anti-Japan content on the internet, and prohibiting all Japan-related protests."[45] Abe's visit to Beijing in the fall of 2006 paved the way for a spate of high-level visits in 2007–8. Chinese premier Wen Jiabao visited Japan in April 2007 and became the first Chinese leader ever to address the Japanese Diet. In his speech

Wen did focus on the history issue, asserting that "the deep scars left in the hearts of the Chinese people cannot be described."[46] When Abe's successor visited Beijing in December 2007, he told students at Peking University: "I would like to convey to all the Chinese people that I am of the firmest conviction that Japan and China should become creative partners who establish a bright future for both Asia and the globe."[47] Following Hu Jintao's visit to Japan in May 2008, a preliminary agreement on energy resource extraction in the East China Sea seemed to have been reached, a not insignificant achievement in the troubled bilateral relationship.

According to Richard Bush, Tokyo had partly sought an agreement because it feared that the start of production in China's Chunxiao field in 2007 could have meant that Japan was confronting a fait accompli. He explains that "Japan succeeded in rebuffing Chinese demands that the Senkaku/Diaoyu Islands be included [in the negotiations], in line with Tokyo's long-standing position that sovereignty over the islands had to be determined before economic cooperation was addressed." Still, Japan was apparently not satisfied with the agreement because the Chunxiao gas field was not offered up by the Chinese as a serious project for "joint development," though another site, the Longjing field that straddles the median line, was suggested for cooperative exploitation. According to James Manicom, the 2008 agreement "does not imply Chinese 'recognition' of the median line. It does, however, imply a degree of flexibility by China."[48]

Another aspect of the agreements from 2007–8 included a set of meetings between the Japan Coast Guard and China's State Oceanic Administration. This nonmilitary communication channel has been identified as crucial because these are frequently the respective bureaucracies controlling ships on patrol in the East China Sea. Unfortunately, these preliminary agreements seemed to fall apart rather quickly, and genuine implementation has stalled indefinitely, not least because of accusations of a "sellout" by conservatives in both Beijing and Tokyo.[49]

Aaron Friedberg takes a cynical view of the progress in China-Japan relations during the years 2006–8. He writes: "Having tried for over a decade to browbeat Japan into passivity, Beijing now had the resources, the self-confidence, and the skill to try to win it over with diplomacy and trade."[50] Indeed, it was not difficult to perceive that Washington's approach aligned with more hawkish elements in Tokyo. For example, "The Bush administration . . . gave quiet encouragement to those [Japanese] who favored constitutional reform . . . [to enable Japan] to send its armed forces far from home and to use them in support of joint military operations."[51] Thus, it is not surprising that new initiatives by the Japanese armed forces were taken with US assistance. The Japanese Air Self-Defense Forces, for example, visited Guam for the first time, allowing their pilots to drop live bombs for the first time ever.[52] The following year, the Japanese defense minister, Ishiba Shigeru, illustrated continuing suspicions regarding Chinese military modernization: "Japan tries to be transparent; . . . I want to see the same transparency from China as well."[53] When, in 2008, the Japan Air Self-Defense Force chief of staff was fired for an offensive essay that justified Japan's World War II campaign in China as a response to "Chinese Communist provocations," it seemed possible that anti-China sentiment existed quite widely in the Japanese armed forces.

The sweeping and unprecedented victory of the Democratic Party of Japan in parliamentary elections in mid-2009 momentarily, at least, raised fundamental questions about Japanese foreign policy. Simultaneously arguing for a restructuring of the US-Japan Alliance and also advocating closer Japan-China ties, Yukio Hatoyama and his party colleagues lacked foreign policy experience but were attempting to move Tokyo in a rather novel direction. From the perspective of Japan-China relations, the Democratic Party of Japan's ascendance seemed to herald a new era of opportunity. Indeed, Hatoyama's first visit to Beijing was made with significant fanfare and concomitant high expectations—which were likely destined to produce disappointment. Indeed, Hatoyama's golden era for China-Japan relations suddenly became just a golden moment as he was swept out of power in Tokyo just nine months after assuming leadership. The major cause of his precipitous exit was apparently his complete inability to deliver on campaign promises regarding US base realignment on Okinawa. In the aftermath of this curious episode, American commentators were inclined toward a triumphal attitude—regarding Hatoyama's views as rather naive.[54] And yet Americans more generally would be wise to reflect on the fact that the same man who had orchestrated a successful political revolution in Japan had in short order been forced to resign, given the problems surrounding one aspect of the US-Japan Alliance. To state the obvious: Hatoyama's premature exit suggests a major disconnect between prevailing political viewpoints in Japan and the emerging role of the alliance in Japanese foreign policy.

Shortly following this political drama in Tokyo, a major crisis developed in China-Japan relations during September 2010. The so-called Trawler Crisis occurred when a Chinese fishing trawler captain maneuvered aggressively against Japanese Coast Guard vessels in the vicinity of the Diaoyu/Senkaku

Islands. The Japan Coast Guard promptly arrested the trawler captain and his crew and impounded the ship. If this had been the end of the crisis, it would simply have resembled a string of similar incidents related to fisheries that have occurred over the last decades. But Beijing did not react well to what it considered to be the rough handling of the trawler and its crew. Not only did it demand their immediate release, but in an unusual step, China arrested a number of Japanese nationals working in China and threatened to pursue charges against them if the fishermen were not promptly released. More unprecedented still was the alleged effort by China to suddenly halt or at least radically slow the importing of rare earths into Japan. These materials were said to be of incredible importance to the health of Japan's economy and, moreover, Japan (and many other countries) had developed a severe dependence on China for imports in this crucial sector. Although Beijing has never confirmed that it deployed this economic leverage against Tokyo, credible Western sources believe that some kind of embargo was put in place, at least temporarily.[55] As Yves Tieberghien writes in a perceptive analysis of the crisis: "[After] China launched an all-out campaign against Japan, . . . Japan awkwardly buckled under the pressure." His analysis, moreover, yields the important conclusion that neither country had sought this test of wills intentionally, but rather it represented a "downward spiral of missed signals, . . . [resulting from] a dynamic interaction between two highly charged domestic political arenas."[56]

In retrospect, this particular incident seems to represent a watershed moment for East Asian security. In Japan sources inside the government released the video of the Chinese trawler appearing to ram a Japanese Coast Guard vessel. Release of this video on YouTube created a new scandal in Tokyo regarding alleged attempts to cover up the true nature of the incident. Particularly in the wake of Hatoyama's downfall, no one wanted to be accused of being "soft on China." Undoubtedly, the rare earths issue compounded fears regarding Japan's economic malaise compared with China's new economic prowess. China was widely assumed, including by decision makers in Washington, to be taking advantage of Japan's relative weakness. Indeed, a pivotal event occurred the following month, in October 2010, when Secretary of State Hillary Clinton visited Japan. In what arguably amounted to a departure from the US policy of neutrality regarding claims to the Diaoyu/Senkaku Islands, she used a technicality of the alliance treaty to assert that the alliance would indeed cover any disputes between China and Japan regarding the disputed claims in the East China Sea.[57] Whether intentionally or not, this seeming clarification of a previously more ambiguous position may in retrospect be seen as one of the first of a number of US geostrategic moves that could later be termed as the US "pivot" to the Asia-Pacific region.[58]

Since March 2011 Japan has been focused on recovery from the devastating earthquake, tsunami, and nuclear energy crisis that took a frightful toll on the island nation. The ultimate strategic and economic consequences of this massive disaster will not be clear for some time, but it is already obvious that the event has further shaken Japan's confidence at a time when the Japanese were already feeling increasingly uncertain about demographic, economic, and security trends. Chinese perceptions of Japan-China relations since 2010 have been relatively pessimistic. Although many Chinese analysts stress the vital importance of Japan-China cooperation for the global economy and the future East Asian order, undercurrents of suspicion seem to predominate, particularly because Tokyo is viewed as colluding with Washington's pivot in a grand design to contain Beijing.

Undoubtedly, the "hot economic relationship, cold political relationship" bespeaks some hopeful sentiment insofar as blossoming and ever-accelerating commercial ties have provided vital ballast to the otherwise volatile relationship. Chinese observers cite with evident pride that in 2002 China surpassed the United States as Japan's largest importer, while in 2007 the Japan-China trade volume exceeded that of Japan-US trade for the first time ever. In 2009 China became Japan's largest export destination. These trade ties create dense networks of interdependence that are amply evident in areas proximate to Japan—for example, in Dalian, where Chinese citizens have been reluctant to engage in anti-Japanese activities given the crucial role of China-Japan trade for that city's development.[59] And yet any major trading development inevitably also yields tensions. Thus, Chinese analysts are concerned about a major trade deficit with Japan, which reached a significant new crest of $55.6 billion in 2010, up 68 percent from 2009, according to Chinese figures. They are troubled that Japanese exports to China are high-value goods, whereas Chinese exports to Japan tend to be low-value and labor-intensive products, such as textiles. Also, the expanded market share for Chinese products is viewed as increasingly difficult. Finally, the Chinese perspective notes that Beijing proposed a free trade agreement with Japan back in 2005, but never received a Japanese response.[60]

The most current geo-economic considerations among the East Asian giants concern the prospects for the so-called Trans-Pacific Partnership (TPP) that is currently advocated by Washington. A paradox is identified by Chinese scholars, who point out that East Asia is the most dynamic region in the global economy, and yet the processes of regional economic integration are "hardly smooth." Regarding the TPP, it is noted that the reasons behind the initiative are not economic but rather political, related to foreign policy calculations and the "American factor" in particular. A Chinese game theoretic analysis of the impact of the TPP on the crucial China-Japan trading relationship yields findings that China and Japan are both better off if either both join the TPP or if both decline to join. Suboptimal outcomes for both economies apparently result if either Japan or China joins, but not both. Even though the analysis is emphatic that the TPP will not generally benefit East Asian economic integration, it is concluded that China and Japan are inextricably linked with respect to trade. A hope is articulated that at some point China and Japan will act like France and Germany in guiding regional economic development.[61]

On the security side, the picture is considerably bleaker, though not devoid of hopeful voices. One Chinese analysis, for example, advocates a China-Japan-South Korea forum as a new regional security model. According to this study, that particular trilateral framework proved useful in the context of the two major crises in 2010—both the trawler incident in the East China Sea and the sinking of the South Korean corvette *Cheonan*. Nontraditional security issues are seen as a key driver for this cooperation, though it is additionally noted that security cooperation on these issues may have significant spillover effects (溢出效应) into more traditional security domains among the three Northeast Asian powers.[62]

A study of Japanese strategy published in 2011 by a Chinese military author is revealing of deepening bilateral tensions in the wake of the 2010 incident in the East China Sea. In general the author maintains that Tokyo has used the incident to promulgate the "China threat theory," boosting military preparations and undertaking a spate of new military exercises as part of a broader strategy to "contain China." The analysis observes that Japanese official publications openly discuss a "China threat," which serves as a justification for a new defense buildup, including increasing Japanese submarine strength from sixteen to twenty-two boats, and also the general building up of forces on Japan's southern flank. It is, moreover, suggested that at least eighteen of the twenty-five joint projects resulting from the "2+2" talks with the United States in June 2011 were directed at countering China. The article additionally describes the "largest ever" joint military exercise between the United States and Japan, which was apparently held in December 2010. As this Chinese author notes, "That this exercise is directed against China is completely obvious." This paper also draws attention to the shift in US policy starting in October 2010 regarding the Diaoyu/Senkaku Islands. The shift from "ambiguous neutrality" to "small-scale intervention" and finally to "emphatic support" for the Japanese claim, according to this analysis, demonstrates Washington's intention to return to the Cold War strategy of the "island chain blockade strategy . . . in order to contain China's rise and damage the strategic environment for China's development." This Chinese author is not oblivious to the dangers in deepening China-Japan tensions, however, and he does make some concrete recommendations for crisis management mechanisms, including a hot line to directly connect coast guard forces operating in the East China Sea.[63]

A 2012 Chinese article examining the Japanese support for the US "return to Asia" also refers to the December 2010 Japanese-US joint exercise as unprecedented in scale, suggesting that this event received wide coverage in China, though it was not even mentioned in the leading US newspapers—a rather disturbing sign.[64] That article goes on to allege collaborative Japanese–American activities to contain China in the South China Sea, but also even in Africa.[65] According to a spring 2012 analysis by the noted People's Liberation Army (PLA) Navy commentator, Captain Li Jie, of the Beijing Naval Research Institute: "The US strategic shift to the East urgently required that Japan provoke a quarrel and create a disturbance. . . . [But] Japan also hopes to draw support from America's enormous power . . . in order to grasp its maritime interests."[66] He decries the "tired and passive reactions" that have hindered China's realization of its maritime rights in the past and—along with research, legal, and enforcement means—he warns that Beijing cannot neglect the appropriate military preparations.[67] Other scholarly writings indicated a widely perceived hardening of Tokyo's outlook toward Beijing.[68] Another paper that illustrates the pessimism among China's specialists on Japan is a study published by the China Academy of Social Sciences, in which the author argues that a "maritime faction" is having an increasingly important influence on Japan's policy toward both the United States and China. According to this analysis, Japan's "maritime faction" believes that (1) maritime states will be challenged by a powerful nation on the Eurasian landmass, (2) that maritime states must form an alliance, and (3) that the maritime states must form a strategic ring of encirclement along the borders of the Eurasian landmass. It is said that these thinkers in Japan reject any cultural association with China and are concerned that China's rise may be quite comparable to that of Germany a century ago.[69]

As discussed at the outset of this chapter, the fall of 2012 witnessed a considerable escalation of the East China Sea dispute. Overall, this escalation has been occasioned by Beijing's dispatch of coast guard vessels to patrol the disputed region in the vicinity of the Diaoyu/Senkaku Islands. From the Chinese perspective, this step was prompted by Japan's initiative to transfer sovereignty of the islets from private to government hands. From the Japanese perspective, the deployment of Chinese patrol vessels appears to be a heavy-handed attempt to alter the status quo. Although this confrontation, which has continued well into 2014, has generally pitted nonmilitary vessels against one another, a couple of troubling incidents between military forces have also occurred in the same area.[70] With the current unsettled political climate in both Beijing and Tokyo, moreover, there is little doubt that the escalating conflict is, at least in part, fueled by internal political dynamics in each capital.

Not surprisingly, Chinese analyses of the unfolding situation are almost universally pessimistic and hawkish in tone. For instance, an article appearing in the influential 学习时报 (*Study Times*) in mid-2013 that examined the US-Japan-China strategic triangle sharply criticizes Japan's behavior as "extremely childish," and likewise asserts that "the US is happy to see certain countries challenge China. These countries serve as American 'pawns' in the effort to contain China." Even as the author calls for greater regional cooperation, he asserts that East Asia has become a region plagued by the risk of interstate war.[71] Suggestive of the internal political dynamics of the unfolding tensions in the East China Sea, prominent pictures of Chinese and Japanese cutters in the contested sea zones constituted front page news in China during the spring of 2013.[72] A PLA Navy captain publicly blamed Washington for the ongoing tensions in the East China Sea, and Chinese military analysts studied the practice of bumping among naval vessels as a tactic in military diplomacy.[73] In the cover story in a naval-affiliated journal from mid-2013, a Chinese analyst claimed that although Japan was accelerating coast guard cutter construction and also transferring some older military vessels into the Japan coast guard, China would, nevertheless, soon have the advantage in numbers.[74] General Luo Yuan, writing in 环球时报 (*Global Times*), anxiously criticized a tendency to follow European pacifist trends that could lead China toward the spread in China of "不抵抗主义" (no resistance-ism).[75]

However, another 2013 analysis by a scholar from the Central Party School suggests that such hard-line viewpoints toward the present crisis in China-Japan relations are widespread in Beijing. In this early review of the Abe administration's policy toward China, the analyst comes to the dire conclusion that "the Japanese government's strategic . . . judgments and . . . goals demonstrate that [Tokyo] regards the rejuvenation of the Chinese nation and the development of its power as a threat to Japanese interests." This analysis frets that Japan is now openly discussing nuclear weaponry and also preemptive strategies. Ultimately, this scholar suggests that a "2:1" (e.g., Japan + the United States vs. China) is not a stable structure of power, and says emphatically that Beijing is "unwilling to allow excessive US intervention in China-Japan bilateral issues."[76] There are moderate Chinese voices on the issue of China-Japan relations, but they are distinctly in the minority.[77]

Late 2013 witnessed yet another significant escalation in Japan-China tensions, as Beijing formally declared in November that it was creating an air defense identification zone (ADIZ) over the East China Sea. Chinese strategists defended the new designation as a "proactive and effective protection against air threats coming from the seaward direction [thus forming] . . . an important link in China's air defense security."[78] However, neither Tokyo nor Washington proved amenable to this argumentation. Not long after the ADIZ was declared, US secretary of defense Chuck Hagel condemned the Chinese initiative "as a destabilizing attempt to alter the status quo in the region."[79] In a less than subtle exercise of continuing US military might, two American bombers then flew directly through the new ADIZ and were not challenged. Preferring the pen to the sword, at least for now, Chinese analysts writing in the official magazine of the Chinese Air Force countered in early 2014 that the United States has the world's largest complex of ADIZs and that Japan's ADIZ (dating from 1969) "is a mere 130 kilometers from China's shoreline" and covers most of the East China Sea. Defending Beijing's action in this case, they note that "[creating an ADIZ] does not alter the nature of international airspace, . . . does not mean an expansion of territorial airspace, . . . [and] certainly is not a no-fly zone."[80]

China-Japan relations continued to spiral downward into the abyss. Appearing at the prestigious Davos World Economic Forum in early 2014, Prime Minister Abe compared the emergent China-Japan rivalry to that between Britain and Germany on the eve of World War I. Predictably, the Chinese did not embrace Abe's historical analogy. For example, one Chinese commentator observed with some irony that Japan had spent the years 1914–18 actively dismembering China (including valuable parts of Shandong Province), with the blessing of the Western powers. However, this critic goes much further, and even compares Abe to Hitler in the Japanese leader's eagerness to alter

Japan's peace Constitution, and also his alleged tendency to lean on nationalism in domestic politics.[81] Also writing in the wake of new tensions fueled by the ADIZ declaration, the Chinese military commentator Li Daguang similarly underlined the threat posed by Abe's determination to press constitutional reform and warned that Tokyo was now pursuing "offensive" and also "long-range" weaponry.[82] Another frequent commentator on strategic affairs, General Peng Guangqian (PLA, retired), writing in an important Chinese academic journal in early 2014, decried Washington's current tendency to have Tokyo do its bidding in the region and warned that "the threat of war becomes more urgent each day!"[83]

It is beyond the scope of this volume to thoroughly investigate Japan's current perceptions of China, but this rendering of Chinese perceptions of Japan and also of the US-Japan alliance clearly reveals a rather acute perception of threat, as well as grave pessimism regarding the direction of the relationship—which is all the more disappointing given some possible signs of progress in the relationship during the years 2006–9.[84] Nevertheless, it bears repeating that some Chinese analysts continue to call for restraint and hope to reform the dangerous instability that currently characterizes the US-Japan-China triangle. Just before the ADIZ controversy, for example, Ren Xiao, director of Fudan University's Center for the Study of Chinese Foreign Policy, bravely and very publicly noted that Japan was gaining much sympathy around the world in present circumstances, in part because it had provided ample "public goods" to the world, for example, by supporting the United Nations.[85] Likewise, an impressively nonconformist article was featured as the lead piece in an early 2014 issue of the Chinese academic journal 日本学刊 (*Japanese Studies*). The author, Shi Yinhong, of People's University in Beijing, does warn of the "right deviation" in Japan's politics and also especially regarding Tokyo's military development. However, Shi also notes that pursuing the isolation of Japan cannot be an end in itself, and that China's complex internal political situation is also partially responsible for the poor state of China-Japan relations. He boldly reminds readers in his conclusion that the "island dispute" (岛争) hardly encompasses the whole of China-Japan relations.[86] Such candid statements from Chinese experts certainly support the hope that there remain unexplored domains and paradigms for compromise in China-Japan relations.

Skepticism abounds regarding the future of Japan-China relations, but one may hope that the recent Xi-Abe meeting, however brief and awkward, may begin a serious process of reconciliation and rapprochement. As one Chinese academic explains, "China has always wanted to be the leader of the Asia-Pacific. To achieve this, it needs the endorsement of Japan. . . . If China wants its policy to go smoothly in Asia, it needs the cooperation of Japan."[87] Unquestionably, the fact that both sides seemed to have different interpretations of the bilateral agreement reached between the two leaders at APEC is not a good sign. Nevertheless, the fact that both sides had agreed to develop a maritime "crisis management mechanism" is a positive step. The fact that the influential scholar Wang Jisi of Peking University has been urging a new approach to China-Japan relations is another good sign.[88] For diplomats coping with the delicate task of bridging the gaping mistrust that now characterizes Japan-China relations and the complex US-China-Japan triangle, a focus on small and tentative first steps—while simultaneously keeping the long-term, more ambitious steps firmly in mind as well—may provide the proper perspective for achieving progress in this relationship that must form the keystone for Asia-Pacific peace in the twenty-first century.

A Cooperation Spiral for the China-Japan-US Triangle

The long, troubled Sino-Japanese relationship is especially ripe for realizing the benefits of a cooperation spiral. This is because the number of actors is not high, but more especially because there are few actual genuine conflicts of interest among Beijing and Tokyo. Both powers seek a stable and prosperous Asia-Pacific region, so that the issues dividing them tend to concern either symbolic politics or the related problem of mistrust, including an evident tendency toward worst case thinking. Michael Yahuda writes: "Neither appears to take into account the national security interests of the other."[89] The United States can help to change this dangerous situation by facilitating a cooperation spiral in this deeply troubled triangular relationship (figure 9.1).

Washington's move 1 on China-Japan relations: The United States should endeavor to decrease the US military presence on Okinawa. In fact, this process is already under way, as some 10,000 US Marines are planned to depart the island over the next two years as part of the base realignment plan agreed to by Tokyo and Washington in 2006.[90] As noted above, the lingering Okinawa issue is a major destabilizing element in the US-Japan Alliance, so much so that the alliance has become a significant issue in Tokyo's domestic politics and even recently precipitated the downfall of Prime Minister Hatoyama. Moreover, the late 2014 election of an "anti-base" governor in Okinawa confirms that the issue is not likely to fade away, as many in Tokyo and Washington

Figure 9.1 Cooperation Spiral: The United States–Japan–China Triangle 合作螺旋：美日中三边关系

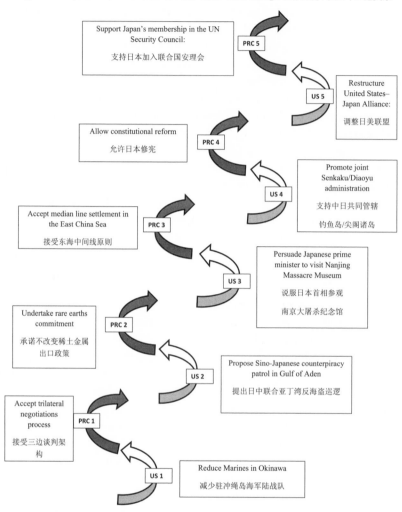

would no doubt prefer. The alignment of forces away from Okinawa is a long-overdue corrective to an unfortunate earlier policy. However, Washington has not realized the full strategic benefits of this realignment. Recognizing that (1) the Marines are not especially well suited for the high-intensity air/sea combat scenarios of East Asia; and (2) that apparently, Australia is now available as a staging area for the Marines, the forces on Okinawa can be cut even further. Yet another strategic rationale for scaling back the US presence on Okinawa is the declining utility of its fixed facilities and airfields, which are now wholly vulnerable to adversary precision missiles and air strikes—an inviting target for preemption—and thus quite destabilizing overall. And yet the proximity of Okinawa to Taiwan would enable the United States to claim that further reductions in the force size at Okinawa were related to declining tensions across the Taiwan Strait. This move, coupled with a linkage to the Taiwan issue, would not only ease tensions in Japanese politics but would also certainly get Beijing's attention with a powerful suggestion that the United States was willing to make hard choices in order to facilitate progress toward a genuine Japan-China rapprochement. Moreover, this step should also initiate a generally more independent foreign policy direction for Tokyo that would benefit Japanese, regional, and global politics. As White writes perceptively: "Japan [is] in the untenable situation of relying for its security on an adversarial relationship between its two most important international partners; . . . the only clear way for Japan to get out of this predicament is to stop relying on America for protection from China."[91]

Beijing's move 1 on China-Japan relations: China should begin to participate in a trilateral summit process with both the United States and Japan. Many leading policy analysts—for example, Michael Swaine—advocate for "minilaterals" to cope with the many economic and security challenges of the Asia-Pacific region.[92] Though the region may ultimately have "too many dialogues" at this point, and this book is somewhat wary about the simple prescription that dialogue will automatically lead to compromise, this particular forum could be uniquely significant and thus deserves special attention. In fact, all sides had already agreed to go ahead with this forum in 2009, when Beijing suddenly "postponed indefinitely."[93] The forum would have the obvious advantage that it is small enough that substance could dominate, and the expectation is that genuine negotiations over tough issues could occur. At a minimum, this dialogue would involve the three largest powers in the Asia-Pacific region. The unusual format could also serve to break the logjams that have often forestalled bilateral meetings among these key actors. Indeed, the not-so-subtle role that Washington should play at such meetings would be not only to reassure the other parties but also to pressure both sides toward mutual accommodation. The reality of this forum's format, however, suggests that it would be difficult for Beijing, which may risk isolation and coming under pressure from the "united front" presented by the US-Japan Alliance. And yet this could form a major opportunity for China to present itself as a "normal" big power, and it may serve as a forum to engage in frank dialogue about the US-Japan alliance and some of China's related concerns. Although Beijing's agreement to actively participate would have an important symbolic value, to succeed the dialogue would need to be iterated over many years in order to build the necessary trust among senior leaders. In this case, it may be wise to take the counsel of the Chinese scholar Wang Jisi and begin trilateral negotiations on less sensitive issues, such as alternative energy sources and energy efficiency.[94]

Washington's move 2 on China-Japan relations: The United States should encourage Japan and China to cooperate in their antipiracy patrols in the Gulf of Aden. The multinational naval effort against piracy in the Gulf of Aden has been cited by many as a potentially important mission for fostering naval cooperation. Though the cost/benefit analysis for the operations as a whole is somewhat open to question, there is no doubt that the threat of piracy is felt by all the major maritime powers. Indicative of a major shift in Chinese national security policy, Beijing elected to send its first small flotilla to the Gulf of Aden in December 2008. Not coincidentally, Tokyo dispatched a similar force to the same area a few months later. Since then, both nations have impressively sustained these efforts, demonstrating together with South Korea that the East Asian powers could make essential contributions to international security in protecting global trade routes. Regarding this development, a senior Pentagon official during the Bush administration is quoted by Richard Bush: "It took Beijing 'about ten seconds' to decide to join the antipiracy effort, he said, with some hyperbole. That Japan took months was 'not bad, but sad.'"[95] This observation actually betrays an all-too-common but rather misguided approach in Washington's assessment of the issue. Rather than fostering competition and disparaging the Japanese for their legitimate inhibitions, US officials would do well to put aside competitive instincts and try to facilitate greater Japan-China military cooperation. Given that Japan and China share nearly identical interests in that region—maintaining vital trade flows—it would be logical for them to cooperate more fully. The importance of the Gulf of Aden as an incubator of naval cooperation is clearly magnified in this case because restraining China-Japan naval competition is so integral to fostering the Asia-Pacific region's peace and stability.

Beijing's move 2 on China-Japan relations: China must agree not to leverage its commercial advantage in rare earth minerals against Japan for political advantage. Unlike the three steps given above, this one would be rather difficult, not least because Beijing does not openly admit to employing such leverage during the 2010 Senkaku/Diaoyu trawler crisis. New research published by Iain Johnston, moreover, casts fresh doubt on whether Beijing really intended to undertake an embargo on rare earths exports to Japan.[96] Whether intentional or not, however, China's reputation, especially in Japan, suffered a major blow. The 2010 Trawler Crisis and the related rare earth controversy can be interpreted as a significant misstep in Beijing's diplomacy because they resulted eventually in the precipitous downfall of the seemingly pro-Chinese prime minister, Hatoyama. Specifically concerning the rare earths issue, Japan's most acute anxiety with respect to China concerns the economic realm, whereas China's recent success has contrasted markedly with poor Japanese economic performance, not to mention the additional challenge of coping with the tsunami and nuclear disaster of early 2011. Therefore, Beijing's alleged deployment of means of "economic warfare" was especially troubling in Japan.[97] Theoretically, markets will eventually adjust as other powers, including the United States, move to balance China's market control. But Japan's high-technology manufacturing will continue to be dependent on China's rare earths for the foreseeable future. Indeed, a spring 2014 assessment suggests that China continues to maintain its dominance of global rare earths markets. The author suggests that current developments point "to the significant advantage China holds in the REE [rare earth element] domain: a competitive presence across the entire REE value chain in addition to very well surveyed and cost-effective mines." Moreover, the same analysis yields that attempts by Japan to form a special rare earths supply relationship with India have not gone smoothly.[98] Therefore, some measured steps by Beijing to recognize a possible earlier mistake will go a long way toward soothing anxieties in Tokyo. To be sure, it is unlikely that stalwart mechanisms could be put in place to credibly "guarantee" that China would not resort to such measures again. However, as with other aspects of this relationship, symbols are of paramount importance, and here a symbolic gesture by Beijing (addressing fear, if not facts) could prompt even more ambitious symbolic gestures by Tokyo to examine much graver historical errors.

Washington's move 3 on China-Japan Relations: Washington must push Tokyo to prompt a breakthrough on the "history issue" with a prime minister's visit to Nanjing and the initiation of negotiations on reparations. Most analysts of China-Japan relations acknowledge the importance of the history issue but treat it as a minor point to be managed. Bush suggests that "Japan's degree of penitence has been far less than that of Germany, the best point of comparison," but he concludes that history must be taken off the table for the present in order to "start with easier matters" and he offers no concrete recommendations on the history issue.[99] To be sure, many Japanese leaders have paid lip service to the issue of making amends for wartime atrocities and damages. The apology by Prime Minister Tomiichi Murayama from the fiftieth anniversary of the war's end in 1995, for example, is often cited by defenders of Japan's current stance regarding history.[100] However, it seems plain that a vague, five-paragraph statement (only one of which is actually dedicated to remorse) that does not even make any mention of China specifically, but rather simply refers to "many nations, . . . particularly Asian nations," would hardly suffice to answer for the deaths of 14 to 15 million Chinese. By contrast, a "Willy Brandt" solution is advocated here, in which the Japanese prime minister takes the "bull by the horns" and grapples with it directly.[101] Contemporary Chinese analyses of China-Japan relations continue to give a high profile to the historical issue and also make note of the positive German example for Japan.[102] As Gilbert Rozman observes: "Japan has failed to bolster its claims to leadership by . . . setting a high moral tone in its treatment of history."[103] To try to make amends properly and emphatically, a Japanese leader would need to do so in Nanjing—site of the most despicable atrocities. Such a trip would have a major potential to significantly alter the character of Japan-China relations. Hatoyama's revolutionary victory for the Democratic Party of Japan in 2009 shows that the wider Japanese body politic may even support an initiative to "reset" relations with China, especially if they understand that such moves will not jeopardize, but rather enhance, security ties with the United States. The visit to Nanjing, difficult as that might be to pull off, will not be enough, and thoughtful reflections on this matter will yield the conclusion that the process, best institutionalized, will have no end point. Indeed, reparations will be an essential component to the accommodation process, as they have been in the German case, where more than $62 billion has been paid out to victims.[104] It is often said that Japan's generosity with loans since 1979 may be considered as reparations, but this is actually misleading. Japanese companies have benefited enormously from these loans, and Japan has also gained a vital position in China's dynamic market from them.[105] These were good investments, plain and simple, and should not be confused with reparations, which have no relation to corporations or financial gain, but genuinely express contrition in a material way. The scholar Reinhard Drifte, who himself praises Tokyo for its generosity with the ODA given to Beijing, has to concede in an article about the 2005 suspension of Japan ODA that "the Japanese government can also not be interested in losing a creditor which so far had always punctually repaid its loans to Japan. This cannot be said of Indonesia; . . . China with its excellent repayment record will be difficult to replace."[106] A useful precedent for US involvement in the East Asian history issue was a 2006 US congressional resolution urging Japan to recognize the rights of South Korean comfort women. The Chinese press observed with great interest, moreover, how, in the spring of 2013, new South Korean president Park Guen-hye successfully pressed the Obama administration to take the history issue more seriously.[107] As recently as the summer of 2013, Beijing has drawn attention to the important US role in the history issue that starkly divides China and Japan.[108] As recently as December 2014, the *New York Times* has seen fit to run an editorial criticizing Tokyo's apparent effort to "whitewash history."[109] Conversely, it is also encouraging, as James Reilly illustrates, that the Chinese leadership has also made efforts to encourage the Chinese people to "remember history, not hatred," even at such sensitive sites as the newly renovated and expanded museum dedicated to the Nanjing Massacre.[110] However, US reluctance to call Japan to account for much more egregious crimes in China (vice those that occurred in South Korea) now imperils the fundamental US interest in facilitating peace and security in the Asia-Pacific region.

Beijing's move 3 on China-Japan relations: China must reign in nationalists on the East China Sea issue, agreeing to the "equidistance" principle overall. Two valid principles for maritime jurisdiction are in competition in the East China Sea dispute, with Beijing favoring the "natural extension of the continental shelf," while Tokyo supports the principle of equidistance for delimiting maritime boundaries. Although the natural extension argument has been recognized by other states (and is often advocated by the United States), Beijing must yield to some extent on this issue, with the recognition that the equidistance principle is widely employed among disputants and is hardly unjust. In effect, China has already endorsed the equidistance principle by only exploring and drilling exclusively on its side of the midpoint line, for example, with its Chunxiao gas field.[111] No doubt, these negotiations will be arduous and painful, but the processes undertaken during the years 2006–9 do suggest that movement is actually possible. The negotiations could also be helped out by "codes of conduct" for air, naval, and coast guard forces in the sensitive region on the pattern of that reached between the United States and China in November 2014—and perhaps also by a general commitment on both sides to demilitarize the contested area.

Washington's move 4 on China-Japan relations: The United States must encourage Japan to accept "joint jurisdiction" regarding the Diaoyu/Senkaku islet dispute.

While gaining the equidistance principle, Tokyo will need to concede the Senkaku/Diaoyu Islands as an area of "joint jurisdiction."[112] Japanese leaders should be willing to concede that point if Chinese leaders have given up the natural extension principle. It is abundantly clear that these islets have the potential to foment major tensions between Beijing and Tokyo, as was evident in the course of 2012 and 2013. It is certainly true that various Chinese scholarly discussions regarding the history and sovereignty of Okinawa only further inflamed tensions by playing on the worst fears of the Japanese regarding the island dispute.[113] However, a kind of restraint still prevails in the policies of both Japan and China. For its part, Tokyo has not sought to occupy the islets; nor, it seems, has it even seriously considered the provocative step of deploying military forces for their defense. And though China's actions in 2012–13 represent an escalation of sorts, Beijing's institutionalization of regular patrols near the islets has been accomplished by unarmed cutters—hardly the most aggressive step that Beijing's leaders could contemplate. Recent US historical scholarship on the various contending claims regarding the Okinawa Reversion Agreement of 1971 has yielded the finding that Washington had formerly designed a kind of "neutrality doctrine" to govern its policy in the East China Sea.[114] *New York Times* columnist Nicholas Kristof, moreover, likely reflects the broader ambivalence among US foreign policy experts regarding the evolving East China Sea confrontation: "In reality, of course, there is zero chance that the United States will honor its treaty obligation over a few barren rocks. We're not going to risk a nuclear confrontation with China over some islands that may well be China's."[115] At present there are no ongoing negotiations, because Tokyo refuses to recognize that a dispute actually exists. Washington must use its influence to initiate these negotiations, which once begun will logically lead to a joint jurisdiction solution.

Beijing's move 4 on China-Japan relations: Beijing should acquiesce to constitutional revision in Japan regarding the role of the Japanese armed forces. Any discussion with Chinese specialists regarding relations and concerns about Japan invariably turns to the subject of Japanese constitutional revision. Article 9 of the Japanese Constitution states explicitly that "the Japanese people forever renounce war as a sovereign right of the nation; . . . [and to that end], . . . land, sea, and air forces, as well as other war potential, will never be maintained."[116] Of course, the reality is that, since 1954, Japan has interpreted this article to mean that it can maintain "self-defense forces." Indeed, among defense analysts, Japan's armed forces are held to be extremely well equipped and capable, even if they do not call themselves "military forces." As a practical matter, Article 9 mainly serves as a political football within Japanese politics, and occasionally may serve to roil US-Japan relations and also China-Japan relations, of course. In terms of weaponry and also employment doctrine, it may have an impact on outcomes on the margins, for example, regarding the lack of land-attack cruise missiles and/or the types of joint exercises that can be performed in cooperation with US forces. China's concerns about Japanese constitutional revision are entirely logical and quite reasonable. However, given the proposed steps to be undertaken by both sides, as outlined above, including the settlement of the main historical and territorial issues, it seems that Beijing could as a result drop all objections to constitutional revision in Tokyo. In that case, Japanese conservatives would be mollified; the issue would no longer poison China-Japan relations; Japan could more easily become involved in global security initiatives; and, finally, the obvious right of self-defense would be clarified. More broadly, such a policy step by Beijing would signal a full acceptance of Tokyo as a "normal country" with legitimate defense concerns and one that must work in partnership with Beijing to ensure peace and security in East Asia and beyond.

Washington's move 5 on China-Japan relations: The United States must move to restructure the US-Japan Alliance, decreasing its salience in recognition of the security dilemma. American analysts have frequently said that China appreciates the US-Japan Alliance because it constrains Japanese defense ambitions and most crucially maintains Japan's nonnuclear status.[117] In this formulation, the alliance prevents the "spiral" conflict result of the security dilemma that might otherwise result from China's growth. This reasoning is outdated, if not entirely obsolete. Since 1995 the capabilities and preparedness of the US-Japan Alliance have been ratcheted up to such an extent that the alliance itself is now triggering a security dilemma that reflects Beijing's acute security anxieties. From China's point of view, it faces not only the prospect of confrontation with the militarily superior United States but also the possibility of being bullied by a United States that is supported and backed up substantially by Japanese military might. These anxieties are amply demonstrated in the articles summarized earlier in this chapter. Many American analysts believe that this striking "imbalance of power" has vital deterrent effects. However, they do not seem to realize that the same imbalance is feeding China's vast appetite for new and more capable military systems. As Hugh White writes: "As long as Japan acts solely in support of America, America is made too strong for China to accept."[118] In order to mitigate the security dilemma in this case, certain steps can be taken to lower the salience of the alliance relationship, including decreasing the relevant deployed US forces and also the pace of exercises. With progress on both the historical issue and also the maritime territorial issue, these steps toward scaling back the alliance would be appropriate and consistent with Japanese security requirements. Such a development would not necessarily cause "Japanese strategy . . . [to] become highly volatile," as some experts have recently forecast.[119] The relationship between Tokyo and Washington might actually come to resemble a more normal alliance relationship—for example, that between the United States and Turkey or that between the United States and Norway, both countries that are proximate to a large neighbor. Let us be clear: The alliance would remain intact, up to and including nuclear guarantees (a special sensitivity), but it could be reduced in significance to reflect the fact that Japan is, in fact, rather secure from external threats. For Tokyo, the restructured alliance would not only lessen the political and economic burdens of current arrangements but would also significantly improve ties with Beijing, and thus allow for the kind of coleadership role in the Asia-Pacific region that is appropriate for Japan.

Beijing's move 5 on China-Japan relations: China must endorse a permanent seat for Japan on the United Nations Security Council. Both China and the United States have come around to a new appreciation of the United Nations, and especially the effective functioning of the UN Security Council (UNSC). Although China has viewed the UN as a useful check on American "hegemony," Washington has been chastened by troublesome unilateral military interventions and is now more inclined toward multilateralism and burden-sharing. For the United States, Japan's entry into the UNSC is clearly beneficial, and Washington is on record supporting this aim.[120] Of course, China is much more reluctant—whether because it will dilute the value of China's vote, because it will suggest that East Asia has more than one leader, or because Beijing fears that Japan will collude endlessly with the United States and other Western powers to further isolate China in the UNSC's deliberations. And yet the UNSC clearly needs further reforms to become effective, and Japanese participation will help give the UNSC additional credibility, as well as enhanced capabilities. Undoubtedly, this would represent a major concession by China to genuinely accept Japan's status as a great power. However, given the proposed Japanese concessions outlined above—including the history issue, the US-Japan Alliance, and joint jurisdiction over the Senkaku/Diaoyu Islands—it is not unreasonable to expect China to offer up such a major "carrot." Indeed, this carrot will be essential to incentivizing Tokyo to pursue a more normal relationship with Beijing.

Conclusion

China-Japan relations have long been stuck in the paradigm of "hot economics, cold politics." To an extent, this reality reflects the complementary aspects of the two economies, but also the natural fears engendered by China's rapid development. What is especially troubling is that the bilateral relationship, already quite strained, seems to have taken a significant turn for the worse since 2010. The possibility of a clash in the East China Sea can hardly be ruled out when armed and paramilitary forces are interacting in bellicose ways on a daily basis. Putting the most cynically realist argument aside—that Washington may seek to benefit from such tensions—enlightened readers will agree with the commonsense conclusion that the United States should not condone increasing tensions between the major powers of East Asia.

The hands-off approach to China-Japan relations has not yielded any significant improvement and seems even to be exacerbating a downward spiral in this crucial relationship. And yet Washington has enormous influence in both Tokyo and Beijing and may seek to build on the foundation—however tentative—that was achieved in the run-up to the November 2014 APEC Summit in Beijing. A well-constructed and genuinely fair process of reconciliation that features concessions on both sides could be employed by Washington to make significant progress in the China-Japan relationship. In particular, Washington must push Tokyo to reexamine and make amends for historical grievances. Japan must also be more flexible in the East China Sea, and a bottom-up review of the US-Japan alliance will be the natural result of improving China-Japan relations. For its part, Beijing will find that prioritizing good relations with Japan will ease tensions throughout the Asia-Pacific region, including with the United States. It must also make major concessions to realize progress, including disavowing the resort to "economic warfare," recognizing the equidistance principle in the East China Sea, and ultimately agreeing to grant Japan a well-deserved permanent seat on the UNSC. The salience of improved China-Japan relations, both for the health and effectiveness of US-China relations and for global order more generally, cannot be overstated.

Notes

1. See, for example, Adam Liff, "Calm in the East China Sea?: What to Make of Shinzo Abe and Xi Jinping's Recent Meeting," *National Interest*, November 12, 2014, http://nationalinterest.org/blog/the-buzz/calm-the-east-china-sea-what -make-shinzo-abe-xi-jinpings-11656.

2. Michael McDevitt, *Sino-Japanese Rivalry: Implications for US Policy*, Institute for National Strategic Studies Special Report (Washington, DC: National Defense University, 2007), 1.

3. 章骞 [Zhang Qian], "日本自卫队将领谈日本'岛屿防卫" [JMSDF Admiral Discusses Japan's "Defense of Islets"], 现代舰船 [Modern Ships], June 2013, 13.

4. Michael D. Swaine, Mike M. Mochizuki, Michael L. Brown, Paul S. Giarra, Douglas H. Paal, Rachel Esplin Odell, Raymond Lu, Oliver Palmer, and Xu Ren, *China's Military and the US-Japan Alliance in 2030: A Strategic Net Assessment* (Washington, DC: Carnegie Endowment for International Peace, 2013), xxi.

5. See, e.g., Andrew Nathan and Andrew Scobell, *China's Search for Security* (New York: Columbia University Press, 2012), 119. They write: "The failure of the imperial strategy proved that Japan could not assure its security on its own." There are many lessons that one could draw from Japan's experience in World War II, but the proposition that Japan is inherently indefensible exaggerates the nature of the problem. Japan was overwhelmed in World War II, because of its imprudent and unwise diplomatic and military strategies.

6. McDevitt, *Sino-Japanese Rivalry*, 6.

7. See, e.g., Gabriele Fahr-Becker, ed., *The Art of East Asia* (Potsdam: Tandem Verlag, 2006), 500.

8. The Mongols, who were proficient in mobile warfare on the vast plains of Eurasia, likely drew upon Chinese Song Dynasty maritime and engineering prowess to launch this invasion fleet. See Louise Levathes, *When China Ruled the Sea: The Treasure Fleet of the Dragon Throne 1405–1433* (New York: Simon & Schuster, 1994), 48–54.

9. Henry Kissinger, *On China* (New York: Penguin Press, 2011), 79.

10. See the discussion regarding Charles DeLong and also General Charles LeGendre given by James Bradley, *The Imperial Cruise: A Secret History of Empire and War* (Boston: Little, Brown, 2009), 184–90.

11. Kissinger, *On China*, 85.

12. See *Illustration of the Decapitation of Violent Chinese Soldiers by Utagawa Kokunimasa*, October 1894, Sharf Collection, Museum of Fine Arts, Boston, MIT Visualizing Cultures, http://ocw.mit.edu/ans7870/21f/21f.027/throwing _off_asia_02/toa_essay04.html.

13. 陈锦华 [Chen Jinhua], *中日关系大事辑览* [Comprehensive Survey of Major Events in China-Japan Relations] (Beijing: People's University Press, 2011), 32.

14. Iris Chang, *The Rape of Nanking: The Forgotten Holocaust of World War II* (New York: Penguin, 1997), 4. A summary of the debate surrounding this book is given

by Peter Gries, *China's New Nationalism: Pride, Politics, and Diplomacy* (Berkeley: University of California Press, 2004), 82–85. An impressively balanced appraisal of Chang's book is made by Daqing Yang, "Review Essay: Convergence or Divergence? Recent Historical Writings on the Rape of Nanjing," *American Historical Review* 104, no. 3 (June 1999): 842–65. This author also shows an impressive and fair acquaintance with current Japanese-language primary and secondary sources, as well as Chinese-language scholarship on the issue.

15. Chen, *Comprehensive Survey*, 46. Peter Gries does an admirable job of surveying Chinese writings, generally from the 1990s, regarding China's evolving historical memory of Japan's aggression; Gries, *China's New Nationalism*. Gries discusses Chinese calculations regarding casualty figures, but not in great detail. He shows that they have tended to increase substantially over the passing years, dating the latest official figure to one given by Jiang Zemin in 1995 (pp. 80-81).

16. Rana Mitter, *Forgotten Ally: China's World War II, 1937–1945* (Boston: Houghton Mifflin, 2013), 5.

17. See the comments by William R. Dodd, US ambassador to Berlin, quoted in ibid., 142.

18. Ibid., 139.

19. Ibid., 142.

20. Ibid., 10, 378.

21. See, e.g., Richard C. Bush, *Perils of Proximity: China-Japan Security Relations* (Washington, DC: Brookings Institution Press, 2011), 6–11. In this generally detailed, sound, and well-researched book of more than 400 pages, there is a seemingly obvious oversight in that the very important and tragic history of the 1930s is given a mere 6 pages and there is no mention of the Nanjing Massacre or other Japanese atrocities.

22. See Renee Jeffery, "When Is an Apology Not an Apology? Contrition Chic and Japan's (Un)apologetic Politics," *Australian Journal of International Affairs* 65 (November 2011): 607, 615.

23. Clarissa Tan, "East vs. East: Asia's New Arms Race," *The Spectator*, April 6, 2013, www.spectator.co.uk/features/8880761/asias-arms-race/.

24. Gries, *China's New Nationalism*, 73.

25. 郑毅 [Zheng Yi], "美国对日本战争反省意识的矫正" [A Correction for American Consciousness concerning Japanese War Introspection], *日本研究* [Japan Studies], no. 3 (2011): 89.

26. June Teufel Dreyer, "The Shifting Triangle: Sino-Japanese-American Relations in Stressful Times," *Journal of Contemporary China* 21 (2012): 410.

27. On this point, see Zou Keyuan, "Sino-Japanese Joint Fishery Management in the East China Sea," *Marine Policy* 27 (2003): 126.

28. Dreyer, "Shifting Triangle," 413.

29. Ezra Vogel, *Deng Xiaoping and the Transformation of China* (Cambridge, MA: Harvard University Press, 2011), p. 298.

30. Paul Smith, "China-Japan Relations and the Future Geopolitics of East Asia," *Asian Affairs*, August 2010, 232.

31. Marie Söderberg, *Japan's ODA Policy in Northeast Asia*, Scandinavian Working Papers in Economics 158 (Stockholm: Scandinavian Working Papers in Economics, 2002), http://swopec.hhs.se/eijswp/papers/eijswp0158.pdf.

32. Pen-Er Lam, quoted by Smith, "China-Japan Relations," 237.

33. Dreyer, "Shifting Triangle," 416; also see 412.

34. Thomas J. Christensen, "China, the US-Japan Alliance, and the Security Dilemma in East Asia," *International Security* 23 (Spring 1999): 61.

35. Erica Strecker Downs and Phillip C. Saunders, "Legitimacy and the Limits of Nationalism: China and the Diaoyu Islands," *International Security* 23 (Winter 1998–99): 135.

36. Christensen, "China," 54.

37. Evan S. Medeiros, Keith Crane, Eric Heginbotham, Norman D. Levin, Julia F. Lowell, Angel Rabasa, and Somi Seong, *Pacific Currents: The Responses of US Allies and Security Partners in East Asia to China's Rise* (Santa Monica, CA: Rand Corporation, 2008), 32.

38. Ibid., 43.

39. Ibid., 47, 54.

40. "Japan Visit Warms Ties with China," BBC, October 8, 2006, http://news.bbc.co.uk/2/hi/4801583.stm.

41. Medeiros et al., *Pacific Currents*, 33.

42. Michael D. Swaine, *America's Challenge: Engaging a Rising China in the Twenty-First Century* (Washington, DC: Carnegie Endowment for International Peace, 2011), 73.

43. E.g., there is no mention of this process by Bush, *Perils of Proximity*, or in the review essay by Jeffery, "When Is an Apology Not an Apology?"

44. 高兰 [Gao Lan], "历史教科书问题: 中日模式与法德模式比较" [The History Textbook Issue: Comparing the China-Japan Model with the France-Germany Model], 日本学刊 [Japan Studies Review], no. 3 (2010): 11, 13–15.

45. James Reilly, *Strong Society, Smart State: The Rise of Public Opinion in China's Japan Policy* (New York: Columbia University Press, 2012), 182.

46. "China PM Seeks War Reconciliation," BBC, April 12, 2007, http://news.bbc.co.uk/2/hi/asia-pacific/6547199.stm.

47. Quoted by Bush, *Perils of Proximity*, 295.

48. James Manicom, "Sino-Japanese Cooperation in the East China Sea: Limitations and Prospects," *Contemporary Southeast Asia* 30, no. 3 (2008): 466.

49. This entire paragraph is drawn from Bush, *Perils of Proximity*, 79–80.
50. Aaron L. Friedberg, *A Contest for Supremacy: China, America, and the Struggle for Mastery in Asia* (New York: W. W. Norton, 2011), 179.
51. Ibid., 105.
52. Medeiros et al., *Pacific Currents*, 55.
53. Quoted by Smith, "China-Japan Relations," 240.
54. See, e.g., Jeffrey A. Bader, *Obama and China's Rise: An Insider's Account of America's Asia Strategy* (Washington, DC: Brookings Institution Press, 2012), 42–47. Bader writes scathingly about Hatoyama's concept of an "East Asian Community" (45–46). He then describes a rather harsh conversation between Obama and Hatoyama at the April 2010 Nuclear Security Summit that apparently "further tightened the political noose around his neck," but then Bader forswears any suggestion that "the US administration had somehow engineered Hatoyama's downfall" (46).
55. Keith Bradsher, "Amid Tension, China Blocks Vital Exports to Japan," *New York Times*, September 22, 2010, www.nytimes.com/2010/09/23/business/ global/23rare.html?pagewanted=all.
56. Yves Tiberghien, " The Puzzling 2010 Diaoyu Crisis: Centrifugal Domestic Politics, Shifting Balance of Power, and Weak Regional Institutionalization," *Harvard Asia Quarterly*, December 24, 2010, available at http://asiaquarterly .com.
57. "Clinton: Senkakus Subject to Security Pact," *Japan Times*, September 25, 2010, www.japantimes.co.jp/news/2010/09/25/national/clinton-senkakus-subject-to -security-pact/.
58. For a description of this incident from within the US administration, see Bader, *Obama*, 106–8. However, this description does not quite clarify the decision, because Bader writes emphatically: "It was absurd to think that China and Japan could have an armed conflict over these rocky islets or that the United States could be drawn in" (p. 107). This conclusion would seem to contradict the administration's reinterpretation of the Treaty provisions that would not cover the islets. A defense of the administration's October 2010 statement—the argument that no alteration in US policy occurred—is given by Mark Manyin, *Senkaku Islands (Diaoyu/Diaoyutai) Dispute: US Treaty Obligations*, CRS Report R42761 (Washington, DC: Congressional Research Service, 2013), www.fas .org/sgp/crs/row/R42761.pdf. The evidence presented in that document is quite persuasive in outlining the US neutrality doctrine regarding the contending claims (pp. 4–5). However, the report's author then relies on the rather specious interpretation that any statements made during the 1970s by US diplomats that apply to Okinawa must also apply to the contested Senkaku/Diaoyutai (p. 5).

A much more comprehensive and scholarly rendering of the evidence is given by Paul Smith, "The Senkaku/Diaoyu Island Controversy: A Crisis Postponed," *Naval War College Review*, Spring 2013, 27–44. This article again reveals reams of evidence illustrating why and how Washington pursued a "neutrality doctrine" but only the thinnest possible evidence regarding a paper trail to support the contention that Article 5 of the US-Japan Treaty would cover the contested islets. Indeed, this conclusion fits with Smith's statement that "more recent American assurances to Japan have been more direct and robust" (p. 40). The root of the problem is the obvious contradiction between the "neutrality doctrine" and the contention that the contested areas are covered by the treaty. To define the problem out of existence may serve short-term policy objectives, but could also be very dangerous for the security of the Asia-Pacific region.

59. Author's interviews, Dalian, October 2010.

60. This entire paragraph is drawn from 刘昌黎 [Liu Changli], "中日贸易的新发展, 新变化及问题" [New Developments, Trends, and Problems in China-Japan Trade], 日本问题研究 [Japanese Research], 25 (April 2011): 16–23.

61. 关权 [Guan Quan], "东亚经济一体化和TPP: 中日之间的博弈" [The Economic Integration in East Asia and TPP: A Game between China and Japan], 东北亚论坛 [Northeast Asia Forum], February 2012, 3–9.

62. This entire paragraph is drawn from 张威威 [Zhang Weiwei], "论中日韩安全合作" [Security Cooperation among China, Japan, and the ROK], 和平与发展 [Peace and Development], August 2011, 22–25.

63. This entire paragraph is drawn from 肖传国 [Xiao Chuanguo], "'钓鱼岛'撞船事件'后日本的战略走向" [Japan's Strategic Direction after the Diaoyu Island "Ship Bumping Incident"], 日本研究 [Japan Studies], March 2011, 72–77.

64. 周永生 [Zhou Yongsheng], "日本对美国'重返亚洲'的军事配合" [Japan's Military Support for America's "Return to Asia"], 现代军事 [Contemporary Military Affairs], February 2012, 31.

65. Ibid., 32.

66. 李杰 [Li Jie, PLA Navy Senior Captain], "要用实质性举措应对钓鱼岛危机" [It Is Necessary to Use Substantive Measures to Respond in the Diaoyu Island Crisis], 现代舰船 [Modern Ships], April 2012, 52.

67. Ibid., 52.

68. See, e.g., 张玉国 [Zhang Yuguo], "野田政权对日美同盟关系的强化" [Improvement of the US-Japan Alliance by the Noda Regime], 国际政治 [International Politics], March 2012, 46–51.

69. 廉德瑰 [Lian Degui], "略论日本'海洋派'的对外战略思想" [On the Foreign Policy Strategic Thinking of Japan's "Maritime Faction"], 日本学刊 [Japanese Studies], January 2012, 10–21.

70. See, e.g., Martin Fackler, "Japan Says China Aimed Military Radar at Ship," *New York Times*, February 5, 2013, www.nytimes.com/2013/02/06/world/asia /japan-china-islands-dispute.html?_r=0.

71. 熊光清 [Xiong Guangqing], "东亚局势: 美中日三边角力" [The East Asian Situation: A Three-Sided Trial of Strength], *学习时报* [Study Times], August 26, 2013, 2.

72. See, e.g., the cover page of *环球时报* [Global Times], April 24, 2013.

73. [Li Jie] (Captain, PLA Navy), "钓鱼岛乱局的'症结' 在美国" [The US Is at the Crux of the Chaotic Situation in the Diaoyu Islands], *现代舰船* [Modern Ships], October 2012, 52; 晓枫, 王薇 [Xiao Feng and Wang Wei], "碰撞承受之重" [The Enduring Importance of Bumping], *兵器知识* [Ordnance Knowledge], November 2012, 21–23.

74. [Zhang Qian], "日本自卫队将领谈日本'岛屿防卫'" [JMSDF Admiral Discusses Japan's "Defense of Islets"], *现代舰船* [Modern Ships], June 2013, 16.

75. 罗援 [Luo Yuan, PLA General], "遏制日本右翼应有'武松打虎'精神" [To Contain Japan's Right-Wing Faction, the Spirit of Wusong the Tiger Killer Is Needed], *环球时报* [Global Times], May 6, 2013, 14.

76. 林晓光 [Lin Xiaoguang], "自民当安倍内阁的对华政策与中日关系" [The Abe Cabinet's China Policy and China-Japan Relations], *和平与发展* [Peace and Development], March–April 2013, 69, 72–73.

77. 蒋帅 [Jiang Shuai], "中日东海大陆架油气资源开发争端解决的新思路" [A New Way of Thinking about Dispute Settlement regarding the Dispute over Oil and Gas Resources between China and Japan on the East China Sea Continental Shelf], *日本研究* [Japan Studies], January 2013, 77–83. Notably, the same issue of this Chinese journal also carries an article by a Japanese scholar advocating a compromise in the territorial dispute.

78. 任筱锋 [Ren Xiaofeng, Captain, PLA Navy], "维护国家领土领空主权和安全的重大举措" [A Major Measure for Protecting the Sovereignty and Security of National Territory and Territorial Airspace] *人民海军* [People's Navy], November 27, 2013, 4. This translation was done by Shazeeda Ahmed and Ryan Martinson of the China Maritime Studies Institute at the US Naval War College.

79. Martin Fackler, "Japan Rejects China's Claim to Air Rights over Islands," *New York Times*, November 24, 2013, www.nytimes.com/2013/11/25/world /asia/japan-rejects-chinas-claim-to-air-rights-over-disputed-islands.html.

80. 张文昌, 苑华锋 [Zhang Wenchang and Yuan Huafeng], "防空识别区: 空防安全的战略预警空间" [Air Defense Identification Zone: A Strategic Early Warning Domain for Air Defense], *空军报* [Air Force News], January 2, 2014, 2. This translation was done by Shazeeda Ahmed and Ryan Martinson of the China Maritime Studies Institute at the US Naval War College.

81. [Qian Wenrong], "一战最重要的教训是什么？ 驳安倍把今日中关系与一战时德英关系类比谬论" [What Are the Most Important Lessons of World War I? A Refutation of Abe's Erroneous Comparison between Contemporary Japan-China Relations and British–German Relations at the Time of World War I] *和平与发展* [Peace and Development], January 2014, 50, 52.

82. [Li Daguang], "安倍的'强大日本'赌局" [Abe's Gamble on a "Mighty Japan"], *当代海军* [Modern Navy], February 2014, 13, 15.

83. 彭光谦 [Peng Guangqian, PLA General-Retired], "调整战略思路，积极应对日本军国化的严峻挑战" [Revise Strategic Thinking, Actively Respond to the Severe Challenge Posed by Japan's Militarism], *现代国际关系* [Contemporary International Relations], January 2014, 15.

84. A current appraisal of these perceptions is given by Swaine et al., *China's Military*, 115–19.

85. 任晓 [Ren Xiao] "中国如何作可亲的大国" [How China Can Become an Amiable Great Power], *东方早报* [Oriental Morning Post], November 14, 2013.

86. 时殷弘 [Shi Yinhong], "日本政治右倾化和中日关系的思维方式及战略政略问题" [Japan's Political Right Deviation and Sino-Japanese Relations, Thought Pattern, and Tactics], *日本学刊* [Japanese Studies], February 2014, 1, 5, 7, 13–14.

87. Zhou Weihong quoted in Simon Denyer and Anna Fifield, "China and Japan Leaders Break Ice with First Meeting, but No Sign of Warmth," *Washington Post*, November 10, 2014, http://www.washingtonpost.com/world/china-and-japan -leaders-break-ice-with-first-meeting-but-no-sign-of-warmth/2014/11/10/acf 10be8-10de-4043-b075-81c7dcee6ca1_story.html.

88. Jane Perlez, "Signs of Hope in Chinese Attitudes toward Japan," *New York Times*, September 11, 2014, http://sinosphere.blogs.nytimes.com/2014/09/11 /signs-of-hope-in-chinese-attitudes-toward-japan/?_r=0.

89. Michael Yahuda, "The Limits of Economic Interdependence: Sino-Japanese Relations," in *New Directions in the Study of Chinese Foreign Policy*, ed. Alastair Iain Johnston and Robert S. Ross (Stanford, CA: Stanford University Press, 2006), 163.

90. Thom Shanker, "US Agrees to Reduce Size of Force on Okinawa," *New York Times*, April 26, 2012, www.nytimes.com/2012/04/27/world/asia/united -states-to-cut-number-of-marines-on-okinawa.html.

91. Hugh White, *The China Choice: Why We Should Share Power* (New York: Oxford University Press, 2013), 87. However, White goes too far in saying that Japan should have nuclear weapons and that "the alliance will cost the United States more than its worth" (p. 88). These ideas are not endorsed here. Rather, as explained below, the US-Japan alliance should be reformed, not abrogated.

Moreover, Japanese nuclear weaponry, though perhaps conceivable in light of recent developments on the Korean Peninsula, should not be necessary, because Japan's national security environment is simply not that dire.

92. Swaine, *America's Challenge*, 366.

93. Bush, *Perils of Proximity*, 286. It is worth noting that it was actually Washington that was initially reluctant about this forum. On the issue of a trilateral meeting on the agenda in 2009 and why China eventually rejected the proposal, see also Swaine, *America's Challenge*, 143–44.

94. Wang Jisi, "The China-Japan-US Triangle," in *Getting the Triangle Straight: Managing China-Japan-US Relations*, ed. Gerald Curtis, Ryosei Kokubun, and Wang Jisi (New York: Japan Center for International Exchange, 2010), 40.

95. Bush, *Perils of Proximity*, 186.

96. Alastair Iain Johnston, "How New and Assertive Is China's New Assertiveness?" *International Security* 37 (Spring 2013): 22–28.

97. Paul Krugman, "Rare and Foolish," *New York Times*, October 17, 2010, www.nytimes.com/2010/10/18/opinion/18krugman.html.

98. Saurav Jha, "China's Rare Earths Advantage," *The Diplomat*, April 29, 2014, http://thediplomat.com/2014/04/chinas-rare-earths-advantage/.

99. Bush, *Perils of Proximity*, 290–92.

100. See "Statement by Prime Minister Tomiichi Murayama 'On the Occasion of the 50th Anniversary of the War's End,'" Japanese Ministry of Foreign Affairs, www.mofa.go.jp/announce/press/pm/murayama/9508.html.

101. A nuanced discussion of this comparison is given by Alexander Lanoszka, "Prime Minister Abe, You're No Willy Brandt," February 13, 2013, *The National Interest*, http://nationalinterest.org/commentary/prime-minister-abe-youre-no-willy-brandt-9874.

102. See, e.g., 楚树龙 [Chu Shulong], "日本国家战略及中国对日战略" [Japan's National Strategy and China's Strategy for Japan], 现代国际关系 [Contemporary International Relations], January 2014, 12.

103. Rozman was quoted by David C. Kang, *China Rising: Peace, Power and Order in East Asia* (New York: Columbia University Press, 2013), 171.

104. "No End in Sight: Germany Has Paid Out More Than 61.8 Billion in Third Reich Reparations," www.ihr.org/jhr/v17/v17n6p19_reparations.html.

105. See, e.g., Yahuda, "Limits," 166; he writes: "It was aid from which Japanese business benefited."

106. Reinhard Drifte, "The Ending of Japan's ODA Loan Programme to China: All's Well That Ends Well," *Asia-Pacific Review* 13, no. 1 (2006): 112.

107. See, e.g., "美国施压安倍收敛历史问题立场" [The US Pressures Abe to Show Restraint regarding the History Issue], 东方早报 [Oriental Morning Post], May 9, 2013.

108. 张健 [Zhang Jian], "日本政治右倾化的历史根源" [The Historical Origins of the Rightward Turn in Japanese Politics], 人民日报海外版 [People's Daily Foreign Edition], August 17, 2013, news.xinhuanet.com/2013-08/16/_116 961599.htm.

109. "Whitewashing History in Japan" *New York Times*, December 3, 2014, http://www.nytimes.com/2014/12/04/opinion/whitewashing-history-in-japan .html.

110. Reilly, *Strong Society, Smart State*, 186–88.

111. For a robust defense of China's refusal to accept the midpoint line, see 苏晓晖 [Su Xiaohui], "东海划界: 日本无理取闹可体矣" [The East Sea Boundary: Japan Is Willfully Provocative Regarding the Latest Proposal], 人民日报海外版 [People's Daily Foreign Edition], August 17, 2013, news.xinhuanet.com/ comments/2013-08/17/c_116977926.htm.

112. On joint jurisdictional zones at sea, see Peter Dutton, "Carving Up the East China Sea," *Naval War College Review* 60 (Spring 2007): 60–61.

113. Jane Perlez, "Calls Grow in China to Press Claim for Okinawa," *New York Times*, June 13, 2013, www.nytimes.com/2013/06/14/world/asia/sentiment -builds-in-china-to-press-claim-for-okinawa.html?pagewanted=all&_r=0.

114. Smith, "Senkaku/Diaoyu Island Controversy," 34.

115. Nicholas Kristof, "Look Out for the Diaoyu Islands," *New York Times*, September 10, 2010, http://kristof.blogs.nytimes.com/2010/09/10/look-out -for-the-diaoyu-islands/.

116. Richard Samuels, *Securing Japan: Tokyo's Grand Strategy and the Future of East Asia* (Ithaca, NY: Cornell University Press, 2007), 45.

117. See, e.g., Andrew Nathan and Andrew Scobell, *China's Search for Security* (New York: Columbia University Press, 2012), 126.

118. White, *China Choice*, 143.

119. Swaine et al., *China's Military*, 276.

120. Karen Travers, "Obama Comes to Japan Bearing Gifts: Support for Japan Taking a Permanent Seat on the UN Security Council and an Invitation to Washington for Prime Minister Kan," ABC News, November 10, 2010, http:// abcnews.go.com/blogs/politics/2010/11/obama-comes-to-japan-bearing-gifts -support-for-japan-taking-permanent-seat-on-un-security-council-an/.

10

THE NEW "FULDA GAP"
Southeast Asia and US-China Relations

★ ★ ★ ★

When Chinese vice foreign minister Cui Tiankai and US assistant secretary of state Kurt Campbell met in Hawaii a couple of years ago for a discussion of developments in Southeast Asia, this hastily called meeting did not reflect the courteous tone and pageantry that characterizes most bilateral summitry. Cui commented: "I believe the individual countries are actually playing with fire, and I hope the fire will not be drawn to the United States."[1] Such bellicose rhetoric has not been employed by diplomats in this relationship since the days of the early Cold War. Strategists in Washington, moreover, seem ever more inclined to view Southeast Asia as the most decisive strategic point in the evolving rivalry—the "Fulda Gap" of an unfolding contest for supremacy in the Asia-Pacific region.[2] During the Cold War, the Central German Plain—the "Fulda Gap"—assumed immense importance in the eyes of many strategists in the superpowers' competition to control the fate of Europe.[3] Some argued that the world contest might be decided by the military forces arrayed across this critical piece of terrain. Is the South China Sea truly the new Fulda Gap of the emergent China-US military and geopolitical rivalry?

US-China tensions in Southeast Asia have hardly abated during the last two years; quite the contrary, unfortunately. Even as the mid-2011 crisis in China-Vietnam relations over the Spratly Islands seemed to cool off, at least temporarily, another significant crisis erupted between China and the Philippines in the spring of 2012 over Scarborough Shoal, or 黄岩岛 (Huangyan

Dao, Yellow Rock Island), and these strains continued into 2014. In mid-2014, another dangerous encounter between Chinese and American military aircraft occurred in the air east of Hainan Island. So bad was the tension recently that a Chinese military editorial elicited coverage on the Chinese international news channel: "Regarding the Huangyan Island issue, China has been patient, not weak, but restrained. However, if there is someone who mistakes China's good intentions for weakness, . . . viewing China as a 'paper tiger,' then he is absolutely wrong."[4] Meanwhile, the US Navy reported that its ship visits to the Philippines in 2012 were up to eighty-eight from fifty-four in 2011, with further expansion sought.[5] Additionally, among the visiting American ships were some of its most advanced nuclear attack submarines. Reacting to Secretary of Defense Chuck Hagel's August 2013 visit to the Philippines, the Chinese press predictably discussed concerns that "the Philippines could become a base for undertaking US military interventions."[6] In mid-2014 the prospect of conflict between China and Vietnam in the South China Sea again appeared disturbingly likely. Seemingly making the case for war, one Chinese commentator has written that there is not necessarily a contradiction between China's peaceful rise and the use of force.[7] There is some hope that a November 2014 bilateral memorandum of understanding agreed between Obama and Xi on "maritime encounters" could mitigate rising tensions. But regrettably, the dark shadow of a possible looming armed conflict in the South China Sea continues to hang over the region.

In some respects, the growing impetus toward strategic competition between China and the United States in Southeast Asia is easily understood. Most fundamentally, this region serves as a crucial bridge between the Indian and Pacific oceans, thus linking Europe, Africa, and the Middle East with East Asia. The importance of this bridge function between other regions is magnified by the fact that the East Asian economies and their related trade linkages have emerged as a major foundation for the global economy more generally. Southeast Asia itself has both robust, developed economies (e.g., Singapore and Australia) and economies that are rapidly improving and show great promise (e.g., Vietnam and Indonesia). The region is, of course, proximate to China, and it also has abundant natural resources and markets that Beijing is eager to exploit. Meanwhile, the United States has long been involved in Southeast Asia, fighting a major war in the region 1965–73, but then later serving as a guarantor of regional stability at the behest of several of the region's states in the fluid international system following the Cold War. US-China rivalry in Southeast Asia has now escalated to the point where an influential Washington think tank declared in early 2012 that the region forms a new, "critical battleground for the transition in global power."[8]

This chapter develops a group of ideas for altering the US-China rivalry dynamic in Southeast Asia toward one of enhanced trust and cooperation that will benefit both the region and also the complex relationship between Beijing and Washington. Before presenting the step-by-step set of concrete proposals that would enable a "cooperation spiral" to begin, some crucial background is presented from both the Chinese and American perspectives, after which the disconcerting events that have gravely increased tensions in the region since 2009 are described in some detail. Again, in using extensive Chinese source material, the concept is to inform readers with respect to Chinese viewpoints. There is no implied endorsement of the assessments in these sources.

Background

Recent headlines detailing new defense cooperation possibilities between the United States and both Vietnam and the Philippines reinforce the necessity to consider East Asian history anew because both these states have been critical to US-China strategic interaction during the twentieth century and even before. Indeed, the conquest of the Philippines by the United States in 1898 was undertaken in part to facilitate America's growing commercial interests in China.[9] A little more than half a century later, Washington sought to contain the influence of Mao Zedong's revolutionary China by supporting South Vietnam against Communist insurgents.

Contemporary Chinese scholarship is grappling with the nature of Chinese interaction with Southeast Asia before the arrival of Europeans in the sixteenth century. That China's trading relations with the states of Southeast Asia were robust is hardly in doubt, given that Manila is said to be built in part upon the ballast stones of Chinese trading junks.[10] A recent Chinese scholarly analysis details how "Southeast Asia's key waters were snatched up . . . [because the Europeans] were hardly satisfied with peaceful trade, but rather pursued aggression by force." It further details how Chinese merchant junks were driven from the region's seas. However, the same account also suggests that the arrival of the Europeans "greatly spurred the sailing ship trade and also closely connected markets in Southeast Asia, China, the Americas and Europe."[11]

A Chinese textbook published in 2010 by Peking University Press as 美国与东亚关系导论 (*An Introduction to the History of US-East Asian Relations*) is also relatively balanced. Regarding the US conquest of the Philippines, the book notes that the United States seized the "opportunity" of the Cuba crisis with Spain for expansion, and also that this seminal event initiated a historical period during which the United States exerted profound influence on Southeast Asia. It is additionally suggested that upward of 200,000 Philippine civilians were killed in the war during the period 1898–1902. However, the Chinese textbook also observes that US colonization was dramatically different from that of Spain, in that it emphasized the building of American-style democratic institutional structures and also an educational system. America's cultural legacy in the Philippines is said to be "huge; . . . Filipinos are Americanized Asians, . . . with American names, . . . dancing to American tunes, . . . and eating American food."[12] It seems that the history of America's colonization of the Philippines is of no small interest in China today.[13]

During the Cold War, it is clear that anticommunism formed an important initial impetus for regional integration and security coordination, a point mentioned but not highlighted by contemporary Chinese scholars, who emphasize the role of the so-called hegemonic system in determining relations among Southeast Asian states in the early Cold War.[14] However, some Chinese scholars are evidently willing to acknowledge that Beijing made certain errors in its diplomacy in Southeast Asia during the Cold War—whether sponsoring revolutionary movements or supporting brutal regimes, such as the infamous Pol Pot in Cambodia.[15] But if these points are quite rare in Chinese historical accounts, a somewhat parallel case of historical amnesia seems evident in Western discussions of the Vietnam War. In this case, it is too often forgotten that US-China strategic maneuvering provided an essential backdrop for the Vietnam conflict, especially in the initial phases.[16]

During the 1970s and 1980s, the Association of Southeast Asian Nations (ASEAN) gradually gained in strength, "defining and redefining Southeast Asia's regional identity and developing norms of collective action," as Amitav Acharya has described the intricate process.[17] In the course of norm and identity construction, Acharya suggests that the collective struggle to reverse Vietnam's 1978 invasion of Cambodia and seek a peaceful resolution of that conflict played an important role.[18] Chinese scholars note that shared concerns about Vietnam helped to break down ASEAN's deep mistrust of China during this period.[19] Combat in the South China Sea in 1988 between China and Vietnam did arouse concerns, but as one detailed US analysis of those events reveals: "Steps taken by rival claimants . . . to exploit the natural resources of the seabed incited Beijing to respond with ever-deeper physical penetrations into the Spratly Archipelago."[20] This event did not alter the trend toward greater regional integration.

The pivotal turning point for China's relations in Southeast Asia came in the years 1989–91. To be sure, the end of the Cold War had a major role in this development. However, Chinese discussions of this period also emphasize the crucial factor of China's internal transformation, including both the 1989 "political disturbance" that dramatically isolated China from the West and also Deng Xiaoping's "Southern Tour," when he pledged to redouble China's commitment to market reforms and to opening to the world.[21] China initiated formal diplomatic relations with Thailand in 1989, Indonesia and Singapore in 1990, and Cambodia in 1993. With the end of the Cold War, "ASEAN regionalism entered a rapid phase of development," inaugurating the ASEAN security dialogue in 1992, the Council for Security Cooperation in the Asia-Pacific in 1993, and the ASEAN Regional Forum in 1994.[22] In another major event for regional security, the US military withdrew from the Philippines in 1992. Nevertheless, more tension in the South China Sea surrounding the Chinese occupation of Mischief Reef in 1994 brought US forces back to the Philippines, albeit on a much more limited basis.[23] Chinese analyses recognize, moreover, that the 1995–96 Taiwan crisis also had an impact on the calculations of ASEAN states vis-à-vis China, but it is claimed that ASEAN members at that time "were paying attention, but were not unduly alarmed since they had already confirmed that Beijing would not resort to force in Southeast Asia."[24] Nevertheless, the same Taiwan crisis created very significant tension in US-China relations, and the shadow of recurring great power rivalry was once again apparent in Southeast Asia as early as the mid-1990s.

US-China strategic interaction in Southeast Asia faced another watershed moment during the 1997 financial crisis, when China extended financial bailout packages to both Thailand and Indonesia, and also resisted the temptation to devalue the Chinese currency. According to one recent Chinese analysis, "At a critical time, China was willing to lend a hand; . . . 1997 became another crucial moment for the [ASEAN-China] relationship."[25] In contrast, a Korean economist recently concluded that Washington did not play a helpful role in that crisis, observing that "much research . . . indicates that the influence of the US in East Asia hinders the development of closer regional economic cooperation."[26]

Another crisis that has been much less discussed, but was potentially even more dangerous, erupted in Southeast Asia in 1999, as East Timor pressed for independence from Indonesia. This particular crisis could have severely alienated Jakarta from the international community, and specifically from the United States and Australia. However, the crisis was adroitly handled through a mature response from Jakarta, as well as the constructive intervention of the UN secretary-general and of Canberra. Beijing's response was low key, but did involve substantive support for intervention by UN peacekeeping troops. China's willingness to send several hundred of these UN "blue helmets" over a period of many years marked a significant step for Chinese foreign policy. According to one Chinese analyst: "The East Timor peacekeeping issue did not block the development of Chinese–Indonesian relations. . . . On the contrary, the issue in large measure accelerated the rapprochement between the two countries." The same Chinese analysis also observes that the East Timor issue in East Asia could also "have followed the same path as the problematic Kosovo intervention. This was the chief reason that [Beijing took] an active role."[27]

The first decade of the new century witnessed major progress in China-ASEAN relations, including both the signing of the Code of Conduct on the South China Sea and a commitment on both sides to build the China-ASEAN Free Trade Area by 2010.[28] To be sure, both these landmark agreements had their associated problems—the former being too vague to resolve issues of contention, and the latter having an impact on myriad "rice bowls," as trade agreements inevitably do.[29] The new closeness between ASEAN and China reflected numerous factors, not least that of proximity and shared cultural heritage. Once seen as dangerous "fifth columns" for Maoist insurgencies, Chinese ethnic communities were increasingly viewed as lubricating the wheels of commerce as regional trade ties flourished. Another key component of China's "charm offensive" in Southeast Asia was its much-improved diplomatic service, wherein Beijing's interests are promoted by experienced and cosmopolitan ambassadors who are not strangers to the regions where they work. Beijing's success in Southeast Asia was sufficiently apparent by 2006 that Joshua Kurlantzick wrote: "Since the late 1990s perceptions of China in Southeast Asia have shifted significantly, so much so that elites and publics in the majority of the ten members of ASEAN now see China as a constructive actor—and potentially, the preeminent regional power."[30]

As implied by Kurlantzick's observation, Washington was viewed as hamfisted, in stark contrast to Beijing's adroit and attentive diplomacy at this time. Despite some brave efforts to reverse the tide, such as the 2004 tsunami relief effort mounted by the US Navy, the war on terrorism and the Iraq War severely damaged the image of the United States in Southeast Asia, especially in key nations with predominantly Muslim populations, such as Indonesia and Malaysia. Efforts to promote and even integrate counterterrorism and sea lane security issues also sometimes backfired. As two Malaysians recently wrote: "Coming so soon after the September 11 incident, the probability of a nexus between terrorism and piracy in the Strait became the rallying cry for the presence of foreign powers in the Strait with offers to patrol the Strait coming from countries such as the US. . . . The littoral states have had to innovate to counter . . . the not-too-covert attempts of foreign powers to grab a strategic toehold in the Strait."[31] Chinese scholars were apparently also suspicious that the United States would succeed in using the war on terrorism to shore up its leadership in Southeast Asia, but these anxieties were not borne out.[32]

The Iraq War, in fact, had a deleterious impact on the United States' relationship with the Philippines, Washington's closest ally in Southeast Asia. Manila had agreed to contribute a symbolic force to go to Iraq (just over 100 personnel), but these forces were abruptly withdrawn after a Philippine truck driver was abducted by insurgents in mid-2004. As one observer notes, "Sino-Philippine security ties underwent a significant upturn after Philippine troops were withdrawn from Iraq in 2004. . . . President Arroyo . . . was playing the 'China card.'"[33] Within a few months, Manila and Beijing had reached both a military cooperation agreement and also the interesting Joint Marine Seismic Undertaking, which involved data gathering, consolidation, and the interpretation of seismic data for about 11,000 square kilometers in the South China Sea.[34] However, the foundation of this newly dynamic relationship was the trade relationship, whereby Manila enjoyed a substantial trade surplus with Beijing.

Nevertheless, consistent with the East Timor analysis above, it is rather clear that Beijing viewed Indonesia as the most pivotal single country in Southeast Asia. According to one Chinese analysis, this prioritization is demonstrated by the fact that Indonesia was the first Southeast Asian state to enter into a "strategic partnership" with Beijing, in the spring of 2005. The same analysis holds that this partnership has strong foundations, including (1) the experience of colonization by the West and a related affinity for nonalignment; (2) their common positions as large, developing economies; (3) strong societal bonds, including both overseas Chinese and also Islam; (4) closely aligned security interests, including prioritizing economic security issues, such as sea lanes of communication; and (5) perhaps most important, a flourishing bilateral trade.[35] A study of the China-Indonesian relationship by a Jakarta specialist yields the somewhat counterintuitive conclusion that

Indonesia's democratization gave a major boost to the bilateral relationship, in part because the Indonesian military—whose influence waned during the democratization process—had always been reluctant to see closer ties between Beijing and Jakarta. It has been observed that because many restrictions on travel have been removed, and "as exchanges of government officials, business persons, and even private citizens have become more frequent, a more positive image of China has begun to merge. Most Indonesians no longer see China as an ideologically threatening state."[36]

The central thrust of China's engagement with Southeast Asia, however, was not actually focused on maritime Southeast Asia, but rather on the Indochina Peninsula. In 2006 China unveiled a proposal for its so-called 一轴两翼 (one axis, two wings) economic development strategy. In this strategy the axis was to be formed by the economic corridor between Nanning and Singapore—a line that more or less bisects the Indochina Peninsula. The eastern "wing" of the concept was to encompass the Gulf of Tonkin / South China Sea area, while the western "wing" referred to the Greater Mekong Subregion initiative.[37] Remarking on the various possibilities for economic integration, one Chinese analysis noted the common approach of regional economies that are "opening up, but doing so gradually," and also underlines the vital role Beijing could play in providing the "public good" of supporting a regional mechanism for financial cooperation.[38] Although some aspects of this plan could be criticized as carrying forward rather particularist provincial interests in China (e.g., Guangxi), the scale, breadth, and pace of infrastructure development—including highways, high-speed rail, and port facility upgrades—suggested a possible epochal change in Southeast Asia's economic landscape.[39]

As this plan started to take shape, in parallel with the major steps envisioned for realizing the China-ASEAN Free Trade Area, the outlook for China-ASEAN cooperation appeared to be extremely promising. Specialists, such as David Kang, have suggested that Asians had perhaps found a way to mitigate the competitive impulse in international politics and that Asian states, contrary to the theoretical suppositions of the dominant realist school, were actually *not* seeking to balance China, especially in Southeast Asia.[40] Surveying regional reactions to China's rise, the RAND Corporation expert (and later senior Obama administration adviser) Evan Medeiros and his colleagues concluded: "It is not in the US interests to take a highly competitive approach to China . . . when interacting with allies and security partners in East Asia."[41]

However, since at least 2008, major concerns have surfaced in Southeast Asia regarding the extent of China's new influence. To take but one example, a report on China-Cambodia relations notes that "to pay its newfound ally [China] for its largesse, [Cambodia] has silently agreed to serve almost every Chinese desire and whim, from making gargantuan land concessions to allowing the building of hydroelectric dams, roads, and bridges."[42] Chinese analysts have themselves understood and emphasized that a core principle of ASEAN has been to prevent the emergence of either an internal or external hegemon.[43] In the last five years, the region has seen a return to intensive great power competition.

Escalating US-China Rivalry in Southeast Asia

In late 2011 the Obama administration unveiled the so-called pivot to Asia as part of a new US defense strategy. Undoubtedly, a major part of this strategy was the implied redirection of resources away from long-term, resource-draining commitments in the Middle East, especially Iraq and Afghanistan. But it is also quite clear that the pivot entails a renewed focus on what has been described in many quarters as a more "assertive China." It is, moreover, apparent that Southeast Asia appears to be developing as something like the "central front" in the emerging US-China strategic rivalry. This section of the chapter reviews how recent developments have carried the region away from a seemingly successful model of security cooperation and regional integration toward a zone of increasing geopolitical tensions. In doing so, the discussion also focuses more narrowly on the most significant flashpoint in the region: the contested claims in the South China Sea.

As noted above, some elements of US-China rivalry were clearly discernible before 2009-10. In particular, the EP-3 incident of April 2001, in which a Chinese F8 fighter maneuvered dangerously close and eventually collided with a US Navy reconnaissance plane, did touch off a serious crisis in US-China relations. The pilot of the Chinese aircraft was actually killed, while the stricken American plane made an emergency landing at a Chinese airbase on Hainan Island. Undoubtedly, the crisis would have generated an extremely intense crisis if the twenty-four members of the American crew had been tragically lost, but fortunately the pilot was able to land the damaged plane successfully at a Chinese air base on Hainan Island. The crew was permitted to return to the United States ten days later, and the aircraft itself was handed back in pieces some months later. What is quite clear in retrospect is that this particular crisis in US-China relations would likely have assumed a much greater importance in the overall security relationship if it had not been for the terrorist attacks of September 11, 2001, which set US national security policy on a decidedly new course—focused on the Middle East.

Before 2009 Chinese assessments of the security situation in the South China Sea appear to have been rather muted, emphasizing the possibilities for negotiated compromise and joint development. Such a tone is clearly evident in an obviously important paper published in China's most prestigious military journal in mid-2008. The author, a professor at China's National Defense University, suggested that "to safeguard the EEZ [exclusive economic zone], it is not usual to employ military forces. If military forces are employed, they will often expand the scope of the incident, causing the situation to become more and more complicated." The piece is quite emphatic in stating that negotiation has been and will remain China's approach to maritime territorial disputes, asserting: "Since the founding of the new China—under the direction of Mao, . . . Deng, . . . Jiang, . . . and Hu—. . . the Chinese government has used the foreign policy instruments of 'negotiations, declarations of differences, and adopting measures to build trust,' . . . which has yielded obvious successes, . . . resolving to a large extent the problems of maritime rivalry and preventing hidden dangers."[44] Because this paper on this topic of great sensitivity was published in such a high-profile journal, there is little doubt that this opinion was also widely held in China's senior military leadership at that time.

Also suggestive of a cosmopolitan approach to the South China Sea in Chinese naval circles were a pair of articles published in the naval-affiliated journal 舰船知识 (*Naval and Merchant Ships*) in late 2007. The two articles, published together, represented a pro/con debate concerning the advisability of taking "control of the Malacca Strait" as a goal of Chinese naval development. The first, pro article asserts: "If an enemy resorted to the use of naval forces to control the Malacca Strait, cutting China's maritime transport links, this would be catastrophic for China's development."[45] This argument is of key relevance for debates about Chinese strategy in the South China Sea, insofar as this sea area is portrayed as a key national maritime transit route, of which the so-called Malacca Dilemma is one critical piece. But illustrative of serious problems with respect to this reasoning is the second, con article, which is considerably longer and takes a skeptical view concerning prospective Chinese Navy efforts to "control the Malacca Strait." The second article argues: "There is no need and there is no ability to deploy forces to take control [of the Strait], nor are the extant, limited threats sufficient to block sea transport. . . . China is not building a mighty navy so that it can follow the Western path of using naval force for military expansion and economic plunder, [so] it will not seek to control the Malacca Strait."[46] Though perhaps tinged by a certain ideological impulse, it is nevertheless clear that some naval strategists in Beijing have been skeptical of any headlong rush into naval expansion in a southward direction.

Several events during 2009 appear to have cumulatively altered the security situation in the South China Sea, which had been relatively tranquil since the 2002 signing of the Code of Conduct among the claimants. First, the so-called *Impeccable* incident of March 2009 witnessed a clutch of Chinese fishing boats (with other official vessels close by) harassing a US surveillance vessel. At the time Chinese analysts were not especially perturbed by the encounter. For instance, the Qinghua University professor Yan Xuetong, who is often viewed as a "hawk" on US-China relations, observed just after the incident: "This is just a symbol of the US being on guard against China; . . . the chance of war breaking out between the US and China is zero."[47] Likewise, Chinese naval commentators offered at the time: "Because there are such controversial points embedded within the Law of the Sea, such maritime confrontations can be said to be 'all in a day's work.' When another incident occurs between Chinese and American vessels, we should not be at all astonished."[48]

Americans, by contrast, responded sharply to the perceived challenge. The *Wall Street Journal*, for example, editorialized that "the Chinese have a knack for welcoming incoming US administrations with these sorts of provocations," and it recommended that President Barack Obama "dispatch a destroyer or two," which he did.[49] One expert summed up the view on this incident prevailing among Western analysts: "In 2009 Chinese vessels carried out dangerous maneuvers to harass American surveillance vessels operating in China's EEZ, but outside its territorial waters. . . . The Chinese position was not supported by the UN Law of the Sea, . . . as signed by the Chinese without reserving their position on this point, nor was it supported by customary international law."[50] Apart from the legal dimensions of this particular incident, one may also speculate that it was related to China's emerging nuclear strategy, because at least some of Beijing's new class of submarines carrying nuclear missiles (known as strategic submarines—literally, ship, submersible, ballistic, nuclear, SSBN) are to be based at Hainan. Recent Chinese naval analyses reinforce the impression that China feels an acute sense of vulnerability in this respect.[51]

Two other events that sharpened Beijing's attention on the region also occurred in the spring of 2009. The first was the announcement from Hanoi that Vietnam would purchase six Russian-made diesel submarines. One Chinese naval strategist had the following reaction to this development: "Although

Vietnam has been equipped with two submarines, . . . nevertheless, this small force of special submarines did not necessarily confer significant submarine experience or talent. . . . Vietnam has undertaken unilateral military, economic, and cultural activities that constitute invasion of the South Sea area by osmosis. Preparations by the Chinese side are inevitable."[52]

At roughly the same time, Vietnam and Malaysia had coordinated to file a joint claim to areas in the South China Sea at the United Nations. China's reaction to that initiative was similarly belligerent. Admiral Zhang Deshun of the Navy Staff is quoted as saying, "Malaysia . . . and such countries are taking this opportunity to make illegal demands, seeking to supersede the legalization of our nation's maritime rights."[53] General Luo Yuan, of the Chinese Academy of Military Sciences, likewise warned: "'Setting aside disputes' does not mean setting aside our sovereignty. . . . China is already not a weak country. . . . It is hoped that related countries will not make a strategic miscalculation."[54] At the same time, a Chinese analysis in an influential Beijing policy journal, 现代国际关系 (*Contemporary International Relations*), warned that a group of "active interventionists" in Washington was seeking to alter the United States' longtime neutral stance toward South China Sea claims.[55]

In the background of increasing regional tensions were growing concerns about a perceived Chinese naval buildup in the region. In this respect the expansion of Chinese naval facilities on Hainan Island is most significant. Although a base has existed for decades at Yulin, the new, larger facility on Yalong Bay just to the east was constructed during the last decade. Some of China's newest and most potent naval platforms have appeared intermittently at this new base. Indeed, the basing of China's first pair of phased-array radar equipped 052C destroyers at the base has been taken as a sign of the fleet's priority focus on the southern flank.[56] Photos of China's second-generation nuclear submarines, including the 093 *Shang*-class SSN and the 094 *Jin*-class SSBN docked at the new base, have also made headlines in recent years.[57] The fact that the base apparently has a large tunnel complex visible in satellite photographs has also set off rumors.[58] The size of the base and its ample, large piers do hint at the possibility of an enlarged Chinese South Sea Fleet, perhaps eventually including an aircraft carrier battle group, in addition to numerous submarines.

It is often observed that the Chinese Navy aircraft carriers operating in the South China Sea could have major symbolic power in intimidating the other, smaller claimants to sovereignty in the area. Moreover, the platform could be useful for extending China's air control into the southern reaches of the South China Sea—a capability that China still seems to lack. The fall 2012 initial testing of Beijing's first aircraft carrier, the *Liaoning*, suggests that this complex capability will soon join China's naval arsenal, albeit at a rather nascent level. Less impressive for pictures, but perhaps more important to the changing "facts on the water," may be the building and deployment in recent years of a large fleet of fast-attack craft (Type 2208) and also a corvette or light frigate (Type 056). The latter vessel seems particularly well suited for operations in the South China Sea. Concerning the latter, *Jane's* reported that well over two dozen units are expected, and that in so doing, the Chinese Navy had a "requirement to increase ship numbers to better enforce territorial and EEZ claims in the East China Sea and South China Sea."[59] Finally, insofar as China wields significant missile capabilities for use against targets ashore and perhaps also at sea, the apparent movement of two missile brigades into the Guangzhou Military Region during 2010, as well as a possible Second Artillery cruise missile brigade and a large over-the-horizon radar system on Hainan, have been reported as a concern.[60]

Still, the sharpest spear in the Chinese navy's arsenal remains the conventional submarine fleet. Here, there has been steady progress, with thirteen *Song*-class submarines launched from 1994 to 2004. Five of the more advanced *Yuan*-class submarines were said to be launched by mid-2010.[61] Advanced *Kilo*-class conventional submarines imported from Russia are readily visible at the Yulin Base in Google Earth imagery. The launch of yet another conventional submarine design in October 2010 has fueled speculation that an "apparent slowdown in naval expansion was a transitory phase while the [Chinese Navy's] submarine fleet appears set to resume its upward trajectory."[62] Indeed, satellite imagery from late 2010 revealed what may turn out to be another new Chinese submarine base off an island southwest of Macau.[63]

Over the course of 2010, the territorial dispute in the South China Sea began to have a tangible, damaging impact on US-China relations. During a March 2010 visit to Beijing by US deputy secretary of state James Steinberg and US National Security Council adviser Jeffrey Bader, a report in the *New York Times* related that they were told that "China would not tolerate any interference in the South China Sea, now part of China's 'core interest' of sovereignty."[64] Apparently, the Chinese officials making these assertions were Vice Minister of Foreign Affairs Cui Tiankai and State Councilor Dai Bingguo.[65] In Bader's recent account of US decision making during this period, published in 2012, he notes "occasional assertions by military and midranking civilian officials to the effect that these waters were of 'core interest' to China."[66] It was also suggested by Secretary Clinton that Dai repeated such statements at the May 2010 meeting of the Strategic and Economic Dialogue.[67] Reviewing policy guidance that "the US took no position on territorial claims to islands in the South China Sea," Bader relates that he was concerned about "a message of passivity" from Washington on this issue.[68] Secretary Clinton's speech to the ASEAN Regional Forum meeting in Hanoi in July 2010 was intended to signal a more US proactive approach to the region. However, after this speech, Chinese foreign minister Yang Jiechi is said to have been surprised and furious.[69] Suggesting a possible ominous turn in the wake of the ASEAN Regional Forum meeting, Chinese chief of the General Staff Chen Bingde was quoted as saying: "We must pay close attention to changes in [regional] situations and the development of our mission [and] prepare ourselves for military struggle."[70] A Chinese military exercise of major significance also apparently took place in early August 2010. It was unusual to deploy elements of the North Sea Fleet and also the East Sea Fleet into the South China Sea. This major exercise was obviously illustrative of growing regional tensions. In another clear diplomatic signal, the first-ever US-ASEAN summit to take place on American soil was held in September 2010.[71]

The great power strains in Southeast Asia only increased during 2011. During the spring, incidents reportedly occurred between Chinese patrol vessels and survey ships from both the Philippines and Vietnam. In the latter instance, which took place in May, it was reported that Vietnamese survey equipment sustained damage. Following this event, significant anti-China protests took place in Hanoi, and the Vietnamese Navy engaged in live-fire drills.[72] The rhetoric from Chinese vice foreign minister Cui Tiankai cited at the beginning of this chapter was delivered in June 2011. The threat of a possible military conflict between China and the United States in Southeast Asia, which is clearly implied by Cui's statement, illustrates the gravity of the evolving situation.

Opinion in Beijing appeared to be turning in a hawkish direction. In mid-2011 Li Shaoning of Peking University, one of China's most prestigious academic institutions, commented that the South China Sea may have untapped energy resources equivalent to one-third of the Persian Gulf—no small prize. He warned ominously: "I think we can give Vietnam a little more time, . . . and hope that they slowly come to understand. But if they continue to be confused, then we have the means to cope with their confusion."[73] An article appearing in 环球时报 (*Global Times*) in November 2011, which said that "if these countries [in Southeast Asia] do not want to change their ways with

China, they will need to prepare for the sound of cannons," received ample press coverage in the West.[74]

Although such statements might be dismissed in some quarters as "banging the gong," discussions by Chinese naval personnel since mid-2010 have suggested that the belligerent tone could actually be more than mere rhetoric. Admiral Hu Yanlin (retired), who recently stepped down as the chief political commissar for the Chinese Navy, asserted: "International anti-China forces are still using the rivalry over the jurisdiction of maritime rights in the Spratly Islands to spoil our relations with neighboring states and further complicating the situation in the South China Sea. . . . The United States, as the fundamental anti-Chinese force, . . . may seek to precipitate a crisis, hoping that internal difficulties could facilitate foreign aggression, or that foreign aggression could cause internal anxiety."[75]

The heightened salience of the South China Sea, in the thinking of the senior Chinese Navy leadership, is further suggested by Admiral Hu's closing comments in the interview, where he proposes that "with respect to activities in the South Sea, . . . [we need to] build the legal basis for the use of non-peaceful means to resolve the rivalry over maritime rights. We are peace-loving, . . . but we also need to make the appropriate plans and preparations."[76] Navy Senior Captain Li Jie wrote a column with a similar tone: "Secretary of State Hillary Clinton brazenly ran to Vietnam, declaring that the resolution of the South Sea dispute and freedom of navigation are US 'national interests' and 'foreign policy priorities,' directly confronting China with this intervention and laying bare [the United States'] determination to adopt a posture that challenges China's 'core interests.'"[77]

A similarly harsh tone was amply evident in the official navy journal 当代海军 (*Modern Navy*), which, while calling for restraint on both sides, also warned: "We in China cannot have restraint without any limits. If Vietnam believes that it can treat Chinese forbearance like so much salt in the South China Sea with its penchant to say anything, then Hanoi has indeed made a strategic error in judgment."[78]

Washington took a number of actions during 2011 to demonstrate its new focus on the South China Sea. In July the United States held a new round of naval exercises with its new strategic partner, Vietnam.[79] For the second year in a row, Vietnamese officials were flown out to the nuclear aircraft carrier USS *George Washington*, as the American battle group was patrolling in the South China Sea.[80] Exercises with the Philippines Navy in the sensitive area off Palawan Island in June 2011 had prompted Chinese army chief

General Chen Bingde to comment that such American military exercises were "extremely inappropriate . . . at this particular time."[81] The United States also transferred a large patrol cutter to the Philippines Navy—now Manila's most advanced warship, despite its age—with the prospect of more such transfers in the future.[82] It was also announced earlier in the summer that the United States would begin basing warships in Singapore for the first time.[83] According to one Washington analyst, "The senior leadership of the US Pacific Command has no illusions regarding the dimension of the emerging challenge."[84] Washington has evidently set about undertaking a newly invigorated effort to "to protect unfettered access to and passage through the South China Sea," as Secretary of State Clinton suggested in a major new policy treatise set forth in early November 2011.[85] Shortly thereafter, President Obama announced in Australia that the United States would begin stationing Marines in Australia, clearly a step intended to "up the ante" in the South China Sea.[86] Although such small forces could hardly be expected to decisively alter the balance of power in the region, the symbolic role of such deployments, whether for Beijing or in various ASEAN capitals, is undoubtedly significant.

Over the course of 2012–13, US-China rivalry in the South China Sea seemed only to intensify. Since the spring of 2012, Beijing and Manila have been at direct loggerheads over the sovereignty of the Huangyan Dao / Scarborough Shoal, located 135 miles west of Luzon. China has seemed to strong-arm the Philippines by employing coast guard cutters and fishing vessels at the reef on almost constant patrol—a capability that the Philippines cannot nearly match. Some conservative news outlets have condemned Washington's reaction as unduly passive; for example, a columnist in *The Economist* opined in September 2013 that "China may have been encouraged by America's failure to respond to China's virtual annexation last year of what it calls Huangyan Island."[87] Even as Manila sought to take the high road by bringing the case to the International Tribunal of the Law of the Sea, Washington and Manila were reported in mid-2013 to be involved in sensitive negotiations regarding increasing the US military presence in the Philippines.[88]

Meanwhile, leading foreign policy experts in Beijing have, in the context of the South China Sea dispute, compared the dispute to the Cuban Missile Crisis, arguing that even if Beijing does not seek "to initiate the use of force, . . . that does not mean that it cannot "employ the military instrument." Given developments in the South China Sea, the Chinese author, moreover, argues that Beijing should readjust its strategy from favoring economic development to safeguarding security.[89] In a report about Philippine accusations regarding the possibility that China was preparing to build structures on the contested reef, another Chinese academic expert opined in fall 2013: "Why must only China alone act with restraint and watch quietly?"[90] Regarding this particular dispute with the Philippines, there did not seem to be much appetite for moderation on the Chinese side. For example, an academic study of the dispute in the prestigious 当代亚太 (*Journal of Contemporary Asia-Pacific Studies*) does usefully compare this dispute with others (Burkina Faso vs. Mali, Benin vs. Niger, etc.) and even talks about the role of new mapping technologies in resolving disputes; but it concludes with a very detailed and emphatic statement of China's sovereign rights over the contested reef.[91] An even harder-line academic analysis of the contesting claims was published in early 2013 in the journal 南洋问题研究 (*Southeast Asian Affairs*). While noting that China continues to insist on bilateral negotiations to resolve the dispute, the author of this piece suggests that "the Chinese side has made all-around preparations if the Philippines escalates the situation; the risk of a clash or conflict exists."[92]

Other Chinese scholarly analyses in 2013 appeared to sound a more hopeful tone. For example, one paper appearing in 国际政治研究 (*International Political Studies*) warned against excessive reliance on military power, emphasizing that "as a signatory of [the UN Law of the Sea], China cannot avoid being constrained by the same treaty." This analysis also directly criticizes China's failure "to the present day to clearly and publicly present the dashed line [in the South China Sea] before the international community."[93] Similarly, another Chinese scholar recently criticized his countrymen for bellicose and uncompromising rhetoric with respect to maritime territorial disputes. Discussing the rather customary Chinese characterization of "Chinese territory since ancient times that cannot be carved up" in an unusually candid manner, this Peking University scholar reminds his colleagues that though this formulation may be useful from a diplomatic point of view, it is simply not scientifically accurate, because Beijing has made many compromises to settle its long land borders.[94] Some early 2014 analyses also carried a rather compromising tone, for example, a detailed article in 财经 (*Finance and Economics*) suggesting that China should not seek to block strong ties between the ASEAN states and either the United States, Japan, or Europe.[95] Likewise, an early 2014 op-ed piece by Wu Shicun, director of the Chinese National South China Sea institute, stated that foreign fears regarding a hypothetical Chinese declaration of an air defense identification zone over the South China Sea were unfounded.[96] Some Western experts apparently believe that China is indeed now moderating its behavior in the region after realizing that it had overreached during the years 2009–11.[97]

And yet there is still reason for ample concern. An intensification of China's confrontation with the Philippines occurred yet again in March 2014, as a large Chinese coast guard vessel interfered with Philippines efforts to resupply a haphazard garrison posted to Second Thomas Shoal (Ayungin/Ren'ai). Gordon Chang, among other American commentators, was quick to claim that Manila was falling victim to Washington's alleged policies of "appeasement." Arguing for a much more forceful US response, Chang writes: "The surrender of the Sudetenland did not work in 1938, and neither did the abandonment of Scarborough in 2012. Once they took that reef, the Chinese, in the second half of last year, began to increase pressure on Second Thomas Shoal. The United States, trying to keep the peace, unintentionally taught the region that aggression works." Chang claims, moreover, that Beijing has also learned from US weakness in both the recent Syrian and Ukraine crises.[98] A mid-2013 Chinese analysis of the China/Philippines confrontation in the South China Sea does indeed support the contention that Beijing has learned lessons from the 2012 standoff over Scarborough Shoal. According to the author, a researcher at the Asia-Pacific and Global Strategy Center at the Chinese Academy of Social Sciences, these lessons included the imperative to establish "actual control" over the contested reef, the employment of maritime enforcement (coast guard) capabilities as the central Chinese forces, and the vital importance of having powerful military forces in the background. In an odd mirroring of Chang's argument, this Chinese author offers a parallel blistering assessment of China's vacillating policies during earlier periods (2010–11), and also warns "Chinese concessions have not supported regional stability; . . . quite the contrary."[99]

During his April 2014 visit to East Asia, President Obama signed a new defense cooperation agreement while in the Philippines. Broaching the issue of the South China Sea rather candidly, he offered: "Given its strategic location, the Philippines is a vital partner on issues such as maritime security and freedom of navigation." Praising the recent impressive efforts undertaken by the US military to assist the Philippines in recovering from a massive typhoon that hit in November 2013, he observed that "the United States will continue to stand with you as you recover and rebuild. Our commitment to the Philippines will not waver."[100] Even before this agreement to intensify cooperation was reached, however, Chinese strategists were already convinced that the Philippines was at the very "core" of the American strategy (战略的核心).

For example, a Chinese analysis counted 250 discreet engagements or joint military exercises between the United States' and the Philippines' armed forces between 2006 and 2010.[101]

Yet Beijing seemed determined to wrest the strategic initiative back from Washington, as only a matter of weeks later, in early May 2014, China deployed a massive drilling exploration rig into a sensitive part of the South China Sea—between the Paracels and the Vietnamese coast. Indeed, recent Chinese assessments regarding offshore energy resources in the South China Sea seem to reinforce Beijing's determination to forcefully uphold what it sees as to its maritime territorial rights and interests.[102] This "Paracels Crisis"—the rig is apparently located 17 miles off the southwest tip of the island group—precipitated a maritime standoff of very significant proportions, with the coast guard and fishing fleets of both China and Vietnam engaging in a range of sustained and risky behavior that apparently resulted in the sinking of at least one small Vietnamese vessel. According to a Chinese report, China had deployed between 110 and 115 vessels to protect the rig, including approximately 35 to 40 patrol cutters and 30 cargo ships and salvage tugs, as well as 40 to 50 fishing boats and 4 warships to complete the protective armada. The same report, moreover, observed that Beijing was seeking compensation for a number of Chinese nationals who had been killed and wounded in anti-Chinese rioting that had accompanied this crisis in Vietnam.[103] Reacting to Beijing's gambit at the annual conference of the International Institute of Strategic Studies in Singapore, "[US secretary of defense Chuck] Hagel told an international security conference that the US 'will not look the other way' when China and others try to restrict navigation or ignore international rules and standards. China's territorial claims in the South China Sea are destabilizing the region, he said, adding that Beijing's failure to resolve such disputes threatens East Asia's long-term progress."[104]

Increasingly frequent reports of Chinese movements around and building activity on certain reefs in the Spratly Islands group, moreover, suggest that Beijing could be adopting a more robust and confrontational approach in 2014.[105] Satellite photos at the time of this writing indicate that Beijing is constructing a three-thousand-meter "island" on Fiery Cross Reef to support an airfield. While it is true that China has been the only claimant to lack an airfield in the Spratlys, this major construction project is said to be "the fourth such project to be undertaken in the Spratly Islands in the last 12–18 months."[106] That could also be the "message" intended by the aggressive air patrolling by Chinese fighters in 2014, which prompted US allegations of reckless and unsafe intercepts in August 2014. Regrettably, China's more muscular approach seems to be overshadowing, at least for now, a promising initiative by President Xi announced in late 2013 to launch a new "maritime silk road" (海上丝绸之路) that seemed to embrace the notion of "putting aside disputes" in the effort to advance win–win development between China and the nations of maritime Southeast Asia.[107] It is difficult to gauge whether or not the newly forceful approach is intended to answer Manila's attempt to bring the dispute before international arbitration or as a response to Obama's recent visit to the region. However, there seems little doubt that current trends point with troubling consistency toward the possibility of a clash of arms.

US-China rivalry in Southeast Asia goes back decades, to the Cold War. Unfortunately, the present rivalry has the potential to be even more dangerous than it was in the past. China's rise has brought about major uncertainties for the region, including the prospect of economic dislocation, environmental degradation, and human rights difficulties, not to mention the stark possibility of Beijing's outright military hegemony. At the same time, there are also questions regarding US intentions—whether concerning new basing arrangements, the effectiveness of US military forces that have evidently been overstretched, or Washington's willingness and ability to exercise leadership.

This atmosphere of uncertainty has created a fertile environment for geopolitical rivalry—one that increasingly renders the concept of "East Asian regionalism" as "totally meaningless," according to one recent Chinese study.[108] Another recent Chinese book calls on Beijing to prepare for a long struggle with Washington over the South China Sea.[109] Misperceptions and a disturbing action/reaction pattern are all too discernible. Thus, for example, the basing of US ships in Singapore, which is viewed as a wholly defensive and rather symbolic policy in the West, is viewed in Beijing as an escalation that endangers China's energy lifeline through the Malacca Strait. Although strategic competition can occasionally produce positive outcomes, it must not be forgotten that strategic rivalry sometimes and—actually rather often—results in war. For instance, a relatively insignificant skirmish over oil exploration or fisheries in the South China Sea between Vietnam and China could quite easily expand into an exchange of blows between the regional naval forces of the United States and China, followed shortly thereafter by theater-level campaign strategies that lead quickly from attacks on area bases to strikes (possibly even with nuclear weapons) against the respective homeland areas. As in 1914, a match strike in a marginal corner of the world could have catastrophic consequences. Preventive diplomacy is urgently needed to make such a dark scenario much more remote than it is unfortunately at present.

A US-China Cooperation Cycle for Southeast Asia

The present "rebalance to the Asia-Pacific" in US foreign policy does not necessarily lead to a good outcome for Southeast Asia—a point made most recently by Singapore's foreign minister, who advised more caution in Washington's dealings with Beijing.[110] Applying the "cooperation spiral" methodology—underpinned by a gradual and reciprocal process of deescalation—will readjust the emphasis of current policy from "hedging" to "engagement," enabling a greater possibility of enhanced regional security and also more stable and effective US-China relations.[111] The steps outlined here focus on the South China Sea as the greatest arena of contention and are also consistent with ideas circulating among ASEAN states regarding the need to achieve "peace by pieces."[112] Confidence-building measures agreed to by Obama and Xi at the Beijing Summit in November 2014 may offer some momentum to this effort to tamp down and reverse the escalation spiral so evident today in the South China Sea. That is not to suggest that the South China Sea is the only domain of Sino-US geopolitical competition in Southeast Asia. The issue of Myanmar, for example, has recently been much discussed as a significant "pawn" on the diplomatic chessboard, especially in the wake of President Obama's historic visit to the country in November 2012. The important issue of Myanmar is actually taken up in the cooperation spiral in chapter 11 on South Asia. Nevertheless, the steps that follow focus on the South China Sea as the most acute and dangerous issue in the region (figure 10.1).

Washington's move 1 in Southeast Asia: The United States should invite China to play a major role at the annual CARAT exercises in Thailand. For the success of the cooperation cycle, it is essential that the initial steps be modest in character and would not require a major course changes in present policies. CARAT, which stands for Cooperation Afloat Readiness and Training, is an ideal venue for the first steps in the cooperation cycle, because the host country is Thailand, which maintains excellent relations with both the United States and China. Moreover, the focus of these exercises is on nontraditional security issues, especially including counterterrorism. These issues have been explicitly embraced by the Chinese Navy, in particular, and by the Chinese military establishment more generally.[113] And these issues have also been identified by China as a critical area for increasing security cooperation with

Figure 10.1 Cooperation Spiral: Southeast Asia   合作螺旋：东南亚

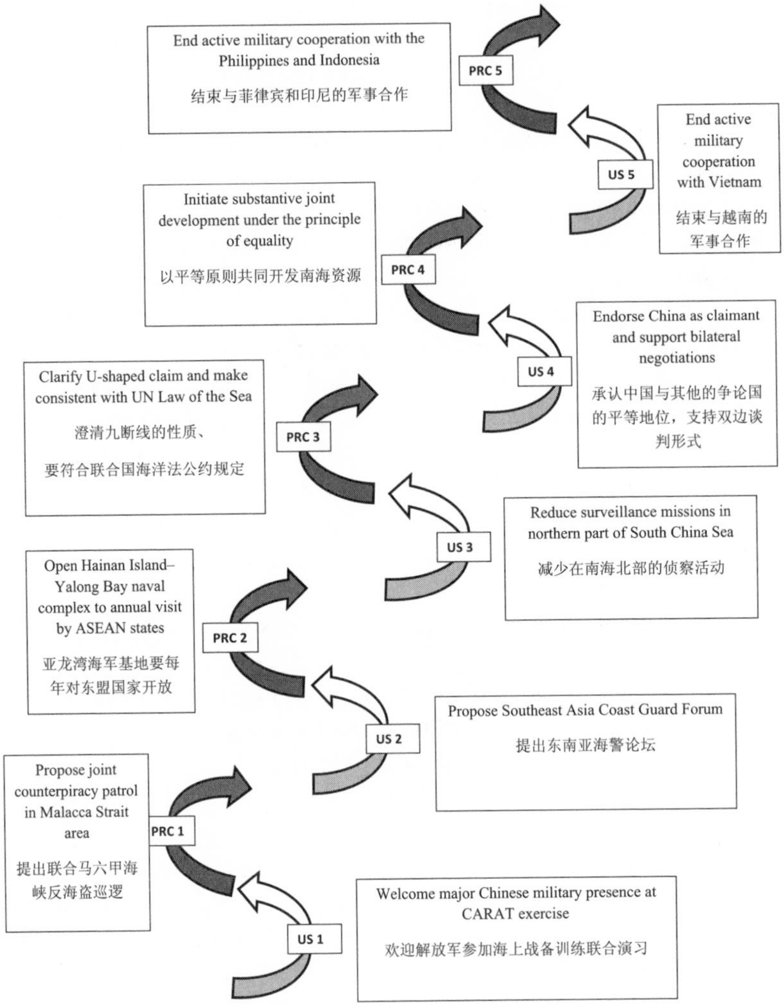

End active military cooperation with the Philippines and Indonesia
结束与菲律宾和印尼的军事合作

PRC 5

End active military cooperation with Vietnam
结束与越南的军事合作

US 5

Initiate substantive joint development under the principle of equality
以平等原则共同开发南海资源

PRC 4

Endorse China as claimant and support bilateral negotiations
承认中国与其他的争论国的平等地位，支持双边谈判形式

US 4

Clarify U-shaped claim and make consistent with UN Law of the Sea
澄清九断线的性质、要符合联合国海洋法公约规定

PRC 3

Reduce surveillance missions in northern part of South China Sea
减少在南海北部的侦察活动

US 3

Open Hainan Island–Yalong Bay naval complex to annual visit by ASEAN states
亚龙湾海军基地要每年对东盟国家开放

PRC 2

Propose Southeast Asia Coast Guard Forum
提出东南亚海警论坛

US 2

Propose joint counterpiracy patrol in Malacca Strait area
提出联合马六甲海峡反海盗巡逻

PRC 1

Welcome major Chinese military presence at CARAT exercise
欢迎解放军参加海上战备训练联合演习

US 1

the ASEAN countries—a focus given additional impetus by China's recent agreement with neighboring Southeast Asian states to jointly patrol the Mekong River Delta following a major crime incident with thirteen Chinese fatalities there in late 2011.[114] Therefore, enhanced Chinese participation in CARAT would be wholly consistent with present Chinese foreign policies and also current Chinese military policies. In fact, China has been invited to CARAT exercises in the past and has actually sent modest delegations of observers. However, the goal in this step would be to initiate a new dynamic with increased Chinese participation, amounting perhaps to the participation of one or more ships or a regiment of soldiers/marines. The fact that Thailand is not a claimant in the South China Sea dispute increases the salience of its potential role as a bridge between the major powers. Indeed, the organizational onus of the exercise should properly be on Bangkok, with the hope that they could cajole Beijing into enhancing participation. China's enlarged participation in the 2014 Rim of the Pacific Exercise in Hawaii suggests that the goal of joining a multilateral exercise in Southeast Asia in a significant manner is hardly out of reach.

Beijing's move 1 in Southeast Asia: China should propose the creation of a regional antipiracy patrol that would have a PLA Navy-US Navy foundation and focus on the crucial Malacca Strait. In this case, the diplomacy would be challenging, but the dividends from building trust and confidence would be substantial. The feasibility of the initiative would be grounded on proven PLA Navy interest and competence in maintaining counterpiracy operations since 2008 in the Gulf of Aden. Moreover, Beijing enjoys strong relationships with the key littoral countries, the so-called MALSINDO states (i.e., Malaysia, Singapore, and Indonesia), that would be crucial to the initiative's success. No doubt the MALSINDO states would be suspicious of increasing great power involvement, but they could likely be convinced of the value if they understood that US-China trust building was an essential goal of the effort. Regional dynamics are now considerably different than a decade ago, when a similar proposal from Washington failed on account of suspicions related to the direction of the global war on terrorism. Critics may additionally counter that piracy in the Malacca area and the South China Sea does not justify such a wide effort. Indeed, all would need to understand that the counterpiracy goal would be decidedly secondary to the goal of trust building. To that end, Beijing would be wise to quickly widen the group to absolutely include the Japanese Navy as well, creating a trilateral core group to work with the MALSINDO states. A clear recognition by Beijing of Tokyo's "core interest" in the Malacca Strait (see chapter 9 on Japan-China relations) could actually be critical to convincing Washington to support the proposal. The fact that Beijing has come around to become a reasonably enthusiastic supporter of the so-called RECAAP initiative—the Regional Cooperation Agreement on Combating Piracy and Armed Robbery against Ships in Asia, which is still mostly sponsored by Tokyo—is a very promising sign in this respect.[115]

Moreover, a Chinese scholar from the prestigious Fudan University recently proposed a framework for trilateral Japan-China-US cooperation in Southeast Asia, suggesting the feasibility of this concept.[116]

Washington's move 2 in Southeast Asia: The United States should propose the creation of a Southeast Asia–Pacific Coast Guard Forum. This step would be relatively simple because it would merely seek to replicate the success of the North Pacific Coast Guard Forum, an organization that has substantially contributed to building working relationships between China's civil maritime authorities and those of the United States, as well as other crucial regional players, including Japan, South Korea, and Russia. In focusing on Coast Guard cooperation, the United States would help to demilitarize maritime security issues in the region and would draw on the very prestigious position of the US Coast Guard, and especially its high reputation in China that has been formed over the last decade.[117] It would, moreover, play to Washington's clear preference for multilateralizing regional security issues. As it would speak to concrete problems of concern in the region (e.g., smuggling, poaching), the initiative would likely receive the enthusiastic support of the ASEAN states. The message from Washington to Beijing would be that the United States welcomes a role for China in regional security and also endorses China's focus on nontraditional security issues and its increased deployment of coast guard cutters to the region as a step that will prevent escalation and the further militarization of the delicate South China Sea issue.

Beijing's move 2 in Southeast Asia: China should invite ASEAN defense officials to carry out annual tours of PLA facilities in southern China, and especially on Hainan Island. This step will go a long way toward addressing the widespread complaint that the PLA is not adequately transparent. Instead of focusing on land forces, which are not of major concern, the focus should be on naval and air forces, and even include missile forces (the Second Artillery). At a minimum, the annual tours should take in both the new major Hainan Island base on Yalong Bay, as well as the South Sea Fleet headquarters at Zhanjiang. The base on Yalong Bay has witnessed a major expansion in the last decade and has therefore been the subject of relentless speculation. This speculation has injured China's regional diplomacy by increasing suspicions regarding the scope and scale of Chinese naval modernization. The initiative should *not* involve US defense officials—which should make it more palatable to the PLA. Rather, by launching an institutionalized approach to substantively improving regional military transparency, Beijing will build trust with its neighbors and deflate exaggerated fears regarding its intentions. This new focus on transparency, along with the multilateral approach, will make this effort meaningful from Washington's perspective.

Washington's move 3 in Southeast Asia: The United States should move to reduce surveillance operations off the Chinese coast, and near Hainan Island in particular. Beijing has long complained that such missions, conducted by specialized surveillance vessels and aircraft, have illustrated Washington's nefarious intentions. China's unorthodox countermeasures—which resulted in the EP-3 incident in 2001, the *Impeccable* incident in 2009, and yet another dangerous incident in August 2014—have not only caused the loss of human life but have also significantly contributed to the major increase in regional tensions during the last decade. Beijing has actually raised the issue to an equal status with US arms sales to Taiwan as creating a major barrier to enhanced overall China-US security cooperation. This sensitivity should not be at all surprising, given China's experience with "gunboat diplomacy," with coastal blockades after 1949, and with the fact that Hainan Island is the site of SSBN testing and future basing. These factors suggest that a move to placate Chinese concerns could reap major dividends for both regional and global security. From Washington's perspective, the legal principle that military activities are permissible within EEZs simply cannot be negotiable. However, standing firm on the principle does not preclude significant reductions in these activities, which hold the potential to seriously improve the security relationship. The United States could feasibly obtain the necessary surveillance data through other means, such as satellite reconnaissance and other less blatant intrusions. Indeed, a recent scholarly and rather comprehensive review of US intelligence operations against China undertaken during the Cold War reveals that such operations may, in fact, yield results that are counter to broader US interests.[118] While the agreement on "maritime encounters" that was reached between Xi and Obama at their Beijing Summit in November 2014 is certainly favorable, its impact on prevailing tensions may not meet expectations, regrettably. The agreement is closely related to a "Code for Unplanned Encounters" agreement reached between the Chinese and US navies back in April 2014. But, as one astute observer notes, that agreement did not prevent the August 2014 encounter between US and Chinese aircraft over the South China Sea, and a fundamental problem with the agreement is that these encounters are "not unplanned."[119] In short, we may wish to think that tensions will dissipate if we develop such "codes of conduct" or "rules of the road," but one cannot remove the strategic, political, and indeed symbolic ramifications of close-in surveillance without addressing the issues both of frequency and more generally of trade-offs in the overall bilateral relationship.

Beijing's move 3 in Southeast Asia: China should act to clarify the precise nature of its claims in the South China Sea, and in doing so should make those claims consistent with the Law of the Sea. At this point, the cooperation spiral begins to deal with the most sensitive and difficult issues, but the aim is not to simply allow for a few years of stability but rather to also seek a more permanent solution to one of the most vexing and also volatile problems in both Chinese foreign policy and US-China relations. The confusion and ambiguity surrounding China's expansive claims are one of the chief causes of the present dispute. Understood in maximalist terms, the so-called U-shaped line of China's claim seems to represent a highly aggressive posture, because it suggests that the ocean in this case be treated similarly to a land border (making no specific reference to maritime legal concepts, e.g., "territorial seas" and "economic exclusive zones"). Iain Johnston's recent scholarship has shown that much of the clamor about "assertive China" is hyperbole, but notes that "more frequent [maritime] patrols, . . . more risk-acceptant action, . . . and more vigorous diplomatic pushback [from Beijing]" have "clearly contributed to an escalation of tension in the East Asian maritime space," suggesting the imperative for Beijing to reform its present posture of ambiguity.[120] Even Chinese maritime legal specialists are challenged to explain the concept, and they readily concede that Chinese specialists disagree about the meaning of the U-shaped line. Two facts, however, should give Beijing confidence regarding these claims: (1) The claim does not derive from the current regime, but rather from the Republican Era; and (2) a modified claim is strengthened by the fact that Taiwan has jurisdiction over the largest island, Taiping Dao / Itu Aba. In other words, Beijing can maintain a rather strong claim, while at the same time modifying this claim to comport with current international norms. Such a move would actually be quite consistent with the other territorial compromises that Beijing has reached in the last two decades.[121] Moreover, as the scholar Michael Gau observed in 2012 in the journal *Ocean Development & International Law*, Beijing has actually been making subtle attempts at finding a compromise: "While the ROC [Republic of China, i.e., Taiwan] has ceased to defend publicly the concept of historic waters in the South China Sea, the PRC seems to have abandoned the position by making negative remarks. The evidence can be found in the 2011 PRC Note Verbale, . . . [which] makes no mention of . . . historic waters. . . . This may justify the view that the PRC has abandoned such an idea so as to facilitate bilateral maritime delimitation negotiations."[122] In other words, China's U-shaped line may continue to exist, but in "harmonized" form, to accord with greater peace and stability in Southeast Asia and between the superpowers.

Washington's move 4 in Southeast Asia: The United States should endorse China's role as a claimant to the Spratlys/Nansha Islands in the South China Sea and should also support bilateral negotiations to facilitate regional stability and peace. In return for Beijing crossing the major hurdle of giving some law-based clarification of its claims, Washington should reciprocate by publicly welcoming China as a legitimate claimant. This is not at all the same as endorsing the Chinese claim itself. It would be to merely suggest that China's claim is on par with those of the other claimants and, consistent with long-standing US policy, making it clear that Washington would not seek to favor any one set of claims over any other. Such a statement would remove China's anxiety over its worst case scenario—namely, that it could be cut out of all the resource riches that exist in the Spratlys/Nansha part of the South China Sea—with the resultant extreme loss of face. Even more important, however, would be Washington's support for bilateral negotiations among the claimants—a process that Beijing has long favored. Such an alteration to current US policy would recognize the simple reality that the complexity of bringing all claimants to the table at once determines that a comprehensive, multilateral solution is simply not feasible—no wonder so little progress has occurred on the issue in the last few decades. Bilateral negotiations have certain advantages, not least that they allow for extended-duration, high-complexity, and one-on-one trust building between leaders. Despite the skepticism, it seems that China's neighbors have actually done quite well in such negotiations.[123]

Beijing's move 4 in Southeast Asia: China must operationalize its policy of "joint development" for the South China Sea, guided by a simple 50/50 split framework. In theory, this step is not so difficult for Beijing, because seeking "joint development" has been official Chinese policy since Deng Xiaoping. In reality, however, joint development has proven difficult—in no small part because it depends on a cooperative disposition on the part of other claimant states. As an example, the Joint Maritime Seismic Undertaking between Beijing, Manila, and Hanoi, which was announced with significant fanfare in late 2005, appears to have been unfortunately shipwrecked on the complex shoals of domestic politics in the Philippines.[124] On the positive side, China will increasingly have the technical capabilities to undertake complex (and deep sea) exploration, which will make joint projects more feasible. A middle split (50/50) will place negotiations between Beijing and various claimants (and their respective corporate interests) within the framework of a fair and equitable distribution of resource benefits. No claimant can then be said to have "won" the South China Sea issue, and yet no claimant will be totally left out of resource exploitation either. It is fully recognized that "the devil is in the details" and that all specific joint development projects will involve inherently complex negotiations. On one hand, ASEAN claimants need to grasp that a peaceful exploitation of resources will not occur unless Beijing is substantially included. On the other hand, Beijing must make sure that joint development is truly "win–win" if cooperation with other claimants is to effectively enhance regional stability. An important and rather more detailed proposal for a joint development solution to the South China Sea dispute that merits wide consideration was recently published as a collaboration between an American and a Chinese scholar.[125]

Washington's move 5 in Southeast Asia: The United States should cease military cooperation with Vietnam. To build a durable regional order in Southeast Asia that is not continually roiling US-China relations will require strategic restraint by both Washington and Beijing. By contrast, recent overtures toward military cooperation between Hanoi and Washington have violated reasonable principles of geopolitical moderation. True, cooperation to date has not ventured far beyond symbolic events, such as port visits, but these activities have fueled very considerable angst in Beijing, and thus introduced a highly unstable variable into US-China relations that did not previously exist.[126] Moreover, there are recent hints, duly noted by the Chinese press, that US-Vietnam defense cooperation may become more serious.[127] It is also not at all clear that military cooperation between Hanoi and Washington will even benefit Vietnamese national interests. For comparison, the small country of Georgia in the Caucasus paid dearly for its vigorous flirtation with the West when it was crushed by the Russian Army in 2008. The same could be said of Ukraine's loss of Crimea in 2014. The central point is that Vietnam has a highly complex relationship with China, but none of the respective issues are directly related to US national security. Bader's observation is revealing on Vietnam's unique role: "No one in the region, with the possible exception of Vietnam, wished to see the United States embroiled in a confrontation with China."[128] Washington's new relationship with Hanoi appears from Beijing's point of view as both opportunistic and threatening. If China began regularized military cooperation and joint exercises with Mexico or Cuba, Americans would perhaps understand the risks of these high-stakes geopolitical poker moves more clearly.

Beijing's move 5 in Southeast Asia: China should cease military cooperation with the Philippines, and also with Indonesia. Manila has very close cultural and historical ties to Washington. Part of a process of stabilizing the Southeast Asia region will entail that Beijing recognizes that the United States has played and will continue to play an important role in regional security. Owing to its proximity, China will naturally have a plethora of economic and security issues to discuss with the Philippines, but these do not depend on an active program of military cooperation. Of course, there should be no limit on non-military institutional cooperation, for example, to improve search and rescue or fisheries coordination that is much needed between the Philippines and Chinese coast guards. It will be much more difficult for Beijing, however, to apply the brakes to the very promising military-to-military relationship that it has developed with Jakarta. This relationship has already evolved to the stage of substantive joint exercises, extensive training, and significant arms purchases. Thus, Indonesia represents a tough case of restraint for China—more on par with the needed American restraint on Vietnam outlined above. Both countries are major regional players that offer favorable geographical positioning and major potential export markets for arms. The inherent instability of geopolitical "games" through involvement with these states in the region has become amply apparent. As Nathan and Scobell observe, "Beijing's growing strength and its preoccupation with its immediate periphery have combined to produce a Chinese soft version of the Monroe Doctrine. . . . Beijing aspires to a buffer zone of stable neighbors, free of great power dominance."[129] Such an arrangement is not actually contrary to US interests. A parallel recognition of "spheres of influence" for each great power in Southeast Asia will create a firmer and more stable foundation for regional peace. And the logic applied here to Vietnam, the Philippines, and Indonesia might indeed be pursued as a broader division of continental Southeast Asia under Chinese leadership, while maritime Southeast Asia might look to a larger constellation of maritime powers, including but not limited to the United States. In this sense, the cooperation spiral does not only rely on building trust and creating stabilizing institutions but also draws on traditional power politics among the great powers. As such, the balance of power may serve rather than undermine regional and global security.

Conclusion

Must the Malacca Strait and the South China Sea inevitably become the "Fulda Gap" of the new Cold War descending on the Asia-Pacific region, as the tense 2014 Shangri-La Dialogue seemed to imply?[130] It is far from the case that this region should emerge at the center of US-China rivalry. Although such a rivalry could serve some parochial short-term interests, no long-term interests in Southeast Asia, or elsewhere, will be served by the deepening of this rivalry. Southeast Asia has seen a remarkable flowering of peace since the end of the Cold War, as the decades-long conflicts on the Indochina Peninsula finally came to a close. The fortunate cessation of this horrendous bloodletting led to the beginning of a new and hopeful chapter in the history of the region, where prosperity is quickly becoming the norm. Historically, Southeast Asians have extensive experience with the injustices of colonialism and with the destruction wrought by great power rivalry. Indeed, the extraordinary development of ASEAN as a regional security and economic institution suggests that local states are fully capable of securing the newfound gains for the region.

However, US-China rivalry in Southeast Asia is now clearly intensifying. On daily Chinese television news shows, analysts dissect Washington's maneuvers in the region to further "contain" China.[131] Similarly, American news reports increasingly feature the plight of Southeast Asians confronting alleged Chinese aggression.[132] To be sure, some voices have emerged to promote caution on both sides of the Pacific, but these voices are still all too rare.[133] A troubling left–right consensus in Washington has now apparently emerged regarding the need to confront China in Southeast Asia.

A half century ago in both Washington and Beijing, national leaders puzzled over how to prevent the perceived clashing of US and Chinese interests in Southeast Asia from resulting in another cataclysm on par with or even exceeding the Korean War, which was seared into their collective memories.[134] It must be hoped that today's Chinese and American leaders will be equally sober in their deliberations, and thus will take positive steps toward compromises that will benefit both their own countries and Southeast Asians.

Notes

1. Edward Wong, "Beijing Warns US about South China Sea Dispute," *New York Times*, June 22, 2011, www.nytimes.com/2011/06/23/world/asia/23china .html?_r=1.
2. During much of the Cold War, Western planners were most anxious about a decisive Soviet strike across the Central German Plain, known as the Fulda Gap in NATO defenses. US political and military strategy during those decades grappled with the difficult problem of how, first and foremost, to blunt such a strike, but also how to convince the Kremlin that it could not possibly win in all related scenarios.

3. This metaphor with respect to the evolving US-China rivalry was first introduced by Robert Kaplan, "Center Stage for the 21st Century," *Foreign Affairs*, March–April 2009, 16–32.

4. "解放军报评论员文章" [Liberation Army Daily Commentator Article], as reported on CCTV News Channel 13, May 10, 2012.

5. Gina Harkins and Sam Fellman, "Navy Wants to Expand Philippine Presence, Create Temporary Base," *Navy Times*, July 27, 2013, www.navytimes.com /article/20130727/NEWS/307270004Navy-wants-expand-Philippine-presence -create-temporary-base.

6. 韩硕, 郑志, 青本 [Han Shuo, Zheng Zhi, and Qing Ben], "美防长在菲律宾大谈'增兵'" [US Defense Secretary Visiting Philippines Discusses "Increasing Forces"], 环球时报 [Global Times], August 31, 2013, 8.

7. 张建刚 [Zhang Jiangang] "专家: 和平崛起与动武不矛盾 维护主权可开枪" [Expert: Peaceful Rise and the Use of Force Are Not in Contradiction—It Is Possible to Open Fire in Defense of Sovereignty] 环球时报 [*Global Times*], June 10, 2014, http://mil.huanqiu.com/observation/2014-06/5015795.html.

8. Patrick M. Cronin and Robert D. Kaplan, "Cooperation from Strength: US Strategy and the South China Sea," in *Cooperation from Strength: The United States, China, and the South China Sea*, ed. Patrick M. Cronin (Washington, DC: Center for a New American Security), 11–12.

9. See, e.g., Walter LaFeber, *The Cambridge History of American Foreign Relations, Volume II: The American Search for Opportunity 1865–1913* (New York: Cambridge University Press, 1993), 156–64.

10. See, e.g., remarks by Philippines President Benigno Aquino III, September 2, 2011, www.gov.ph/2011/09/02/president-aquino-speech-at-the-philippines -eastern-china-business-forum-september-2-2011/. See also 杨静林 [Yang Jinglin], "古代中非关系与贸易" [Relationship and Trade between China and the Philippines in Ancient Times], 东南亚纵横 [Around Southeast Asia], June 2010, 73–76.

11. 赵文红 [Zhao Wenhong], "试论近代早期欧洲殖民者对东南亚海上贸易格局的影响" [Impact of European Colonizers on the Situation of Southeast Asia's Maritime Trade in the Early Modern Period], 东南亚纵横 [Around Southeast Asia], September 2011, 47, 52.

12. This paragraph drawn from 张小明 [Zhang Xiaoming], 美国与东亚关系导论 [An Introduction to the History of US-East Asian Relations] (Beijing: Peking University Press, 2010), 59–60.

13. See, e.g., 候洁 [Hou Jie], "论美国对菲律宾南部摩洛人的殖民统治" [American Colonial Rule on Moro in the Southern Philippines], 东南亚研究 [Southeast Asian Studies], January 2008, 67–72; and 陈衍德, 杨宏云 [Chen Yande and Yang Hongyun], "美国的新殖民主义与菲律宾民族主义

的回应: 1898–1935" [The United States' New Colonialism and the Philippine Nationalistic Response, 1898–1935], 东南亚研究 [Southeast Asian Studies], April 2008, 41–47.

14. 郑先武 [Zheng Xianwu], "东南亚区域间主义的历史考察" [A Historical Examination of Regionalism in Southeast Asia], 南洋问题研究 [Southeast Asian Affairs], no. 146 (February 2011), 23. Conversely, it is also worth noting that Chinese scholars are starting to undertake serious historical research into US-China strategic interaction in Southeast Asia during the Cold War. See, e.g., 翟韬 [Zhai Tao], "美国对东南亚华人宣传政策的演变 1949–1964" [The Evolution of US Propaganda Policy toward the Ethnic Chinese in Southeast Asia, 1949–1964], 美国研究 [American Studies Quarterly], January 2013, 117–37; and 刘雄 [Liu Xiong] "国家安全与华侨利益的双重考量: 论新中国对东南亚华侨政策的演变, 1949–1960" [National Security and the Dual Key Considerations for Overseas Chinese: A Discussion on the Evolution of China's Policy toward Overseas Chinese in Southeast Asia, 1949–1960], 中共党史研究 [Research on Communist Party History], June 2013, 38–48.

15. Xie Tao, "Back on the Silk Road: China's Version of a Rebalance to Asia," *Global Asia 9*, no. 1 (Spring 2014), www.globalasia.org/Issue/ArticleDetail/548 /back-on-the-silk-road-chinas-version-of-a-rebalance-to-asia.html.

16. On the perceived Chinese threat to Southeast Asia in the early 1960s, see, e.g., Lawrence Freedman, *Kennedy's Wars: Berlin, Cuba, Laos, and Vietnam* (New York: Oxford University Press, 2000), 301 .

17. Amitav Acharya, *Constructing a Security Community in Southeast Asia: ASEAN and the Problem of Regional Order* (London: Routledge, 2001), 8.

18. Ibid., 96–98.

19. 曹云华 [Cao Yunhua, ed.], 东南亚国家联盟: 结构运作与对外关系 [The Alliance of the Southeast Asian Countries: Structure, Activities and Foreign Relations] (Beijing: China Economic Publishing House, 2010), 155.

20. Lieutenant Michael Studeman, "Calculating China's Advances in the South China Sea: Identifying the Triggers of 'Expansionism,'" *Naval War College Review* 51, no. 2 (Spring 1998), 69. Another account is by John Garver, "China's Push through the South China Sea: The Interaction of Bureaucratic and National Interests," *China Quarterly* 132 (December 1992): 99–128.

21. 魏玲 [Wei Ling], "国内进程不对称互动与体系变化: 中国, 东盟与东亚合作" [Domestic Progress, Asymmetric Interaction and System Change: China, ASEAN, and East Asian Cooperation], 当代亚太 [Journal of Contemporary Asia-Pacific Studies], June 2010, 58–59.

22. 郑先武 [Zheng Xianwu], "东南亚区域间主义的历史考察" [A Historical Examination of Regionalism in Southeast Asia], 26.

23. Renato Cruz de Castro, "The US-Philippine Alliance: An Evolving Hedge against an Emerging China Challenge," *Contemporary Southeast Asia* 31, no. 3 (2009): 404–5.

24. [Cao Yunhua, ed.], 东南亚国家联盟: 结构运作与对外关系 [The Alliance of the Southeast Asian Countries: Structure, Activities, and Foreign Relations], 155.

25. 魏玲 [Wei Ling], "国内进程不对称互动与体系变化: 中国, 东盟与东亚合作" [Domestic Progress, Asymmetric Interaction and System Change: China, ASEAN, and Asian Cooperation], p. 61.

26. Hyoung-Kyu Chey, "The Changing Political Dynamics of East Asian Financial Cooperation: The Chiang Mai Initiative," *Asian Survey* 49, no. 3 (May–June 2009): 453.

27. 牛仲君 [Niu Zhongjun], "中国参与东帝汶维和的原因级立场分析" [China's Peacekeeping Operations in East Timor: History and Analysis], 外交评论 [Foreign Policy Commentary], April 2007, 50–51.

28. For a recent favorable appraisal of the China-ASEAN Free Trade Area's impact on regional trade flows by an economist in Malaysia, see Evelyn S. Devadason, "ASEAN-China Trade Flows: Moving Forward with CAFTA," *Journal of Contemporary China* 19 (September 2010): 653–74.

29. A late 2012 study by two Fudan University economists may suggest that Chinese scholars are concerned about the economic dislocations in neighboring countries due to China "export expansion." 罗长远, 张军 [Luo Changyuan and Zhang Jun], "中国出口扩张的创新溢出效应: 以泰国为例" [The Innovative Spillover of China's Export Expansion: The Example of Thailand], 中国社会科学 [Social Sciences in China], November 2012, 57–80.

30. Joshua Kurlantzick, "China's Charm Offensive in Southeast Asia," *Current History*, September 2006, 270.

31. Mohd Nizam Basiron and Sumathy Permal, "Regional Maritime Security Environment: The Malaysian Perspective," in *Southeast Asia and the Rise of Chinese and Indian Naval Power: Between Rising Naval Powers*, ed. Sam Bateman and Joshua Ho (London: Routledge, 2010), 91.

32. 郑蔚康 [Zheng Weikang], "菲律宾对东盟政策中的美国因素" [The Influence of the United States on the Philippines' Policies toward ASEAN], 东南亚研究 [Southeast Asian Studies], May 2009, 63.

33. De Castro, "US-Philippine Alliance," 411.

34. Ibid.

35. 许利平 [Xu Liping], "战略伙伴关系框架下的中国: 印尼合作: 基础现状与趋势" [China-Indonesia's Cooperation under the Framework of the Strategic Partnership: Basis, Status Quo, and Trends], 东南亚研究

[Southeast Asian Studies], March 2011, 56. On the interesting issue of Indonesia-China cooperation on the issue of sea lane security, see, e.g., James Hardy, "China Offers Indonesia Coastal Radars," *Jane's Defense Weekly*, May 16, 2012, 16.

36. Rizal Sukma, "Indonesia-China Relations: The Politics of Re-engagement," *Asian Survey* 49 (July–August 2009): 604.

37. 古小松 [Gu Xiaosong], "广西在中国-东盟交流合作中的地位和作用" [Guangxi's Position and Role in China-ASEAN Communication and Coopera-tion], 东南亚纵横 [Around Southeast Asia], November 2008, 21–27.

38. 李海江, 丁文丽 [Li Haijiang and Ding Wenli], "湄公河次区域经济发展现状与金融合作研究" [Research on the Economic Developing Status and Financial Cooperation of the Greater Mekong Subregion], 南亚纵横 [Around Southeast Asia], October 2008, 17.

39. Regarding these many projects, see, e.g., Thomas Fuller, "A Highway That Binds China and Its Neighbors," *New York Times*, March 30, 2008, www.nytimes.com/2008/03/30/world/asia/30iht-road.1.11530886.html; and Anthony Kuhn, "Full Speed Ahead for China's Rail Links with Its Neighbors?" *NPR Morning Edition*, June 14, 2011, www.npr.org/2011/06/14/137111321 /full-steam-ahead-for-chinas-rail-links-abroad.

40. David Kang, *China Rising: Peace, Power, and Order in East Asia* (New York: Columbia University Press, 2009), 126–52.

41. Evan Medeiros, Keith Crane, Eric Heginbotham, Norman D. Levin, Julia Lowell, Angel Rabasa, and Somi Seong, *Pacific Currents: The Responses of US Allies and Security Partners in East Asia to China's Rise* (Santa Monica, CA: RAND Corporation, 2008), 246.

42. Sigfrido Burgos and Sophal Ear, "China's Strategic Interests in Cambodia: Influence and Resources," *Asian Survey* 50 (May–June 2010): 237–38. A less pessimistic analysis of China's aid activities in Cambodia is given by James Reilly, "A Norm-Taker or a Norm-Maker? Chinese Aid in Southeast Asia," *Jour-nal of Contemporary China* 21 (January 2012): 80–81.

43. 韩发展, 王学玉 [Han Fazhan and Wang Xueyu], "化解东盟国家对中国撅起疑虑" [Defusing ASEAN States' Misgivings toward China's Rise], 东南亚纵横 [Around Southeast Asia], August 2011, 24.

44. 孙景平 [Sun Jingping], "新世纪新阶段海上安全战略断想" [Notes on Maritime Security Strategy in the New Period in the New Century], 中国军事科学 [China Military Science], June 2008, 77, 79.

45. 易海冰 [Yi Haibing], 中国海军要控制马六甲海峡 [The Chinese Navy Should Seek to Control the Malacca Strait], 舰船知识 [Naval and Merchant Ships], November 2007, 24.

46. 一业 [Yi Ye], "中国不应该控制马六甲海峡," [China Should Not Seek to Control the Malacca Strait], *舰船知识* [Naval and Merchant Ships] November 2007, 26–28.

47. "专家: 南海事件不足道中美战争可能性为零" [Expert: The Chance of the South China Sea Incident Leading to a US-China War Is Zero], *环球时报* [Global Times], March 13, 2009.

48. 潘泽岗 [Pan Zegang], "碰撞: 从'无瑕'号事件看中美近海对抗" [Collision: A Look at the US-China Confrontation in the Near Seas from the Vantage Point of the "Impeccable" Incident], *舰船知识* [Naval & Merchant Ships], May 2009, 19.

49. "Lost on China: A Bad Treaty Leads to a Naval Scrap," *Wall Street Journal*, March 11, 2009, http://online.wsj.com/article/SB123672918272489143 .html.

50. Michael Yahuda, "China's New Assertiveness in the South China Sea," *Journal of Contemporary China* 22, no. 81 (2013): 447. For an in-depth discussion of the related legal arguments on both sides, see Peter Dutton, ed., *Military Activities in the EEZ: A US-China Dialogue on Security and International Law in the Maritime Commons*, China Maritime Study 7 (Newport: Naval War College Press: 2010), www.usnwc.edu/Research---Gaming/China-Maritime-Studies -Institute/Publications/documents/China-Maritime-Study-7_Military -Activities-in-the-.pdf.

51. See, e.g., 游民 [You Min], "中国如何防范美国核潜艇" [How China Can Guard against US Nuclear Submarines], *舰船知识* [Naval & Merchant Ships], July 2013, 32–37.

52. 朱伟祺 [Zhu Weiqi], "'基洛'潜艇驶入越南再思考" [Reevaluating the Arrival of Kilo-Class Submarines into Vietnam], *现代舰船* [Modern Ships], July 2009, 6, 9.

53. "南海军情特报" [Special Military Intelligence Report on the South China Sea], *军事世界* [Inside Defense], May 2009, 21.

54. Ibid.

55. 蔡鹏鸿 [Cai Penghong], "美国南海政策剖析" [Analysis of US Policy toward the South Sea], *现代国际关系* [Contemporary International Relations], September 2009, 1–7.

56. James Bussert, "Hainan Is the Tip of the Chinese Navy's Spear," *Signal Magazine*, June 2009, www.afcea.org/signal/articles/anmviewer.asp?a=1968&print =yes.

57. L. C. Russell Hsiao, "China's New Submarines and Deployment Patterns: Aimed at the South China Sea?" *China Brief* 10, issue 21 (October 22, 2010): 1.

58. Thomas Harding, "Chinese Nuclear Submarine Base," *Telegraph*, May 1, 2008, www.telegraph.co.uk/news/worldnews/asia/china/1917167/Chinese-nuclear-submarine-base.html.

59. Ted Parsons and Mrityunjoy Mazumdar, "Photos Provide Clues for Chinese 'Type 056' Corvette Design," *Jane's Navy International*, December 2010, 4.

60. Russell Hsiao, "PLA Posturing for Conflict in the South China Sea," *China Brief* 10, issue 16 (August 5, 2010): 2.

61. Ted Parsons, "Launch of Mystery Chinese SSK Fuels Submarine Race in Asia," *Jane's Navy International*, October 2010, 4.

62. Hsiao, "China's New Submarines," 2.

63. Andrei Chang, "PLA Navy South Sea Fleet Constructing New Submarine Base," *Kanwa Asian Defense Review Online*, no. 74 (December 2010): 10–11.

64. Ed Wong, "Chinese Military Seeks to Extend Its Naval Power," *New York Times*, April 23, 2010, www.nytimes.com/2010/04/24/world/asia/24navy.html.

65. Ian Storey, "China's Missteps in Southeast Asia: Less Charm, More Offensive," *China Brief* 10, issue 25 (December 17, 2010): 5.

66. Jeffrey A. Bader, *Obama and China's Rise: An Insider's Account of America's Asia Strategy* (Washington, DC: Brookings Institution Press, 2012), 105. However, earlier in this account, he seems to say that the "core interest" comment never occurred (p. 77).

67. Storey, "China's Missteps," 5.

68. Bader, *Obama*, 104.

69. John Pomfret, "US Takes a Tougher Tone with China," *Washington Post*, July 30, 2010.

70. L. R. Hsiao, "PLA Posturing," 1–2.

71. Satu Limaye, "America's Bilateral Relations with ASEAN: Constraints and Promise," *Contemporary Southeast Asia* 32 (2010): 312.

72. "Vietnam in Live Fire Drill among South China Sea Row," BBC, June 13, 2011, www.bbc.co.uk/news/world-asia-pacific-13745587.

73. 新天 [Xin Tian], "破解南海迷局: 李晓宁看南海问题" [Penetrating the Confusing Situation in the South China Sea: Li Xiaoning's Views on the South China Sea Issue], 军事文摘 [Military Digest], July 2011, 9.

74. Charles Scanlon, "South China Sea Tensions Rattle China's Neighbors," BBC News, November 3, 2011, www.bbc.co.uk/news/world-asia-pacific-15578083.

75. Admiral Hu Yanlin (ret.), interview reported in "海军上将眼中的中国海洋战略" [Chinese Maritime Strategy from the Perspective of a Navy Admiral], 现代舰船 [Modern Ships], October 2010, 11.

76. Ibid., 13.

77. [Li Jie, PLA Navy senior captain], "美国频繁军演习的叵测用心" [The Inexplicable Motive behind Frequent US Military Exercises], 现代舰船 [Modern Ships], October 2010, 60.

78. 高卫民 [Gao Weimin], "南海问题: 各方要谨慎应对" [The South China Sea: All Sides Need to React Prudently], 当代海军 [Modern Navy], July 2011, 54–57.

79. Patrick Barta, "US-Vietnam in Exercises amid Tensions with China," *Wall Street Journal*, July 16, 2011, http://online.wsj.com/article/SB1000142405270 23042238045764474127484655574.html.

80. Jacob Moore, "USS *George Washington* Welcomes Aboard Vietnamese Guests," August 1, 2011, www.c7f.navy.mil/news/2011/08-august/021.htm.

81. "US-China Spat over South China Sea Military Exercises," BBC News, July 11, 2011, www.bbc.co.uk/news/world-asia-pacific-14097503.

82. "Philippine Navy Acquires Hamilton Cutter," May 13, 2011, www.philippine embassy-usa.org/news/1682/300/Philippine-Navy-Acquires-Hamilton-Cutter /d,phildet/.

83. Craig Whitlock, "Navy's Next Stop in China Will Set China on Edge," *Washington Post*, November 18, 2011, www.washingtonpost.com/blogs/checkpoint -washington/post/navys-next-stop-in-asia-will-set-china-on-edge/2011/11/18 /gIQAzY7wYN_blog.html.

84. Marvin Ott, "Deep Danger: Competing Claims in the South China Sea," *Current History*, September 2011, 241.

85. Hillary Clinton, "America's Pacific Century," *Foreign Policy*, November 3, 2011, www.foreignpolicy.com/articles/2011/10/11/americas_pacific_century ?page=0,3.

86. "Obama Visit: Australia Agrees US Marine Deployment Plan," BBC News, November 16, 2011, www.bbc.co.uk/news/world-asia-15739995.

87. "Flaws in the Diamond: In the Different Disputes in the East China Sea and South China Sea, China's Aims Are the Same," Banyan Column, *The Economist*, September 21, 2013, 46. An even more strident critique is by Gordan Chang, "China and the Biggest Territorial Grab since World War II," *Forbes*, June 2, 2013, www.forbes.com/sites/gordonchang/2013/06/02/china-and-the-biggest -territory-grab-since-world-war-ii/.

88. "US, Philippines in Talks on US Military Presence in Philippines," UPI, July 12, 2013, www.upi.com/Top_News/World-News/2013/07/12/US-Philippines -in-talks-on-US-military-presence-in-Philippines/UPI-75241373658529/# ixzz2gTvsIWyv.

89. 阎学通 [Yan Xuetong], "从南海问题说到中国外交调整" [Calling for a Revision of Chinese Foreign Policy from the South China Sea Issue], 中国外交 [Chinese Foreign Policy], April 2012, 58.

90. 韩硕, 邱永峥, 刘畅 [Han Shuo, Qiu Yongzheng, Liu Chang], "菲律宾称中国在黄岩岛建设施" [Philippines States That China Is Building Facilities at Huangyan Island / Scarborough Shoal], 环球时报 [Global Times], September 4, 2013, 3.

91. 张卫彬 [Zhang Weibin], "国际法庭确定领土边界争端中地图证据份量考: U形线地图在解决南沙群岛争端中的作用" [Consideration Given to Maps by the International Court in Settlement of Border Disputes: The Role of the U-Shaped Line in Resolving the Dispute over the Spratly Islands], 当代亚太 [Journal of Contemporary Asia-Pacific Studies], May–June 2012, 117–30.

92. 孔令杰 [Kong Lingjie], "中菲关于黄岩岛领土主权的主张和依据研究" [A Comparative Study of the Arguments of China and the Philippines on Sovereignty over Huangyan Island / Scarorough Shoal], 南洋问题研究 [Southeast Asian Affairs], January 2013, 19–20.

93. 高风 [Gao Feng], "南海争端与'联合国海洋法公约'" [The South China Sea Dispute and the "United Nations Law of the Sea"], 国际政治研究 [International Political Studies], March 2013, 154–55.

94. [Zhang Qingmin], "中国解决陆地边界经验对解决海洋边界的启示" [Lessons from China's Resolution of Its Land Borders for Resolving Its Maritime Border Issues], 外交评论 [Foreign Policy Review], April 2013, 9.

95. [Cai Tingyi], "'角力'东盟" [The "Tussle" for ASEAN], 财经 [Finance and Economics], January 13, 2014, 35.

96. [Wu Shicun], "外界不必臆测南海防空识别区" [The Outside World Need Not Conjecture Regarding an Air Defense Identification Zone for the South China Sea], 还球时报 [Global Times], January 3, 2014, 15.

97. Yahuda, "China's New Assertiveness," 458.

98. Gordon Chang, "Appeasing China," March 19, 2014, *The National Interest*, http://nationalinterest.org/print/commentary/appeasing-china-10073.

99. 张结 [Zhang Jie], "黄岩岛模式与中国海洋威权政策的转向" [The Huangyan Model and the Shift of China's Maritime Strategy], 东南亚研究 [Southeast Asian Studies], no. 4 (2013): 29.

100. "Remarks by President Obama and President Benigno Aquino III of the Philippines in Joint Press Conference," April 28, 2014, White House Office of the Press Secretary, www.whitehouse.gov/the-press-office/2014/04/28/remarks-president-obama-and-president-benigno-aquino-iii-philippines-joi.

101. 张景金 [Zhang Jingjin], "美非同盟强化及其在美国亚太再平衡战略中的作用" [The Strengthening of the US-Philippines Alliance and Its Function in America's Rebalance Strategy to the Asia-Pacific], 南洋问题研究 [Southeast Asian Affairs], January 2014, 1–2.

102. 李金蓉, 朱瑛, 方银霞 [Li Jinrong, Zhu Ying, Fang Yinxia], "南海南部油气资源勘探开发状况及对策建议" [The State of the Exploration and Development of Oil and Gas Resources in the Southern Part of the South China Sea and Policy Suggestions], 开发与管理 [Ocean Development and Management], April 2014, 12–15; 朱伟林, 米立军, 高乐, 钟锟, 高阳东 [Zhu Weilin, Mi Lijun, Gao Le, Zhong Kun, and Gao Yangdong], "认识和技术创新推动中国近海油气勘探再上新台阶" [The Innovation in Knowledge and Technology Has Given Impetus to Reaching a New Stage in Hydrocarbon Exploration Off China's Shores: A Review of 2013 Offshore Exploration in China], 中国海上油气 [China Offshore Oil and Gas], February 2014, 1–8. A full translation of the first article given here was completed by the China Maritime Studies Institute at the Naval War College by Shazeeda Ahmed and Ryan Martinson.

103. 方晓 [Fang Xiao], "越南急造新执法下水, 中国要越放弃幻想停止西沙挑衅" [Vietnam Is Hastily Building Cutter Patrol Craft, China Wants Vietnam to Abandon Its Fantasies and Halt the Paracels Challenge], 东方早报 [Oriental Morning Post], June 6, 2014, A16.

104. "China Is Destabilising Southeast Asia, US Defence Secretary Says," *The Guardian*, May 31, 2014, www.theguardian.com/world/2014/may/31/china-is-destabilising-south-east-asia-us-defence-secretary-warns.

105. Floyd Whaley, "Philippines Reports Chinese Ship Movements around Disputed Reefs," *New York Times*, June 5, 2014, www.nytimes.com/2014/06/06/world/asia/philippines-reports-chinese-ship-movement-around-disputed-reefs.html?_r=0.

106. James Hardy and Sean O'Connor, "China Building Airstrip-capable Island on Fiery Cross Reef," Jane's, November 20, 2014, http://www.janes.com/article/46083/china-building-airstrip-capable-island-on-fiery-cross-reef.

107. See, e.g., 陈武 [Chen Wu], "发展好海洋合作作伙伴关系" [Facilitate the Partnership of Maritime Cooperation], 东南亚纵横 [Around Southeast Asia], January 2014, 3–5; 刘新生 [Liu Xinsheng] "携手打造新 '海上丝绸之路'" [Join Hands to Create a New "Maritime Silk Road"], 东南亚纵横 [Around Southeast Asia], February 2014, 3–5.

108. 罗辉 [Luo Hui], "东亚地区主义的模式与路径分析" [East Asian Regionalism: Pattern and Path], in 新兴大国与传统大国: 博弈中的合作 [New-Type Great Powers and Traditional Great Powers: Cooperation within a Game], ed. 黄仁伟 [Huang Renwei] (Beijing: Current Events Press, 2010), 125.

109. 郑泽民 [Zheng Zemin], 南海问题中的大国因素 [The Great Power Factor in the South Sea Issue] (Beijing: World Knowledge Press, 2010), 104.

110. Shaun Tandon, "Singapore Warns US on Anti-China Rhetoric," Agence France-Press, February 8, 2012, www.google.com/hostednews/afp/article/ALeq

M5g1hvgGhNFvi9d_VR2RrRRLT7HyWg?docId=CNG.bd4020d80f3778c
303ff226bde78f155.391.

111. Although "hedging" should be deemphasized, especially within the region, some adjustments in US military forces are still required to hedge against the worst case scenario of great power conflict. Regarding such adjustments, see Lyle Goldstein, "Resetting the US-China Security Relationship," *IISS Survival* 53 (April–May 2011): 109–11.

112. Saw Swee-Hock, Sheng Lijun, and Chin Kin Wah, *ASEAN-China Relations: Realities and Prospects* (Singapore: Institute of Southeast Asian Studies, 2005), 16.

113. See, e.g., 田中 [Admiral Tian Zhong, PLA Navy], "海军非战争军事行动的特点 类型及能力建设" [Special Characteristics Categories and Capabilities of Naval Military Operations Other Than War], *中国军事科学* [China Military Science], no. 3 (2008): 25–30. On Chinese views of nontraditional security, see Lyle J. Goldstein, ed., *Not Congruent, but Quite Complementary: US and Chinese Approaches to Non-Traditional Security* (Newport: Naval War College Press, 2012).

114. See Edward Wong, "China and Its Neighbors Begin Joint Mekong Patrol," *New York Times*, December 10, 2011, www.nytimes.com/2011/12/11/world /asia/china-and-neighbors-begin-joint-mekong-river-patrols.html.

115. On RECAAP, see its official website, www.recaap.org/Home.aspx.

116. 祁怀高 [Qi Huaigao], "东亚区或合作领导权模式构想: 东盟机制下的中美日合作领导模式" [A Leadership Model Proposal for East Asian Regional Cooperation: China-US-Japan Co-leadership Model under the ASEAN Framework], *东南亚研究* [Southeast Asian Studies], April 2011, 55–59. A recent appraisal of China's interests in the Malacca Strait is given by 唐冲, 李志斐 [Tang Chong and Li Zhifei], "马六甲海峡安全问题与中国的政策选择" [The Malacca Straits Security Problem and China's Policy Options], *中国外交* [Chinese Foreign Policy], April 2013, 58–63. Interestingly, this analysis does explicitly recognize the "Japan factor" in US calculations (p. 59), and thus may illustrate Beijing's recognition of the importance of a trilateral initiative in this particular sphere. This piece also is noteworthy for its emphasis on the terrorist and piracy threats to the Malacca Strait; and the importance for Beijing of maintaining strong relations with Malaysia, Singapore, and Indonesia; as well as the general importance of the Chinese Navy and its ability to patrol in and around this crucial maritime chokepoint (pp. 58–59, 62–63).

117. Lyle Goldstein, "China as a New Maritime Partner? The US Coast Guard is Opening the Door to a Cooperative Relationship with China," *USNI Proceedings* 133 (August 2007): 26–31.

118. Bob Bergin, "The Growth of China's Air Defenses: Responding to Covert Overflights, 1949–1974," *Studies in Intelligence* 57, no. 2 (June 2013): 19–28.

119. Mark J. Valencia, "The New US-China MOU on Air and Maritime Encounters," *Diplomat*, November 17, 2014, http://thediplomat.com/2014/11/the-us-china-mou-on-air-and-maritime-encounters/.

120. Alastair Iain Johnston, "How New and Assertive Is China's New Assertiveness?" *International Security* 37 (Spring 2013): 46.

121. M. Taylor Fravel, *Strong Borders, Secure Nation: Cooperation and Conflict in China's Territorial Disputes* (Princeton, NJ: Princeton University Press, 2008), 300. This argument was recently made explicitly by RADM Yin Zhuo in an interview; see "学者: 钓鱼岛摩擦中美方加入斡旋很有价值" [Scholar: The US Intervention into the Diaoyu Island Tension with an Offer to Mediate Could Have Great Value], 新华网 [Xinhua News Net], January 4, 2011.

122. Michael Sheng-Ti Gau, "The U-Shaped Line and a Categorization of the Ocean Disputes in the South China Sea," *Ocean Development & International Law* 43 (2012): 62–63.

123. See, e.g., the discussion regarding negotiations and agreements with Kazakhstan, Kyrgyzstan, and Tajikistan in ibid, 160–66.

124. De Castro, "US-Philippine Alliance," 414.

125. Mark Valencia and Hong Nong, "Joint Development Possibilities: What, Where, Who, and How?" *Global Asia*, Summer 2013, 102–9.

126. 李忠林 [Li Zhonglin], "试析中越关系中的美国因素" [An Analysis of the US Factor in Sino–Vietnamese Relations], 亚非纵横 [Asia & Africa Review], April 2011, 52. Even this rather moderate analysis views recent development of US-Vietnam relations as "a strengthening of Washington's containment strategy toward China."

127. See, e.g., 海矛 [Hai Mao], "越南欲采购P-3C反潜巡逻机" [Vietnam Desires to Purchase P-3C Antisubmarine Aircraft], 中国国防报 [China National Defense News], April 23, 2013, 14.

128. Bader, *Obama*, 103.

129. Andrew J. Nathan and Andrew Scobell, *China's Search for Security* (New York: Columbia University Press, 2012), 169.

130. See "Shangri-La Dialogue 2014: Abe Gives Shangri-La Keynote," https://www.iiss.org/en/events/shangri-s-la-s-dialogue.

131. See, e.g., CCTV 13, "环球视线: 美泰联手多国展开亚太最大军演" [Global View: The US and Thailand Lead the Asia-Pacific's Largest Multilateral Military Exercise], February 8, 2012, featuring Admiral Yin Zhuo (ret.) analyzing CARAT exercises in Thailand, http://news.cntv.cn/world/20120208/124694.shtml.

132. Mary Kay Magistad, "Philippines Wary of China's Aggressive Stance in the South China Sea," *PRI's The World*, www.theworld.org/2012/02/philippines-china-energy/.

133. See, e.g., 张励 [Zhang Li], "经济外交与中国—东盟区域合作: 内涵, 实践, 与效用" [Economic Diplomacy and Regional Cooperation between China and ASEAN: Connotation, Practice and Effectiveness], *东南亚纵横* [Around Southeast Asia], September 2011, 65.

134. On US and Chinese crisis decision making in the early 1960s, see Lyle Goldstein, "When China Was a Rogue State," *Journal of Contemporary China* 12 (November 2003): 739–64.

11

ALTER EGO
India and US-China Relations

Acentral theme of this book is that China's growing power will force the United States and other powers to make strategic readjustments and to reach political accommodations with China. This "shadow of the future" is starkly and crisply provided by dramatic economic growth charts that demonstrate China's economy surging ahead of the United States' economy in the near future, just as it surpassed Japan's economy several years ago. This future is not completely assured, but it is highly likely. And yet the same trend lines also document the parallel, if somewhat more gradual, ascent of India. Given India's more transparent and institutionalized systems of governance, and also its higher population growth rate, many observers are inclined to see India as surpassing China in several measures of national power, including aggregate gross national product, in the second half of the twenty-first century.[1]

India became a full-fledged nuclear power in 1998. It has now enjoyed more than two decades of medium to high economic growth rates. Indian high-technology companies are beginning to show promise as well. Meanwhile, New Delhi has begun to flex its muscles in regions outside its immediate neighboring areas, such as the South China Sea—a development that has proven quite unnerving for Beijing. And India has emerged as the world's largest importer of weaponry—now including significant arms purchases from the United States, as well as from its traditional supplier, Russia. This trend has been duly noted in Chinese military circles.[2] Viewing the prospects for rivalry between these two ascending giants, Robert Kaplan has written:

[In the] heart of maritime Asia, . . . the Strait of Malacca is the Fulda Gap of the twenty-first century, . . . where the spheres of naval influence of India and China meet."[3]

Unlike China's fraught relationship with Japan, relations between New Delhi and Beijing are relatively calm at this point, as suggested by the reasonably successful first summit meeting between Xi and Prime Minister Narendra Modi in September 2014. Each country's leadership appears to be focused on securing mutual economic benefits from the burgeoning trade relationship. It is amply clear that as China adopts its new foreign policy to pursue the "New Silk Road" orientation the evolving role and disposition of India will be crucial. However, there are signs of growing rivalry, as well as definite points of friction. The docking of Chinese submarines in Sri Lanka during September and November 2014 caused a stir in Indian national security circles. To boot, there is also the still-aching wound of the 1962 war, which creates intense lingering suspicion on the Indian side. In addition, Chinese military strategists are wary of the prospects for an informal alliance between the United States and India. This concern will be amply demonstrated in the course of this chapter. As in the chapters preceding this one, an extensive set of Chinese sources are presented, but discussion of these sources does *not* imply agreement with these analyses. Although intense Sino-Indian rivalry has yet to materialize, therefore, it is not at all too early to consider how a cooperation spiral could help to mitigate the most destabilizing elements within the China-India-US strategic triangle, seeking to bring peace and development to a long-troubled, but extremely promising, region.

Background

Conventional explanations of Chinese history often portray China as isolated and self-absorbed, neglecting one of history's most comprehensive transcivilizational evolutions: namely, the spread of Buddhism from India into China. This process began in the second century BC and continued over one thousand years, as reflected most spectacularly in the vast cave complex of Dunhuang in Gansu Province. That Indian Buddhism in China was often refracted through a Tibetan cultural lens throughout that process makes the interconnections between these three civilizations all the more crucial. Besides the famous Silk Road, the Indian and Chinese civilizations were also connected by major maritime routes. It is well known that Zheng He's early Ming expeditions around the Indian Ocean cannot be described as exploratory missions because, indeed, these routes were well known to Chinese seafarers at the time.

China and India shared a similar fate in the nineteenth century—a common legacy that still affords some elements of a common outlook on world politics among contemporary strategists in both New Delhi and Beijing. Even as Indians and Chinese were marginalized in world affairs during the "Great Game" and other related contests among the great powers, the two civilizations began to rub up against one another in troubling ways. Kaplan discusses the foreign policy of Lord George Curzon, the viceroy of India from 1899 to 1905, with evident enthusiasm and in the hope that modern Indian strategists will define a new "forward" strategy.[4] But it is essential to realize that Curzon's legacy was not uniformly positive—for example, with respect to Tibet, as described in an academic history:

> Curzon . . . convinced London in 1903 to permit an expedition to enter Tibet to force negotiations. The Tibetans refused to negotiate with this expedition, so its British officers . . . led their Indian troops deeper and deeper into Tibet. . . . The Tibetan military attempted to block their advance, and a series of battles ensued in which the Tibetans were easily defeated, suffering losses of over a thousand troops. In the battle of Guru alone, between six hundred and seven hundred Tibetan troops were killed in a matter of minutes. No match for the invaders, the British force entered Lhasa . . . on August 3, 1904. They were the first Western troops ever to conquer Tibet. Throughout this period the Chinese government (through its *amban*) urged the thirteenth Dalai Lama to negotiate with the British expeditionary force to prevent their further advance, . . . but . . . the Dalai Lama . . . ignored these admonitions.[5]

Immediately after the founding of the People's Republic of China in 1949, the Chinese army made the conquest of Tibet an urgent priority—a military operation that coincided with the entry of Chinese forces into the Korean conflict. Initially, and "contrary to popular belief in the West, [Mao Zedong] pursued a policy of moderation in Tibet."[6] However, the situation became more and more polarized during the 1950s, as initial attempts were made at "socialist transformation."

Another factor in the escalating tensions in Tibet was the effort by the US Central Intelligence Agency (CIA) to train and arm Tibetan guerilla fighters.

This effort began operations in earnest during 1957. In its initial development, it was essential to keep the effort outside the purview of the Indian government, so operations were mounted from East Pakistan (later, Bangladesh), Bhutan, and Nepal.[7] A recent history of CIA operations in Tibet, written by two people who had been involved in the operations, reports not only on the "infectious enthusiasm" of the Tibetan patriots but also, all too frequently, on their tragic loss due to exposure in the harsh climate or capture, often followed by execution. There were even circumstances when "by capturing radiomen and forcing them to continue sending messages, Communist intelligence agencies duped the CIA ... into sending more agents and supplies, with both deadly and embarrassing results."[8] In John Garver's classic account of Sino-Indian relations, *Protracted Contest*, he contends that "the Tibetan issue was central in the deterioration of Sino-Indian relations which culminated in the 1962 war." Noting the conspicuous role of CIA operations supporting Tibetan insurgents in the escalating tensions, Garver observes: "Whatever the actual extent of Indian complicity with US covert operations may have been, *Beijing believed* that Nehru knew of and cooperated with CIA efforts" (emphasis added).[9]

The border war of 1962 was not much noticed in the West because it was short in duration, but also particularly because it occurred at the exact same time as the Cuban Missile Crisis. However, the war's influence on Asian geopolitics has been both broad and of long duration. The war set India on a path toward nuclearization, spurred New Delhi's increasing tilt toward Moscow, and dramatically solidified the entente between Islamabad and Beijing that exists to this day as one of the most salient and durable features of the South Asian security environment. A relatively recent Western account of the conflict observes that the "natural conditions [in the arena of combat] were arguably as harsh as any in the history of warfare." In a rather remarkable feat of arms that featured not only surprise but also impressive logistics preparations and tactical flexibility, the Chinese "[People's Liberation Army] destroyed the fighting strength ... of three brigades of the Indian Army ... [and] mauled five others."[10] The war is receiving new attention in Chinese military circles. For example, a special edition of 兵工科技 (*Ordnance Industry and Science Technology*) in mid-2011 carried half a dozen articles, including new interviews with veterans, a survey of the war's logistics challenges, an update on the border status quo, and a review of India's most advanced air combat fighters. The lead article evinces little disposition to alter Beijing's conventional view of the conflict: "Confronted by the expansionist policies of the Indian government, and multiple violent provocations, . . . China was forced to undertake this war . . . that struck a blow against India's strategy of regional hegemony . . . and won 50 years of peace on our country's western border."[11] Recent Chinese scholarship on the war has puzzled over why Chinese deterrence signals were apparently misread in New Delhi,[12] and also, somewhat troublingly, on how the 1962 war could be a model for coping with current challenges to Chinese sovereignty.[13]

In the years following the 1962 war, China again made its geostrategic weight felt when it threatened to intervene in the India/Pakistan conflict of 1965. Coming a year after China's first nuclear test, New Delhi's level of anxiety regarding China was extremely acute at this time. Adding to this anxiety, no doubt, was the Karakoram Highway linking China and Pakistan, which opened in 1971. However, during the second India/Pakistan conflict in 1971, China's support for Pakistan was considerably more limited.[14] Although China did not seem to react with special alarm to India's initial nuclear test in 1974, Garver observes that the "evidence suggests that Chinese assistance to Pakistan's nuclear program began only after India's nuclear test. . . . India's demonstration of a nuclear explosion capability, coming seventeen months after Pakistan's dismemberment, underscored the possibility that India could dominate Pakistan."[15] After a major crisis along the tense, contested Himalayan border in 1986, Sino-Indian relations suddenly improved with the breakthrough visit of Indian president Rajiv Ghandi to Beijing the following year. During this visit, Beijing agreed not to interfere in the Kashmir issue, in exchange for Indian assurances that New Delhi would not meddle in the Tibet issue.[16]

After the end of the Cold War, Sino-Indian relations continued to warm, despite worsening turmoil in Indo-Pakistan relations. China's response to the nuclear tests of 1998 was "restrained," and during the 1999 Kargil War, Beijing seems to have rejected direct appeals from Islamabad for firm support. However, China's trend toward neutrality in South Asia may have ended with the September 11, 2001, terrorist attacks against the United States, because of both escalating geopolitical rivalry in Central Asia and deepening US-Indian strategic ties.[17] One Chinese perspective on US-Pakistan relations notes that a definite "亲印" (kiss India) tendency was already quite visible in US policy during the late 1990s, and also underlines the US threat after the 9/11 attacks to "炸回到旧石器" (bomb it back to the Stone Age) as critical to securing Islamabad's cooperation within the war on terrorism.[18] During the serious 2001–2 crisis in Indo-Pakistani relations, "China showed a more pro-Pakistan tilt, . . . as opposed to its arguably neutral stance during the Kargil Conflict."[19]

As part of a new "look East" policy, India began to turn greater attention toward its eastern flank, beginning in earnest in 2004 with the construction of a new Indian Air Force base in the Andaman/Nicobar Islands, which are proximate to the Malacca Strait.[20] In parallel, a Chinese scholarly analysis admitted in 2007 that China-Myanmar military and security cooperation had been "continuously strengthened over the previous decade. That cooperation apparently included modernizing Myanmar's naval facilities (e.g., with the upgrading of radar systems) at Sittwe, Coco, Hianggyi, Kyaukpyu, Mergui, and Zadetkyi Kyun. This Chinese analysis warned that "India's desire and determination to join hands with the United States and Japan to restrain Chinese activities in the Indian Ocean is more obvious with each passing day."[21]

Such sentiments were also apparent among Chinese military thinkers at that time. Thus, the December 2008 cover story of the Chinese Navy magazine 当代海军 (*Modern Navy*) drew attention in a series of articles to the increasing threat posed by New Delhi's ever-closer military alignment with Washington. One of these stories emphasized the unprecedented scale of US-Indian military exercises, which have been taking place every year since 2004. These exercises were said to involve a wide variety of US military equipment and to have a secondary motive of selling advanced hardware to India.[22] Another article in the same issue emphasized the fact that a major theme of the Malabar naval exercises is antisubmarine warfare, suggesting that the target of the exercise—China—was "extremely obvious." This Chinese Navy author observed: "The Malabar exercise has not only become the most important method by which the United States draws India into the Asia-Pacific alliance system, but also a key mechanism for strengthening the alliance and the military cooperation between various alliance partners. This time the shifting of the Malabar exercise from the Indian Ocean to take place in the sea areas off of China has completely exposed the real goal of the US to actively construct an 'Asia Pacific Alliance of Democracies' in order to contain a rising great power."[23]

President Obama's fall 2010 trip to Asia—during which he visited only democratic states, including India, Indonesia, South Korea, and Japan— seemed to suggest that Beijing's suspicions regarding an "alliance of democracies" might have some basis in reality. Meanwhile, New Delhi's so-called countercontainment strategy was taking form; it apparently includes among its initiatives an increased Indian strategic profile in the South China Sea, with particular emphasis on strengthening India-Vietnam military cooperation.[24] Even as China emerged as India's largest trading partner, and as the two Asian giants have found some common cause on various sensitive questions such as climate change, the unmistakable tendency toward escalating geopolitical rivalry is all too apparent in the early twenty-first century.

Sino-Indian Rivalry Comes of Age

It is beyond the scope of this research effort to comprehensively survey the US-India-China strategic triangle from all angles. But some contribution toward an understanding of the current dynamics of this key triangle, especially for Western readers, can be gained from looking at important Chinese writings on this issue.

Undoubtedly, a major issue of discussion with respect to Sino-Indian rivalry has been the potential for maritime rivalry between these two states with simultaneously rapidly expanding naval capabilities. As Kaplan details in the book *Monsoon*, "The Chinese had a port and road system in [Myanmar]. They were building bunkering facilities in Sri Lanka. They had footholds in the Seychelles and Madagascar . . . and hoped Gwadar in Pakistan would be a friendly harbor." But he concludes, after extensive interviews with Indian strategists, that "India was not about to let China and Pakistan guard, or indeed block, its entrance to the Gulf of Oman from Gwadar, for this would create for India a 'Hormuz dilemma,' the equivalent to China's 'Malacca dilemma.'"[25] He describes the so-called string of pearls strategy in considerable detail throughout *Monsoon*, and he even makes visits to most of the Chinese "pearls." However, it should be noted that the term "string of pearls" is not of Chinese origin, but rather was coined by the defense consulting firm Booz Allen in a 2004 report. On his investigative trip to Gwadar, Kaplan does not find a secret Chinese naval base in the making, but rather just "poor Baluch fishermen and their families." Instead of a hotbed of geopolitical scheming between Chinese and Americans, he instead finds red hot tensions between Baluchs and Punjabis as the dominant political theme. A detailed study by the naval analyst Daniel Kostecka casts serious doubt on Beijing's alleged strategy to control the Indian Ocean.[26]

And yet the reality on the ground has not halted the groundswell of journalistic and academic writings on the so-called string of pearls strategy—by US and Indian strategists in particular.[27] This firestorm of interest bespeaks the simple fact that rivalry sells, but Kaplan's important caveat has been too often ignored: "One cannot caution enough how subtly this game will have to be played."[28] Not surprisingly, Chinese scholars have been ever more forceful in making denials regarding the supposed string of pearls strategy. Ye Hailin, a respected Chinese specialist on South Asia, responded as follows in Shanghai's 东方早报 (*Oriental Morning Post*) in the autumn of 2012:

> Of course, China has no such "string of pearls strategy," and China's "Indian Ocean strategy" is certainly not of this character. It is simply impossible that China could have such an approach directed at expanding its military influence for the purpose of protecting its sea lanes. This line of scheming, which has been extremely dependent on the resources and encouragement of foreign countries, is greedy and also vicious. Chinese officials, scholars, and journalists have discussed—and most often been forced to discuss—the theme of "China's strategy in the Indian Ocean" and have commonly made the following . . . points: China is extremely dependent on foreign energy supplies so that the security of sea lines of communication is very important for China; however, China will not therefore undertake to expand its military activities in the Indian Ocean, and certainly will not seek a path toward military hegemony; so the "String of Pearls strategy" exists wholly in the realm of fiction.[29]

Ye does go on to assert that it is completely normal and natural for any country to seek to protect its maritime supply routes, but he dismisses the "militarization" often reported in the Indian and Western media reports as "见怪不怪" (a threat that disappears when confronted). Demonstrating a new urgency for Beijing to dispel related rumors, official Chinese spokesmen offered official denials in early 2013. Defense Ministry spokesman Geng Yansheng called the rumors "a distortion of the facts that seeks to sow discord between China and neighboring states," while Foreign Ministry senior official Luo Zhaohu emphasized that the Gwadar initiative was "a purely economic project."[30] Nevertheless, the idea of Chinese military bases in the Indian Ocean cannot quite be ruled out when the Chinese themselves are actively debating the issue. For instance, an editorial posted to the website of 环球时报 (*Global Times*) in early 2013 made a somewhat surprisingly strong argument for setting up a system of Chinese military bases in the Indian Ocean. This editorial sees no great distinction between "海外基地" (foreign bases) and "海外战略支撑点" (foreign strategic support points), but it does see an urgent requirement for Beijing in this respect that increases daily. The rationale for this change in China's foreign policy is said to be the so-called Malacca Dilemma, whereby 80 percent of China's oil is said to transit the narrow Malacca Strait connecting the Indian and Pacific oceans. Interestingly, the authors of this editorial suggest that such overseas Chinese military facilities in the Indian Ocean could facilitate not only ongoing counterpiracy activities but also humanitarian aid activities and counterterrorism operations. Thus, they may support China's efforts to enhance its role as a "responsible great power" by enabling it to better "提供国际公共安全产品" (provide public security goods).[31] Such statements are sure to give Western and Indian military analysts much fodder for debate, but such ideas in the Chinese media—which at this point lack any official endorsement, not to mention evidence on the ground of military facilities in development—hardly seem to be the Chinese threat that some apparently see looming in the Indian Ocean.

Chinese strategists focused on South Asia are evidently most concerned with the evolving role of the United States, and thus Washington's relatively new focus on the Indian Ocean region has prompted significant anxiety among these strategists. For example, a recent Chinese study of the United States' evolving strategy for the region in the prestigious journal 国际问题研究 (*International Studies*) concludes that America's aim of "controlling the Indian Ocean is not simply about enabling complete access to [the region's] abundant resources, but allows the use of the transport corridors as a lever to control other states." The pillars of American policy in the Indian Ocean are said to be to (1) promote Indian regional and global leadership, (2) seek to improve US ties to South Asian and Southeast Asian states, (3) consolidate and strengthen the US military presence on Diego Garcia, and (4) lead multilateral responses to nontraditional security threats in the region. This analysis comes to a disturbing conclusion: "The US seeks to spoil the strategic environment for China's peaceful rise, raise the specter of the 'China threat,' put pressure on the security of China's maritime transport nodes, and create more problems between China and the coastal states of the Indian Ocean region."[32]

Unquestionably, Chinese military analysts, who previously perhaps were not overly concerned with Indian military might, are now paying close attention to India's buildup. Chinese appraisals in the naval sphere logically pay considerable attention to India's expansive aircraft carrier program. Illustrating the obviously competitive nature of the simultaneous buildup among the two Asian giants at somewhat comparable levels of naval development, an early 2013 report made light of India's very first indigenous aircraft carrier. This report especially noted that France and Italy have played a major role in its construction and that the ship would deploy Russian MiG-29 fighters and not an indigenous fighter jet, unlike the Chinese *Liaoning* aircraft carrier.[33] Of greater concern to Beijing's military planners has been the quite unprecedented sale of twelve P-8I antisubmarine aircraft from the United States. Not only do these aircraft represent the world's cutting-edge platform in the crucial domain of antisubmarine warfare, but there is also a major concern that "their central mission will be to watch the activities of the Chinese Navy in the Indian Ocean." And there is also a deeper anxiety that the United States is drawing the Indian Navy into its wider regional antisubmarine system that also relies on Japan and South Korea. According to this Chinese analysis, the sale "will result in exercises in the domain of antisubmarine warfare that will yield closer bilateral naval cooperation."[34] A detailed Chinese examination of India's military activities in the Andaman and Nicobar Islands notes the steady deployments of Indian ships and aircraft to the easternmost part of the Indian Ocean. According to this Chinese analysis, New Delhi's move to place unmanned aerial vehicles in the area was justified as necessary to combat piracy in the area, but this is described as simply an "excuse." Rather, the real intent of such deployments proximate to the Malacca Strait is interpreted to be a threat: "[India] may simply pull a bit on the rope, tighten the knot, and this will make certain countries uncomfortable." This area is seen as a 跳板 (springboard) for future Indian exertions into the Pacific.[35]

Consistent with the Chinese concerns articulated above are Beijing's especially acute anxieties about India's increasing military presence in the South China Sea region. According to one detailed Chinese analysis of India's increasing profile in the region, "India has actively entered the South China Sea with the obvious intention of containing China." It is also suggested that, in the course of difficult border negotiations and related tensions, New Delhi is using the South China Sea issue to apply "pressure for the purpose of gaining a strategic advantage in the border negotiations." Attempting to explain Indian actions more fully, this Chinese analyst explains: "India believes that Chinese naval power is rapidly developing and has already reached into the Bay of Bengal. If China succeeds in realizing its claims in the South China Sea, then it will come through the Malacca Strait and challenge India in the Bay of Bengal." In other words, India is seen as attempting to block China's entry into the Indian Ocean. Moreover, it is emphasized in this Chinese analysis that this process is being encouraged by the United States, as then–secretary of state Hillary Clinton is alleged to have openly stated during her visit to India in July 2011.[36]

Whether Washington has intended it or not, Beijing holds the perception that the India card has been played against it. Thus the China-India rivalry has become a major component of the spiraling China-US rivalry. The dynamic is quite familiar from the US-Japan-China triangle, and just as disturbing. Even though that triangle may have more immediate points of friction and much deeper historical wounds (see chapter 9), a similar triangle involving India could be more consequential for the future of world politics, given the dynamic growth trajectories of both Asian giants. Therefore, instead of pouring gasoline on the China-India rivalry, Washington should be looking for ways to bridge the widening gap between New Delhi and Beijing. China and the United States share numerous goals in South Asia, not least the imperative of preventing Pakistan from becoming a failed state. In Central Asia there are also a variety of cooperative opportunities for the United States and China. Even as the United States departs Afghanistan, a detailed Chinese analysis of the situation advocates that China play an increasing role through the vehicle of the Shanghai Cooperation Organization (SCO). Operating from a principle that "阿人治阿" (Afghans should rule Afghans) and that the United Nations should be at the core of guiding external involvement, this analysis advocates that the SCO should make a definite contribution. Notably, it does not advocate excluding the United States from Central or South Asia in the future.[37]

With respect to China-India relations, it is not difficult to find optimistic Chinese perspectives—that is, sincere believers in the concept of "Chindia." In a phenomenon familiar to US-China relations, the bilateral China-India relationship has the essential ballast of ballooning trade. From under $5 billion in 2000, this trade grew to exceed $70 billion in 2011, when China suddenly emerged as India's top trading partner. The power of these figures was recently demonstrated in an article in the influential Chinese magazine 财经 (*Finance and Economics*), which turned the notion of an India/China rivalry in a transformed Myanmar on its head: "During the nineteenth century, the English had sought to create land transport links connecting India and China through [Myanmar], but it was not realized. But after [Myanmar's] economic opening up, land links between India and China will be opened for the first time ever. Whether it is China linking to the Indian Ocean or India 'looking to the East,' . . . China and India must both in the future invest more in building [Myanmar's] transportation foundation."[38] In other words, Myanmar (and other issues standing between China and India) can become a basis for cooperation instead of rivalry.

President Xi's trip to India in September just a few months after Modi assumed office is suggestive of Beijing's acute desire to set the relationship on a positive track. Xi brought with him a hundred Chinese businessmen with the not-too-subtle message that China desires to upgrade the economic relationship further. But surely it was in the back of Xi's mind as he arrived in New Delhi that Modi had just returned from Tokyo. Asian geopolitics are in full bloom, so it seems. According to some reports, Xi's entire visit was overshadowed by new tensions on the Sino-Indian border.[39] The challenges in this vital relationship should not be underestimated. But Washington can play a role in facilitating a constructive relationship between New Delhi and Beijing, as outlined below.

A Cooperation Spiral for the United States and China in South Asia

Washington's move 1 in South Asia: The United States should not encourage India's entry into the volatile South China Sea and should urge India to forswear any intention to build a military base in Vietnam (figure 11.1). Over the last few years, India has developed ever-closer ties with Vietnam, including a robust military component that even touches such sensitive domains as submarine warfare. Indeed, if India makes a major effort to train Vietnam's nascent submarine force, then this could constitute a major thorn in China's side during the coming decades. As a clever part of New Delhi's strategy of "countercontainment" that effectively retaliates for China's close military ties with Pakistan, one must observe that there is some justice and likely effectiveness in India's "game." However, this is a dangerous game to play—especially for the Vietnamese, who cannot hope to compete in military power with China; nor can they rely on India to save them from an "angry dragon." Therefore, though New Delhi will no doubt continue to play the Vietnam card, it must be cautious, and the United States could play the useful and mature role of urging India to be cautious. Nor can it be ruled out that China's "routine" port visits of submarines to Sri Lanka have become part of this precarious spiral of new tensions. To continue nurturing a cooperative dynamic in the South Asia region, New Delhi would be wise to rule out building any military bases in Vietnam. Of course, New Delhi most likely never had such intentions—and this will make such a concession all the more easy to swallow for Indian strategists. But in Beijing, this step will count—the better to help China realize that responsible behavior with respect to Pakistan and Sri Lanka will be rewarded.

Figure 11.1 Cooperation Spiral: The United States–India–China Triangle 作螺旋：美印中三边关系

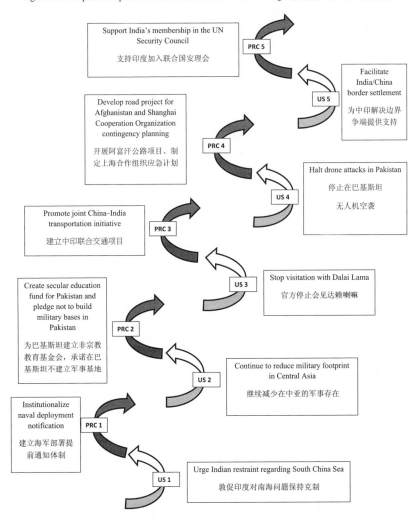

Beijing's move 1 in South Asia: China should promote a naval deployment notification system with India. It is apparent that maritime rivalry is now at the heart of tensions rising between the two Asian giants. Some US strategists have begun to wisely question whether such a maritime rivalry is truly consistent with long-term US interests, as too many Western analysts have long assumed.[40] The tendency toward maritime rivalry may simply be an inherent aspect of rapidly rising powers that have the resources and nationalist aspirations to build powerful navies. However, the volatile brew of vulnerable sea lanes, constricted strategic chokepoints, contested maritime claims, and testy third parties suggests that the Sino-Indian naval rivalry could quite easily escalate into hostilities. One could consider numerous ways to decrease mistrust in the maritime relationship, but the occasional, symbolic joint exercise or port visit cannot be considered sufficient to the task. A more concrete solution would be to develop a system for notifying all the relevant parties about significant naval exercises (i.e., those involving more than two vessels), but the notification would only apply to one another's major zone of respective maritime interest. Thus Beijing would notify New Delhi of major naval activities in the Indian Ocean. Likewise, New Delhi would reciprocate with information on deployments to the Western Pacific (east of the Malacca Strait). Although, ideally, such an informal naval confidence-building mechanism would also include the activities of submarines, that step would perhaps stretch the burden of trust to the breaking point, and so this initiative would be best focused on surface vessels. Nevertheless, in a surprising and quite unprecedented development in December 2013, Beijing seems to have informed New Delhi about the first-ever deployment of a Chinese nuclear submarine to the Indian Ocean. Although the Indian media reacted with predictable alarm to this development, a deeper analysis may yield the encouraging conclusion that China's defense leaders strongly perceive a need to maintain good relations with India.[41] Nevertheless, whatever goodwill might have resulted from that unusual prior notification seems to have been overshadowed by the multiple dockings of Chinese submarines in Sri Lanka during the second half of 2014. As one Indian commentator wrote, "The presence of Chinese submarines across Palk Straits has deeply disturbed the government which is making another call to Lankan authorities, this time to convey strong displeasure."[42] Considering that both navies have wide ambitions for regular deployments into the other nation's core, proximate zone of interest, this trust-building mechanism could be of growing importance. Because China's naval modernization has been extraordinarily rapid in recent years, it would be highly appropriate and encouraging to see this initiative come from Beijing as a way to cool tensions in the waters off South Asia.

Washington's move 2 in South Asia: The United States should continue to reduce its military footprint in Central Asia. For some years the United States has been drawing down its military forces in Central Asia. In 2005 US forces departed from a major base in Uzbekistan. The significant decision to close the Manas

Base in Kyrgyzstan, made in December 2013 (the actual closing was in June 2014), though under significant pressure from the host country, represents another major milestone in this process. The United States must rein in its commitments due to its overstretched resources as the war in Afghanistan winds down. If represented positively, the withdrawal from the facilities in Kyrgyzstan can actually benefit US-China relations (and also relations with Russia) and not just economize on scarce resources. After all, Chinese strategists have long considered, to a considerable extent at least, the US presence in Central Asia as part of a broader effort to encircle and contain China. Similar steps that are explicitly sensitive to China's quite reasonable concerns regarding the security of its western flank would also be appropriate. This is particularly important, given heightened sensitivity in Beijing in the wake of several attacks by the Uighur Muslim minority, both in restive Xinjiang Province and also further afield, including deadly attacks in 2013–14 in Kunming and even in the heart of Beijing. Indeed, an especially troubling scenario for Chinese strategists is the possibility of a fusion of external and internal threats; the most obvious example would be if the United States were to undertake covert aid to Uighur separatists or attempt such aid as "horizontal escalation" to coerce Beijing in the midst of a maritime conflict (e.g., the South China Sea).[43] To allay these Chinese concerns, Washington should take the further step to strictly limit the size of its footprint at the still-sprawling US air base at Bagram in Afghanistan. An *Air Force Magazine* exposé from late 2012 discussing the future of that base reveals the dizzying array of platforms that have operated from this facility—including heavy bombers and electronic warfare aircraft, not to mention all conceivable types of special operations helicopters. The temptation in Washington to maintain a "rapid influx" capacity at a facility just over 300 miles from the western Chinese border will undoubtedly arise among Pentagon planners during the years to come. However, this temptation should be resisted, as it apparently was when the decision was made to close the Kyrgyzstan base in late 2013. The Bagram facility should be either closed or kept at minimum operating capacity, consistent with President Obama's plan to reduce US troops in Afghanistan to about a thousand attached to the embassy in Kabul by the end of 2016.[44] This reduced regional footprint in Central Asia will not only support a more sustainable global posture but may also enable improvements to be made in US-China security cooperation in Central and South Asia.

Beijing's move 2 in South Asia: China must step up in Pakistan by making a major commitment to secular education and also by dispelling rumors regarding a future Chinese military base. China's image in Pakistan would be improved if it was not tied so closely to the Pakistani military and if its development projects were not all so closely tied to the effort to enhance China's trade position in South Asia and the Middle East. These efforts, to be sure, do constitute a benefit for both Pakistan and China. However, they are not nearly ambitious enough to engender a fundamental turnaround in Pakistan's prospects. Instead of military and infrastructure projects (which may continue), a new focus is required: on secular education—the major bottleneck in Pakistan's development process. Pakistan's literacy rate stands at an appalling 46 percent. A Chinese program focused on improving education in Pakistan would focus on high school and college—effectively, training the teachers who will change Pakistan in one generational leap. The program would require at least $1 billion to set up and run myriad schools, but most important to pay for sending tens of thousands of Pakistanis abroad to study for one or more years. An essential way to build goodwill from this project would be to institutionalize a system whereby a third of the students go to China, a third to Europe, and a third to the United States. By "spreading the wealth" with this program, Beijing would be simultaneously supporting a close ally, keeping a close watch on its other investments, and building goodwill with both the United States and India. At the same time, to underline that its primary motive in South Asia is commercial and not military, Beijing should put in writing its promise not to convert its Gwadar port initiative or any other locations in Pakistan into military bases. Although it is logical for Chinese forces to make occasional visits, and seek logistical support, a "base" would imply hardened facilities for munitions, security personnel, and so on. A base, moreover, would also mean facilities designed to be defended in wartime. It should be quite easy for China to make such pledges and to offer the necessary proof to dispel these harmful rumors.

Washington's move 3 in South Asia: The United States should cease presidential visits with the Dalai Lama. This book has concentrated primarily on geopolitics and not on human rights as a factor in the US-China relationship. More is said about the intertwining of these two issues in the book's conclusion (chapter 12). However, there is no question that Washington could provide a major impetus for a cooperation spiral vis-à-vis Beijing with respect to South Asia by taking the significant step of ceasing presidential visits with the Dalai Lama. By taking this step, America would be acknowledging its recognition that the Tibetan question has been a core debilitating issue in Sino-Indian relations since the 1950s. Moreover, it would signify US recognition that clandestine

US operations played a significant role in exaggerating these tensions during the height of the Cold War in Asia, as was outlined above in the background section of this chapter. In the fall of 2009 President Obama decided not to meet with the Dalai Lama before his visit to Beijing—a tacit recognition that this meeting would damage US-China relations.[45] Rather than an issue of tactics and timing, however, a more permanent solution that altogether removes such visits from the president's calendar is now quite appropriate. Far from improving the lot of most Tibetans, such visits may constitute what the Tibet expert Melvyn Goldstein calls "bad friend syndrome"—perpetuating a situation of hostility without any prospect of resolution. Americans may continue to support Tibet in their own private capacities, but the appearance of US government support for this quite blatantly anti-Chinese cause should be halted for the purpose of energizing US-China cooperation in South Asia.

Beijing's move 3 in South Asia: China should initiate a program of infrastructure construction, especially in Myanmar, that would decisively link China and India. The Asian giants are separated by the massive wall of the Himalayas and the Tibetan Plateau. Although it is true, to some extent (as in this case), that good fences make good neighbors, undoubtedly these natural barriers also hinder robust trade and societal links. As discussed above, such ideas were indeed proposed (if informally) in the Chinese magazine *Finance and Economics* during mid-2012. A "pan-Asian high-speed rail link" connecting Kunming to New Delhi, as part of a much larger network stretching further west, has been considered since at least early 2010.[46] However, a network directed at increasing the connectivity of India-Myanmar-Bangladesh and China deserves special focus and consideration. This should include rail and road networks that connect via mid-Myanmar and South Myanmar routes directly through to Chittagong and Dhaka, and also Kolkota. Such extensive routes would powerfully complement a northern route connecting Kunming and New Delhi. Undoubtedly, hawks will howl that such links could serve as future "invasion routes," and environmentalists will howl about degraded ecosystems. Nevertheless, these concerns should be easily dealt with when one considers the massive economic benefits that would accrue from bringing advanced systems of transportation infrastructure to this desperately poor region. It is also clear that Chinese engineering prowess would be crucial to the execution of such a project, and yet the technology and expertise do exist. India would have the difficult task of putting aside its pride and envy and seeing the advantages of modernizing its hitherto backward Northeast. The United States could play a constructive role in facilitating the difficult negotiations, assembling the capital, and also making sure that local concerns are taken into account in this massive project. An initial meeting of the Bangladesh-China-India-Myanmar (BCIM) grouping to discuss the proposed Kunming to Kolkata economic development corridor actually took place in December 2013 in Kunming.[47] The end result—a China-India trade relationship "firing on all cylinders"—could provide a major stabilizing force for India-China relations for the twenty-first century and beyond.

Washington's move 4 in South Asia: The United States should cease all drone attacks in Pakistan. These drone attacks, which were perhaps justified in the years immediately after the 9/11 attacks and during the hunt for Osama bin Laden, are now a major hindrance to effective US diplomacy in South Asia and are playing a clear role in radicalizing Pakistani politics. Beyond the obvious negative impact of widespread collateral damage that has been reported to result from such attacks, there is also the close association between drones and US diplomacy that is having a deleterious impact on the US image worldwide, but especially in the Islamic world and plainly within Pakistan itself. What does this issue have to do with US-China relations? In fact, a US-Chinese partnership pursuing the two nations' shared interest in Pakistan's stabilization and future prosperity must constitute a fundamental plank of future US-China cooperation in South Asia. For this partnership to be effective in accomplishing this difficult yet all-important task, the drone campaign in Pakistan must be halted. It is worth reminding Americans at this point that of the nineteen hijackers who executed the 9/11 terrorist attacks, not a single one was from Pakistan (or Afghanistan, for that matter). Moreover, the Pakistani Taliban did not exist before 2001, but rather came about as a by-product of the war in Afghanistan. China will not wish to actively collaborate with the United States in South Asia until the drone attacks are stopped, and US development aid to Pakistan will also not be truly effective until this polarizing issue is definitively settled. Drone attacks may need to continue elsewhere, but they should be given additional oversight and scaled back significantly everywhere.[48]

Beijing's move 4 in South Asia: China must step up in Afghanistan by taking responsibility for modernizing Afghanistan's road network and also by developing the Shanghai Cooperation Organization's contingency planning for peacekeeping operations. More than a few American strategists have noted in recent years the sad, but likely all too true, irony that US blood and treasure were being sunk into Afghanistan, but that China would reap the benefits in terms of exploiting the country's vast mineral wealth and gaining new markets for its goods.[49] Although China and Afghanistan share a small border, Beijing has been rather cautious about getting involved with that troubled nation to date—no doubt reflecting a certain risk aversion, but also a desire not to be entangled with the troubled US and NATO efforts. Given the relatively rapid pullout of US forces during the period 2014–16, accompanied by the conspicuous decision to improve the climate of US-China relations by withdrawing forces from Kyrgyzstan and scaling down the base at Bagram in Afghanistan, China should step up in Afghanistan and increase its provision of public goods. A brilliant aspect of the Chinese development model puts a premium on transportation infrastructure, and roads in particular. US-led road-building projects in Afghanistan have been enormously expensive yet have yielded quite limited success.[50] But it is absolutely true that roads have a huge potential to rapidly improve the lives of Afghans by connecting markets. They may also help to bring an end to the country's endemic warlordism and civil strife by aiding the regime in Kabul and fostering a sense of Afghan national identity. Given China's vast experience with road building in Central Asia's difficult terrain, there is no question of feasibility. Just as important, China has the will to make this effort succeed given that it will be gaining crucial access to new and proximate markets. Of course, there will be issues with security arrangements, but Beijing has never had problems with a few practical handouts to grease the wheels of commerce, and it has the workers and engineers willing to work in dangerous conditions. China will *not* intervene unilaterally with military force in Afghanistan, and its due caution is well considered. However, as suggested in the Chinese analysis of the SCO's role in Afghanistan described above, the readiness of the SCO to deploy peacekeeping forces into the troubled region for humanitarian purposes in grave circumstances, with the UN's mandate, will be a welcome barrier against future disasters in Afghanistan.

Washington's move 5 in South Asia: The United States should prod India to accept the "East/West swap" of claimed territory on the China/India border. The India-China border remains tense and frozen in a Cold War posture of enmity, because of unresolved claims dating back to before the Sino-Indian War of 1962. Indeed, tensions have flared on the border as recently as April 2013 and even somewhat inexplicably during September 2014 in the midst of the first Modi-Xi summit.[51] In the western sector India claims a significant territory called Aksai Chin, whereas in the eastern sector China claims an even larger territory that is now a province of India called Arunachal Pradesh. According to Garver, Beijing has offered a similar deal to New Delhi at least twice: a swap of India's claim in exchange for China's claim. In other words, the status quo on the border would be maintained, and both major claims in the west and the east would be dropped. India has rejected this offer on both occasions, arguing that it does not recognize China's claim in the east. In an era when both China and India wield not only powerful conventional forces but also increasingly robust nuclear forces, war between the Asian giants is increasingly unthinkable—especially when it could now erupt over a glacier or a remote valley that is generally uninhabited. Given the enormous stakes involved, it is time for Beijing and New Delhi to reach a compromise on the border through negotiations. Again, Washington may play a useful role in facilitating this compromise, which would have major benefits for regional security and the global economy, given the ever-increasing status of the two contesting parties.

Beijing's move 5 in South Asia: China should endorse India as a permanent member of the UN Security Council. Having made considerable gains in cooperation with the United States and India—such as ending presidential visits with the Dalai Lama, some limits on Indian naval activities east of the Malacca Strait, the withdrawal of US forces proximate to the sensitive Chinese border in Xinjiang, and finally India's compromise regarding the border—Beijing should finally be willing to make the major concession of allowing New Delhi to join the UN Security Council as a permanent member. Such a step is only natural, in that it recognizes India's growing global power and responsibilities. However, it is also profoundly in China's interest, because this step will help to bring about the multipolar world that Beijing often says that it seeks. Moreover, by elevating the status of India on the world stage, this move will help to take some of the edge off the nationalism of India, which otherwise could play the victim card and assume a more aggressive stance. And as with the process of finally welcoming Japan to the Security Council (a step advocated in the cooperation spiral in chapter 9), it would be assumed that a UN Security Council that more fully reflects the actual structure of world power (vice reflecting the European dominance of the early twentieth century) will be much more effective in resolving the major problems of international security that arise in the coming centuries.

Conclusion

With the dramatic ascendance of Narendra Modi to the post of India's prime minister in a sweeping victory during the spring of 2014, new risks and new opportunities alike seemed to pervade the uncertain diplomatic milieu that followed this epochal shift in New Delhi's politics. For its part, Beijing quickly recognized the imperative to try to establish an immediate rapport with the new leader.[52] However, the perils for this somewhat troubled bilateral relationship should not be underestimated, given the simmering tensions of the last few years. President Xi moved quickly to cement his ties with the new Indian leader. Apparently, as Chief Minister of Gujarat, Modi visited China five times and was impressed by China's rapid economic modernization. In Beijing, Modi is viewed as a leader who can deliver on reforms to the Indian economy. But there are myriad problems as discussed in this chapter, not least that India seems potentially "ambivalent" about China's "New Silk Road Strategy" at the outset.[53] Chinese and Indian diplomats will have their hands full in handling this difficult relationship, but the United States also has a definite role to play.

Confronted by the troubling specter of these two huge Asian tigers glowering at one another suspiciously, with each trying to show the other one that it is stronger, Washington could cynically choose to egg them on and 坐山观虎斗 (sit on the mountain watching the tigers fight). Alternatively, Washington could take the more mature and responsible road of seriously attempting to help them reconcile. The former traditional "realist" approach may appeal to those who think that China can be surrounded, hemmed in, and generally contained. But that is not the approach advocated in this book, which assumes that the result of such a strategy would likely be a repetition of the misery caused by the catastrophic wars and wasteful rivalries of the twentieth century. Yet sadly, as demonstrated by the Chinese sources surveyed above, the sense in Beijing is that Washington and New Delhi are actively conspiring to hinder and strangle China's rapid ascent.

However, it is not hard to see that in the failures of current policies in Pakistan and Afghanistan lie the very seeds for enhanced cooperation between the United States and China, which could not only help bring greater security to the entire South Asian region but also increase trust in the troubled US-China-India triangular relationship. India, as the unchallenged leader of the South Asian region, would be wise to realize that it has everything to gain from an increasingly stable Afghanistan and Pakistan, as well as a more constructive US-China relationship that enhances security in South Asia.

Notes

1. This conclusion was suggested, e.g., in the 2012 report of the US National Intelligence Council. See, e.g., Jason Overdorf, "India's Growth to Surpass China's by 2030: Report," *Global Post*, December 11, 2012, www.globalpost

.com/dispatches/globalpost-blogs/india/india-faster-growth-us-economy -developing.

2. 蔡吕良 [Cai Luliang], "印度成为世界最大武器进口国" [India Has Become the World's Largest Weapons Importing Country], 人民海军 [People's Navy], December 20, 2011.

3. Robert Kaplan, *Monsoon: The Indian Ocean and the Future of American Power* (New York: Random House, 2010), 261.

4. Ibid., 183.

5. Melvyn C. Goldstein, *The Snow Lion and the Dragon: China, Tibet, and the Dalai Lama* (Berkeley: University of California Press, 1997), 23–24.

6. Ibid., 52.

7. Kenneth Conboy and James Morrison, *The CIA's Secret War in Tibet* (Lawrence: University Press of Kansas, 2002), 33, 76, 154–55, 187, 196.

8. Ibid., 211.

9. John Garver, *Protracted Contest: Sino-Indian Rivalry in the 21st Century* (Seattle: University of Washington Press, 2001), 60–61.

10. Cheng Feng and Larry Worzel, "PLA Operational Principles and Limited War," in *Chinese Warfighting: The PLA Experience since 1949*, ed. Mark Ryan, David Finkelstein, and Michael McDevitt (London: M. E. Sharpe, 2003), 188, 193.

11. 刘俊学 [Liu Junxue], "高原凯歌" [Song of Triumph from the High Plateau], 兵工科技 [Ordnance Industry Science Technology], no. 16 (2011): 9.

12. 刘会军 [Liu Huijun], "威摄视角下的中印边界争端研究" [China-India Border Dispute: A Study from a Deterrence Perspective], 南亚研究 [South Asia Studies], no. 3 (2011): 1–28.

13. 李向前 [Li Xiangqian], "从领土主权之重看一九六二年中印边界反击作战决策" [Decision Making for the Counterattack in Self-Defense along the Sino-Indian Border in 1962 in Light of the Supremacy of Territorial Sovereignty], 中共党史研究 [CCP History Research], May 2012, 77.

14. Garver, *Protracted Contest*, 201.

15. Ibid., 325.

16. See, e.g., Jian Yang and Rashi Ahmed Siddiqi, "About an All-Weather Relationship: Security Foundations of Sino-Pakistan Relations since 9/11," *Journal of Contemporary China*, July 2011, 566.

17. Ibid., 567–71.

18. 安高乐, 吴明 [An Gaole and Wu Ming], "论9/11巴美对恐怖主义的认识和与政策演变" [Evolution of US and Pakistani Views on Terrorism and Related Policies since 9/11], 江苏科技大学学报 [Journal of the Jiangsu University of Science and Technology], September 2011, 70,73.

19. Yang and Siddiqi, "About an All-Weather Relationship," 570.

20. 楚水昂 [Chu Shuiang], "安达曼：印度扼守马六甲的锁钥" [The Andamans: India Guards the Strategic Gateway to Malacca], 现代兵器 [Modern Weaponry], May 2012, 10–14.

21. 林锡星 [Lin Xixing], "中缅石油管道设计中的美印因素" [US and Indian Influences on the Sino-Myanmar Oil Pipeline Proposal], 东南亚研究 [Southeast Asian Studies], May 2007, 34.

22. 李娴 [Li Xian], "美印联合军演规模空前" [US-Indian Join Military Exercises Are of an Unprecedented Scale], 当代海军 [Modern Navy], December 2008, 12–14.

23. 万佩华 [Wan Peihua], "美印日'马拉巴尔09'军演耐人寻味" [The US-India-Japan "Malabar 09" Military Exercise Provides Food for Thought], 当代海军 [Modern Navy], December 2009, 15–18.

24. Iskander Rehman, "Keeping the Dragon at Bay: India's Counter-Containment of China in Asia," *Asian Security* 5 (2009): 114–43.

25. Kaplan, *Monsoon*, 127–28.

26. See Daniel J. Kostecka, "Places and Bases: The Chinese Navy's Emerging Support Network in the Indian Ocean," *Naval War College Review* 64 (Winter 2011): 59–78, www.usnwc.edu/getattachment/0ecf6fde-e49e-485a-b135-c240a22e8a13/Places-and-Bases--The-Chinese-Navy-s-Emerging-Supp.

27. See, e.g., Michael Green and Andrew Shearer, "Defining US Indian Ocean Strategy," *Washington Quarterly*, Spring 2012, 175–89.

28. Kaplan, *Monsoon*, 126.

29. [Ye Hailin], "瓜达尔港与中国南亚战略" [Gwadar Port and Chinese Strategy in South Asia], 东方早报 [Oriental Morning Post], September 4, 2012, 15.

30. "国防部：所谓'珍珠链'包围圈纯属子虚乌有" [Defense Ministry: The So-Called "String of Pearls" Containment Ring Is Complete Nonsense], 中评社 [China Review News], February 28, 2013, www.zhgpl.com/doc/1024/5/3/5/102453595.html.

31. "中国须在印度洋建战略支撑点，确保海外利益" [China Needs to Build Strategic Sustaining Points in the Indian Ocean to Support Its Overseas Interests], 环球网 [Global Times Net], January 8, 2013, http://news.xinhuanet.com/world/2013-01/08/c124201984.htm.

32. 时宏远 [Shi Hongyuan], "美国的印度样政策及对中国的影响" [The US Indian Ocean Strategy and Its Impact on China], 国际问题研究 [International Studies], no. 4 (2012): 68, 73–76, 79.

33. 仲永龙 [Zhong Yonglong], "印度国产航母荒废一年后重新开工" [After a Year of Neglect, Work Begins Again on China's Indigenous Aircraft Carrier], 环球时报 [Global Times], January 25, 2013.

34. [Du Chaoping], "借力补网: 印度引进P8I及对中国海军的影响" [Borrow Strength to Fix the Net: The Impact of India's Introduction of the P8I on the Chinese Navy], 舰载武器 [Shipborne Weapons], December 2011, 14, 20.

35. [Chu Shuiang], "安达曼: 印度扼守马六甲的锁钥" [The Andamans: India Guards the Strategic Gateway to Malacca], 现代兵器 [Modern Weaponry], May 2012, 14.

36. 方晓志 [Fang Xiaozhi], "试论印度加入南海问题的战略动因及发展前景" [A Tentative Analysis of the Strategic Motives of India's Involvement in the South China Sea Issue and Its Future Evolution], 和平与发展 [Peace and Development], December 2012, 51, 53.

37. 余建华 [Yu Jianhua], "阿富汗问题与上海合作组织" [The Afghan Question and the Shanghai Cooperation Organization], 西亚非洲 [West Asia and Africa], April 2012, 56–73.

38. 胡维佳 [Hu Weijia], "中面印经贸互连" [Trade Interconnections between China, Burma, and India], 财经 [Finance and Economics], July 16, 2012, 69.

39. Annie Gowen, "Troops Face Off at China-India Border as Nation's Leaders Meet," *Washington Post*, September 18, 2014, http://www.washingtonpost.com /world/troops-face-off-at-india-china-border-as-leaders-of-nations-meet/2014 /09/18/a86e7b8a-1962-4446-b80c-f038a57527f3_story.html.

40. See Evan Braden Montgomery, "Competitive Strategies against Continental Powers: The Geo-Politics of Sino-Indian-American Relations," *Journal of Strategic Studies* 36 (2013): 76–100. This paper advocates for Washington to stir up "continental rivalry," vice "maritime rivalry," between the two rising Asian giants. That is not at all the approach taken in this book. Indeed, the "competitive strategies" approach seems mistakenly to assume away the possibility that facilitating India-China cooperation might be the most effective way to promote US interests in the Asia-Pacific region.

41. See Sandeep Unnithan, "Hidden Dragon on the High Seas," *India Today*, March 21, 2014, http://indiatoday.intoday.in/story/china-nuclear-powered -attack -submarine-south-china-sea/1/350573.html.

42. Sachin Parashar, "Sri Lanka Snubs India, Opens Port to Chinese Submarine Again," *Times of India*, November 2, 2014, http://timesofindia.indiatimes.com /india/Sri-Lanka-snubs-India-opens-port-to-Chinese-submarine-again/article show/45008757.cms.

43. See, e.g., 顾正龙 [Gu Zhenglong], "助推新疆暴恐活动频发的境外因素" [Pushing the Increasing Number of Terrorist Activities in Xinjiang: The External Factor], 军事文摘 [Military Digest], May 2014, 22–26.

44. Karen DeYoung and Missy Ryan, "Afghan Mission for U.S. to Continue Under New Authorities," *Washington Post*, November 22, 2014, http://www

.washingtonpost.com/world/national-security/white-house-gives-commanders
-broader-authority-to-support-afghan-troops/2014/11/22/8741f2fc-724e
-11e4-ad12-3734c461eab6_story.html.

45. For insight into the Obama administration's calculations on this matter, see Jeffrey A. Bader, *Obama and China's Rise: An Insider's Account of America's Asia Strategy* (Washington, DC: Brookings Institution Press, 2012), 75. Bader describes the "kabuki-like diplomatic discussion with the Chinese on Tibet," followed by "outraged commentaries" by American conservatives because of miscues during the "prearranged photo op." One is left wondering how such ideological efforts actually comport with US strategic interests.

46. Ananth Krishnan, "China Wants High-Speed Rail Link to India," *The Hindu*, March 14, 2010, www.thehindu.com/news/international/china-wants-high speed-rail-link-to-india/article244282.ece.

47. Ananth Krishnan, "China Wants India to Play Key Role in 'Silk Road' Plan," *The Hindu*, August 10, 2014, http://www.thehindu.com/news/international /world/china-wants-india-to-play-key-role-in-silk-road-plan/article6301227.ece.

48. President Obama implied that US drone strikes would be reduced and "heavily constrained," in a speech in the spring of 2013 at the National Defense University. See "Remarks by the President at National Defense University," May 23, 2013, www.whitehouse.gov/the-press-office/2013/05/23/remarks-president -national-defense-university.

49. See, e.g., Robert Kaplan, "Beijing's Afghan Gamble," *New York Times*, October 6, 2009, www.nytimes.com/2009/10/07/opinion/07kaplan.html.

50. See, e.g., Alissa Rubin and James Risen, "Costly Afghanistan Road Project Is Marred by Unsavory Alliances," *New York Times*, May 1, 2011, www.nytimes .com/2011/05/01/world/asia/01road.html?pagewanted=all&_r=0.

51. Harrison Gardiner, "India and China Vow to Cooperate on the Border," *New York Times*, May 20, 2013, www.nytimes.com/2013/05/21/world/asia /india-china-border-issues.html?_r=0; and Jason Burke and Tania Branigan, "India-China Border Standoff Highlights Tensions before Xi Visit," *The Guardian*, September 16, 2014, http://www.theguardian.com/world/2014/sep/16 /india-china-border-standoff-xi-visit.

52. Bruce Einhorn, "China Tries to Woo India's Prime Minister, Narendra Modi," *Bloomberg Businessweek*, June 10, 2014, www.businessweek.com/articles /2014-06-10/china-tries-to-woo-indias-prime-minister-narendra-modi.

53. Harsh V. Pant, "Why Xi Jinping's Visit to India Is Significant," BBC, September 16, 2014, http://www.bbc.com/news/world-asia-india-29217667.

12

CONCLUSION: REBALANCING THE REBALANCE

Mitigating Strategic Rivalry in U.S.-China Relations

Of late, US-China relations seem to be on a more secure footing. The November 2014 Obama-Xi Summit in Beijing appears to have produced some tangible outcomes on a wide variety of pressing issues, from climate change to visa restrictions to trade in high technology. There was even an accord on military confidence-building and the Prime Minister of Japan, America's foremost ally in Asia, managed to shake hands with the Chinese president. But don't believe the hype.

US-China relations remain mired in suspicion regrettably. While any forward progress is welcome, of course, the steps cited above are mostly symbolic, representing, for the most part, repackaging of longheld policies rather than genuine negotiated compromises. The measures emerging from the late 2014 summit will unfortunately not stabilize the relationship over the long term, nor provide definitive solutions to the most grave issues confronting the relationship and global security more generally. These measures may simply move the relationship from deeply fraught to extremely tense and will do little to break down the veritable chasm of strategic mistrust that presently divides Washington and Beijing. In the strategic realm, since 2011 Washington has embarked on a "rebalancing to the Asia-Pacific," while Beijing seems ever more determined to press its maritime claims and simultaneously believes that the United States is determined to contain and stifle China's rise. Most troubling of all, the military establishments in both the United States and China each appears to hold that they must earnestly prepare for rivalry and even direct conflict.

Although, for the moment, the relationship is still guided by pragmatists, there is no denying a certain intense loathing—extant in the larger body politic, but also felt intensely among political elites and bureaucrats in the corridors of power. This hostility was born of historical enmity, cultural divergence, and above all ideological estrangement. When geopolitical rivalry, undergirded by the "natural laws" of realism, is added to this volatile mix, conflict between the United States and China may appear to be dauntingly overdetermined.

The shadows of mistakes made a hundred years ago before World War I should inform our sober deliberations today. Responsible scholars, strategists, and policymakers on both sides of the Pacific must endeavor to reduce US-China tensions, lest this relationship repeat the tragedy of great power politics, with devastating consequences. This book is part of such an effort, and thus it seeks to chart a viable path of partnership through the implementation of "cooperation spirals" that will provide concrete policy benefits to both sides and to the world community more generally, and thus provide the substantive framework for "new great power relations," a term that should be embraced and not rejected by Washington as explained in chapter 1. The gradual and reciprocal nature of the cooperation spirals suggests that the process itself, or "model," is so self-evident and intuitive as part of basic human interaction that it does not require extensive theoretical elaboration. But the impulse toward compromise or mutual accommodation that the cooperation spirals embody is informed by Kissinger's wise observation that neither China nor the United States is any longer sufficiently strong to impose solutions upon the other. Yet neither superpower is well practiced in the difficult process of negotiating compromises with an equal.[1]

The essence of the argument made in this book is that China must make a comprehensive effort to increase the transparency of its national security apparatus, reform some of its long-held claims, and influence certain partners to conform to international norms. In a series of deescalatory steps, the United States should reciprocate by limiting the scope of its military deployments and military engagement activities, particularly but not only in the Asia-Pacific region. Together with its still-extant military superiority, a thorough acquaintance with the deeper history of US-China relations (chapter 2) should enable and inspire Washington to lead in initiating a series of cooperation cycles. After all, it was American ships that patrolled the Yangtze River for nearly a century after 1854 and not Chinese ships patrolling the Mississippi River. The transformative nature of Taiwan–Mainland interactions since 2008 (chapter 3) provides an extraordinary opportunity to demonstrate the promise of the cooperation cycle and break this Gordian knot that has long impeded enhanced US-China cooperation. Economic relations (chapter 4) provide vital ballast for the relationship and have yielded remarkable benefits to both societies, while environmental cooperation (chapter 5) is now extremely promising and will likely take center stage in future relations as the world community grapples with the impending challenge of climate change. A proposal is made suggesting that Washington accept a per capita emissions standard if China will agree to join a climate change treaty with intrusive verification procedures. In the developing world (chapter 6), it is suggested that if Beijing were more transparent in its aid, financial, and arms trade transactions, Washington would likely agree to embrace China's coleadership—for example, in leading key institutions such as the World Bank.

The second half of the book focuses more narrowly on areas of acute geopolitical tensions between the superpowers. Washington's flexibility and forbearance on the Taiwan question should prompt Beijing's closer attention to the global menace of nuclear proliferation. The discussion of superpower strategic interaction in the Middle East (chapter 7) holds that active Chinese support for positive signals emerging from Tehran could be reciprocated by US pressure on Israel with respect to its nuclear weapons capabilities, along with greater restraint in the Persian Gulf more generally. A novel approach regarding the North Korean proliferation challenge is described (chapter 8), wherein Washington actually seeks a closer relationship between Beijing and Pyongyang rather than striving for the latter's isolation, in order to strive for a more stable and secure Korean Peninsula. With respect to the precarious China-Japan relationship (chapter 9), a series of compromises is advocated that is newly attentive to history, divides disputed territory, reforms the US-Japan alliance, and also enables Japan to join the UN Security Council as a permanent member. Superpower mutual accommodation in Southeast Asia (chapter 10) suggests that Washington should support a bilateral "joint development" formula in exchange for Beijing's agreement to reform the "nine-dash line" claim. As with the Japan discussion, China is beckoned into a more constructive triangular relationship with India (chapter 11) that also yields New Delhi a seat on the UN Security Council, while committing the United States to a somewhat reduced military footprint in Central and South Asia. Hardly any of the compromises mentioned here would be easy, although most are so plainly in that state's interest that they might adopt these measures irrespective of any hypothetical "cooperation cycle." However, there can be little doubt that the path of compromise and peace will require leaders of conviction and bravery. Unfortunately, the "China-bashing syndrome" now seems an endemic phenomenon of contemporary American politics (and journalism); and, moreover, it seems that America-bashing is also, predictably, widely popular in China today.[2]

Munich Redux?

The criticism sure to be leveled at this book is that it allegedly advocates "appeasing" China: satisfying many of Beijing's long-standing gripes regarding the US alliance system, while only receiving "piddling" and unenforceable promises of enhanced transparency and pressure on various partners (e.g., Iran) in return for Washington's restraint. As noted in the book's introduction, such criticism tends to be ideological in nature and is not adequately attentive to the reciprocal dynamics of the proposed cooperation cycles. Not only are they intended to ensure balanced, two-way accommodation, but their step-by-step nature assures that confidence is built in preliminary "baby steps," before the major and more difficult steps are even attempted. There is no built-in assumption, moreover, that steps are irreversible, and some backsliding is practically inevitable given the ambitious task of making progress on a multitude of complex issues simultaneously. For American readers, a casual glance at some of the compromise measures asked of Beijing within the cooperation cycles—from agreeing to verification procedures for carbon emissions, to accepting a midpoint delimitation in the East China Sea, to opening its new giant naval base on Hainan Island to regular visits by personnel from the Association of Southeast Asian Nations (ASEAN), to legalizing genuinely independent labor unions, to granting both Japan and India permanent seats on the UN Security Council—reveals that these measures will hardly be easy concessions to which China can agree. It must be stated emphatically: There is no argument in this book for unilateral concessions. Such an arrangement would only engender anger and insecurity.

But even if the applicability of the appeasement critique is unwarranted in this case, it is worth probing the question further with respect to US-China relations. For Aaron Friedberg, "the strategic and domestic political objections to appeasement are obvious . . . and overwhelming." He continues, "Despite claims that it would reduce the risk of war, cutting a deal over the heads of democratic allies with a strong, authoritarian China would strike many Americans as both imprudent and immoral." He is concerned that concessions "might simply embolden [Beijing] to press for more and, by signaling US weakness, could encourage aggressive behavior by other authoritarians in Asia and elsewhere." He closes his discussion of appeasement by returning to the realist conception of the balance of power, suggesting that "unchecked Chinese domination of East Asia could give it preferred access to . . . the region's . . . vast resources. . . . From a secure base, China could project power into other regions, much as the United States was able to do from the Western Hemisphere."[3]

Hugh White's counterargument holds that "the lesson people draw from [Munich regarding appeasement] . . . is a harsh one: The only way to make sure we do not give away too much is to give away nothing. This line of reasoning is emotionally satisfying and can be good politics, but it is based on some important fallacies and leads to bad policy." He further explains that the fallacies are "there is no chance that if America just stands firm, China will go away, and everything will keep on as it has been until now." He seems to be saying here that it is simply impossible that a much more powerful "risen" China will accept the former status quo. A clear irony in this respect that arises from Friedberg's discussion of state ambitions is his evident fear that China might do exactly what the United States has done. Indeed, some perspective in understanding China's rise is gleaned from the American experience of about a century ago. Between 1890 and 1920, the United States resorted to force on a significant scale: thirty-five times in Latin America—an average of more than once a year.[4] Put against that record, China's increased parading of coast guard vessels and the occasional resort to water cannons hardly seems very "assertive." Thus, Friedberg's own analogy, which is actually quite appropriate, seems to undermine his major concerns. Not only has China proven relatively benign in interactions with its immediate neighbors—Russia's use of force against both Georgia in 2008 and Ukraine in 2014 may be another point of comparison in this respect—but there is hardly a shred of evidence suggesting that China is seeking to "project power into other regions . . . from a secure base." True, some Chinese strategists are presently arguing for such power projection capabilities, and the topic of foreign "bases" or simply "outposts" has been broached, but their sharpest arguments are by and large couched in the context of a major threat posed by the US alliance system against China— suggesting that "Thucydides' trap" has indeed been sprung. Fortunately, these proposals have not yet been acted upon in Beijing, leaving out the possibility that the action/reaction escalation spiral or "doomsday machine" can still be halted and even reversed.

Returning to White's robust counterargument to the appeasement critique: "The other mistake is that there is no midpoint between conceding nothing and conceding everything." He states that the best remedy to prevent the problem of the adversary with an insatiable appetite (akin to Nazi Germany) is to "define clearly in advance just how far one is willing to go, . . . and to explain clearly to Beijing where that point is, when that point has been reached, and what happens if China keeps pushing beyond it."[5] Here, it can be stated unequivocally that White's call for clear, logical, and defensible American "red lines" in the Asia-Pacific region is fully endorsed.[6] Similarly, Steinberg and O'Hanlon are correct in arguing: "Clarity about red lines is a key element of deterrence designed to reduce the danger of miscalculation."[7] Critics of policies that promote compromise are sure to respond that any compromises could weaken deterrence and hence cause the war they are trying to avert. This argument is not without a certain merit, so there is an imperative to establish realistic and genuine red lines, but also to accomplish compromises in a gradual and reciprocal manner. The problem of conveying excessive weakness is recognized here, and, as discussed below in more depth, military strength is a crucial requirement for effective and stable compromise.

A couple more points about the appeasement critique—which perhaps is better described as the "appeasement cudgel"—with respect to Washington's China policy need to be made. First, those deploying this critique should be aware that the most eminent historian of conflict and great power rivalry in the early twentieth century, Paul Kennedy, has explicitly denounced the widespread use of the tortured Munich analogy for addressing contemporary foreign policy dilemmas. He states that "it is sometimes very smart to take one step back." And then he provides numerous examples where conciliatory policies proved successful, ranging from Britain's long-time appeasement of the United States to Washington's final move to "abandon the colossal encumbrance of Vietnam" in the 1970s. He makes this argument in the context of a broader call for the United States to "trim our sails and no longer try to bestride the world like a colossus. . . . We shall make a concession here, a concession there, though hopefully it will be disguised . . . as 'power sharing' and 'mutual compromise,' and the dreadful 'A' word will not appear."[8] One could spend an entire book describing the rather gaping differences between contemporary China and Germany's bloody rise. But most leaders will be familiar enough with the two respective leaders' biographies to understand well that Xi Jinping is no crude, racist, angry, uneducated Austrian corporal. Rather, Xi is an engineer whose family suffered terribly during the mass hysteria and radicalism of the Cultural Revolution. He has few connections with the military, and he lived briefly in Iowa. Betraying his rather liberal and even pro-Western worldview, he has sent his only child to be educated at Harvard. The Munich analogy exaggerates the lessons of a single historical case, and now scholars of international security do not even believe the historical record supports those supposed lessons.[9]

A final reason why the "appeasement cudgel" should not be applied to attempts at mutual accommodation in the US-China context concerns the global balance of power. Let us recall that this seems to be at the heart of Friedberg's disquiet regarding China's rise. Realists, including Kissinger as well as this author, also view the global balance of power as the final guarantor of security, and ultimately of peace. In 1938 British leaders confronted major gaps in their own defenses and what they perceived as a perilous military imbalance favoring Germany, such that they were negotiating with a gun to their heads. No such circumstances apply in the present situation. The United States retains military superiority in almost all critical domains, whether with respect to submarines or nuclear weapons. Even projecting decades into the future, when China's economy (and thus defense spending) could be substantially larger than that of the United States, Washington will be able to count on the fact that Canberra, Tokyo, and New Delhi—not to mention Seoul, Hanoi, Jakarta, and many other capitals in close proximity to China—will all be making efforts to match Chinese military power. As White observes, Beijing is hardly strong enough to dominate in East Asia, even if it wanted to. Thus, the United States is in a very strong, almost unassailable strategic position. It has the strength to make judicious and reasonable compromises for the sake of peace. With this in mind, it is worth considering the words of Winston Churchill, the leader most associated with standing against appeasement, before the House of Commons in December 1950: "Appeasement in itself may be good or bad according to the circumstances. Appeasement from weakness and fear is alike futile and fatal. Appeasement from strength is magnanimous and noble and might be the surest and perhaps the only path to world peace."[10]

A Worthy and Capable Partner?

Beyond the strategic aspects of whether and how to try to cooperate with China, there are additional questions regarding whether the United States should genuinely work with China despite its dismal human rights record, and also whether China is truly capable of delivering on its commitments. The human rights question is not a small one for US-China relations, and some readers may be surprised that this book has generally not delved deeply into this issue, with just a few minor exceptions. In part, this simply reflects the limits of space and the fact that the issue is well covered in other scholarly efforts, as well as by Western newspapers. But there is, in addition, a conviction presented here that human rights should not be a major issue in US-China relations. Such a course is anathema to most Americans, even within the foreign policy elite. Friedberg is quite accurate in asserting that "to most Americans, China's human rights violations are not only intrinsically wrong but also a powerful indicator of the true, morally distasteful (some would say 'evil') nature of the Beijing regime. . . . The possibility of a warm, trusting and stable relationship is remote, to say the least. Moral judgments about domestic behavior aside, democracies also tend to regard nondemocracies as inherently untrustworthy and dangerously prone to external aggression."[11]

By contrast, the view of this author is again much closer to White's perspective on the Chinese regime. He notes:

> The people of China have a lot to complain about. . . . Pressure for . . . political change in China could easily grow. . . . [But] China is not like many other authoritarian countries. Its government is repressive, but unlike many repressive governments it has delivered genuine benefits to its people. In China today many hundreds of millions of people lead much better lives than their parents could have ever imagined, with better housing, better education, better health care, better clothes, more freedom to travel, and better economic prospects. Only in the West, where we take such things for granted, do such momentous improvements in material welfare seem politically unimportant.[12]

Both Kissinger and Swaine argue that the democratization of China should not be Washington's policy objective.[13]

Four basic reasons support this hands-off approach to democratization in China. First and most obviously, it will not be feasible to achieve a solid working relationship if Washington is simultaneously pursuing "regime change" against the Communist regime in Beijing. Indeed, American leaders seem to underestimate the degree to which the US focus on human rights tends to degrade the quality of relations across the board, given that distrust has become the defining principle on both sides. Moreover, there may be a

dangerous tendency among the Chinese national security elite to view ideo-
logical challenges from Washington as directly coordinated with strategic military challenges.[14] Then there is the question of leadership time and energy.
This problem was illustrated very clearly when US secretary of state Hillary
Clinton devoted most of her spring 2012 visit to Beijing for the Strategic and
Economic Dialogue to dealing with the blind dissident Chen Guangcheng.
To be sure, she enjoyed generally positive reviews in the American press after
securing his release to go to the United States, but predictably the summit
achieved little progress on the key issues of nuclear proliferation and climate
change. The third reason to limit the role of human rights in America's China
policy is that it seems quite hypocritical to single out China for special criticism when the United States manages to quietly and yet very actively cooperate with states that have even worse human rights records, such as Saudi
Arabia. Most important, perhaps, there is the problem that a firm human
rights agenda actually seems to undermine the very agenda that it is seeking
to promote. China is quite clearly liberalizing, for example, with regular demonstrations taking place to protest corruption and environmental problems.
However, these threats can be easily quashed by the government if they can
be tarred as tools of Western interests. The ironic truth, therefore, seems to be
that these movements will be much more potent without Western interference
of any kind. China is moving in a pluralist direction, to be sure, but it must
be allowed to find its own path toward enlarged freedoms.[15] Perhaps this is
why at the recent APEC Summit in Beijing President Obama was at pains to
make clear that the United States had no role in the Hong Kong protests. As
discussed in chapter 3, such democratic aspirations will have largest impact on
China's democracy debate if the West refrains from involvement to the maxi-
mal extent. Moreover, the faltering of the Arab Spring in 2013, especially in
Egypt, suggests that democratization may be a highly unstable and occasionally even tragic process if it occurs too rapidly or before certain preconditions,
such as basic norms and "rules of the political game," are agreed upon.

A final, well-elaborated critique of enhanced US-China cooperation was
made by Elizabeth Economy and Adam Segal in the august pages of *Foreign
Affairs* in mid-2009.[16] They took the Obama administration to task for what
they considered to be a naive and unsustainable policy toward China of "more
cooperation on more issues more often." While admitting to the "undeniable
logic" of enhanced US-China cooperation, they criticized such efforts as constituting a "Group of Two mirage," because the attempt to reach such a functional bilateral relationship would "raise expectations for a level of partnership

that cannot be met and [would] exacerbate the very real differences that still exist between Washington and Beijing." Economy and Segal are critical of "empty frameworks for dialogues and never-ending dialogues," and they see the need to lower expectations given "mismatched interests, values, and capabilities." This article does make a number of insightful observations, including the assertion that "Washington [must] change its behavior, too," and more particularly, that world opinion may be most crucial to coaxing Beijing toward reform on the most difficult issues. This book, moreover, is sympathetic to the now-common critique of US-China relations that "dialogues" may be necessary but are hardly sufficient, and so only a very few further dialogues are proposed herein, including the crucial trilateral dialogues encompassing both India and Japan together with the United States and China.

However, this important article, which may well have had an influence in the downward lurch of relations between Washington and Beijing since late 2009, contains at least three major flaws. The first is a tendency to miss the forest for the trees by lumping all issues together. Thus, Americans may well be disturbed by low-quality dairy products or pet food originating in China, but markets have a way of sorting such issues out themselves, and these issues simply cannot be on par with the imperatives to prevent great power conflict, to halt nuclear proliferation, and to develop a global system to effectively regulate carbon emissions. On the issue of whether Beijing is competent to be a cooperative partner because it is allegedly "incapable of following through"— a rather arrogant supposition—one may simply recall the headlines from India during the last two years—whether regarding tainted school lunches or extensive instances of aggression against women or submarine explosions— to realize that the United States does not and should not simply weigh the competence of states in deciding whether to actively cooperate with them. A second major flaw concerns the article's failure to account for modern Chinese history and, in particular, the major chip that the Chinese carry on their collective shoulders due to the "century of humiliation." The reason why this is a devastating shortfall for this particular argument is that Economy and Segal's core recommendation is that Washington cope with Beijing by closely coordinating with both Tokyo and various European states. Although informal diplomatic coordination is always useful, one can see the problem of this policy direction when one simply considers that just over a century ago it was the same agglomeration (various European states, the United States, and Japan) that were overseeing a massive combined assault on the walls of Beijing during the Boxer "Rebellion." Such obtuseness with respect to history, and the rather obvious repercussions of related and hardly disguised diplomatic schemes to lever multilateral pressure against China, are largely to blame for the rising tensions in East Asia since 2009. A final flaw in the article is that it takes a very static, conservative approach to the Chinese regime, reflecting perhaps a thin understanding of Chinese perspectives. In fact, as demonstrated below, though many Chinese foreign policy analysts are both angered and anxious regarding perceived attempts by the United States to "contain" China's rise, a vocal majority seeks further progressive reform of Chinese foreign policy and also enhanced cooperation with the United States.

A Final Look at Evolving Chinese Perspectives

While Beijing has been steadily increasing its capabilities and sophistication for promoting Chinese viewpoints, even daring to take out full-page advertisements in the *New York Times* on a regular basis, it is still very worthwhile to sample the immense offerings of the contemporary Chinese media and academic debate concerning US-China relations. Indeed, this book has offered readers a uniquely broad and deep probe into Chinese thinking on a variety of issues by examining Chinese-language writings from the leading thinkers within each chapter and thus spanning a very wide range of issues, from environmental policy to regional security and development issues. Recall that presenting these perspectives does *not* imply agreement with these viewpoints. Disturbingly, the analyses surveyed in the preceding chapters, though open to new US-China cooperative endeavors, generally betray rising concern over the developing US-China rivalry in their various respective sectors of focus.

Indeed, as discussed throughout much of this book, it is hardly difficult to find examples of major Chinese anxiety and bitterness regarding US policy in the Asia-Pacific region. Occasionally, the Western media put down such sentiments either to the highly insecure machinations of what they consider to be an inherently unstable regime, or alternatively suggest that these are the isolated views of a very select group of Chinese media outlets that adhere to a very nationalist orientation. However, these common practices tend to understate the wider extent of anti-American sentiment in China. Indeed, one 2012 Chinese scholarly analysis underlines the wide basis of anti-Americanism in China (that it is said parallels a similar anti-China basis in the US body politic). The same analysis yields that hawkish parties on both sides of the Pacific tend to see a US-China war as all but inevitable.[17] An early 2013 analysis of the prospects for "new-type great power relations" suggested that few think an actual US-China armed conflict could occur in the coming decades, but that "conflict and competition are increasing. People have the reasonable fear that, even as Chinese and US power becomes more equivalent, that competition and tensions will further intensify." This analysis highlights the detrimental role of continual US interference in China's domestic affairs and sees Washington's connivance and support in the various challenges that Beijing is said to confront from its neighbors.[18] As one might expect, Chinese military journals are quite full of articles that anxiously describe new US military capabilities, for example, Conventional Prompt Global Strike (a project discussed specifically in the next section of this chapter).[19] Strategic pessimism and anxiety are evident among senior Chinese military officers, such as retired general Peng Guangqian and retired admiral Yang Yi.[20]

Although press coverage in China of the May 2013 Sunnylands Summit between Obama and Xi generally adopted a positive and constructive tone, undercurrents of major, lurking tensions were again not difficult to discern. For example, one commentary published in Shanghai's *Oriental Morning Post* at the time of the summit warned: "From its founding to the present day, American history has always been a history of struggling against an enemy," and also observed that a clear message to Xi in the summit's California location is that the United States is and will remain a Pacific power.[21] A lengthy commentary in the influential *Study Times* that followed the summit also noted that the Obama administration's "rebalancing" had complicated US-China relations, suggested that the "rebalance" was already being rebalanced by Secretary of State John Kerry's frenetic diplomacy around the Middle East, but also observed that tensions between Beijing and Washington in the Asia-Pacific region were intensifying "on a daily basis."[22] Leading Chinese experts on US-China relations sounded newly alarmed regarding recent developments. Yuan Peng, for example, concludes in a mid-2012 analysis that Washington was "seeking to draw together the support and strength to contain China's rise, limit its maritime expansion, and prevent any giving way to a new system of shared power in the Asia-Pacific."[23] Although counseling against an emotive reaction, the Peking University scholar Zhu Feng also asserted in mid-2012: "The US 'Asia-Pacific pivot' is quite obviously an attack [冲击] against China."[24] Another mid-2012 analysis, this time from the director of international strategy at the Central Party School, Liu Jianfei, tellingly begins by observing that many opinions have surfaced recently suggesting that Chinese diplomacy has been "too weak" and should presently shift its priority from "development" to "security," given the extant challenges from neighbors and threats from various great powers.[25] In 2014 it was not difficult to find harsh critiques of the US 'rebalance to the Asia-Pacific,' whether in official military literature or among foreign policy analyses.[26] Thus, a mid-2014 issue of 世界经济与政治 (*World Economics and Politics*) carried as its lead article an appraisal of the "rebalance" that warns that the policy had been hijacked by the American military-industrial complex and consequently militarized. The author cautions, moreover, that the "Asian alliance tail is wagging the American dog" and that this phenomenon threatens to make China into an enemy of the United States.[27] Another article from mid-2014 by a Peking University professor in the same journal suggests that US-China rivalry is "spreading to all areas of the Asia-Pacific," and that both sides are pursuing 针锋相对 (tit-for-tat) strategies in the military domain.[28] Another 2014 article, this time the leader paper by a group of military authors publishing a designated PLA research project, explores "US Restrictions on Chinese Seapower." For these authors, China does not just confront "遏制" (containment) by the United States, but something perhaps even more bellicose: "围堵" (a condition of being under siege) or even "掣肘" (a condition of being held by the elbows). For the purpose of restricting Chinese naval power in the eastern, southern, and western flanks, Washington is said to be constructing a "超长防线" (super long line of defense) that stretches from the Aleutian Islands to the Persian Gulf. Among their conclusions, for example, is that American strategists are seeking to use the India-China territorial dispute on land to "牵制" (pin down) China by diverting its attention away from the maritime flank. In this rather dark portrayal of US-China strategic interaction, the authors recommend robust improvements to China's anti-submarine warfare capabilities and also its nuclear forces.[29]

Conversely, the balance of opinion among Chinese scholars and strategists in China is that China has no alternative but to try to seek a more positive and constructive relationship with the United States. For example, Liu Jianfei's analysis mentioned above argues emphatically against revising China's foreign policy doctrine to counter the US "rebalancing to Asia." He suggests that the threat to China should not be exaggerated—noting, for example, that the nature of the US-Japan Alliance has not changed substantially from its earlier form and, moreover, that China's fundamental security can still be assured.[30] Another influential foreign policy thinker, Cui Liru, similarly argued in late 2011 that the probability of China getting into a war with a major power had significantly decreased in the new century.[31] Senior Chinese foreign policymakers, such as Cui Tiankai, have attempted to improve the climate of US-China relations. In a speech in July 2012, Cui identified maintaining peace and stability in Asia as a top priority for US-China relations and stated that China rejects "枝独秀" (a single branch blooms alone) and thus would not pursue prosperity or security at the expense of others.[32] Contrary to the concerns of some Western analysts that China's rapid rise would lead to overconfidence, Chinese strategists, including military strategists, do not see a favorable military balance, and they generally appear to see "US decline" as overhyped.[33] Some academic Chinese writings have even broached concepts of a greater fusion between Chinese and US strategic interests. For example, the lead article in the prestigious Chinese academic journal 当代亚太 (*Journal of Contemporary Asia-Pacific Studies*) made the unconventional argument that strong security ties between the United States and various countries in the Asia-Pacific region allow them to be more relaxed regarding close economic relations with China.[34] In an even more unusual line of argumentation in China, the Peking University scholar Wang Yizhou argues that China can learn some lessons from the experience of other great powers, especially that of Great Britain and also the United States. In a somewhat remarkable passage, he argues that "England's rise was accompanied by a high degree of navigational exploration and market-oriented trade—the ocean became the British Empire's 'high frontier'; when American power came to the fore, [it] promoted . . . the building of the United Nations and such international organizations." He calls upon China's leaders to correct the unflattering image abroad of China as a "跛足巨人" (lame giant) by turning in earnest to the provision of global "public goods."[35] In 2014 the well-known Chinese strategist Jin Canrong published a comprehensive study of "new type major power relations" that concluded, based on a number of prevailing conditions, that Washington and Beijing would not ultimately go down the well-worn path of great power rivalry.[36] In sum, this brief survey of selected Chinese writings on US-China relations reveals that there is very ample suspicion regarding US policies toward China, and yet there remains a very substantial segment of informed opinion in China that wants to work constructively with Washington to build a more peaceful and prosperous world order.

A Final Cooperation Spiral Focused on the Larger Strategic Relationship

Washington's move 1 in the larger strategic relationship: The United States should initiate a "bottom-up review" of Taiwan policy with a stated goal of increasing flexibility (figure 12.1). Taiwan has long been at the very center of US-China tensions, for historical, ideological, and strategic reasons, as discussed at length

Figure 12.1 Cooperation Spiral: The Larger Strategic Relationship 合作螺旋：中美关系大局

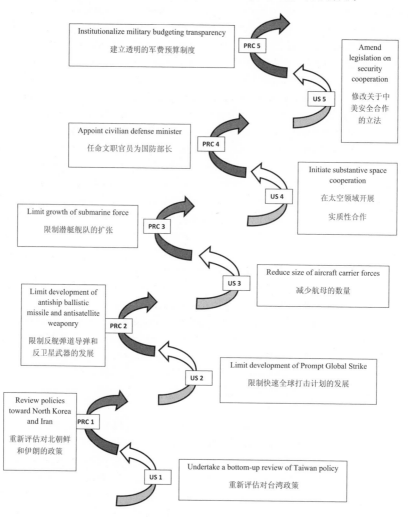

in chapter 2 and particularly chapter 3 of this book. In deference to the issue's extreme importance for improving US-China relations, chapter 3 reveals this book's first cooperation spiral that seeks to take advantage of the post-2008 rapprochement in cross-Strait relations to achieve major gains in US-China relations. The cooperation spiral advocated in chapter 3 suggests a process like all the others in the book of reciprocal accommodation, featuring major concessions on the Chinese side, including but not limited to pulling missile forces back from the Taiwan Strait area, restricting amphibious capabilities, and eventually even renouncing the use of force against Taiwan. Relative gains (see chapter 1), however, will generally favor China with regard to this issue, so that Washington would naturally favor some kind of geopolitical compensation for its flexibility regarding a central "core interest" of Beijing. Many Western experts will be skeptical about such an approach. For example, the scholar Tom Christensen has written recently that "there is a basic intellectual problem with the view that US-China cooperation is built on a horse trade of sorts."[37] Presenting the framework elaborated in these pages, that particular viewpoint clearly is not shared here. "Horse trading," it turns out, is a central element of effective diplomacy. In fact, the pervasiveness of Christensen's reluctant view may partially explain the many logjams that persist in US diplomacy and that afflict US-China relations in particular. In choosing to take a more flexible approach to Taiwan that overtly favors peace and integration, the United States will indeed be pursuing its own national security interests following the sound logic of scholars, such as Glaser, Gilley, and Saunders (see chapter 3). But Taiwan is such a fine "horse" that the United States should be rewarded for adopting a newly constructive position on the issue; and such a strategic "exchange" of benefits, especially with respect to "core interests," will indeed be of great importance to those seeking to reform Washington's longtime Taiwan policies.

Beijing's move 1 in the larger strategic relationship: China should undertake a bottom-up review of its policies toward nuclear proliferation, enhancing its pressure on both North Korea and Iran. China does not have robust defense relations with any provincial-sized entities claimed by the United States, so an exactly equivalent "trade" is out of the question, of course. But the genius and creativity of effective diplomacy are to look for approximate equivalents in other dimensions of bilateral diplomacy. Undoubtedly, nuclear nonproliferation has occupied a central spot in US national security policy since at least 1991. Two major wars have been fought for this purpose with Iraq, and several others have been contemplated. Undoubtedly, nuclear proliferation could be called a core interest of the United States. Clever critics will, of course, argue (following Christensen's logic) that the key violator states of Iran and particularly North Korea are actually greater threats to China's interests than they are to the United States. This is true enough from a simple, rational perspective, but international relations are neither simple nor entirely rational. A more holistic perspective that encompasses historical path dependency and various material interests yields the clear conclusion that Beijing is evidently less concerned about nuclear proliferation in both these circumstances, even while still somewhat alarmed. The basic position adopted in this book is closer to that of Washington—that nuclear nonproliferation is completely vital to global security. Therefore, whole chapters have been devoted to both the Iran nuclear question (chapter 7) and the North Korean nuclear question (chapter 8), as well as the various pathways to constructive US-China cooperation with respect to these key issues. A small but definite step forward on this key issue was the inaugural meeting of the US-China Nonproliferation Joint Working Group on November 3, 2014 in Beijing.[38] As advocated in both these chapters, China's approach would not be the application of ever more sanctions against Tehran and Pyongyang. That would likely be counterproductive. Rather, Beijing would dangle some of its own carrots combined perhaps with a little bit of "stick" as well. Most important, China could provide a vehicle to act as a "trusted agent" with respect to nuclear inspections by even creating its own agency for enforcing nonproliferation—complete with the requisite technical capabilities. This would not be the first time that the Taiwan issue had been intertwined with both the North Korean and Iran issues. But such a "horse trade" will be enormously beneficial to both the superpowers, and also to global security more generally.

Washington's move 2 in the larger strategic relationship: The United States should eliminate or strictly limit the Conventional Prompt Global Strike (CPGS) program. This book has quite purposefully focused on diplomatic challenges first and foremost, while relegating military analysis to the background. However, there is no question that certain military issues are highly relevant to US-China relations, and so a few questions regarding deployments and weapons systems have been considered in the preceding chapters. The overall configuration of each respective military (force structure, posture, and doctrine) will be critical to setting the relationship on a stable path for the twenty-first century. Moreover, scholars of international relations have generally agreed that the "cult of the offensive" that may naturally permeate military organizations has contributed to the outbreak of great power conflict in the past, most obviously in 1914.[39] As suggested in the previous section, the CPGS program is viewed with alarm in China and is causing Chinese military strategists to consider their own version of CPGS, including hypersonic strike vehicles, as well as other countermeasures, such as much enlarged nuclear forces generally. An obvious reason that this program could be extremely destabilizing in a genuine US-China military crisis is the threat to Chinese command and control, early warning, and nuclear forces that CPGS poses. These weapons, therefore, may well put Beijing in an early "use'm or lose'm" situation that could lead to rapid nuclear escalation. Other reasons to scrap the program are that the United States hardly lacks for alternative, effective delivery systems (whether bombers or cruise missiles), and obviously there is the cost issue as well. Congress has already evidently shown some wise reluctance with regard to this program, but scrapping it could yield some benefit for US-China strategic stability.[40] It could also yield a reciprocal move by Beijing if negotiated skillfully by US diplomats.

Beijing's move 2 in the larger strategic relationship: China should eliminate or strictly limit its development of antiship ballistic missiles (ASBM) and also antisatellite (ASAT) weapons. These two weapons systems have fostered copious hand-wringing at the Pentagon over the last decade. ASAT weapons are more widely understood, because China undertook to make a public test of the system in January 2007. This test was doubly controversial because, in addition to demonstrating China's ability to threaten US satellite systems, it also created a significant amount of space debris and thus violated widely held norms with respect to weapons testing in space. The ASBM issue remains more speculative, though many US national security experts and leaders believe that China already possesses such a system.[41] The revolutionary aspect of this weapons system is that its speed and range may be sufficiently potent as to render almost all large naval surface combatants obsolete. Specifically, the weapons system has been discussed as a first-order threat to aircraft carriers, the primary capital ships of the US Navy and the basis for much of its fighting doctrine. It is as yet unclear why China has not elected to test this innovative ASBM system, though one may speculate that rumors of the weapons' existence have, in and of themselves, served Beijing's purposes well. Unlike the US CPGS program discussed above, Chinese military leaders may be even more reluctant to part with these two programs, given that they have less redundancy in strike capabilities. Then there are inevitably problems of transparency and verification, which could be particularly thorny for attempts to limit these systems. One could hypothetically imagine levels of Chinese compliance in this case, ranging from Chinese accession to the Intermediate Nuclear Forces Treaty[42]—a step that could have myriad positive effects on China's image and security environment—to the much more modest step of not overtly testing and fielding such systems. Chinese hawks will doubtless argue that such systems are crucial to China's evolving deterrence posture, but a wiser perspective in China would understand that such systems also feed the approaches of zero-sum strategic thinking, arms racing, and hair trigger alert postures, not to mention contributing to a continued blurring of nuclear and conventional conflict scenarios. Steinberg and O'Hanlon make a similar set of recommendations with a related helpful analysis—for example, on the difficult issue of verification.[43]

Washington's move 3 in the larger strategic relationship: The United States should significantly trim its force of aircraft carriers. There are good reasons to undertake this reform of US Navy force structure irrespective of US-China relations. These reasons include chiefly cost, vulnerability, and larger global strategy. Regrettably, the new X-47 carrier-launched unmanned aircraft program—closely watched in China—appears set to give the "big decks" another lease on life. However, removing some piloted aircraft may mitigate costs and risks to an extent, but it is unlikely to overcome the full weight of a rational cost/benefit calculus that points to the necessity of force reductions. The simple truth is that given the vast and lethal array of cruise missiles now wielded by even less sophisticated prospective opponents, aircraft carriers only really make sense in low-intensity combat operations or humanitarian operations. Given those constraints, there is no reason why the US Navy aircraft carrier force could not be reduced from eleven to between four and six vessels—an enormous savings in resources. Our chief concern here, however, is what role such reductions might play in US-China relations, and especially in strategic interaction in the Asia-Pacific region. There is reason to believe that this role could be significant, because (1) of the tremendous symbolic import of aircraft carriers, (2) China has now produced its first genuine aircraft carrier with more to follow, and (3) Beijing's historical sensitivity to "gunboat diplomacy." American "hawks" will undoubtedly fret that American deterrence is being undermined by such force reductions, but this displays their ignorance regarding aircraft carriers' vulnerability in contemporary naval warfare. US diplomats would rather be wise to put a positive spin on this sensible force reduction by citing not only technological change but also Washington's welcome of a more multipolar world.[44]

Beijing's move 3 in the larger strategic relationship: China should undertake to strictly limit the dimensions of its rapidly modernizing submarine fleet. Although, as discussed above, aircraft carriers are rather antiquated and therefore are somewhat ancillary to the naval balance of power, the same cannot be said about modern submarines—the true capital ships of contemporary navies. They are nearly impossible to detect and include enough firepower in some cases to destroy whole nations. The future dimensions of the Chinese submarine force (and also that of the United States), matters a great deal to stabilizing the two nation's nascent rivalry in the Asia-Pacific region. No wonder that upstart naval powers all around the Pacific Rim seem to be purchasing submarines at a record pace.[45] The rapid modernization of China's submarine fleet has played a role in this interactive strategic dynamic, to be sure, but it should be noted that the Chinese Navy is rising quickly from a rather low initial base. Moreover, its growth can hardly be called hurried, for example, when compared with that of the Soviet Navy, which completed the construction of an incredible ninety-one diesel submarines in 1955 and fourteen nuclear submarines in 1970.[46] And yet even the moderate pace of China's modernization of its submarine force has unnerved both smaller neighbors and the traditional naval powers. At this point, the Chinese submarine force is made up of about fifty-five submarines, while the US Navy has almost seventy. But the illusion of parity quickly dissipates as one realizes the very substantial advantages that nuclear submarines possess almost across the board in naval combat and that all US Navy submarines are nuclear, but only a small proportion of Chinese submarines are nuclear. Still, China's evidently ambitious effort in undersea warfare could achieve near parity within fifteen to twenty years if current trends persist. This progression in itself is likely to be somewhat destabilizing, but if China were to reach for outright superiority, that could precipitate a highly dangerous strategic competition on par with the Cold War. To date, Chinese leaders have wisely seemed to keep the country's navalists in check; but given such dangers, and the enormous sums that both countries have and will spend on such weapons, specialists on both sides would be wise to give serious thought to proposals for naval arms control. Indeed, the interwar period's much-criticized Washington Treaty system proved to be mostly a victim of faulty verification procedures that are generally no longer an issue, thanks to modern surveillance technologies.

Washington's move 4 in the larger strategic relationship: The United States should initiate substantive space cooperation with China. As with naval power, space power is certain to be a formidable currency of geopolitics in this century and those that follow. American dominance in space has served as a key tool in enabling the "unipolar moment" since the collapse of the USSR. It is now relatively clear, however, that Beijing has its own major aspirations in space and, moreover, that China seems to have substantial prowess in the field of rocketry, in addition to growing expertise on satellites, remote sensing, and related capabilities. Recent or planned achievements for China in this realm have included becoming only the third country to launch a human into space, establishment of a satellite navigation system independent of the Global Positioning System, surpassing the United States in commercial satellite launches, building a space station, and landing a probe on the moon. In addition, the January 2007 Chinese ASAT test demonstrated how space weaponization can fuel tensions between the superpowers. This test may also demonstrate the perils of Chinese space scientists laboring in relative isolation. Unfortunately, a 2011 law adopted by the US Congress prohibits the National Aeronautics and Space Administration (NASA) from pursuing cooperation with China. As Michael Krepon wisely wrote regarding the Obama–Xi Sunnylands Summit in May 2013: "Press reports of their deliberations include no mention of discussions about space cooperation. If true, this reflects a poverty of imagination among their advisers and an agenda that is too filled with contentious issues to include a bold cooperative venture in space."[47] NASA administrator Charlie Bolden strongly advocates for this cooperation, and he has sparred with Congress over this issue on several occasions.[48] Undoubtedly, US-China space cooperation could have some of the benefits of the 1975 Apollo–Soyuz docking in terms of providing a symbolic impetus for bilateral cooperation more generally. But it could also enable projects—for example, a Mars mission— that are simply too prohibitively expensive for one space power to undertake independently.

Beijing's move 4 in the larger strategic relationship: China should reform its leadership system to permit the appointment of a civilian defense minister. As with many of the recommendations in this book, this reform is independently consistent with China's national security interests, irrespective of any connection to US-China relations. This is because military bureaucracies are distinct, in terms of both the enormous resources at their command and also the particular esprit de corps and unique perspective that the hierarchy and training naturally bring about. For these reasons, militaries wield massive clout in almost every country, but particularly within great powers. Therefore, a civilian cadre that oversees the armed forces is quite imperative to organize, control, and direct the military in the nation's best interest—one that supersedes the narrow parochial interests of the armed forces themselves. The power of the Chinese military (the People's Liberation Army, PLA) within the larger Chinese leadership is a subject much debated in Western foreign policy circles. It is often noted that China's foreign policy structure lacks a "national security council" where military chiefs are forced to make their arguments in front of a wide variety of civilian advisers. Although the author's many interactions with the PLA do suggest a high degree of professionalism in the force, a number of civil/military incidents during the last decade hint at possible problems with China's civilian control. A list of such incidents might include, to name a few: close calls with US military units in December 2013 and August 2014, the unveiling of the J20 aircraft during US secretary of defense Robert Gates's trip to China (2010), the harassment of US surveillance vessels (2009), military operations in support of disaster relief related to the Wenchuan earthquake (2008), and, perhaps most prominently, the ASAT test (2007). From the Chinese point of view, the best reason for this reform could simply be to improve China's image. After all, Chinese defense leaders simply stand out awkwardly at major gatherings of defense leaders when they are surrounded by states that have civilian defense leaders. A gradual movement in a reformist direction might convert the relatively weak defense minister portfolio into a civilian job, leaving the more powerful chief of staff portfolio for uniformed personnel, while a greater shift from military to civilian power could occur over a number of years. Under the current system, Western observers are quite consistently blaming the allegedly aggressive Chinese military for troubling hiccups in the relationship and, whether or not the allegation is true, this is not a healthy phenomenon for US-China relations over the long term.

Washington's move 5 in the larger strategic relationship: The United States should reform the National Defense Authorization Act of fiscal year 2000 that places significant restrictions on military-to-military exchanges. If China were to successfully reform its policies toward nuclear proliferators, agree to limit certain threatening weapons capabilities, and move toward greater civilian control of the PLA, the way would certainly be cleared in Washington for major breakthroughs in further developing the vital relationship between the two respective armed forces. To date, military cooperation has been stilted and awkward, following a pattern of generally ad hoc, nonsubstantive meetings. In a signal of just how awkward this relationship remains at present, China not only dispatched four ships to participate in the RIMPAC 2014 multinational naval exercises in Hawaii, but also sent an intelligence collecting ship separately to conduct surveillance on the exercise as well. This approach, not surprisingly, did not sit well with many Americans. For example, Representative Randy Forbes (R-VA) stated, "It is clear their first trip to RIMPAC should be their last."[49] Both sides have occasionally suspended the military-to-military relationship. American critics have frequently alleged that military engagement simply helps PLA capabilities, with no discernible payoff for US interests. But this view is shortsighted, and most US leaders (including those within the military) have supported direct engagement efforts with the PLA. It is actually the US side that learns more from engagement activities, for the simple reason that the United States is a highly transparent society, so the basic Chinese understanding of US military operations, weaponry, and doctrine is already extremely high, irrespective of engagement activities, as amply demonstrated by a close reading of Chinese military journals. Apart from which side gains a better understanding of the other, these activities are crucial to building habits of trust and cooperation at the staff and operational military level, where there is so clearly a paucity of trust at present. Indeed, this author's observation is that promising military cooperation initiatives often suffer a "death by a thousand cuts" because mid-level bureaucrats are reluctant to pursue engagement efforts even when approved by senior leadership. Port visits and the like have occurred, with a positive uptick in these activities occurring in 2013–14, but this embryonic level of military engagement simply will not suffice to keep the peace in the twenty-first century.

Beijing's move 5 in the larger strategic relationship: China must move into line with global norms on military transparency by publishing specific information on its weapons programs, and also especially in the area of military budgeting. Transparency has been a theme of this entire book, and a number of specific measures have been already proposed to increase Chinese military and also diplomatic transparency in order to allay various fears from neighboring states regarding its intentions. For example, with respect to the South China Sea dispute, it was proposed that opening the giant nuclear submarine base on the southern tip of Hainan Island to frequent visits by ASEAN defense personnel could allow the United States to reduce the intensity of its military posture in Southeast Asia (see chapter 10). However, Beijing should seek to leap the last major hurdle in establishing "new-type great power relations" by moving into full conformity with global norms regarding transparency—given US flexibility on Taiwan, US willingness to limit its naval superiority, and a new impetus from Washington to substantively increase the quality of military-to-military engagement, as advocated in this cooperation spiral. China has long argued that transparency is a tool of the strong against the weak, and that China's security depends on hiding its true capabilities. This argument was logical in the 1960s, when China was extremely weak and vulnerable; but it is no longer applicable today, when its armed forces are much stronger in all dimensions—even surpassing those of the United States in certain capabilities, as discussed in the book's introduction. As Chas Freeman explains: "Transparency advertises strength, which is why we have liked it and, up to now, the Chinese have not. Increasingly, however, they do."[50] To be sure, Beijing has made major progress in military transparency over the last decade, and these achievements should be duly noted: a defense ministry spokesman, an informative and accessible website, and myriad military diplomatic engagements that have brought the PLA out of isolation and into the global community on a very regular basis. Beijing has, moreover, published a series of defense white papers that are reasonably clear and specific, and apparently are quite comparable to others published in the Asia-Pacific region.[51] Still, a major barrier to US-China trust in the military security domain lies in the fact that little is known about Chinese weapons' capabilities, and even less about China's weapon development and procurement plans. It has become quite usual to learn about new major weapons systems, whether stealth fighters or submarines, from photos mysteriously appearing on the Web. Such revelations without any official explanations only feed mistrust and fear surrounding China's rise. To skeptics, such revelations only confirm their notion that China is laying the groundwork for regional hegemony by "biding its time and hiding its capacities." The most effective way to counter this line of theorizing is to continue to open the PLA, its impressive weapons development complex, and even the related budget ledgers and plans to outside scrutiny. China need not fear this process of 开放 (opening up) because it is in line with its other national policies, its military intentions are benign, and its military modernization program is moderate in scope. The unveiling of China's first aircraft carrier in 2012–13 may, in some respects, serve as a model for China's enhanced adherence to global norms of transparency. Chinese military writings in the 2013–14 time frame, moreover, suggest that the PLA itself understands the imperative for greater military transparency in order to better support Chinese foreign policy.[52]

Pivot to a New Cold War?

Military incidents and crises are unfortunately becoming more common in US-China relations. Since the mid-1990s, the relationship has witnessed the 1995–96 Taiwan Strait crisis, the 1999 Belgrade bombing incident, the 2001 EP-3 crisis, the 2006 *Kitty Hawk* incident, the 2007 ASAT test, and the 2009 *Impeccable* incident. Since 2010, tensions have intensified on the Korean Peninsula, in the East China Sea, and also in the South China Sea. When the Obama administration took office in 2009, it inherited the policies of the Bush administration, which had sought to subordinate problems in the Asia-Pacific region to the "global war on terrorism." Although the inevitable focus on the Middle East following the September 11, 2001, terrorist attacks on America created an atmosphere of uncertainty in the Asia-Pacific region, the general policy direction on China of encouraging Beijing to become a "responsible stakeholder" is now widely perceived as reasonably successful. The Obama administration's early policy formulation aiming at "strategic reassurance" appeared to be a worthy successor to Zoellick's important formulation. Unfortunately, this very promising policy direction has been quite inexplicably dropped like a stone and replaced by the "pivot to the Asia-Pacific," a formulation later repackaged as a "rebalancing to the Asia-Pacific."

This initiative, which may stand as the most proactive and coherent and consequently the most important foreign policy legacy of the Obama administration, was unveiled in the fall of 2011 in major policy statements by Obama and Secretary Clinton, and has diplomatic, informational, economic, and military components. In its most ideal form, the strategy is most concentrated on the nonmilitary aspects of American power and, as such, represents "smart power"—doing more with less. The concept is that the world's most dynamic economies are in Asia, and therefore, the United States must reassert its influence in the region, especially by expanding free trade networks (e.g., the Trans-Pacific Partnership), but also by providing diplomatic "boots on the ground"—faithfully attending the myriad regional multilateral talk shops that had been neglected to some extent in the previous administration. Although some shoring up of US prestige has seemed to occur under the new strategy, the reality of the "rebalancing" has regrettably fallen far short of expectations. As one of the leading thinkers on US-China relations, Kenneth Lieberthal, wrote in 2013: "Unfortunately, at this point [Obama's rebalancing] strategy is in danger of actually enhancing rather than reducing bad security outcomes. . . . It is therefore time to rebalance judiciously the rebalancing strategy."[53] The rebalancing strategy has many readily identifiable problems, but perhaps the most damaging is its tendency toward militarization. This has occurred, by and large, because the large and well-resourced military (and military-industrial complex) has jumped at the evident opportunity to "counterbalance" the alleged "peer competitor." In other words, the policy has served to justify an impressive parade of weapons programs, as well as an intensified regimen of military exercises.

An important critique of the "rebalancing" was published in the journal *Foreign Affairs* at the end of 2012. In this piece, China expert Robert Ross succinctly described the policy's shortcomings: "The new US policy unnecessarily compounds Beijing's insecurities and will only feed China's aggressiveness, undermine regional stability, and decrease the possibility of cooperation between Beijing and Washington." Ross asserts that Washington has turned to "costly initiatives whose force is disproportionate to the threat from China," and he squarely blames Secretary Clinton's clumsy diplomacy in Southeast Asia during mid-2010: "US Secretary of State Hillary Clinton . . . directly inserted the US into these legally complex disputes. In July 2010 in Hanoi, after extensive discussions with all the claimants to the islands except China, Clinton declared US support for the negotiating positions of the Philippines and Vietnam."[54] A parallel analysis could also be made regarding Clinton's October 2010 embrace of Japan's position regarding the contested islands in the East China Sea (see chapter 9). Although Ross may be incorrect in underrating China's military capabilities and also tends to exaggerate Beijing's economic problems, his overall conclusion is sound and worthy of close attention: "The Obama administration's pivot has not contributed to stability in Asia. Quite the opposite: It has made the region more tense and conflict-prone. . . . The outbreak of hostilities in the region will become a real possibility, as China pushes back."

Through the hundreds of Chinese-language articles examined in this book, there is a plainly evident common theme: Most Chinese foreign policy and defense specialists are convinced that Washington seeks to contain and even derail China's rise. Bilateral tensions have built up in almost all global regions but are most acute in East Asia for now. These tensions are deeply rooted and have been amply described in each chapter of this book. The case regarding "opportunity costs" accruing from major US-China tensions has also been made, including, but hardly limited to, nuclear proliferation, various humanitarian crises from Syria to Sudan to Myanmar, and, of course, regarding climate change. True, some movement is discernible on the critical climate change front, and it has been encouraging to see some degree of cooperation, albeit modest, between China and the United States in coordinating responses to the Ebola Crisis. But the question that needs to be continually asked is whether more US-China cooperation could be undertaken to address more global challenges. Arguments over uninhabited rocks should not distract from these larger imperatives, but that has largely been the case to date, unfortunately.

Skeptics will inevitably counter that the major cause of East Asian tension is China's "assertive" behavior. However, sophisticated strategists should immediately understand that the attempt to figure out "who started it?" is a blame game dripping with subjectivity that will not yield any serious conclusions. China is a great power that has always been moderately "assertive," except perhaps a century ago, when it was literally a "failed state." A simple beta test on the "assertive China" thesis is to see that China resorted to the significant use or demonstration of force in the 1950s (Korea), 1960s (against India), 1970s (against Vietnam), 1980s (against Vietnam), and in the 1990s (in the Taiwan crisis). Another interesting beta test on the "assertive China" thesis is to examine a period in American history that is somewhat comparable. A century ago, the United States was a "risen" power, completing its "manifest destiny," and taking up a new, uncertain, and unprecedented role on the world stage. In 1846–47, a border dispute with Mexico eventually yielded six new states (including California) for the brash American Republic. As noted earlier in this chapter, between 1890 and 1920, the United States conducted no less than thirty-five significant military interventions in Latin America. During that period, US troops also took the lead role in storming the ancient walls of Beijing—a troubling event that is commemorated in the very first room of China's newly refurbished Party History Museum (and is discussed in some detail in chapter 2). Thus, Western analysts, who term contemporary Chinese foreign policy "newly assertive," not only lack perspective regarding patterns in the Chinese use of force but also appear unable or unwilling to view such accusations in comparative perspective—that is, relative to the rise of other great powers in modern history. Parading coast guard cutters that employ water cannons in contested sea zones cannot objectively be termed "assertive" in any meaningful way. In an obvious contrast, Russia's invasion of Georgia in 2008 and its annexation of Crimea in 2014 clearly constitute assertive behavior. Perhaps America's greatest fear is that China's behavior will simply replicate that of America a century ago? Such a realization should result in some circumspection and hopefully a new maturity in Washington's approach to the Asia-Pacific region. Indeed, a good model to study may well be that of Great Britain as it sought to reach a modus vivendi with an ever more powerful and self-confident United States a century ago.

Several additional problems with the "rebalancing to the Asia-Pacific" need still to be briefly addressed, even if they cannot be elaborated here in great detail. Above, the diplomatic opportunity costs were briefly touched upon. But one must also consider the straightforward financial costs of the pivot, because resources are finite. This will mean that the defense budget cannot be trimmed to support "nation building at home"—schools, bridges, and the like. It will mean that the US armed forces (and likely the Chinese PLA) will continue to emphasize war-fighting and deterrence capabilities at the expense of key nontraditional security missions, including peacekeeping, disaster relief and coping with pandemic outbreaks. It will mean that US aid projects are focused on countries on the other side of the world (e.g., Myanmar) rather than those needy countries next door (e.g., Haiti). It will also mean that certain poor, developing countries (e.g., the Philippines), but also certain developed but strained countries (e.g., Japan), will devote unnecessary sums to developing major weapons systems to deter or fight China versus other national priorities. This trade-off emerged in stark relief in the fall of 2013, when it was announced that Manila was considering major new defense outlays—for example, frigates and submarines—even as the country's third-largest city on the island of Mindanao was enveloped in the bloody chaos of a resurgent insurrection. After the tragedy of the massive typhoon hitting the Philippines in October 2013, one wonders if sufficient funds in Manila will be devoted to making the island archipelago genuinely more resilient for facing increasingly powerful storms. Or rather, such obviously urgent imperatives might regrettably be sacrificed in the name of defense preparedness and safeguarding national sovereignty.

Yet another problem with the "rebalancing to the Asia-Pacific" has been the extent to which it has been pushed and shepherded along by "third parties." These third parties are regional states concerned to protect the status quo in the face of a rapidly rising China and a United States that is evidently undergoing an identity crisis after two failed conflicts in the Middle East. Essentially, leaders and diplomats from various East Asian states—but above all those from Japan, the Philippines, Vietnam, and Singapore—have exercised a significant influence on Washington—urging it in increasingly desperate tones to "stand up to Beijing's bullying." American susceptibility to such arguments reflects an apparent psychological desire to be perceived as playing a vital or "indispensable" role in global security—at bottom, the simple human need to be needed and liked, actually. What a pleasant break from vitriolic debates over fiscal and social problems to be told emphatically by East Asian leaders that US moral and strategic leadership is imperative and then to bask in the consequent adulation. In any contest with Beijing, these states are perceived as "underdogs," and they may also benefit from liberal antipathy to the Chinese regime, even though several of these countries cannot actually be termed democracies. Then, there is the fact that these small states are frequently more focused on direct policy outcomes (e.g., a given joint statement or joint military exercise)—and thus are able to successfully apply pressure on US officials, who may hold a less certain and more ambiguous disposition regarding various regional disputes. These regional appeals, which the author has witnessed on more than a few occasions, form the "demand signal" that Obama administration officials claim is the driving force behind the pivot. This somewhat subtle and rather insidious diplomacy exercised by various officials (and often retirees) from third-party states is not quite irrational, but is certainly short-sighted because their respective countries will hardly benefit from increased US-China tensions. Where current US strategists have gravely miscalculated is in reasoning that US national security interests in the Asia-Pacific are simply equivalent to the sum of the concerns of all allies and partners. Indeed, the worst outcome of those tensions would certainly be catastrophic for them, because their countries would be the most likely blood-soaked battleground for any US-China military contest. In general, these countries are quite mistaken if they think that the American public is prepared to go to war with China over uninhabited rocks. Regrettably, it seems that in recent strategic deliberations, Washington has too often been "played" by odious nationalist and parochial interests in these allied and partner states.

But are these countries not sincerely frightened by "scary" China? Children talk of monsters hiding under the bed or in the closet as "scary," and these fears are almost always irrational—even as they are natural and wholly understandable. At the national level, moreover, "scare" tactics may be used to advance the interest of certain domestic political groups within front-line countries. Overall, we may wish to be empathetic to these various regional concerns—even as we might be empathetic to the fears of a child—but we should not confuse this empathy with sound and rational foreign policy. A more thoughtful perspective understands that (1) China's rise will inevitably occasion some anxiety and instability; (2) China's military buildup is largely driven by its historical experience of invasion and vulnerability; (3) Beijing has not resorted to the major use of force in more than three decades; and (4) most fundamentally, China may quibble over various rocks and reefs with neighbors, but it is emphatically not likely to invade either Honshu or Luzon, nor even Okinawa or Palawan. The role of scholars here needs to be to help separate rational and irrational fears and responses.

Apart from the "free-riding" aspects of current and evolving defense arrangements in the Asia-Pacific region that are disturbing and contrary to US national interests, there is the problem that US partners and allies should benefit US national security and not form a strategic liability that could drag a reluctant Washington into wars over matters of no strategic consequence. An "offshore balancing" approach to US foreign policy, based on caution and on purely defensive arrangements, would better serve US national security interests. After all, China is rising into a thicket of strongly capable and strong-willed powers that are hardly ready to bend to Beijing's will. Australia, Indonesia, Vietnam, Japan, and India have all indicated a clear willingness—even an eagerness—to confront various Chinese claims and policies. The argument by various "hawks" that these states will cave to Beijing without robust American backing seems unwarranted. Moreover, the further claim that these states would subsequently "bandwagon" with China against the United States is even more grossly misleading. In other words, there is no possibility that China could turn the tables in the all-important global balance of power against the United States. As White states: "While [China] is strong, it is not *that* strong" (emphasis added); and Chinese leaders understand this fact in spades.[55]

A final deleterious myth propagated by various "hawks" is the notion that any reforms to American strategy and related commitments will inevitably collapse the entire structure of East Asia and even global security. This notion is patently false, and the US strategic position has inevitably been strengthened by various adjustments, whether undertaken during the Cold War, such as the withdrawal of US bases from Taiwan, and even more obviously the total US pullout from Vietnam, or after the Cold War, such as the 40 percent drawdown in US troops from the Korean Peninsula undertaken by George W. Bush.[56] In actuality, alliances and security arrangements are strengthened by reforms that bring their means and goals in conformity with global and regional power and political realities. Such reforms would actually help the "credibility" of American commitments. However, the United States should only undertake the resort to arms when actual national interests are at stake and not for the sake of credibility alone. In fact, a recent reexamination of the role of credibility concerns among US decision makers in the Cuban Missile Crisis concludes: "This approach to foreign policy was guided—and remains guided—by a . . . school-playground view of world politics rather than the cool appraisal of strategic realities. It put—and still puts—America in the curious position of having to go to war to uphold the very credibility that is supposed to obviate war in the first place."[57] As Steinberg and O'Hanlon conclude: "The abstract fear of dominoes falling does not require that every perceived provocation be fully rebuffed by force."[58]

Unfortunately, rivalry has a powerful self-reinforcing dynamic that may make the credibility argument seem logical, whether in seeking out new security commitments or within crises. The arguments of those pushing for aggressive and noncompromising solutions gain force in a climate of nationalism, xenophobia, and sensationalism, perhaps especially where pithy bloggers or outrageous video clips may outweigh prudence and the careful examination of facts viewed within a larger historical context. Smaller countries, moreover, may push their parochial viewpoints, exaggerating the will and capabilities of the superpowers to determine regional outcomes in their favor, pushing the region to the brink of disaster. Powerful military-industrial complexes on both sides of the Pacific will no doubt see a mortal threat in the other that leads them to ask for ever larger percentages of national wealth to push the boundaries of science in the name of national defense. Uniformed personnel on both sides, perhaps driven by a "cult of the offensive," could argue for greater "forward" deployments and even for "shock and awe"–type destabilizing first strikes. In short, the tendencies toward rivalry are multifarious and potent. This brings us to the final problem with the "rebalancing strategy to the Asia-Pacific." It posits no special initiative, institutions, or mechanism to control and mitigate the US-China rivalry that is now developing into full and perilous bloom. To the contrary, the strategy feeds upon rivalry and then inflames it further.

Of Archdukes and Sand Pebbles

One hundred years ago—after a period of remarkable peace, scientific achievement, and economic growth—Europe was set alight by the assassination of an archduke, by misperception, by nationalism, and by faulty military strategy. This unexpected but catastrophic explosion went on to kill tens of millions of people and, thereafter, foment the pathological hatreds, both between and within societies, that precipitated bloodletting on an even greater scale in the revolutions and the second global cataclysm among the great powers that followed hard upon the first. The same scenario could all too easily unfold in contemporary Asia. A century hence, our ancestors may discuss the many disastrous "wars surrounding the rise of China," even as we discuss today the catastrophic conflagrations surrounding Germany's rise. Perhaps nuclear weapons and economic interdependence will prevent such an outcome? Maybe, or maybe not.

Great power rivalry is a force of nature that is nearly impossible to control. Its dynamics are amply clear in contemporary US-China relations. However, thinking and responsible people need not accept war, rivalry, and the inability to cooperate as inevitable outcomes. The imperative to prevent an apocalyptic World War III, the obvious dangers of regional conflict flowing from nuclear proliferation, and the ever-clearer menace of global warming must inspire us to collectively struggle against the inexorable drive toward intensified US-China rivalry. One model to escape this perverse dynamic is provided in this book in the form of "cooperation spirals," which are built on the principles of gradualism, reciprocity, and mutual compromise. This model can be adapted to restrain all aspects of US-China rivalry, from the South China Sea to the Korean Peninsula and from economic tensions to climate change negotiations. Such steps toward compromise can be debated and altered, reversed and reformulated. Here, one hundred steps are suggested; but there are thousands of alternative steps that need to be suggested, examined, and refined. Indeed, Steinberg and O'Hanlon's 2014 book usefully proposes a whole panoply of alternatives, ranging from traditional arms control efforts to a "cyber risk reduction center," which deserve careful consideration and might also fit well into "cooperation spirals."[59] I do not for a minute underestimate the difficulties involved in negotiating these painful compromises, which will necessarily involve "games" on at least two levels, international and domestic.

Half the steps recommended here are directed toward Beijing, and the other half are directed toward Washington. Symmetry makes for a balanced and elegant model. Many recommendations for Beijing involve greater transparency, and many recommendations for Washington involve a less militarized and reformed alliance posture in the Asia-Pacific region. Invariably, the policy proposals directed at Washington are more specific because, as an American, the author has a more intuitive grasp of American diplomacy and what reforms could be made. Chinese diplomats and scholars are best positioned to understand where various Chinese foreign policy reforms could serve the cause of mutual compromise.

These reflections on the necessity of compromise are not the musings of a naive dreamer but rather are the candid judgments of a national security professional, who has observed the ever-accelerating tendency toward rivalry in US-China relations with growing disquiet. This author has an established record of strongly advocating appropriate defense programs, for example, in support of a larger and more capable US Navy submarine fleet.[60] Where the United States should "speak softly and carry a big stick," it has instead regrettably more frequently "spoken loudly and carried a small stick." This book has focused on "speaking softly," while appreciating that the size of the stick is not irrelevant.

To be sure, Washington must pursue a "hedge" against the worst case. But a hedge is by nature a secondary issue that seeks in a low-key manner to manage risk with respect to a low-probability outcome. It is, by definition, not the major thrust of national policy. By contrast, the current situation dominated by the "pivot" and "Air–Sea Battle" quite mistakenly takes this competitive strategy as the central policy direction.

To guide the United States in a more positive direction, the country will require leaders imbued with the wisdom attained from a careful reading of history. Many have drawn attention, as this book has, to the important centenary of World War I as a potent focal point for such reflections. However, another era of history that is much less discussed and heralded, but is cut directly from the rich fabric of US-China interactions, may be even more important for those leaders to meditate on as they go about making the hard choices that may well determine the future course of world order. As spelled out in chapter 2 of this book, one hundred years ago, US Navy vessels roamed widely through the waters, especially along the main rivers, of China. Nowhere is there a more incisive and profound accounting of America's difficult relationship with China—cultural, economic, strategic, and yes, racial—than in Richard McKenna's *The Sand Pebbles* (1962). The account is fictional, but undoubtedly reflects McKenna's extensive experience as a "river rat" serving with the US Navy in China over a period of years.

The hero of this odyssey, set along the rivers and lakes between Wuhan and Changsha deep in China's interior during the decade following the Great War, is the US Navy sailor Jake Holman. He is not in China long before he learns that "the Chinese hate and despise you." In attempting to understand his mission there, he and his shipmates conclude that "China is like Indian country in the old days in the States. . . . The businessmen and the missionaries are the settlers." Undoubtedly, Holman is beguiled by various aspects of Chinese culture, not least "all the best food Holman had ever eaten."[61] Unlike his shipmates, Holman is able to look across cultures, and he thus establishes an incredibly strong bond of friendship with a Chinese "coolie" shipmate, whom Holman admires intensely. With evident devotion, he teaches his Chinese shipmate all he knows about the practical engineering of ship engines—the highest form of religion in Holman's worldview.

A powerful climax of the novel is reached when a shore party from Holman's US Navy ship must stare down a squad of troops from the Chinese Nationalist (Kuomintang) Army seeking to requisition property from an American school in Changsha:

> "A small misunderstanding I'm afraid," the older man said. "Ensign Bordelles, may I present Major Liu of the National Chinese Army?"
> Bordelles in his white and gold bulked much larger than the slender Chinese officer in neat green. No one moved for a second. Then, to

avoid saluting first, Bordelles held out his hand. Treaty people did not salute warlord officers. Bordelles went up on his toes, leaning a bit, in an effort to crush Liu's hand. Liu's face did not show anything.

"What is your mission here, Mr. Bordelles?" he asked.

"My mission is to ask you that, Mr. Liu," Bordelles said. "This compound is American property. You can't just *lafoo* it."

"The English word is 'commandeer'" Liu said. "This is Chinese soil. I have already shown Mr. James my authority under Chinese law to commandeer this school for a battalion headquarters."

His voice was quiet, but he was tense. It was very tense and quiet in the courtyard. Mr. James said something about the Chefoo Convention. Bordelles stepped nearer Liu and looked steeply down on him.

"May I see your authority?" he asked, just as quietly.

"No." Liu stepped back. "You have no right even to be here, in uniform and under arms," he said. "I will have you and your men escorted back to your consulate. If necessary, I will post a guard to see that you stay there."

Bordelles jerked visibly at almost every word. His eyes stared and his lips tightened. The Sand Pebbles shuffled their feet, getting set. All the colors were brighter. Bordelles spoke slowly.

"Let me warn you, Mr. Liu. Any interference on your part with me and my men in the performance of our lawful duty will constitute an act of war against the United States of America." He paused, to let that soak in. "If your superior officers are not prepared to go to war against America, they will probably disavow your action and make amends." His eyes holding Liu's eyes, he drew his forefinger slowly across his throat. "It has happened before," he said.

Liu was pale, too. He did not flinch. Holman felt numbly that two great, groping giants were touching fingertips. When Liu spoke, his English was slurred from tension, but his voice was still quiet.

"All too often before, but we have had enough of that now," he said. "I will quote your own history to you, Mr. Bordelles. If you mean to have a war, let it begin here."

You know, it could, Holman thought suddenly. Bordelles' nostrils were white and flaring, and all his cheerful farmer look was gone. Liu spoke a command and the green-clad soldiers began to form up. They all had rifles, and the noncoms had Mauser machine pistols in the wooden scabbards. There were at least four squads of them. Custer's Last Stand, Holman thought. Remember the Alamo. It did not seem to have anything to do with him personally.

"You may have your men sling arms, or you may have them lay down their arms," Liu said.

Bordelles was silent as stone. *Please. Please, gentlemen*, the two missionaries were saying. *Be reasonable. Make allowances.*

"You may go under escort, or you may go under full arrest," Liu said. "That is all the choice I will give you, and you must make it now."

The missionaries slipped away. Bordelles stood frozen. Time seemed stopped. Liu spoke in Chinese. The noncoms echoed, and the green soldiers fixed bayonets. The sudden hedge of bright, sharp steel was like an electric shock that started time again. A veil came over Bordelles' face. He turned half left.

"Sling arms," he ordered, in a choked voice.[62]

The United States' difficult relations with China in our own time are certain to prompt similarly tense standoffs and will require comparable restraint—not to mention another painful psychological adjustment, not unlike that experienced by Holman and his shipmates in the passage given above. But for America, there is no viable alternative to meeting China halfway.

Notes

1. Henry Kissinger, "Power Shifts," *IISS Survival* 52 (December 2010–January 2011): 212.
2. See, e.g., "Lexington: The China-Bashing Syndrome," *The Economist*, July 14, 2012.
3. Aaron L. Friedberg, *A Contest for Supremacy: China, America, and the Struggle for Mastery in Asia* (New York: W. W. Norton, 2011), 254.
4. See, e.g., "An American Lake: The Navy and Marines in Central America," in *The Naval Institute Historical Atlas of the US Navy*, ed. Craig L. Simonds (Annapolis: Naval Institute Press, 1995), 124.
5. Hugh White, *The China Choice: Why We Should Share Power* (New York: Oxford University Press, 2013), 164–65.
6. Unfortunately, US leaders have muddled the credibility of red lines in recent years by both overuse and failure to subsequently back them up. The key is to reduce ambiguity, but just as important to form the red line in the maximally defensive posture, so as not to aggravate tensions. With respect to maritime claims, for example, the United States should state very clearly that contested claims are outside the US defense perimeter. Meanwhile, there is the obvious point that direct attacks against the home islands of allied states will constitute a

crossing of Washington's red line. Such clear, defensive policies would promote restraint and negotiations to resolve disputes. Above all, they would prevent unwanted escalation over "rocks."

7. Steinberg and O'Hanlon, *Strategic Reassurance*, 10.

8. Paul Kennedy, "A Time to Appease," *The National Interest*, June 28, 2010, http://nationalinterest.org/article/a-time-to-appease-3539.

9. See, e.g., Norrin M. Ripsman and Jack S. Levy, "Wishful Thinking or Buying Time? The Logic of British Appeasement in the 1930s," *International Security* 33 (Fall 2008): 148–81.

10. "Address to the House of Commons, December 4, 1950," in *Churchill Speaks: Winston S. Churchill in Peace and War: Collected Speeches, 1897–1963*, ed. Robert Rhodes James (New York: Chelsea House, 1980), 937; cited by Ripsman and Levy, "Wishful Thinking," 153.

11. Friedberg, *Contest*, 42.

12. White, *China Choice*, 42.

13. Michael D. Swaine, *America's Challenge: Engaging a Rising China in the Twenty-First Century* (Washington, DC: Carnegie Endowment for International Peace, 2011), 376–78; Henry Kissinger, *On China* (New York: Penguin Press, 2011), 526.

14. See, e.g., Admiral Hu Yanlin (ret.), interview reported in "海军上将眼中的中国海洋战略" [Chinese Maritime Strategy from the Perspective of a Navy Admiral], 现代舰船 [Modern Ships], October 2010, 11.

15. Regular evidence for this conclusion is found in the pages of the liberally inclined Chinese magazine 财经 [Finance and Economics]. E.g., the August 27, 2012, issue ran an astonishing cover story on China's system of labor camps—a system that has subsequently been significantly reformed.

16. Elizabeth C. Economy and Adam Segal, "The G-2 Mirage," *Foreign Affairs* 88 (May–June 2009): 56–72.

17. 林利民 [Lin Limin], "未来十年中美关系的'范式'选择与中国对美战略" [The Choice of Paradigms for US-China Relations and China's Strategy toward the US], 国际关系学院学报 [Journal of the University of International Relations], February 2012, 5.

18. 牛新春 [Niu Xinchun], "关于中美'新型大国关系' 的几点思考" [A Few Thoughts Related to the "New-Type Great Power Relations" between China and the US], 和平与发展 [Peace and Development], February 2013, 2–3, 10–11.

19. See, e.g., 梁熠, 罗小明, 蔡业泉 [Liang Yi, Luo Xiaoming, and Cai Yequan], "美国战略打击力量体系发展及其影响与启示" [Development of American Strategic Strike Forces and Their Effect], 军事运筹与系统工程 [Military Operations Research and Systems Engineering], December 2011, 30.

20. See comments made at a December 22, 2012, forum as reported by 候李光 [Hou Liguang], "未雨绸缪话国家安全风险" [Repairing the Roof before the Rain: A Discussion of National Security Risks], 国防科技工业 [Defense Industry Science and Technology], January 2013, 38–39.

21. 刘迪 [Liu Di], "习奥会: 超越G2" [The Xi–Obama Summit: Going beyond G-2], 东方早报 [Oriental Morning Post], May 29, 2013.

22. 高祖贵 [Gao Zugui], "中美新型大国关系构建启步" [Initial Thoughts on Constructing New-Type Great Power Relations between China and the US], 学习时报 [Study Times], June 10, 2013.

23. 袁鹏 [Yuan Peng], "中美: 新"两极对立?" [China and the US: New Bipolar Antagonists], 中国外交 [Chinese Foreign Policy], April 2012, 60.

24. 朱锋, 周新政 [Zhu Feng and Zhou Xinzheng], "奥巴马政府亚太战略调整冲击中国外交与安全" [An Onslaught on China's Diplomacy and Security from the Obama Administration's Adjustment to Its Asia-Pacific Strategy], 和平与发展 [Peace and Development], June 2012, 1, 6.

25. 刘建飞 [Liu Jianfei], "关于近几年中国外交的反思" [Thoughts on Chinese Diplomacy in Recent Years], 中国外交 [Chinese Foreign Policy], July 2012, 10, 12.

26. See, e.g., 查长松, 李大光 [Cha Zhangsong and Li Daguang], "'空海一体战'下的美武器装备亚太布势" [The Tendency in US Military Equipment Deployments under the Concept of "Air–Sea Battle"], 当代海军 [Modern Navy], March 2014, 55–57.

27. 阮宗泽 [Ruan Zongze], "美国'亚太再平衡'战略前景论析" [The US "Rebalance toward Asia": Quo Vadis], 世界经济与政治 [World Economics and Politics], April 2014, 13–4, 156.

28. 胡波 [Hu Bo] "中美在西太平洋的军事竞争与战略平衡" [The China-US Military Competition and Strategic Balance in the Western Pacific Ocean] 世界政治与经济 [World Economy and Politics] (May 2014), 64–84.

29. 杨震, 周云亨, 王萍 [Yang Zhen (PLA), Zhou Yunheng, Wang Ping (PLA)] "论后冷战代美国对中国海权发展的制约" [On the US Restriction of China's Seapower in the Post-Cold War Era] 东北亚论坛 [Northeast Asia Forum] (July 2014), 3–14.

30. Ibid., 11, 13.

31. 催立如 [Cui Liru], "关于中国国际战略的若干思考" [A Few Thoughts Related to China's International Strategy], 现代国际关系 [Contemporary International Relations], November 2011, 2.

32. 催天凯 [Cui Tiankai], "中美在亚太的良性互动" [The Positive Interaction between China and the US in the Asia-Pacific Region], 国际问题研究 [International Studies Research], July 2012, 9.

33. See, e.g., "朱成虎, 孟凡礼" [Zhu Chenghu, PLA General, NDU, Meng Fanli, NDU], "简论美国实力地位的变化" [Some Thoughts on US National Power and Its Status], 美国研究 [American Studies], Summer 2012, 29–42; and also 徐 焰 [Xu Yan, PLA General, NDU], "中美经济, 军事实力的差距有多大" [The Gap in Economic and Military Power between China and the US], 中国外交 [Chinese Foreign Policy], October 2012, 60–62.

34. 周方银 [Zhou Fangyin], "中国撅起, 东亚格局变迁与东亚秩序的发展方向" [China's Rise, the Transformation of East Asian Structure, and Directions for the Development of the East Asian Order], 当代亚太 [Journal of Contemporary Asia-Pacific Studies], October 2012, 15.

35. 王逸舟 [Wang Yizhou], "中国需要大力拓展 '高边疆' 和提供国际公共产品" [High Time for China to Vigorously Expand the 'High Frontier' and Provide International Public Goods], 中国外交 [Chinese Foreign Policy], September 2012, 3–5.

36. 金灿荣, 赵远良[Jin Canrong and Zhao Yuanliang], "构建中美新型大国关系的条件探索" [Exploring and Taking Advantages of Favorable Conditions to Establish a New Model of Major Country Relations Between China and the United States] 世界经济与政治 [World Economics and Politics], March 2014, 50–68.

37. Thomas J. Christensen, *The Need to Pursue Mutual Interests in US-PRC Relations*, US Institute of Peace Special Report 269 (Washington, DC: US Institute of Peace Press, 2011), 5.

38. "Fact Sheet: President Obama's Visit to China," White House, November 11, 2014, http://www.whitehouse.gov/the-press-office/2014/11/11/fact-sheet-president-obama-s-visit-china.

39. Stephen van Evera, "The Cult of the Offensive and the Origins of the First World War," *International Security* 9 (Summer 1984): 58–107.

40. Amy Woolf, *Conventional Prompt Global Strike and Long-Range Ballistic Missiles: Background and Issues*, CRS Report for Congress R41464 (Washington, DC: Congressional Research Service, 2013), www.fas.org/sgp/crs/nuke/R41464.pdf.

41. Bill Gertz, "China Has Carrier-Killer Missile, US Admiral Says," *Washington Times*, December 27, 2010, www.washingtontimes.com/news/2010/dec/27/china-deploying-carrier-sinking-ballistic-missile/.

42. This idea is promoted by Mark Stokes and Dan Blumenthal, "Can a Treaty Contain China's Missiles?" *Washington Post*, January 2, 2011, www.washingtonpost.com/wpdyn/content/article/2010/12/31/AR2010123104108.html.

43. Steinberg and O'Hanlon, *Strategic Reassurance*, 170–71, 209.

44. A fascinating glimpse into the current debate in China over the strategic value of aircraft carriers is given by 许可 [Xu Ke], "简析美国'航母外交'实践及对我启示" [A Brief Analysis of the US Practice of Carrier Diplomacy and Its Revelations for China], 亚非纵横 [Asia and Africa Review], November–December 2013, 38–43. This appraisal credits "carrier diplomacy" with preventing escalation in many circumstances.

45. See, e.g., Wendell Minnick, "Asia's Naval Procurement Shows Major Growth," *Defense News*, May 19, 2013, www.defensenews.com/article/20130519 /DEFREG03/305190004/Asia-s-Naval-Procurement-Sees-Major-Growth.

46. Norman Polmar and Jurien Noot, *Submarines of the Russian and Soviet Navies, 1719–1990* (Annapolis: Naval Institute Press, 1991), 281–84, 290–300. Interestingly, Chinese naval analysts have examined the Soviet submarine development experience in great detail and have concluded that too-rapid development resulted in major problems over the long run.

47. Michael Krepon, "US Space Cooperation with China," *Space News*, July 8, 2013, www.spacenews.com/article/opinion/36172us-space-cooperation-with-china.

48. Mark Matthews, "NASA, Lawmakers at Odds on Cooperation with China," *Orlando Sentinel*, July 16, 2013, www.spacenews.com/article/opinion/36172 us-space-cooperation-with-china.

49. Randy Forbes quoted in William Wan, "Chinese Spy Ship Lurks around U.S.-led Pacific Naval Drills," *Washington Post*, July 21, 2014, http://www .washingtonpost.com/blogs/worldviews/wp/2014/07/21/chinese-spy-ship-lurks -around-u-s-led-pacific-naval-drills/.

50. Chas W. Freeman Jr., *Interesting Times: China, America, and the Shifting Balance of Prestige* (Charlottesville, VA: Just World Books, 2012), 161.

51. Michael Kiselycznyk and Phillip C. Saunders, *Assessing Chinese Military Transparency* (Washington, DC: National Defense University Press, 2010).

52. See, e.g., 候小河, 陈舟 [Hou Xiaohe and Chen Zhou], "试论建立军事互信" [On Building Military Mutual Trust], 中国军事科学 [China Military Science], March 2013, 33–42; and 陈铎, 江河 [Chen Duo and Jiang He], "开放军事采购, 我们准备好了吗?" [Opening Up Military Acquisition: Are We Well Prepared?], 人民海军 [People's Navy], February 26, 2014, 4.

53. Kenneth Lieberthal, "Memorandum: Bringing Beijing Back In," *Foreign Policy*, January 17, 2013, www.brookings.edu/research/papers/2013/01 /bringing-beijing-back-in.

54. Robert S. Ross, "The Problem with the Pivot: Obama's New Asia Policy Is Unnecessary and Counterproductive," *Foreign Affairs* 91 (November–December 2012): 72, 77–78.

55. White, *China Choice*, 145.

56. Ross, "Problem with the Pivot," 78.
57. Benjamin Schwarz, "The Real Cuban Missile Crisis: Everything You Think You Know Is Wrong," *The Atlantic*, January–February 2013, 78.
58. Steinberg and O'Hanlon, *Strategic Reassurance*, 121.
59. Ibid., 209–11.
60. See, e.g., Lyle Goldstein and Shannon Knight, "Wired for Sound in the Near Seas," *USNI Proceedings*, April 2014, 56–61; Lyle Goldstein and Shannon Knight, "Sub Force Rising," *USNI Proceedings*, April 2013, 40–44; Lyle Goldstein, "China Confronts Long-Standing Weakness in Anti-Submarine Warfare," *China Brief* 11, no. 14 (July 2011); Gabriel Collins, Andrew Erickson, Lyle Goldstein, and William Murray, "Chinese Evaluations of the USN Submarine Force," *Naval War Review*, Winter 2008, 68–86; and Lyle Goldstein and William Murray, "Undersea Dragons: China's Maturing Submarine Force," *International Security*, Spring 2004, 161–96.
61. Richard McKenna, *The Sand Pebbles* (Annapolis: Naval Institute Press, 1962), 18, 78, 83.
62. Ibid., 339–40.

INDEX

Figures are indicated by "f" following page numbers.

Abe, Shinzo, 225, 232–33, 240–41, 242–43
accountability, need for, 11
Acharya, Amitav, 266
Acheson, Dean, 50, 64
Afghanistan, 169, 315, 319, 322–23, 325
Africa. *See* developing world; *individual countries by name*
African Union, 151
AFRICOM, 142, 146, 155–56
agriculture, 116–17
AIDS, President's Emergency Plan for AIDS Relief, 150
Air Force, US, 34–35
Air Force Magazine on Bagram base in Afghanistan, 319
air pollution, 79, 112, 116, 120, 125–26
Air–Sea Battle strategy of Pentagon, 7, 362
American exceptionalism, 31–35
American Institute in Taiwan, 62–63
America's Challenge: Engaging a Rising China in the 21st Century (Swaine), 8

Andrade, Tonio, 47–48
Angola, 139, 141
antipiracy. *See* piracy
Anti-Secession Law (China), 55
antiship ballistic missiles (ASBM) and antisatellite (ASAT) weapons, 347–48, 351, 353
antisubmarine. *See* submarines
appeasement, 15, 16, 71, 280, 333–36
Arab Spring, 163, 170–71, 182, 338. *See also* Middle East
arms sales: arms embargo on China, 100–101, 167; to India, 305; to Latin America, from China, 143, 154–55; to Middle East, from China, 167; to Taiwan, 56, 59, 65–66, 67–68, 77n57
Arrow War (or Second Opium War), 30
Asian Financial Crisis (1997–98), 83, 267
Asia pivot, 7, 271, 283, 330, 341, 354–58, 362
"assertive China" thesis, 271, 288, 334, 355–56

371

Association of Southeast Asian Nations (ASEAN), 266–68, 283, 292; China-ASEAN Free Trade Area, 268, 270; Code of Conduct on South China Sea, 268, 273; inspection proposal for tours of PLA facilities in southern China and on Hainan Island, 286–87, 352; Regional Forum (1994), 267; Regional Forum (2010), 276; and Taiwan crisis, 267

Athens vs. Sparta, 19–20

Australia, 99, 102, 201, 244, 264, 268, 278, 359

averting catastrophe, 2–3, 360–64. *See also* cooperation spirals for US-China relations; debate on how to respond to China's rise; US-China rivalry

Axelrod, Robert, 12–13

Bader, Jeffrey, 7, 23*n*20, 77*n*57, 130, 131, 224*n*80, 257*n*54, 257*n*58, 275–76, 290, 329*n*45

Bagram base in Afghanistan, 319, 323

Bahrain, 163, 171, 182–83

battle of. *See name of specific battle*

Beijing Consensus, 153, 157

Benghazi embassy attack (2012), 163

Berkeley–Qinghua partnership, 120–21

Bilateral Investment Treaty (BIT), 95

Blair, Dennis, 213

Blumenthal, Daniel, 59

Boxer Rebellion (1900), 27, 32, 41, 228, 339

BP oil spill (2010), 109, 123

Brautigam, Deborah, 140

Brazil, 130, 131, 141

Britain: imperialism of, 29, 307, 343; US relations with, 143, 335

Buddhism, spread from China to India, 306

Bush, George W.: Asia-Pacific policy of, 353; "Axis of Evil" speech (2002), 199; Iran policy of, 180; North Korean policy of, 199, 201, 209; and Taiwan defense, 63; withdrawal of US troops from Korean Peninsula, 359

Cairo Conference (1943), 63–64, 166

Cambodia, 126, 266, 271

Campbell, Kurt, 224*n*80, 263

CARAT (Cooperation Afloat Readiness and Training) exercises in Thailand, proposed US invitation for China to participate in, 283–85

Carnegie Endowment for International Peace study on US-Japan-China triangle, 226

Carter, Jimmy, 198, 212

CCP. *See* Chinese Communist Party

Centers for Disease Control (US), 117

Central Asia, 164, 315; US military footprint in, proposed reduction of, 318–19, 332. *See also* India; Pakistan

Central Intelligence Agency, US. *See* CIA

CFIUS (Committee on Foreign Investment in the United States), 94

Cha, Victor, 196, 200, 202, 218

Chao Liang, 10

Chen Bingde, 276, 278

Chen Guangcheng, 338

Chen Shuibian, 52

Chen Siqing, 90, 92

Cheonan incident (2010), 201–3, 205, 209, 212, 215, 221*n*43, 238

Chiang Kai-shek, 35, 49, 51, 228, 230

China, relations with other countries and international dealings. *See* historical legacy for US-China relations; US-China rivalry; *specific countries and regions*

China Academy of Social Sciences study on maritime faction, 239

China and Iran: Ancient Partners in the Post-Imperial World (Garver), 166

The China Choice: Why America Should Share Power (White), 9–10

Chinese Communist Party (CCP): anti-American policy, 35; and labor movement, 100; in Taiwan, 68

Chinese immigrants in United States, violence against, 32

Chinese nationalism, 13

Chinese National Museum (Beijing), 27, 33, 356

Christian missionaries, 31–32, 33

Churchill, Winston, 336

CIA (US Central Intelligence Agency): estimates of Great Leap catastrophe by, 37–38; Tibetan operations of, 38, 307–8

civilian defense minister in China, proposal for, 350–51

Clapper, James, 213

climate change, 20, 113, 115, 116, 121, 127–31; global climate change agreement, proposals for, 129–31; proposal for Chinese to agree to legally binding international agreement, 127–28, 332

Clinton, Bill, 17, 168, 198, 224*n*80

Clinton, Hillary, 23*n*20, 85, 146, 236, 276, 277, 278, 314, 338, 354–55

coal, 113–14, 130–31

Coast Guard (China), 119, 151

Coast Guard (Japan), 234, 236

Coast Guard (US), 119, 150

Coast Guard cooperation, 286

Cold War, 1–2; and Japan-China relations, 229–30; linkage as concept during, 17; and Middle East, 166; revolutionary movements during, China's support for, 139; and Southeast Asia, 266–67, 282, 294*n*14; sphere of influence as concept during, 18, 25*n*49; surveillance operations off Chinese coast during, 287; understanding of, as aid in current US-China relations, 40; and Vietnam War, 39, 266

Committee on Foreign Investment in the United States (CFIUS), 94

Conflict Management and Peace Science (journal), 12

constructivist tradition, 14

Contest for Supremacy (Friedberg), 6–7, 13

Conventional Prompt Global Strike (CPGS) program, 341, 346–47

Cooke, Merritt, 113, 121

cooperation spirals for US-China relations: as applied by the author, 2, 14; balance in, 333; and constructivist tradition, 14; in developing world, 147–57, 148*f*; in economic relationship, 93–102, 94*f*; to enlarge strategic relationship, 343–53, 344*f*; first move to come from United States, 41; in India, 316–24, 317*f*; in Japan, 243–52, 244*f*; on Korean question, 191–92, 210–18, 211*f*; and liberal tradition, 14; and linkage, 17, 18; in Middle East, 177–85, 178*f*; as opposite of escalation spirals, 2, 12, 13; overview of, 12–19, 331; and realist principles, 14; in Southeast Asia, 283–91, 284*f*; sparking debate and negotiation on best structure for, 21; and spheres of influence, 17–18; in Taiwan situation, 60–69, 61*f*, 332; void in scholarship on cooperation, 12

Copenhagen summit (2009), 113, 130, 131

corporate green scorecard program, 129

corruption, 98, 103, 140, 156, 338

Council for Security Cooperation in the Asia-Pacific, 267

CPGS (Conventional Prompt Global Strike) program, 341, 346–47

credibility: of Chinese sources, 16; in Cuban Missile Crisis, 359; of red lines, 65, 335, 364*n*6

Crowe Memorandum (1907), 8

Cuban Missile Crisis (1962), 139, 154, 359

Cui Tiankai, 263, 275, 276

Cultural Revolution, 37, 117, 196–97, 230, 335

currency geopolitics, 82, 87, 89, 101–2

Curzon, George, 307

Cushing, Caleb, 29

Dai Bingguo, 275–76

Dalai Lama, 38, 307, 320–21, 324

Dalian oil spill (2010), 109, 123

Daqing Yang, 255*n*14

Davos World Economic Forum, 241

debate on how to respond to China's rise, 6–12; as author's purpose to spark, 21; Bader's recommendations, 7; Chinese voices, importance of listening to, 10–12, 24*n*46; Friedberg's recommendations, 6–7; Kissinger's recommendations, 7; lack of strategy, 6; military vs. nonmilitary responses, 9; Obama's policy, 7; Steinberg and O'Hanlon's recommendations, 8–9; Swaine's recommendations, 7; White's recommendations, 9–10

defense and deterrence policies, 7

deforestation, 116

delinkage policy, 17

Democratic Party (Japan), 235, 248

Democratic Progressive Party (DPP, Taiwan), 52, 54–55

Deng Xiaoping, 82–83; and environmental damage, 111; joint development initiatives under, 267, 289; and North Korea, 197; Southern Tour pledge to open China to world, 267; visit to Japan (October 1978), 230–31

deterrence, 7, 20, 347, 348, 356; "active deterrence," 218; "dual deterrence," 51; nuclear deterrence, 85; of red lines, 335

developing world, 15, 137–62, 332; African Union, urging China's support of, 151; arms sales to Latin America from China, proposed cap for, 143, 154–55; bilateral dialogue focused on Africa, proposal for, 152–53; Chinese perspectives on, 142–47; competition among superpowers over, 137; cooperation spiral for US-China relations in, 147–57, 148*f*; dangers to Chinese working in Africa, 146; fisheries enforcement patrol for African waters, proposal for, 150–51; foreign aid and investment projects, proposals for China's conformance to norms

in, 156–57; historical background, 138–42; military medicine, proposed joint US-China engagement in, 147–49, 161*n*37; peacekeeping initiatives in, 141; termination of AFRICOM, proposal for, 155–56; unease of US over China-Africa cooperation, 146–47; UN peacekeeping operations, proposed US commitment to, 151–52; World Bank president, proposal of Chinese candidate for, 153–54. *See also* AFRICOM

Diaoyu/Senkaku Islands: crisis (fall 1996), 231; crisis (fall 2010), 225, 235–36, 238, 247; crisis (fall 2012), 240; Japanese plan to retake if seized by China, 232; joint jurisdiction proposal for, 249–50; sovereignty negotiations over, 234; US policy regarding, 239, 257–58*n*58

diplomacy, 7; "carrier diplomacy," 368*n*44; Chinese diplomacy characterized as "weak," 341–42; costs of, 356; informal diplomacy, 339; North Korea-US diplomatic relations, proposal for, 215; pre–World War I American diplomacy, 33. *See also* reciprocity

The Diplomat (magazine), 16

distrust between China and United States, 3–4, 337

Dragon Mart (Dubai), 164, 169

drone attacks in Pakistan, 19, 329*n*48; proposal for United States to terminate, 322

Du Halde, Jean-Baptiste, 81

Dulles, John Foster, 230

Durban Summit (2009), 113, 127

Dutch East India Company, 48

Du Wenlong, 208

East Africa rail network, 145

East China Sea: air defense identification zone (ADIZ) over, 4, 241, 242; crisis with Japan (2012), 225; energy drilling in, 232, 234; equidistance proposal for,

249; fishing ban, 118; ships patrolling in, from both China and Japan, 234; territorial disputes over, 19, 240, 355; US involvement in, 56, 355. *See also* Diaoyu/Senkaku Islands

East Timor, 267–68, 269

East Turkestan Independence Movement, 169

Ebola Crisis (2014), 137, 147, 149–50, 155, 157, 355

Eclipse: Living in the Shadow of Economic Dominance (Subramanian), 86–87

economic aspects of Taiwan-Mainland relations, 53, 54. *See also* trade

economic aspects of US-China relations, 14, 79–108, 332; background, 81–88; Chinese investment in US, proposed policy changes for, 93–95; Chinese perspectives on, 88–93; Chinese vs. US economy, size of, 3, 6, 86–87, 103, 305, 336; cooperation spiral for, 93–102, 94f; currency and renminbi, 82, 87, 89, 101–2; and Deng's focus on economy, 82–83; destabilizing growth of China, 80; and global economic landscape, 89; high technology sales to China, proposed easing of, 100–101; intellectual property rights (IPRs), Chinese enforcement of, 97; and Mao's economic failure, 82; and rebalance of Chinese economy, 80, 86, 87, 88, 89, 91; saving rate in US, need to increase, 97–98; and service sector, 88; tensions of 1990s, 84; trade unions in China, proposal for, 100; transparency in Chinese major corporations, need for, 98–99; visa-free travel between China and US, proposal for, 96–97. *See also* trade

Economic Cooperation Framework Agreement (ECFA), 53

The Economist: on Africa-China relationship, 140; on Iranian nuclear issue, 179; on Middle East engagement of China, 164; on US saving rate, 98

Economy, Elizabeth, 111–12, 125, 338–39

education in Pakistan, 320

Egypt, 155, 163, 170, 338

Eisenhower, Dwight, 38, 51

Elgin, Lord, 30

energy challenges, 113–14; clean energy agreement, 120; coal, 113–14, 130–31; fracking technology, 177; natural gas from US, proposed sale to China, 177; nuclear energy, 114–15; oil imports from Middle East, 168–70, 176, 177; oil transit through Malacca Strait, 313; renewable energy, 114

environmental issues, 15, 109–36, 332; air-quality monitoring by US Embassy, proposal to curtail, 125–26; background, 110–13; bifurcation of negotiations, proposal for agreement to, 126–27; carbon capture and sequestration, 121; Chinese environmental measures, 111–12, 338; cooperation spiral for US-China relations, 123–31, 124f; corporate green scorecard program, proposal for, 129; from crisis to opportunity, 118–23; dam-building agreements, proposals for, 126; and Deng's policies, 111; emissions control, 113–16, 332; environmental protest movements in China, 122; global climate change agreement, proposals for, 129–31; green technologies and initiatives, 112, 114, 121; high-speed rail (HSR) network, proposal for, 128–29; and linkage, 17; and Mao's policies, 111; maritime spill mitigation, proposals for, 123–24; oil spills, 109, 123–24; spillover dangers of China's environmental crisis, 113–18; State Environmental Protection Agency (SEPA), proposed expansion of, 124–25; waste disposal, 117. *See also* air pollution; climate change; fisheries

EP-3 incident (April 2001), 271, 287, 353

escalation spirals, 12

"evil" characterization of Chinese regime, 13, 337

Fairbank, John, 28, 29, 41, 81
First Nation people and Canadian dam building, 126
fisheries, 118–19, 150–51
Fisheries Law Enforcement Command (FLEC, China), 119
fishing methods, 117–18
Flying Tigers (World War II), 34–35
Foot, Rosemary, 39
Forbes, Randy, 351
Foreign Affairs: on Obama policy toward China, 338–39, 354–55; on Taiwan situation, 58–59
Foreign Policy on China's growing involvement in Africa, 157
Forum on China-Africa Cooperation (2006), 149–50
fracking, 177
Freeman, Chas, 19, 46, 70–71, 352–53
Friedberg, Aaron, 6–7, 13, 234–35, 334–35, 336, 337
Fulda Gap, 263, 292, 292n2, 306

G-2. *See* Group of Two
Garver, John, 70, 166, 167–68, 170, 308, 309
Gates, Robert, 60, 351
Gau, Michael, 288
GE installations of wind turbines, 121
Geng Yansheng, 312
Georgia, Russian use of force in, 290, 334, 356
Ghandi, Rajiv, 309
Gilley, Bruce, 58, 67–68, 345
Global Asia (journal), 13
global environment, 123–31
Golden Central Triangle, 89
good governance, 145
Gorbachev, Mikhail, 82
Grant, Ulysses, 48–49
Great Leap Forward, 37, 111, 140, 196, 204

great power relations, 5, 331, 360. *See also* Cold War; US-China rivalry
Group of Two (G-2), 15, 16, 153, 338
Guam base of US military, 60–62
Gulf of Aden, 150, 164, 180, 246, 285
Gulf of Mexico oil spill (2010), 109, 123
Gulf of Oman, 311

Hagel, Chuck, 241, 264, 281
Hainan Island, 264, 271, 274, 275, 286–88, 352
Haiti, 141, 357
Han Chinese, 42n9
Hanit incident (2006), 172, 182
Hatoyama, Yukio, 235, 236, 243, 247, 248, 257n54
health care: military medicine, proposed joint US-China engagement in, 147–49; naval hospital ship (Chinese), sent to Africa and Latin America, 148–49. *See also specific diseases*
hedging policy, 283, 302n111, 361
He Di, 50
Heritage Foundation, 23n20
Hezbollah, 181–82
Hideyoshi's invasion of Korea, 192
high-speed rail (HSR), 128–29, 136n65; connecting Kunming to New Delhi, 321
historical legacy for US-China relations, 14, 26–45; in 1950s and 1960s, 38–39; and American exceptionalism, 31–35; American role in mid-nineteenth-century China, 27–30, 356; from brief collaboration to intense conflagration, 35–39; British imperialism in, 29–30; opening of China by Nixon, 39–41; origins of, 28–31, 331; Philippine conquest by United States, 32, 265, 266; pre–World War I American diplomacy, 33; pre–World War II US policy, 34; understanding as basis for US to lead in cooperation cycles, 331, 339; US Navy Yangtze Patrol, 29–30, 331, 362; and World War II, 34–35

HIV/AIDS, President's Emergency Plan
for AIDS Relief, 150
Homeland Security Department, US, 96
Hong Kong, 68–69, 338
Hong Xiuquan, 31
Hua Guofeng, 167
Huai River, 111–12
Huangyan Island, 264, 278
Hu Jintao, 89, 171, 186; Jang meeting
with (2012), 208; visit to Japan (2008),
234
human rights, 15, 215, 218, 336–38
Hu Yanlin, 277
hydropower, 114

IAEA (International Atomic Energy
Agency), 183, 215, 217
immigration from China to United States,
96–97
Impeccable incident (March 2009), 273,
287, 353
imperialism: of Britain, 29, 307, 343; in
Chinese history, 29, 40; of United
States, 335, 356
India, 15, 305–29, 332, 359; 1962 war
with China, 306, 308–9; arms sales
to, 305; carbon emissions of, 131;
Chinese perspectives on, 308–9,
310, 312–13; Chinese role in India/
Pakistan conflicts (1965 & 1971),
309; Chinese vs. Indian economy,
size of, 305; competence of, 339;
cooperation spiral for US-China
relations in, 316–24, 317*f*; economic
development corridor proposed for
Kunming to Kolkata, 322; Himalayan
border crisis (1986), 309; historical
background, 306–11; infrastructure
construction program, proposal for,
321–22; Kargil War (1999), 309,
310; military capabilities, buildup of,
313–14; naval deployment notification
system, proposal for, 317–18; nuclear
development of, 305, 309; population
growth of, 130; Security Council,
proposed permanent membership on,
324, 332; Sino-Indian rivalry, 306,
311–16, 328*n*40; and South China
Sea, 305, 314, 316; territorial dispute
on China/India border, proposal to
resolve, 323–24; trade with China,
315, 322; US alliance with, 306,
309, 339, 342; Vietnam military
cooperation with, 311, 316
Indian Ocean, 310–13, 318
Indochina Peninsula, economic
development strategy for, 270
Indonesia, 164, 249, 267, 269–70,
359; and East Timor, 267–68, 269;
limitation of of military cooperation
with China, proposal for, 290–91; and
Malacca Strait, 285, 302*n*116
informal diplomacy, 339
intellectual property rights (IPRs), 97
Intermediate Nuclear Forces Treaty, 347
International Atomic Energy Agency
(IAEA), 183, 215, 217
International Security (journal), 12, 24*n*42,
59, 85
International Tribunal of the Law of the
Sea, 278
Iran, 164–65, 167, 169–71; Chinese
influence on, to reduce tensions with
United States and Israel, 181–82,
183, 184–85, 332; effect of improved
US relations with, 176–77; nuclear
weapons in, 171–76, 179, 183, 186,
345–46; oil imports from, 176; regime
change as objective, proposal for US
to renounce, 179–80, 183; sanctions
against, 176, 180–81, 183
Iran-Iraq War, 167
Iran-Turkey agreement (2010) on nuclear
research, 174–75
Iraq War, 169–70, 182, 199, 205, 268,
269
Israel, 163, 167, 172, 175, 182, 184–85,
332

Jane's on Chinese naval capabilities, 275

Jang Song Taek, 208

Japan, 15, 225–62, 332; antipiracy initiatives in Gulf of Aden, proposal for Japan to join in, 246; China-Japan-South Korea forum proposed, 238, 261*n*93; Chinese perspectives on, 237–39, 240–43, 250; constitutional revision as to role of armed forces in, proposal for, 250–51; cooperation spiral for China-Japan-US triangle, 243–52, 244*f*; disaster recovery after earthquake and tsunami (March 2011), 237; hands-off approach of United States toward China-Japan relations, 226–27; Hideyoshi's invasion of Korea, 192; historical background, 49, 227–32; historical study effort highlighting differences between Chinese and Japanese approaches, 233, 255*n*15; history issue, needing breakthrough with China on, 247–49; invasion of China (1937–45), 228–29; joint military exercises with United States, 238–39; and Malacca Strait, 285, 302*n*116; model of US-Japan trade relations, 92; new era of China-Japan relations, 232–43; and North Korea, 200; and nuclear weapons, 260*n*91; overseas development assistance to China, 231, 248; rare earth minerals, proposal that China not leverage its advantage in, 236, 246–47; Security Council, proposed permanent membership on, 252, 332; self-defense forces of, 226, 232, 250–51; and Taiwan, 48–49, 55, 228, 231–32; tourism from China to, 233; trade with China, 233, 237; trilateral summit of Japan, China, and United States, proposal for, 245–46; US-Japan Alliance, 71, 229, 231, 235, 242, 243, 245, 246, 251–52, 260*n*91, 332, 342; US troop withdrawal from Okinawa, 243–45; Yasukuni Shrine visits as issue for China, 229–30, 232.

See also Diaoyu/Senkaku Islands; East China Sea
Japan Socialist Party, 232
Jiang Zemin, 83, 232
Jilin poultry plant tragedy (2013), 100
Jin Canrong, 343
Johnson, Louis, 50
Joint Marine Seismic Undertaking (China, Philippines, and Vietnam), 269, 289

Kang, David, 192, 270
Karakoram Highway (China and Pakistan), 309
Kargil War (1999), 309, 310
Kashmir, 309
Kennan, George, 18
Keohane, Robert, 12–13
Kerry, John, 179, 341
Khrushchev, Nikita, 139, 196
Kim Dae-jung, 199
Kim Il-sung, 36, 50, 193–94, 196–97, 198
Kim Jong-il, 197, 198, 200, 202, 224*n*80
Kim Jong-un, 209
Kissinger, Henry, 8, 39, 40, 52, 81, 230, 331, 336, 337
Kitty Hawk incident (2006), 353
Koizumi, Junichiro, 232
Korean peninsula. *See* Korean War; North Korea; South Korea
Korean War, 1, 35–37, 50; Chinese perspectives on, 193–96; military history project on, proposal for, 210–11
Kuomintang (KMT), 43*n*34, 47, 50, 54, 55, 70, 166, 228
Kuwait, 166–67
Kyoto Protocol, 126–27
Kyrgyzstan, 319, 323

labor movement in China, 100
Lagos–Mombasa highway project, 151
Latin America. *See* developing world; *individual countries by name*
Lee Denghui, 52
Lee Myung-bak, 201, 202, 209, 221*n*43

liberal tradition, 14
Libya, 156, 163, 164, 170, 171, 199
Li Daguang, 242
Li Hongzhang, 48–49
Li Jie, 39, 239, 277
Li Keqiang, 145, 207
Lin Biao, 36
Lin, Justin Yofu, 81, 82, 86, 154
linkage, 13, 17, 18
Li Shaoning, 276
Li Weijian, 171
Liu Hongwu, 144
Liu Jianfei, 341
logging ban, 112, 116
Lu Feng, 115, 116
Luo Yuan, 195, 240, 274
Luo Zhaohu, 312

MacArthur, Douglas, 1
Malacca Strait (Malacca Dilemma), 115,
    272–73, 282, 285–86, 302*n*116, 306,
    310, 313, 314
Malaysia, 269, 274, 285, 302*n*116
Mali, 141, 155
MALSINDO states (Malaysia, Singapore,
    and Indonesia), 285, 302*n*116
Mao Zedong: on avoiding military conflict
    with United States, 51; and economic
    growth, 82; and environmental
    damage, 111; and Great Leap Forward,
    37; and Japan-China relations, 230; on
    Khrushchev in Cuban Missile Crisis,
    139; and Korean War, 36, 194; on
    Qing Dynasty, 33; reaction to foreign
    derision of China, 33–34; on shelling
    Kuomintang-occupied offshore islands,
    166; and Tibet conquest, 307; and
    Vietnam War, 265
maritime pollution, 109, 117–18, 123–24.
    See also fisheries
maritime security, 10, 48. *See also* East
    China Sea; South China Sea; *individual
    countries by name*
Maritime Silk Road, 164, 282
Marshall, George, 35

Ma Xiaojun, 115
Ma Ying-jeou, 47, 53–55, 70
McKenna, Richard, 362
McNamara, Robert, 153
Medeiros, Evan, 270
Mekong River Delta, patrolling of, 284
methodological issues of research, 16
Mexican War (1846–48), 143, 356
Mexico, competing in international trade,
    141
Middle East, 15, 332; arms sales to,
    167; Bahrain base of US Fifth Fleet,
    proposal to close, 182–83; bilateral
    counterterrorism center, proposal
    for China to fund, 178–79; Chinese
    attention to, 163–64, 186; Chinese
    perspectives on, 57, 170–77; in Cold
    War, 166; cooperation spiral for
    US-China relations in, 177–85, 178*f*;
    Hezbollah receiving arms from Iran,
    proposal for China to get Iran to halt,
    181–82; historical background, 165–
    70; Hormuz Patrol squadron, proposal
    for, 180; Iran regime change, proposal
    for US to renounce as objective, 179–
    80, 183; Iran sanctions, proposal for
    US to ease, 180–81, 183; Israel nuclear
    disarmament, proposal for, 184; natural
    gas from US, proposed sale to China,
    177; oil imports from, 168–70, 176;
    rebalancing power structure in as goal,
    186; recognition of Israel, proposal
    for China to abet, 184–85; western
    penetration of Persian empire, 166.
    See also nuclear weapons; *individual
    countries by name*
military: and African security issues,
    146; aircraft carriers, proposal to limit,
    348; antiship ballistic missiles (ASBM)
    and antisatellite (ASAT) weapons,
    proposal to eliminate, 347–48; China's
    focus on development of, 56; China
    vs. United States, 3, 19; civilian
    defense minister in China, proposal
    for, 350–51; Conventional Prompt

military (*continued*)
  Global Strike (CPGS) program, 341,
    346–47; Hormuz Patrol squadron,
    proposal for China to provide, 180;
    incidents and crises, frequency of,
    353–54; India's buildup of capabilities,
    313–14; India-Vietnam military
    development, 311, 316; Japan's self-
    defense forces, 226, 232, 250–51;
    joint India-US military exercises, 310;
    joint Japan-US military exercises,
    238–39; joint Philippine-US military
    exercises, 281; joint Vietnam-US
    naval exercises, 277–78; military
    medicine, proposed joint US-China
    engagement in, 147–49, 161n37;
    National Defense Authorization Act
    (FY 2000), restrictions on military-
    to-military exchanges, 351–52;
    overseas US bases, 9, 19, 60–62,
    182–83, 212–13, 216–17, 235,
    243–45, 278; Pakistan bases, Chinese
    not to undertake, 320; Philippines,
    US military presence in, 264; Rim
    of the Pacific Exercise (2014), 285,
    351; South China Sea, Chinese and
    other countries' buildup in, 273–75;
    South Korean naval and armed forces,
    201–4; strength as prerequisite to
    compromise, 335; Taiwan-China
    military security agreement, proposal
    of, 62; transparency, need for China
    to increase, 352–53; US retrenchment
    needed, 331. *See also* submarines
Ming Dynasty, 48, 82, 192
Minnan Hua (Taiwan dialect), 70
Missionaries in China, 31–32, 33, 42n19
mitigating strategic rivalry, 330–69. *See
    also* US-China rivalry
Modi, Narendra, 306, 316, 324
Mongol invasions, 227, 254n8
Monroe Doctrine, 142–43, 291
Monsoon (Kaplan), 311
Montreal Protocol to ban ozone-depleting
    chemicals, 111

Mugabe, Robert, 140
multipolarization, 18
Munich analogy for foreign policy, 335–36
Murayama, Tomiichi, 248
Myanmar, 126, 156, 283, 310, 311, 315,
    321–22, 357

Nairobi terrorist attack on West Gate Mall
    (2013), 155
Nanjing Massacre (1937), 49, 228–29,
    233, 248–49, 255n21
NASDAQ, 98–99
Nathan, Andrew, 66, 73–74n21, 254, 291
National Aeronautics and Space
    Administration (NASA), 350
National Defense Authorization Act (FY
    2000), 351–52
NATO, 292n2, 323
Needham, Joseph, 81
neoliberals vs. neorealists, 12
neutrality doctrine, 236, 250, 257–58n58
New Silk Road Strategy, 2, 144, 164, 306,
    325
New York Stock Exchange, 98–99
New York Times: forum on US-China
    relationship, 40; on Japan's failing to
    confront World War II history, 249
Nigeria, 155
Niu Jun, 51
Nixon, Richard M., 17, 39, 212, 230
North Korea, 15, 191–224; 1950s'
    advantage to South Korea, 196; 1960s'
    playing China and Russia against one
    another, 196–97; Chinese involvement,
    need to take significant role, 192,
    214–15, 218–19; Chinese perspectives
    on, 205–8; Chinese troop presence
    in, proposal for, 213–14; cooperation
    spiral for US-China relations in,
    191–92, 210–18, 211*f*; evolving
    situation with provocations toward
    South Korea, 192–210; as failure of
    US-China relations, 191; food shortage
    in, 209; Four-Power Yellow Sea Patrol,
    proposal to form, 211–12; historical

background, 2, 192–201; intertwined with Chinese communist movement, 193; leadership change of 2011, effect of, 192; likelihood of government's collapse in, 218; missile technology in, 172, 207; naval incidents with South Korea, 201–3; nuclear development in, 175, 192, 198, 199, 201, 206–8, 214–15, 332; nuclear disarmament of, China's ability to assist in, 217–18, 345–46; possible unification with South, 209–10, 218; power shift from US to China on Korean Peninsula, 203, 332; sanctions on, 206; Sino–North Korean Defense Treaty (1961), proposal to reinvigorate, 213–14; and Sony Crisis (2014), 218; trade with China, 206, 208–9, 218; upset over US opening relations with China, 197; US diplomatic relations with, proposal for, 215; US negotiations with, proposal for, 214. *See also* Korean War

North Pacific Coast Guard Forum, 286

North–South Agreement on Reconciliation, Non-Aggression, and Exchanges and Cooperation (1991), 198

North Vietnam. *See* Vietnam War

Noryang Point, battle of (1597), 192

nuclear energy, 114–15

Nuclear Non-Proliferation Treaty, 183, 184, 199

Nuclear Security Summit (April 2010), 257n54

nuclear weapons: in China, 39; Chinese review of nuclear proliferation policies, proposal for, 345–46; in India, 305, 309; in Iran, 171–76, 179, 183, 186, 345–46; in Iraq, 198; in Israel, 175, 184, 332; in Japan, 260n91; in North Korea, 175, 192, 198, 199, 201, 206–8, 214–15, 345–46; and Taiwan situation, 50–51, 332; US-China Nonproliferation Joint Working Group, 346

Obama, Barack: on Afghanistan troop reduction, 319; African visit of (2013), 137; Asian trip of (2010), 310; Asia pivot as policy of, 7, 271, 354–58; Asia policy inherited from Bush, 353–54; on Australia as station for US Marines, 278; China policy of, 7, 23n20, 338–39; on China's financial rise, 85; on China's investment in United States, 93; on drone strikes, 329n48; and environmental regulation, 115, 130; Iran policy of, 179, 180; and Japan's failing to confront World War II history, 249; meeting with Hatoyama (April 2010), 257n54; meeting with Hu (2009), 120; meeting with Xi Jinping (June 2013), 4, 341; Myanmar visit of (2012), 283; North Korean policy of, 201, 209, 224n80; on Philippine defense cooperation agreement, 280; on South China Sea provocation, 273, 280; Taiwan policy of, 56, 66; trade relations with China, 92, 101. *See also* Obama-Xi Summit (November 2014)

Obama and China's Rise (Bader), 7, 23n20, 77n57

Obama-Xi Summit (November 2014), 4–5, 20, 330; confidence-building measures, 283, 330; environment and climate accord, 110, 113, 116, 122–23, 127, 128, 131; maritime encounters in South China Sea, 264, 287; omission of space cooperation, 350; technology transfer, 101; trade and tariffs reduction, 95

Obuchi, Keizo, 232

O'Hanlon, Michael, 8–9, 18, 46, 65, 335, 348, 359, 361

oil sales. *See* energy challenges

oil spills, 109, 123–24

Okinawa Reversion Agreement (1971), 250

Olympic Games: Summer 2008, 112, 179; Taiwan's participation, 64–65

one-child policy, 111, 130
Open Door policy, 33
Operation Praying Mantis of 1988 (US Navy), 167
Opium War, 28–29, 42*n*7, 81
ozone-depleting chemicals, 111, 125

Pakistan, 19, 215; Chinese relations post 9/11 attacks, 309–10, 316, 320; Chinese role in India/Pakistan conflicts (1965 & 1971), 309; secular education, need to commit to, 320; stability in, 325; US drone attacks in, proposal to terminate, 322; US policy on, 315
Panetta, Leon, 208
Pang Zhongying, 10
Park Chung-hee, 197, 216
Park Guen-hye, 249
peacekeeping initiatives in developing world, 141, 151–52, 186, 268
Pearl River Tower, 119–20
Peking University textbook on US history in Asia, 28, 31, 32, 265–66
Peloponnesian Wars, 19
Peng Dehuai, 194, 195
Peng Guangqian, 242, 341
People's Liberation Army (PLA), 36, 50, 195, 286–87, 308, 350–53
Persian Gulf War, 182, 198
Persian Spring. *See* Middle East
Peterson Institute for International Economics, 53
Pettis, Michael, 80, 86, 87, 91, 98, 102
Philippines: defense cooperation agreement with United States, 280; defense spending of, 357; and Iraq War, 269; Joint Marine Seismic Undertaking with China, 269, 289; joint military exercises with United States, 281; military cooperation agreement with China, 269; rollback of military cooperation with China, proposal for, 290–91; strained relations with China, 263, 267, 276, 278–80; US conquest of, 32, 265,

266; US military presence in, 264, 267, 278
piracy, 146, 150, 180, 246, 269, 285–86, 302*n*116, 313, 314
Platt, Stephen: *Autumn in the Heavenly Kingdom*, 30–31
pluralism, Chinese move toward, 338
Pollack, Jonathan, 196–97, 198
Pol Pot, 266
Power, Samantha, 137
power transition in world politics, 20
President's Emergency Plan for AIDS Relief, 150
Protracted Contest (Garver), 308
Putin, Vladimir, 11, 186

Qiang Zhai, 38
Qiao Gen, 91
Qin Dynasty, 33
Qing Dynasty, 30, 31, 33, 48, 70, 82, 111, 166

RAND Corporation study of US ground force reductions, 217
rare earth minerals, Chinese advantage in, 236, 246–47
realist form of cooperation, 14, 39, 331
rebalancing strategy to the Asia-Pacific. *See* Asia pivot
RECAAP initiative (Regional Cooperation Agreement on Combating Piracy and Armed Robbery against Ships in Asia), 285
reciprocity, strategy based on, 13, 14, 331, 345
recommendations for US-China relations. *See* cooperation spirals for US-China relations
red lines, credibility of, 65, 335, 364*n*6
regime change as US objective: in China, importance of US to abandon, 337–38; in Iran, proposal for US to renounce, 179–80, 183
Regional Comprehensive Economic Partnership, 92

renewable energy, 114

Ren Xiao, 242

Rice, Condoleezza, 200

Rim of the Pacific Exercise (2014), 285, 351

Roh Mo-hyun, 199, 200

Romney, Mitt, 85

Roosevelt, Alice, 33

Roosevelt, Franklin Delano, 152

Roosevelt, Theodore, 33

Rouhani, Hassan, 163, 175, 176, 183

Rumsfeld, Donald, 212

Russia: aggressiveness of, 11; arms sales to India, 305; comparison of China's and Russia's economy, 82; Georgia, use of force in, 290, 334, 356; US relations with, 3, 65. *See also* Ukraine Crisis

Russo-Japanese War (1904–5), 192

Ryukyu Islands, 48–49

The Sand Pebbles (McKenna), 362–64

SARS epidemic (2003), 112

Saudi Arabia, 167, 170, 175, 182, 215, 338

Scarborough Shoal, 263

secular education in Pakistan, 320

Sekaku Island. *See* Diaoyu/Senkaku Islands

self-criticism, need for, 11

Shanghai Communiqué, 63, 73–74n21

Shanghai Cooperation Organization (SCO), 315, 322–23

Shen Dingli, 10, 208

Shigeru, Ishiba, 235

Shi Lang Doctrine, 48

Shi Xiaodong, 57, 62

Shi Yinhong, 242

Sierra-Leone China Friendship Hospital, 150

Singapore, 99, 264, 270, 278, 285, 302n116

Sino-Japanese War (1894–95), 192, 228

Sino-Soviet alliance and Korean War, 37

Six-Party Talks (2003), 199, 214, 217, 218

Song Dynasty, 227, 254n8

Songhua River, 112

Sony Crisis (2014), 218

South Asia, 164. *See also* India

South China Sea: Beijing conference (mid-2013) on, 57; Chinese naval and air buildup in, 274–75, 281–82; Chinese perspectives on, 272–73, 275–77, 278–79, 282; Code of Conduct on (2002), 268, 273; combat between China and Vietnam in (1988), 266; as "core interest" to China, 275–76; drilling exploration rig placed by China in, 281; energy exploration in, 84; fishing ban, 118; *Impeccable* incident (March 2009), 273, 287, 353; and India, 305, 310–11, 314, 316; joint development proposal for 50/50 split framework, 289–90; Paracels Crisis (May 2014), 281, 287; security situation in, 273; Taiwan-Mainland coordination of policies over, 62; territorial disputes over, 19, 274, 288–89; US approach to, 23n20, 56, 264, 274, 276–77, 355; Vietnam and China engaging in risky behavior in (2014), 281; Vietnam and Malaysia filing UN claim to areas in, 274; volatility of, 282–83; warships in, 4

Southeast Asia, 15, 263–304, 332; antipiracy patrol for Malacca Strait, proposal for, 285–86; CARAT (Cooperation Afloat Readiness and Training) exercises in Thailand, proposed US invitation for China to participate in, 283–85; China's "charm offensive" in, 268; compared to Fulda Gap, 263, 292, 292n2; cooperation cycle for US-China relations in, 283–91, 284f; escalating US-China rivalry in, 271–83; hedging policy in, 283, 302n111; historical background, 265–71; Indochina Peninsula, economic development strategy for, 270; inspection proposal for tours of PLA facilities in southern China and on Hainan Island, 286–87, 352;

Southeast Asia (*continued*)
  and Iraq War, 268, 269; limitation of
  Philippine and Indonesian military
  cooperation with China, proposal for,
  290–91; limitation of US military
  cooperation with Vietnam, proposal
  for, 290; Southeast Asia–Pacific Coast
  Guard Forum, proposal for formation
  of, 286; strained US-China relations
  in, 263–65; US surveillance operations
  off China coast, proposal to reduce,
  287–88. *See also* South China Sea;
  individual countries by name
South Korea: *Cheonan* incident (2010),
  201–3, 205, 209, 215, 221*n*43, 238;
  China-Japan-South Korea forum
  proposed, 238, 261*n*93; Chinese
  perspectives on, 203–5; Chinese
  relations with, 201, 205; "comfort
  women" issue in, 193; foreign policy
  falling into three factions, 205; military
  transparency mechanism, proposal
  for China to institute, 215–16; naval
  prowess of, 203–4; North Korean naval
  attacks on, 201–2; partial withdrawal
  of US forces from, proposal for, 212–
  13, 216–17; possible unification with
  North, 209–10, 218; US alliance with,
  201, 204–5, 218; withdrawal of US
  nuclear weapons from (1991), 198. *See
  also* Korean War; North Korea
South–South pivot. *See* developing world
South Sudan, 140, 145
space cooperation with China, proposal
  for, 349–50
spheres of influence, 17–18, 25*n*49
Spratly Islands, 263, 277, 281, 289
Sri Lanka, 306, 311, 316, 318
Stalin, Joseph, 36, 194
State Environmental Protection Agency
  (SEPA, China), 124–25
State Oceanic Administration (China),
  234
Steinberg, James, 8–9, 18, 65, 275, 335,
  348, 359, 361

Stillwell, Joseph, 35
Strait of Hormuz, 172, 174, 175, 177, 180
*Strategic Reassurance and Resolve: US-China
  Relations in the 21st Century* (Steinberg
  & O'Hanlon), 8–9, 18, 65
submarines, 273–75, 306, 316, 318,
  361; antisubmarine aircraft, 154,
  314; Chinese modernization of fleet,
  proposal to limit, 348–49; Japanese,
  238; nuclear attack submarines, 60,
  175, 264, 274; South Korean, 203–4;
  Soviet development problems, 368*n*46;
  strategic submarines of China, 273; US
  Navy, 203
Subramanian, Arvind, 86, 102
Sudan, 140, 141, 145, 158*n*11
Sunflower Movement, 54
Sunni vs. Shiite Islam, 171
Sunnylands summit (June 2013), 4, 341,
  350
Swaine, Michael, 8, 68, 245, 337
Syria, 163, 164, 170, 181, 186, 280

Taft, William, 33
Taiping Rebellion, 30–31, 41
Taiwan question, 14, 15, 46–78, 332;
  228 incident (1947), 50; in 1950s, 38,
  50–51, 195, 230; "1992 Consensus,"
  52; 1995–96 crisis, 52, 169, 231, 353;
  2000–10 strained relations, 52, 63;
  alliance strains caused by US position
  over, 71; amphibious invasion, need for
  China to reduce possibility of, 66–67,
  77*n*58; arms sales to Taiwan, 56, 59,
  65–66, 67–68, 77*n*57; background,
  47–52; calming of tensions over,
  46–47, 69–70; Chinese perspectives
  on, 55–58; confederation, proposed
  peace treaty process to form, 68–69;
  confidence-building maritime security
  exercises of Taiwan and Mainland,
  57, 62; cooperation spiral for, 19,
  60–69, 61*f*, 332; and Guam base
  of US military, 60–62; in Japan-
  China relations, 228, 232; Japanese

colonization of, 48–49, 55; as key to improved US-China relations, 46; and Korean War, 50; Ma's election and accommodation policies, 52–60; military security agreement, proposal of, 62; in Nixon administration, 39–40; objections to concessions to China, 71–72; pre-Korean War, 36, 50; recognition of Taiwan's international presence, proposal for China to accept, 64–65; removal of Chinese missiles from short-range locations, proposal for, 63, 76–77n55; soft power of Taiwan, effect in Mainland, 69; and South China Sea claims, 288; Taiwan Strait Crisis of 1962, 51; US abetting Taiwan's unification, 63–64; US disclosure of defense ties with Taiwan, proposal for, 62–63; US perspectives on, 58–60; US review of Taiwan policy to increase flexibility, proposal for, 343–45

Taiwan Relations Act (US), 58

Taku Forts, battle of (1859), 30

Talas, battle of (751 CE), 165

Taliban, 169, 322

Tamerlane, 166

Tang Dynasty, 81, 165

Tang Jiaxuan, 200

Tanzania–Zambia Railway Authority (TAZARA), 139–40

Tao Wenzhao, 51

Tattnall, Josiah, 30

technology export controls, 7

terrorism, 146, 169, 175, 178–79, 186, 232, 268–69, 309; and CARAT (Cooperation Afloat Readiness and Training) exercises on nontraditional security issues, 283–85

Thailand, 267, 283–85

third-party relations, 15–16

Three Gorges Dam, 114

Thucydides' trap, 19–20, 334

Tiananmen Square Massacre (1989), 52, 83, 231

Tianjin City Museum, 32

Tibet, 306, 307–8, 309, 320–21, 329n45

Tolley, Kemp, 29–30, 33

tourism between Mainland and Taiwan, 53

town and village enterprises (TVEs), 111

TPP. *See* Trans-Pacific Partnership

trade: between Africa and China, 140, 144; China-ASEAN Free Trade Area, 268, 270; between India and China, 315, 322; between Indonesia and China, 269; between Japan and China, 233, 237; between Latin America and China, 141; between Mainland and Taiwan, 53; between North Korea and China, 206, 208–9, 218; between South Korea and China, 216; tariffs reduction (2014), 95; tensions between US and China, 90–91; trade deficit and US saving rate, 98; between US and Japan in 1990s, 92. *See also* economic aspects of US-China relations; Trans-Pacific Partnership

trade unions, 100

Trans-Pacific Partnership (TPP) trade pact, 90, 91–92, 99–100, 237–38, 354

transparency, need for China to increase, 361; corporate transparency, 98–99; dam-building practices, 126; emissions control, 116; fisheries agreements, 151; investment projects in developing world, 156; military transparency mechanism, 215–16, 235, 286, 331–32, 347, 352–53

Trawler Crisis (2010), 235, 247

Treaty of Friendship between China and Japan (1978), 230

Treaty of Shimonoseki (1895), 49

Treaty of Wangxia (1844), 28, 29

Triple Intervention, 228

Truman, Harry, 1, 36, 50, 64, 195

trust, building of, 12, 337

Tsvangirai, Morgan, 140

Tunisia, 163, 170

Turkey, 171, 174–75, 252

Uighur Muslim minority, 319

Ukraine Crisis (2014), 3, 11, 17, 65, 186, 280, 290, 334, 356

unilateral concessions, reasons to avoid, 333

United Nations: China's membership in, 51; driftnet fishing prohibition in North Pacific, 119; guiding role of, 315; Law of the Sea, 273, 288; peacekeeping operations, 141, 151–52, 268; Security Council, 173, 252, 324, 332; Security Council Resolution 1718, 206; US promotion of, 343; Vietnam and Malaysia filing claim to South China Sea areas, 274

unmanned aerial vehicles, 314

UNOCAL, 84, 93, 177

US-China Nonproliferation Joint Working Group, 346

US-China rivalry, 1; ability of United States to work with China, 336–40; and arms race, 3; challenges for, 330–31; Chinese perceptions of, 340–43; dire predictions based on, 20; distrust in, 3–4, 337; military incidents and crises, frequency of, 353–54; and offshore balancing approach to US foreign policy, 358–59; and proxy conflicts, 3; self-reinforcing dynamic, 359–60; third-party pressure on United States, 357–59; World War III, imperative to prevent, 360–64. *See also* cooperation spirals for US-China relations; debate on how to respond to China's rise

US consulates in China, 26

US history, Chinese scholars' view of, 55–56

US relations with other countries and regions. *See specific countries and regions*

USS *Plymouth*, 30

USS *Powhatan*, 30

USS *Pueblo* incident (1968), 197

Uzbekistan, 318

Venezuela, 154

Versailles Treaty (1919), 49, 228

Vietnam, 359; economic growth of, 264; India-Vietnam military cooperation, 311, 316; joint naval exercises with United States, 277–78; rollback of US military cooperation with, proposal for, 290; Russian-made submarines, purchase of, 273–74; in South China Sea territorial dispute, 274, 355; strained relations with China, 263, 264, 266, 276, 281

Vietnam War, 38–39, 264, 265, 335

visa-free travel between China and US, proposal for, 96–97

Wachman, Alan, 47, 48, 50

Wall Street Journal on Chinese provocations in South China Sea, 273

Wang Jisi, 3–4, 246

Wang Nan, 174

Wang Ning, 175

Wang Qingxin, 83

Wang Yizhou, 343

Ward, Frederick, 30–31

War to Resist America. *See* Korean War

War with Mexico (1846–48), 143

Washington Consensus, 153, 157

Watts, Jonathan, 116, 117, 119–20

weapons. *See* military; nuclear weapons; submarines

Wen Jiabao, 208, 233–34

When a Billion Chinese Jump: How China Will Save Mankind—or Destroy It (Watts), 119

White, Hugh, 9–10, 251, 260n91, 334–35, 336, 359

wind power, 114, 121

Wolfowitz, Paul, 145, 153

World Bank, 145, 153–54, 332

World Health Organization, 64

World Trade Organization (WTO), 64, 83, 90, 92, 100, 121

World War II, 34, 49, 226, 235, 254; Tokyo War Crimes Tribunal, 230

Wu Shicun, 279
Wu Xinbo, 10

Xian Incident (1936), 228
Xie Zhenhua, 127
Xi Jinping: African visit of (2013), 137, 143; background and character of, 335–36; on capping carbon emissions, 118; on Central Asian trade, 164; father of, in Cultural Revolution, 37, 335; interest in modern history, 40, 45*n*61; and Japan-China relations, 225; on Korean War, 194–95; "Leadership Cadres Should Read Up on History" (speech 2011), 40–41; meeting with Abe (2014), 242–43; meeting with Modi (September 2014), 306, 316, 323, 325; meeting with Obama (June 2013), 4, 341; meeting with Park (June 2014), 216; on North Korea, 207; on Southeast Asia and trade, 282. *See also* Obama-Xi Summit (November 2014)

Yalong Bay base, 274, 286
Yan Baoxing, 203
Yancey, John, 1
Yang Jiechi, 276
Yang Yi, 341
Yangtze River, 114, 117, 119, 331
Yan Xuetong, 273
Yasukuni Shrine visits, 229–30, 232
Ye Hailin, 312
Yellow Sea, 203, 209, 211–12
Yeonpyeong Island, 201, 215
Yin He (Chinese ship), 167–68
Yuan Peng, 57, 341
Yu Hongyuan, 115–16

Zhang Deshun, 274
Zhenbao Incident, 39
Zheng Chenggong, 48
Zheng He, 138, 166, 306–7
Zhou Enlai, 51, 197
Zhu Feng, 341
Zhu Rongji, 83

ABOUT THE AUTHOR

Dr. Lyle J. Goldstein is an associate professor in the China Maritime Studies Institute (CMSI), which was established at the US Naval War College in Newport, Rhode Island, in 2006 to study China's maritime development and also improve maritime cooperation with China. He served as the founding director of CMSI from 2006 to 2011. For this service, he was awarded the Superior Civilian Service Medal by the US Navy. The assessments expressed by the author in this book are his own and do not represent the views of the US Naval War College, the US Navy, or any other agency of the US government.

He is the author of *Preventive Attack and Weapons of Mass Destruction* (2006), the CMSI monographs *Five Dragons Stirring up the Sea* (2010) and *Chinese Mine Warfare* (2009), and co-editor of six books: *China's Future Nuclear Submarine Force* (2007); *China's Energy Strategy* (2008); *China Goes to Sea* (2009); *China, the United States, and 21st-Century Sea Power* (2010); *Chinese Aerospace Power* (2011); and *Not Congruent, but Quite Complementary: U.S. and Chinese Approaches to Nontraditional Security* (2012). He is also a regular contributor to *The National Interest*.

Goldstein received his B.A. from Harvard University, an M.A. from Johns Hopkins University's School of Advanced International Studies, and his Ph.D. from Princeton University. He also studied at Beijing Normal University.